COUNSELING AND PSYCHOTHERAPY
WITH PERSONS WITH
MENTAL RETARDATION AND
BORDERLINE INTELLIGENCE

COUNSELING AND PSYCHOTHERAPY WITH PERSONS WITH MENTAL RETARDATION AND BORDERLINE INTELLIGENCE

Douglas C. Strohmer
Louisiana State University
Medical Center

H. Thompson Prout
Florida State University
(Editors)

Clinical Psychology Publishing Co., Inc.
4 Conant Square
Brandon, Vermont 05733

Library of Congress Cataloging–in–Publication Data

Counseling and psychotherapy with persons with mental retardation and
 borderline intelligence / Douglas C. Strohmer, H. Thompson Prout,
 editors.
　　　p.　cm.
 Includes bibliographical references and index.
 ISBN 0–88422–121–0 (hardcover) : $39.50
 1. Mentally handicapped—Mental health. 2. Mentally handicapped—
 Counseling of. 3. Psychotherapy. I. Strohmer, Douglas C., 1945–　.
 II. Prout, H. Thompson, 1947–　.
 [DNLM: 1. Mental Retardation—psychology. 2. Mental Retardation—therapy. 3. Psychotherapy—methods. 4. Counseling—methods.
 300 C855 1994]
 RC451.4.M47C53　1994
 616.85'880651—dc20
 DNLM/DLC　　　　　　　　　　　　　　　　　　　94–12016
 for Library of Congress　　　　　　　　　　　　　　　　CIP

Library of Congress Catalog Card Number: 94–12016
ISBN: 0–88422–121–0

[CPPC]　4 Conant Square
　　　　Brandon, VT 05733

Cover Design: Sue Thomas
Printed in the United States of America.

CONTENTS

CONTRIBUTORS

Douglas C. Brown
Department of Psychology
James Madison University

Randy L. Cale
Private Practice
Albany, New York

Harriet C. Cobb
Department of Psychology
James Madison University

Randy Elston
Rehabilitation Counseling Program
East Central University

William Gunn
Department of Community
  and Family Medicine
Duke University Medical Center

Edward M. Levinson
Department of Educational Psychology
Indiana University of Pennsylvania

Johnny L. Matson
Department of Psychology
Louisiana State University

Michael Peterson
Developmental Disabilities Institute
Wayne State University

H. Thompson Prout
Psychological Services Program
Florida State University

Jay A. Sevin
Department of Psychology
Louisiana State University

Paul M. Spengler
Department of Counseling Psychology
Ball State University

Douglas C. Strohmer
Department of Rehabilitation Counseling
Louisiana State University
  Medical Center

1 ISSUES IN COUNSELING AND PSYCHOTHERAPY

H. Thompson Prout and
Douglas C. Strohmer

Counseling and psychotherapy have long been a standard option in the treatment of emotional problems in the general population of persons without mental retardation. In many cases, psychotherapy is seen as the treatment of choice, or the first option. Despite the fact that individuals with mental retardation experience the same type and range of emotional disorders as the nonretarded population, the choice of counseling or psychotherapy as a viable treatment option is rarely considered with this population. In fact, Reiss, Levithan, and McNally (1982) have identified the emotionally disturbed population of individuals with mental retardation as one of the most underserved populations in terms of receiving mental health services.

As professionals working in mental retardation services, we have been both frustrated and somewhat amused by the decision-making process within the mental health community. Time and time again, we have seen that children and adolescents who also possess less well developed cognitive abilities are readily taken into treatment by mental health centers and private practitioners. Yet, we have also observed the hesitancy, reluctance, and direct opposition that these same service providers exhibit when faced with a client with mental retardation. More often than not, it appears that the traditional mental health providers try to avoid providing counseling and psychotherapy services to individuals with mental retardation. For instance, we have seen the same mental health center provide services for a 9-year-old child, yet reject services for an individual with mental retardation who functions cognitively at the 9-year-old level. If one client at the 9-year-old level (i.e., the child) can benefit from counseling or therapeutic services, it seems reasonable that an adult at the 9-year-old level (i.e., the adolescent or adult client with mental retardation) could also benefit from these services.

It is the working hypothesis of this book that counseling and psychotherapy constitute a viable treatment option in dealing with the emotional and adjustment problems of persons with mental retardation. It is hoped that this book will foster more interest in providing counseling and psychotherapy services for the population of individuals with mental retardation. We find a combination of Kazdin's (1988) and Corsini's (1989) definitions of psychotherapy best represents what we include in our definition of psychotherapy and counseling. These elements of counseling and/or psychotherapy include:

- A formal or special interaction between two (or more) individuals, typically a "client" and a "counselor" or "therapist," where one party is specifically seeking help for ameliorating distress or dealing with a particular problem.

- The therapist or counselor applies a set of procedures or techniques or provides a set of conditions with the aim of alleviating the distress or solving the problem, with a theoretical base underlying the therapist's activities.

- The focus of the interaction may be on cognitive, affective, attitudinal, and/ or behavioral factors.

- Typically, the client describes the problems and issues related to the distress or concern, with the counselor or therapist responding with interactions that apply techniques or set conditions for amelioration of the concern or distress.

As Kazdin (1988) notes, psychotherapy includes a wide range of interventions, both from a theoretical and technique viewpoint. Excluded are interventions that do not include formal interactions between the client and counselor, typically interactions that fall in the operant behavior modification or behavioral consultation frameworks where the procedures or techniques are not delivered or conducted by the counselor or therapist. The purpose of this chapter is to review and present issues that relate generally to the provision of counseling and psychotherapy services to persons with mental retardation. Because this area has historically been ignored in the professional literature, many of these issues are somewhat speculative or biased, or are parallel to other developments in the general treatment of persons with mental retardation.

The Client with Mental Retardation:
Who Is Appropriate for Counseling? What Are His or Her
Characteristics?

An important issue in determining which client with mental retardation might profit from counseling or psychotherapy is the individual's level of retardation. For the most part, the provision of counseling and psychotherapy services will be directed toward those individuals with mental retardation who are at or above the 6- or 7-year-old cognitive level. This is often described in the child and adolescent psychotherapy literature as a minimum level of cognitive development to be able to profit from direct therapeutic intervention. Selecting this minimum level of cognitive development thus limits the provision of therapeutic services to those adolescents, older children, and adults who are in the upper moderate to mild ranges of mental retardation. It should be noted that this group makes up by far the largest percentage of those individuals who carry a mental retardation diagnosis. Although technically no longer a classification of mental retardation, we also include those with borderline intelligence in this group. Although some have written both in the mental retardation and child psychotherapy literature that there are techniques (e.g., play therapy) that can be used with those at even lower levels of development, it is our opinion that the provision of therapeutic services to clients below the 6- to 7-year-old level will in most cases not be beneficial. Thus, most individuals in the moderately mentally retarded range, and virtually all of those in the severely and profoundly retarded ranges, would not be candidates for direct therapeutic intervention.

As Sevin and Matson report in Chapter Two, the individual with mental retardation is susceptible to the full range of emotional disorders. Although it is generally accepted that many of the more severe psychiatric disorders (i.e., the psychoses) are usually not treatable by counseling or psychotherapy, a large percentage of disorders are seen as treatable with counseling and psychotherapy, either directly or as an adjunct to other treatments. Related to our working hypothesis, we feel that if counseling and psychotherapy is a viable option for treating a specific emotional disorder in a nonretarded person, it then should be considered as a viable option for treating the same disorder in a person with mental retardation. For example, the use of cognitively based therapy for the treatment of depression is well established. Yet, this is rarely used as an option for treating depression with individuals with mental retardation.

In addition to recognizing the fact that the population of individuals with mental retardation presents a full range of emotional and behavioral problems, it is useful in therapy to understand the characteristics and nature of the life of the client with mental retardation. As indicated above, the focus of this book is on the moderately and mildly retarded older child, adolescent, and adult. This range includes individuals who are typically at a cognitive developmental level from 6 to 7 years to 12 to 13 years. In general, there is a lack of adequate life span developmental data on this group. However, we are struck by the similarity between the issues faced by the adult population of individuals with mental retardation and those faced by adolescents with "normal" intelligence in the course of their development. Naturally, there are significant differences, but the overlap is striking. If one peruses any of the general textbooks on adolescent development and psychology, it is clear that the contents could also serve, with some limitations, as guidelines for working with adolescents and adults with mental retardation. Consider the following general similarities between the life issues faced by adolescents without mental retardation and by adults with mental retardation:

- Both are not living independently and are dependent on some authority person(s) to direct their lives.
- Both tend to be in settings during the day where their activities are supervised.
- Both have cognitive limitations, particularly in terms of problem solving, impulse control, and more concrete thought.
- Both are struggling with issues of independence, identity, peer groups, vocational choices, sexual identity, and dealing with authority figures.
- Both are often referred by others and may enter counseling/therapy involuntarily.

In our own clinical work we have counseled both adolescents and adults with mental retardation—we have found the problem-solving tasks and life issues facing these populations to be very similar. We do *not* imply that adults with mental retardation should be treated as adolescents—rather, that the body of psychological knowledge gathered concerning adolescents may provide a useful reference point for clinical work with individuals with retardation.

Elements of "Good" Therapeutic Interventions

The chapters in this book discuss a variety of interventions with persons with mental retardation. Although preferences for certain techniques and guiding theories will be evident, there are a number of elements of good therapeutic practice that cut across theoretical boundaries. We feel that consideration of these elements is important and that they should always be kept in mind, regardless of theoretical perspective, orientation, or utilization of specific techniques.

Counseling/Therapy Should Be Developmentally Appropriate

With cognitively and developmentally limited clients, it is necessary to develop direct interventions that are appropriate for the client's language and cognitive levels. In the area of language, this necessitates consideration of vocabulary, level of complexity of questions, and the nature of therapeutic leads directed at the client. Simpler language and briefer and more straightforwardly answered questions are indicated. The counselor/therapist may need to be more diligent in determining both what the client means by his or her language and whether the client understands the language used by the counselor. We once worked with a client who kept referring to his "depressions," and we assumed that he was describing problems commonly attributed to clinical depression—sadness, unhappiness, etc. On checking, the client was describing a fairly classic case of acute anxiety episodes. We initially had failed to clarify the client's meaning of the word "depressions." Once the clarification was made, treatment with this individual proceeded very smoothly.

The other aspect of development that has therapeutic implications is the client's level of cognitive development. Piagetian theory may be useful here in guiding interventions. Dougherty and Moran (1983) note that most adults with mild retardation will achieve Piaget's cognitive developmental level of concrete operations, but not the more advanced level of formal operations. Individuals at the concrete level of cognitive development basically think in the here and now. Individuals who are functioning at this level do not tend to think abstractly, to test hypotheses about the world, or to understand the concept of probability. Given that most all individuals with mental retardation tend to fall in the concrete level of cognitive development, it will be critical in counseling that the focus be on more real-life experiences and here and now issues. This need to be more concrete in counseling would seem to suggest the viability of more direct problem solving, modeling, and role playing. Generalization of counseling gains to issues outside of therapy, and more abstract personal problem solving, is less likely to be successful. In reviewing the major theories of psychotherapy (e.g., Corsini & Wedding, 1989), one notes considerable discussion of client changes that would require the attainment of formal operations. This focus on formal operations makes the routine use (as applied with "normal" IQ adults) of these theories with clients with mental retardation of questionable validity.

"Inelegant" Goals

The limitations noted above may restrict the type of goals that counselors can develop with their clients. Without considering these limitations counselors may have a tendency to set goals that are too high or perhaps too optimistic for their cognitively limited clients.

Rational-emotive therapy provides a useful distinction of types of goals in therapy (Grieger & Boyd, 1980). "Elegant" goals are those in which the client will not only be able to apply the problem solving he or she learned relative to the original referral concern, but will also be able to generalize it to other life areas. For example, a woman presents problems relative to the stresses of dealing with the people with whom she works. In therapy, she is able to understand her co-workers better and develop some new behaviors for her interpersonal relations. She is thus able to resolve the original work-related referral concern. However, she finds that she is also able to apply some of her new skills and perceptions with her family and in other areas of her life. She has been able to generalize. This generalization and more global improvement in her functioning represent a more "elegant" goal attainment. It represents a preventive or positive mental health intervention in that it also reduces the tendency of the client to become disturbed.

Implicitly, elegant goals involve formal operations. Individuals at the concrete level of cognitive development may be limited in their ability to attain "elegant" goals. Frequently counseling will need to focus on inelegant goals (i.e., those in which the client is able primarily to resolve the specific problem brought to counseling; in the example above, the inelegant goal would be improvement in her work situation). With clients with mental retardation, "inelegant" goals may frequently be the most appropriate. Although not as lofty as elegant goals, the inelegant goals may be more realistic. Further, this improvement in specific situations and the resulting stress reduction are likely to impact on other areas of clients' lives. Thus, we feel inelegant goals are appropriate for the population of individuals with mental retardation; and, further, that the accomplishment of such goals is a significant success in counseling and should be viewed as such.

Style and Foci

The need to be more concrete with clients with mental retardation dictates that the content of therapeutic discussion have a specific-problem, here-and-now focus. Historical reconstruction of personal events, as well abstract analyses or projections into the future, are likely to be unproductive. Further, the problem focus needs to be specific in nature. The role of "insight" in behavior change and improved emotional functioning has often been questioned even in interventions with nonretarded populations. With clients with mental retardation, pursuing a goal of insight may be even more unproductive. In general, it does not appear that a goal of "insight" is appropriate, particularly in the sense of insight associated with psychoanalytic or dynamic perspectives. Insights that *directly* lead to understanding of specific, current behaviors may have a role in counseling/therapy. In general, the counselor's therapeutic style will also be more active. The counselor/therapist may take a more directive role in focusing the content of the sessions. There may be a more active conversational exchange between client and counselor/therapist, and there may be more "activities" (e.g., role playing, modeling) in the therapy sessions.

Expression-Fostering Techniques

The language and cognitive limitations inherent in mental retardation may make traditional "talking" interventions more difficult. The less articulate client with mental retardation may feel uncomfortable in verbally oriented sessions. Anxiety may impede interaction and clients may have difficulty finding the correct language to express their thoughts and feelings. The counselor/therapist is faced with two tasks: (1) providing the client with a language or way to communicate thoughts, feelings, and concerns and (2) providing avenues and activities to encourage expression.

The first task, in effect, is teaching the client some basic skills or tools that he or she will need to engage in the therapy/counseling process. Initially, this may mean explaining what the general purpose of the meetings will be and why the client is entering into the counseling relationship. More specifically, however, it will involve teaching clients ways of describing their emotions and thoughts. This may involve teaching them some "emotional language" that goes beyond "I feel good" or "I feel bad," or teaching clients the meanings and uses of words like "sad," "angry," "nervous," etc. An additional, useful tool is to teach clients the differences between thoughts and feelings. We have often found that when clients are asked a question that calls for an affective response, a nonaffective response results. For example, a client was asked, "How do you *feel* about what your roommate did to you?" and responded, "I thought it was a lousy thing to do." We have found that teaching clients the thought/feeling distinction facilitates gaining a clearer picture of clients' problems both for the counselor/therapist and the client.

Counselors and therapists may also wish to make use of the range of expression-promoting techniques that include nonverbal components. The client may need assistance in discussing certain issues and tying emotions and thoughts to certain situations. Drawing, role plays, puppet play, games, and mutual-storytelling techniques rely less on verbal interchange and allow nonverbal expression. Further, these activities may provide more concrete content for the client to relate to emotionally and cognitively. For example, a client who has difficulty describing concerns about his or her family may have an easier time doing this while completing a family drawing that may provide a base for discussion. Similarly, providing the client with a "stimulus" picture that is relevant to his or her current situation may allow him or her to express emotions that are otherwise untapped.

Multimodal Approaches

The work of Lazarus (1976, 1981) is often recognized as a viable and preferred technique for conducting therapeutic interventions with nonretarded populations. Further, this approach cuts across a number of theoretical orientations. Lazarus uses as a base the *BASIC ID* which describes seven *modalities* or areas that could be problematic or influencing the client's functioning.

B	=	**B**ehavior
A	=	**A**ffect
S	=	**S**ensation
I	=	**I**magery
C	=	**C**ognition
I	=	**I**nterpersonal
D	=	**D**rugs/**D**iet

Briefly, Lazarus supports assessment across modalities to assess referral concerns comprehensively. By assessing across modalities, practitioners are less likely to omit significant components of a problem, focus solely on one area, or be too narrow in choice of treatment targets. Following assessment, the practitioner can then prioritize concerns, choose the most efficacious point(s) for intervention, and match targets with specific interventions. We will discuss this issue later, but there has been a tendency among clinicians to underassess some social-emotional problems among clients with mental retardation, and perhaps focus too much on overt behavioral concerns. The utilization of the *BASIC ID* combats this tendency and opens up a wider array of treatment options. We support this multimodal philosophy as a sound base for clinical work and suggest that it may be a particularly useful orientation for work with persons with mental retardation.

Involvement with "Significant Others"

Persons with mental retardation generally live in systems where their behavior is influenced, and in some cases controlled, by others. Counseling and psychotherapeutic interventions should not ignore these systemic factors, and counseling should not occur in isolation from these aspects of the clients' lives. Therapeutic interventions will interface with families and those who provide services for persons with mental retardation. Family interventions (Chapter Seven) and consultation issues (in this chapter) are discussed later in this volume.

Developmental Adaptations

As will be seen in the subsequent chapters in this book, there are very few counseling and psychotherapeutic techniques designed or developed specifically for persons with mental retardation. Yet, this "special" population requires special consideration in the development of therapeutic interventions. This paucity of techniques dictates that the generic therapeutic approaches be developmentally adapted for persons with mental retardation. In fact, much of the discussion in later chapters focuses on developmental adaptations.

As discussed above, interventions need to be developmentally appropriate for the client. Two general methods exist for developmental adaptation of techniques for use with persons with mental retardation. The first is to alter directly the techniques that would be used with a nonretarded person of the same age. This may involve simplifying the language utilized, making the concepts discussed in therapy more concrete, fostering a more active client role, reducing the number of ideas discussed, changing the nature of outside (i.e., homework) therapy assignments, etc. Experienced therapists who work with nonretarded clients often gauge their therapeutic work by their client's ability to understand and process the content of therapy and make these types of changes as they progress in therapy. With persons with mental retardation, these adaptations are likely to be more planned and extensive. Rather than intuitively responding to the client's reactions in therapy, the therapist who works with clients with mental retardation may a priori plan the nature and level of content for the sessions.

The second option involves utilization of child and adolescent counseling and psychotherapy techniques within normalization considerations. A wide array of therapeutic techniques have been applied and found useful with child and adolescent populations (Brown & Prout, 1989; Kazdin, 1988). For example, Brown and Prout (1989) delineate applications of behavioral, reality, rational-emotive, psychodynamic/psychoanalytic, Adlerian, person-centered, and systems theories for working with child and adolescent populations. These child and adolescent techniques have, in most cases, already been adapted for less cognitively developed individuals and have been formulated based on developmental considerations. In many cases, they can either be directly applied with persons with mental retardation of all ages or require less modification/adaptation than the similar adult techniques. This second option, however, *must* take into consideration normalization issues. The principle of normalization (Wolfensberger, 1972) calls for persons with mental retardation to live and work in the community in as close to what is considered "normal" conditions as possible. This includes providing access to community services and resources and treating the individual in an "age-appropriate" manner. We have seen some mental health professionals, unfamiliar with the population of individuals with mental retardation, treat adult clients with mental retardation like small children. This clearly is not normalizing. Thus, if the professional decides to utilize techniques designed for children and adolescents, he or she should balance the choice and application of techniques with normalization considerations. Adult clients with mental retardation should be treated as much like adult nonretarded clients as possible. The utilization of play techniques with adults with mental retardation, in most cases, would not be normalizing. Although there may be some instances where therapists may choose childlike interactive techniques, these approaches should only be used after the consideration of normalization issues and, perhaps, trials of less childlike techniques. Further, it should be noted that the principles of normalization are consistent with the growth and personal-fulfillment philosophies espoused in many of the various theoretical orientations to therapy.

Points of Role Conflict

The delivery of counseling and psychotherapy services often places practitioners in situations where there may be potential role conflict. This is particularly true for professionals working in agencies where they may perform multiple roles (e.g., counselor, administrator, consultant, placement specialist, vocational evaluator). Additionally, professionals who also work with families of handicapped individuals may find themselves in dual roles involving services to both the individual and the individual's family.

The issues with family interventions are more fully discussed in Chapter Seven. However, the professional may find him/herself in conflicts between and among the agency, the family, and the individual client. Family concerns and desires may be in conflict with the agency and/or the individual. The professional may find the question "Who's the client?" a somewhat cloudy issue. Professionals who deal frequently with families may find it useful to identify their allegiances clearly early in their counseling and to inform parties of any constraints and limitations to family counseling and consultation. Such delineation is important from both ethical and treatment effectiveness perspectives.

The agency-based professional who performs multiple roles is also likely to encounter role conflicts. Professionals providing counseling and psychotherapy services to an individual may also be asked to provide or participate in other services for the individual. For example, we counseled with a young man in a community residence about self-esteem and sexuality issues. At the same time that counseling services were being provided, we were asked to develop a behavioral plan to deal with some problem behaviors in the community residence. This involved participating in a team meeting to discuss the young man and "imposing" a plan that might involve some consequences not viewed as desirable by him. Later, we were asked to participate in a placement meeting about this same young man in which decisions were being made about his move to a more independent, less-restrictive apartment setting. Again, the subtle influence of the confidential prior counseling relationship was difficult to put aside in making objective decisions. The roles of counselor/ therapist vs. behavior manager and/or counselor/therapist vs. decision maker may be difficult to keep separate, yet may place the professional in conflictual and even potentially unethical positions. One immediate role conflict involves the issue of "sharing" information from the counseling sessions with other team members. Clearly, it is *unethical* to reveal this information in the staff or team meeting. Yet, on a more subtle level, information gathered in the counseling sessions could potentially influence the decisions about the nature of a behavior plan. Professionals should inform their clients of their other obligations and roles within an agency. An additional role conflict involves the establishment of an open, caring relationship with the client, while at the same time being involved with implementing negative consequences. It is best to inform all parties of the potential role conflicts and where possible to avoid situations that would foster this type of problem. The clear solution in these situations is to maintain only one type of relationship with a client, although given the extensive nature of the services provided to individuals with mental retardation, this solution is not always a practical one.

Types of Counseling and Psychotherapy Problems

As mentioned previously, persons with mental retardation present the full range of psychological disorders and social-emotional problems. They also present in counseling with a broad range of problems and concerns. Two studies have assessed the types of concerns addressed in counseling and psychotherapy with persons with mental retardation.

Wittmann, Strohmer, and Prout (1989) used an open-ended questionnaire and asked a variety of "counselors" who work with persons with mental retardation to list the problems they most commonly encounter in counseling persons with borderline intelligence and clients with mental retardation. It was stressed that the focus was on problems the clients *wanted* help with, not the counseling problems or referral concerns presented by the population of individuals with mental retardation. The "counselors" were predominantly bachelor's- and master's-level trained professionals who worked in residential and workshop settings. The responses were categorized by type of concern or problem presented. Based on the percentage of all responses, the most frequent problem areas were:

Interpersonal Concerns	22%
General Psychological Functioning	18%
Work	12%
Sexuality	6%
Family	5%
Residential Living and Adjustment	5%
Behavior	4%
Financial and Material Resources	4%
Accepting and Coping with Disability	4%
Dealing with Authority Figures	4%

Many other problems and concerns were noted, but all were mentioned in less than 4% of the responses.

In a similar study, Jacobson and Ackerman (1989) surveyed psychologists (members of the American Association on Mental Retardation's Psychology Division) about their services to persons with mental retardation and psychiatric impairments. They asked the respondents to indicate whether they addressed certain aspects of adjustment in counseling and psychotherapy with persons of different levels of mental retardation. They found the following percentages of psychologists who acknowledged that these aspects were addressed in counseling and psychotherapy with clients with borderline intelligence and with mild/moderate mental retardation.

Aspect	Borderline Intelligence	Mild/Moderate Retardation
Adaptation to Current Living Situation	62%	78%
Adaptation to New Living Situation	59%	70%
Motivation for Learning	42%	45%
Peer Group Relationships	66%	77%
Familial Relationships	57%	62%
Self-Control of Unacceptable Behavior	69%	85%
Improving Self-Advocacy	43%	45%
Interpersonal or Social Skills Enhancement	68%	85%

Performance on Assessment Measures	27%	31%
Personality Functioning	45%	46%
Improving Employability	46%	49%
Career or Employment Planning	36%	32%
Responsiveness to Supervision or Direction	54%	32%

As can be seen, these two studies suggest many similar concerns even though they approached the question from somewhat different vantage points and methodologies. More important, it is clear that persons with mental retardation present a wide range of problems, concerns, and issues that need to be dealt with in counseling and psychotherapy. In fact, these lists might be useful clinically in assessing problem areas for individual clients.

Clinical Judgment Issues

Conceptually, thorough and accurate diagnosis and assessment are key ingredients to the planning of successful interventions. Although the link between assessment and treatment may be tenuous at times, rational assessment/intervention interface is a desirable goal for practitioners. Erroneous clinical judgment can lead to failure to recognize a problem or disorder or result in the implementation of inappropriate treatments. The work of Steven Reiss and his colleagues (Levithan & Reiss, 1983; Reiss, Levithan, & Syszko, 1982; Reiss & Syszko, 1983) points to one area of clinical judgment bias. They coined the term "diagnostic overshadowing" to describe a tendency for clinicians and professionals to downplay or ignore mental health problems when they are aware that the client or patient functions in the mentally retarded range. In a series of analogue studies, they presented professionals with identical case studies with the exception that in one case the individual was described as having an IQ in the mentally retarded range, and in the other, the person's cognitive functioning was described in the average range. When the subject of the case study was described as having mental retardation, the clinicians were less likely to diagnose an emotional disorder and to recommend appropriate therapeutic intervention. This is likely to translate to an actual underdiagnosing of emotional problems in the population of individuals with mental retardation and create difficulties in obtaining mental health services.

Alford and Locke (1984), using a similar methodology, focused more specifically on treatment recommendations and found clinicians were more likely to recommend behavioral treatments for persons with mental retardation as opposed to other intervention options. This is also a form of clinical judgment bias in that the range of potential treatment options may be restricted in the clinician decision making about the client. As noted previously, counseling and psychotherapy are often not thought of as viable options by some—the mental retardation label may inappropriately rule out this option.

The studies noted above may be limited due to their analogue nature. Our experience, however, suggests that overshadowing may be even more of a factor in actual clinical practice. We once interviewed a woman with mild mental retardation who was referred by her apartment supervisor because of general moodiness. During an interview, she cried constantly, described poor eating and sleeping patterns, spoke of her low self-esteem and hopelessness, and related thoughts of suicide. Behavioral data supported what appeared to be an almost "textbook" presentation of clinical depression, in the moderate to severe depression range. It was decided to refer her to a local psychiatrist for a second evaluation. The psychiatrist was provided with a summary of the initial interviews and behavioral reports, and the client's behavior in the second interview was similar to her previous interview. The consult sheet was returned to the referring agency with the following notation: "Diagnosis: Mental retardation with behavioral problems. Recommendation: Use a reward system." We would like to think that this is an atypical response to clients with mental retardation. Unfortunately, this type of overshadowing occurs too frequently.

Sovner and Hurley (1986) have also described factors that affect the diagnosis of psychiatric disorder in persons with mental retardation. They describe "pathoplastic" factors which distort the effects of personality and intelligence upon the presentation of psychiatric disorders. In effect, the cognitive impairments of mental retardation modify the nature of the symptoms of the psychiatric disorder. The more severe the cognitive impairment, the greater the influence on the symptoms. These factors include *intellectual distortion* due to diminished ability to think abstractly and communicate intelligibly; *psychosocial masking,* which refers to the concrete content and lack of imagination in symptom presentation; *cognitive disintegration*, which may result in behavioral regression or even more limited cognitive functioning due to poor coping mechanisms and reaction to stress; and *baseline exaggeration*, in which general deficits and maladaptive behaviors may significantly increase under stress. Any one of these factors may alter the nature of the clinical presentation of disorders when compared to the typical presentation in nonretarded persons. Further, this limits the utility of typical diagnostic procedures that are used with the general population. Sovner and Hurley specifically note the limitations of the traditional clinical interview with persons with mental retardation and the need to rely more on information provided by caregivers. Sovner and Hurley also feel that current psychiatric criteria (i.e., *DSM-III-R*) are inadequate when dealing with persons with mental retardation because the pathoplastic factors may make detection of certain clinical features difficult.

Treatment Efficacy: An Error in Logic?

As will be seen throughout this book, there is relatively little "good" empirical research on the efficacy of counseling and psychotherapy with persons with mental retardation. Historically, there has been a general conclusion that counseling and psychotherapy have not been shown to be effective with persons with mental retardation (e.g., see the reviews of Sternlicht, 1965; Nuffield, 1983; and Matson, 1984). Many of these studies on the efficacy of counseling and psychotherapy with persons with mental retardation were done in the 1950s, 1960s, and 1970s. There are many issues related to this failure to show effectiveness, including many methodological concerns. Perhaps as a result of this research many general books on counseling and psychotherapy do not discuss mental retardation, or rule out consideration of counseling and psychotherapy with persons with mental retardation. Matson (1984) notes that mental retardation routinely is used to eliminate potential subjects from general psychotherapy efficacy studies. The general conclusion is that counseling and psychotherapy with persons with mental retardation has been viewed as ineffective *due to the mental retardation.*

It is interesting to note that at roughly the same time the research seemed to indicate that counseling and psychotherapy were ineffective with persons with mental retardation, the debate was raging about the general effectiveness of counseling and psychotherapy. Eysenck's (1952, 1966) and Rachman's (1971, 1973) reviews of therapy effectiveness with adults and Levitt's (1957, 1963, 1971) similar reviews with children concluded that psychotherapy was generally ineffective or not much more effective than no treatment. Athough this view has changed in recent years (e.g., see Kazdin, 1988), the earlier research *seemed to blame the techniques* and not the populations studied.

We believe that the interpretation of ineffectiveness of therapeutic interventions with persons with mental retardation suffered a "kill the messenger" error in logic. The two lines of research occurred at approximately the same time. When psychotherapy was found to be ineffective with persons with mental retardation, the analyses attributed this ineffectiveness to the limitations of persons with mental retardation. However, when psychotherapy was found to be generally ineffective, the analyses attributed the ineffectiveness to the inadequacy of the techniques. Thus, we have two essentially similar empirical findings with two different interpretations of the data. Although we cannot point to a series of studies that clearly supports the effectiveness of counseling and psychotherapy with persons with mental retardation, we do not feel that current research negates potential efficacy. In effect, we feel it was *incorrect logical reasoning* that blamed the failure to show effectiveness on the subjects with mental retardation. As a result we feel quite strongly that the issue of the general effectiveness of counseling and psychotherapy with persons with mental retardation remains unanswered.

Counseling: A Client's Perspective

We close this chapter with a few quotes from clients with mental retardation we have counseled. The first set are from beginning counseling sessions and demonstrate the need to understand the client's view of counseling. Typically, we ask clients why they have been sent to talk to us. A few responses from different clients:

- "I don't know why I'm here."
- "You're going to get me out of trouble."
- (Hostile Client) "You're the bozo they sent me to . . . I'm not going to let no shrink read my mind."
- "They keep saying I'm screwed up. You're going to unscrew me."
- "You are the doctor and you know all the answers."

Not unlike individuals without retardation who come for counseling, our clients with mental retardation are at cross-purposes with us or unclear about the nature of counseling and therapy. This lack of clarity, incompatible goals, or direct opposition are likely to serve as starting points of the therapeutic process.

As we neared the end of an approximately 6-month counseling relationship with a man with mild mental retardation named Michael, we asked him to describe his view of the counselor and the counseling process. Michael, 32, had a measured IQ of 62 and had been referred for anger problems and general interpersonal difficulties. A combined approach of cognitive-behavioral, problem-solving, and affective techniques had resulted in decreased and less intense outbursts and improved interpersonal functioning. Additionally, the relationship between client and counselor was quite positive. When asked to describe his view, Michael paused for a few minutes and replied:

A special kind of friendship . . .

A really special friend...

Someone you can talk to about most anything—things that really bother you . . .

It helps you find better ways to act . . .

Helps you know about other people and why they act funny
sometimes . . .
Someone you can tell things to and they won't always be judging on you—
and they won't blab it around . . .

Again, not unlike nonretarded individuals who come for counseling, Michael
needed a relationship built on trust, understanding, and a willingness on the part of
the counselor to adjust counseling to meet his needs. In this case he was able to find
such a relationship, and understood it and appreciated it. It is our hope that the
material presented here and in the chapters to follow will help other counselors
allow other Michaels to find similar help and support.

The Organization of this Book

The remainder of this book focuses both on specific counseling and
psychotherapeutic techniques as well as some related areas of the professional
literature. The chapter on psychopathology acquaints the reader with the range of
social-emotional problems presented by individuals with mental retardation,
followed by a discussion of ways of assessing these problems. In effect, these two
chapters address the questions "What are our clients' problems?" and "How do we
describe and/or quantify the problems?" The next two chapters focus on individual
counseling and psychotherapy, contrasting and describing both behavioral and
more traditional approaches to intervention. The chapters on group interventions
and family approaches describe a broader array of techniques from different
theoretical viewpoints. Finally, we conclude with a chapter on vocational counseling—although vocational counseling is not often considered a "psychotherapeutic"
technique, we feel that this area is often an ignored component in developing
programs focused on promoting general emotional adjustment.

References

Alford, J. D., & Locke, B. L. (1984). Clinical responses to psychopathology of mentally
retarded persons. *American Journal of Mental Deficiency, 89,* 195-197.
Brown, D. T., & Prout, H. T. (Eds.). (1989). *Counseling and psychotherapy with children
and adolescents* (2nd ed.). Brandon, VT: Clinical Psychology Publishing.
Corsini, R. J. (1989). Introduction. In R. J. Corsini & D. Wedding (Eds.), *Current
psychotherapies* (4th ed., pp. 1-16). Itasca, IL: F. E. Peacock.

Corsini, R. J., & Wedding, D. (Eds.). (1989). *Current psychotherapies* (3rd ed.). Itasca, IL: F. E. Peacock.

Dougherty, J. M., & Moran, J. D. (1983). The relationship of Piagetian stages to mental retardation. *Education and Training of the Mentally Retarded, 18*, 260-265.

Eysenck, H. J. (1952). The effects of psychotherapy: An evaluation. *Journal of Consulting Psychology, 16*, 319-324.

Eysenck, H. J. (1966). *The effects of psychotherapy*. New York: International Science Press.

Grieger, R., & Boyd, J. (1980). *Rational-emotive therapy: A skills-based approach*. New York: Van Nostrand Reinhold.

Jacobson, J. W., & Ackerman, J. J. (1989). Psychological services for persons with mental retardation and psychiatric impairments. *Mental Retardation, 27*, 33-36.

Kazdin, A. E. (1988). *Child psychotherapy: Developing and identifying effective treatments*. New York: Pergamon.

Lazarus, A. A. (1976). *Multimodal behavior therapy*. New York: Springer.

Lazarus, A. A. (1981). *The practice of multimodal therapy*. New York: McGraw-Hill.

Levithan, G., & Reiss, S. (1983). Generality of diagnostic overshadowing across disciplines. *Applied Research in Mental Retardation, 4*, 59-64.

Levitt, E. E. (1957). The results of psychotherapy with children: An evaluation. *Journal of Consulting Psychology, 21*, 186-189.

Levitt, E. E. (1963). Psychotherapy with children: A further evaluation. *Behavior Research and Therapy, 60*, 326-329.

Levitt, E. E. (1971). Research on psychotherapy with children. In A. E. Bergin & S. Garfield (Eds.), *Handbook of psychotherapy and behavior change* (pp. 474-493). New York: Wiley.

Matson, J. L. (1984). Psychotherapy with persons who are mentally retarded. *Mental Retardation, 22*, 170-175.

Nuffield, E. J. (1983). Psychotherapy. In J. L. Matson & J. A. Mulick (Eds.), *Handbook of mental retardation* (pp. 351-368). New York: Pergamon Press.

Rachman, S. (1971). *The effects of psychotherapy*. Oxford: Pergamon Press.

Rachman, S. (1973). The effects of psychological treatment. In H. J. Eysenck (Ed.), *Handbook of abnormal psychology*, (pp. 273-298). New York: Basic Books.

Reiss, S., Levithan, G., & McNally, R. (1982). Emotionally disturbed mentally retarded people. *American Psychologist, 37*, 361-367.

Reiss, S., Levithan, G., & Syszko, J. (1982). Emotional disturbance and mental retardation: Diagnostic overshadowing. *American Journal of Mental Deficiency, 86*, 567-574.

Reiss, S., & Syszko, J. (1983). Diagnostic overshadowing and experience with mentally retarded persons. *American Journal of Mental Deficiency, 87*, 396-402.

Sovner, R., & Hurley, A. D. (1986). Four factors affecting the diagnosis of psychiatric disorders in mentally retarded persons. *Psychiatric Aspects of Mental Retardation Reviews, 5(9)*, 1-3

Sternlicht, M. (1965). Psychotherapeutic techniques useful with the mentally retarded: A review and critique. *Psychiatric Quarterly, 39*, 84-90.

Wittman, J. J. P., Strohmer, D. C., & Prout, H. T. (1989). Problems presented by persons of mentally retarded and borderline intellectual functioning in counseling: An exploratory investigation. *Journal of Applied Rehabilitation Counseling, 20*, 8-13.

Wolfensberger, W. (1972). *The principle of normalization.* Toronto: National Institute on Mental Retardation.

2 AN OVERVIEW OF PSYCHOPATHOLOGY

Jay A. Sevin and Johnny L. Matson

Persons with mental retardation are susceptible to the same range of behavioral and emotional disorders as are nonintellectually impaired persons. Yet surprisingly few clinicians and doctors have concerned themselves with the emotional development of persons with mental retardation as a group. The high incidence and variety of emotional maladjustment in the population with mental retardation has become recognized more in recent years. Initial studies have suggested alarmingly high rates of mental illness in persons with mental retardation (Penrose, 1962; Rutter, Tizard, Yule, Graham, & Whitmore, 1976). Several studies have reported rates four to six times greater than those for the general population. Thus, agreement exists among mental health professionals today that there is a need for more research in this area.

There has been a strong link between mental illness and mental retardation throughout history. In fact, prior to the 17th century, no distinction was made between the two disorders (Rosen, Clark, & Kivitz, 1976). As a result, persons with mental retardation and those with emotional disturbance received the same treatment and the same stigma. The tendency to see these two conditions as a single disorder may have in many cases been due to apparent similarities between psychotic reactions and the behavior of individuals with more severe mental retardation (Beier, 1964). Nevertheless, the differentiation of mental retardation from psychopathology gradually began to take place during the 19th century. Most classification systems came to distinguish between the two disorders based on the presence or absence of the individual's potential for reasoning and complex thought

(Lewis & MacLean, 1982). The presence of cognitive deficits has remained at the core of all subsequent definitions of mental retardation. Still, it was not until 1886 that a legal distinction was made between mental retardation and mental illness in England.

It was during the late 1880s that the first studies were published reporting the coexistence of emotional disturbances and mental retardation within individuals. Several cases of psychotic, mentally retarded children were reported. Also, during this period there appeared the first reports of affective disorders in persons with mental retardation (Clouston, 1883; Hurd, 1888).

At the turn of this century, most prominent professionals in this country held the view that there existed some inherent link between mental subnormality and delinquency, crime, and other behavioral disorders (Beier, 1964; Fernald, 1908). This view, coupled with the then popular theory that mental retardation was solely the result of genetic inheritance (Ollendick & Ollendick, 1982), led to a period of strict segregation and frequent sterilization of persons with mental retardation.

To counter the stigma of mental retardation, the 20th century has been marked by the attempt of many professionals in the field to divorce mental illness from mental retardation. These efforts were probably necessary at first, in order to compensate for the harshness of previous views. However, this separation has resulted in the tendency to view mental retardation and psychiatric disorders as nonoverlapping conditions. There exists at present a sharp division between social and delivery services for individuals with mental illness and persons with mental retardation. Thus, the tendency has been to ignore the social and emotional development of persons with mental retardation in order to treat cognitive/ intellectual deficits. It is only in recent years that a few clinicians in the field have begun to assert that the emotionally disturbed have the same rights to counseling and psychotherapy as do the nonretarded emotionally disturbed.

Despite studies suggesting high incidence and a broad range of emotional disorders among persons with mental retardation, many important topics such as etiology, assessment, and treatment of psychopathology in this population are only beginning to be investigated. Other important issues such as the adaptive signifi-cance of pathological behavior and effects of institutionalization on mental illness are also in need of study. In addition, certain specific disorders such as substance abuse, somatiform disorders, and most of the psychosexual disorders have gone almost entirely unexplored with persons with mental retardation. Much of the existing literature is anecdotal and conjectural. Only a handful of studies have utilized empirical procedures and scientifically sound methods. Thus, work in this field is still in its early stages.

In this chapter, the authors will attempt to present a descriptive overview of psychopathology in persons with mental retardation. Both theoretical issues and research findings from past literature will be discussed. A comprehensive review of all studies dealing with psychopathology in persons with mental retardation is well beyond the scope of this chapter. However, a broad survey of significant findings and research trends will be presented. Finally, the chapter will define particular areas in need of study and offer suggestions for future research.

The first part of this chapter will provide an overview of the major issues relevant to emotionally disturbed persons with mental retardation. This review will include a look at prevalence data, a summary of the major theoretical models of psychopathology in persons with mental retardation, and a discussion of personality traits and life events that play a role in the emotional disorders of this population. Finally, diagnosis and treatment models will be discussed.

The second section of the chapter deals with the specific types of psychopathology in persons with mental retardation that have been studied. This section will focus on anxiety disorders, affective disorders, psychoses, disorders of impulse control, and personality disorders. Incidence, etiology, treatment methods, and presenting symptoms will be discussed in relation to the specific disorders. Also, various classification systems will be evaluated. Due to the broad nature of this chapter, the reader will frequently be referred to other sources for more detailed discussions of particular issues.

Definitions

In dealing with psychopathology in persons with mental retardation, attempts to integrate and compare the findings of various studies are frequently complicated by the different definitions of psychopathology and mental retardation employed by the authors. For reasons of clarity, mental retardation and psychopathology are defined in this chapter according to the *Diagnostic and Statistical Manual-III* (APA, 1980), presently the most widely used classification system of emotional disorders. According to *DSM-III/DSM-III-R*, the essential features of mental retardation are:

(A) Significant subaverage general intellectual functioning: an IQ of 70 or below on an individually administered IQ test (for infants, since available intelligence tests do not yield numerical values, a clinical judgment of significant subaverage intellectual functioning). (B) Concurrent deficits or impairments in adaptive behavior, taking the person's age into consideration. (C) Onset before the age of 18. (pp. 40–41)

The classifications of mild, moderate, severe, and profound mental retardation are also used in accordance with *DSM-III/DSM-III-R*. In this chapter definitions of specific emotional disorders and terms of psychopathology are also used according to *DSM-III/DSM-III-R*, except when reporting specific findings of an author who used a different diagnostic system or when specifically discussing another system of classification.

Issues in Psychopathology

In general, previous studies dealing with emotional disturbances in persons with mental retardation have fallen into one of several categories. Some studies have attempted to establish prevalence rates of psychopathology in the population with mental retardation. Some studies have discussed various etiological considerations or theoretical models of emotional disturbances that are of importance for persons with mental retardation. A very few studies have concerned themselves with assessment and diagnosis of disorders, and smaller numbers have attempted to assess the efficacy of treatment models. This section will review some of the most relevant theories and salient findings in each of these areas.

Prevalence

The study of psychopathology in persons with mental retardation becomes increasingly important in light of the existing prevalence data. Virtually every study examining prevalence has supported the assertion of greater rates of psychiatric disorders in persons with mental retardation than in the general population (Lewis & MacLean, 1982). In the following studies, diagnoses of emotional disorders were made according to the standard psychiatric manuals in vogue at the time.

Most early prevalence studies were conducted in institutional settings. Penrose (1938), in a study of 1,280 cases of mental retardation, reported 132 cases of psychoneuroses and perversions, 48 cases of schizophrenia, and 24 cases of affective psychoses. Pollock (1944) reported that of 444 persons with mental retardation in New York state hospitals, approximately 40% had experienced one or more transient psychotic episodes. Also, approximately 18% of this sample were diagnosed as schizophrenic. In a population of newly admitted or readmitted patients in a state institution, Neuer (1947) identified seven cases of manic-depressive psychoses and 39 cases classified as neurotic, characterized by restlessness, anxiety, enuresis, and compulsive behavior. The presence of psychiatric disorders probably increases the likelihood of a person with mental retardation being institutionalized (Lewis & MacLean, 1982; Saenger, 1960). Therefore, the above rates may reflect selection biases and are not generalizable to the noninstitutionalized population with mental retardation. In addition, institutionalization itself may contribute to emotional disturbances and maladaptive behavior.

Investigating very different populations, Dewan (1948) and Weaver (1946) examined army recruits and draftees found to have mental retardation. Dewan (1948) reported that of Canadian Army recruits diagnosed as having mental retardation, 47% were found to be emotionally unstable by psychiatric examination. Only 20% of a nonretarded control group were found to be emotionally unstable. Also, Weaver (1946) reported that of 8,000 wartime soldiers with IQs less than 75, 47% of the males and 38% of the females were discharged for emotional disorders. These two studies are of particular interest due to their uses of large, noninstitutionalized samples of adults.

Syzmanski (1977) found emotional disturbances in 54% of 132 children referred to a clinic for individuals with developmental disabilities in a general pediatric hospital. Chazan (1964) studied children with mild mental retardation in an educational placement setting and found the rate of emotional disturbances to be twice as great as that in a control group of children in normal classes. Chess and Hassibi (1970), studying 52 noninstitutionalized children from middle-class families, reported 13 cases of reactive behavior disorders, one case of psychosis, one case of neurosis, and 11 subjects that exhibited signs of cerebral dysfunction. These studies all depict higher rates of psychopathology in children with mental retardation.

Phillips and Williams (1975) evaluated the records of 100 children with mental retardation referred to a psychiatric clinic for assessment of the severity of their mental retardation. Thirty-eight percent of these children were diagnosed as psychotic and exhibited "autistic, mute, or disturbed communication; severely disorganized behavior with self-abusive, uncontrolled outbursts; and distorted interpersonal relationships" (p. 23). Of the 62 nonpsychotic children, 49 were classified as having other behavioral disorders or personality disorders. Among the nonpsychotic children, major symptoms as noted by parents fell into three categories: (a) aggression (44%), (b) poor social relations (43%), and (c) developmental lags (44%). Only 13% were not diagnosed as having some behavioral disorder. A comparison of these children with 79 children without retardation indicated little difference in the types of psychopathology suffered. This study is of particular clinical importance because it gives descriptive data as well as general diagnoses.

It is possible that persons with mental retardation may often overlap diagnostic categories and that less severe cases are sometimes arbitrarily defined. One problem has been that personality disorders are infrequently distinguished from classic psychiatric disorders in persons with mental retardation (Beier, 1964). Craft

(1959) attempted to make this distinction in a study of 314 adult inpatients. They found that only 7% of their sample could be classed as emotionally disturbed whereas 33% showed personality disturbances. Other investigators (Donaldson & Menolascino, 1977; Humphreys, 1940; Weaver, 1946) have also indicated a high incidence of personality disorders in persons with mental retardation, but empirical data are not referenced.

Koller and his colleagues (Koller, Richardson, & Katz, 1983) made the first attempt at gathering prevalence data across the life span of 192 persons with mental retardation. In a study of a 5-year birth cohort, young adults with mental retardation and their parents were interviewed to assess behavioral disorders during distinct periods over the first 22 years of life. Approximately 60% had suffered from some emotional disturbance in each age period assessed. Emotional disturbances were found to be more frequent among females in postschool periods. Antisocial behavior was more common in males both in childhood and postschool periods.

Finally, the Isle of Wight studies (Rutter, 1971; Rutter, Tizard, & Whitmore, 1970; Rutter et al., 1976) represent perhaps the best data available regarding prevalence of emotional disorders in persons with mental retardation. Subjects included 2,199 children with mental retardation in a 9- to 11-year-old cohort. Thirty percent were rated as emotionally disturbed by parents; 42% were rated as disturbed by teachers. These findings are five to six times the rate of emotional disturbances found in a randomly selected control group. In a subgroup of children with severe and profound mental retardation, 50% were diagnosed as emotionally disturbed compared to only 7% in the general population. Diagnosis was determined by clinical observation and interviews with parents. These studies are highlighted by their use of multiple methods of assessment and control groups of persons without mental retardation.

From existing studies it is impossible to assess the prevalence of psychiatric disorders in persons with mental retardation with any great precision. As stated above, rates of psychopathology found in institutionalized populations probably exceed those in noninstitutionalized populations because emotional disturbances may play a role in the decision for institutionalization. In fact, identification of mental retardation, especially milder degrees, is probably more likely to occur in the presence of behavioral disturbances (Lewis & MacLean, 1982). Second, differences in prevalence rates can be attributed to differences in the diagnostic criteria utilized, emphases of the studies, and methods of assessment used. Craft (1959) points out that there are certain inherent difficulties in dual diagnosis where one condition may be partly dependent on the other.

Nevertheless, certain conclusions become evident from the above studies. First, psychopathology occurs in the population with mental retardation much more frequently than in the general population. Second, the full range of emotional disturbances found in the general population are found in the population with mental retardation in varying degrees. Virtually every sample studied reported higher rates of a wide variety of emotional disorders. Third, at least in some cases, the constellation of pathological behaviors exhibited by individuals with mental retardation are the same as those exhibited by emotionally disturbed persons without mental retardation. The field of dual diagnosis would be greatly enhanced by future studies which consider prevalence rates in relation to control groups without mental retardation and which provide not only diagnostic labels but also more detailed descriptions of the subjects themselves.

Models of Psychopathology

Several models of psychopathology currently exist, due mainly to five major theories: psychoanalytic, behavioral, sociological, existential, and biological (Akiskal & McKinney, 1975). Yet, although these theories have been thoroughly investigated in relation to the general population, they have infrequently been applied to persons with mental retardation as a group. There are several ways of addressing psychopathology in persons with mental retardation from a theoretical standpoint. One way is to take traditional theories of psychopathology and to apply them to the population with mental retardation. Traditional theories may apply equally well to persons with mental retardation. However, it is important to note that although the behaviors displayed may be similar and the same etiological factors may play a role in the emotional disturbances of persons with or without mental retardation, it may not be safe to assume that the dynamics leading to psychiatric illness are identical in both (Konarski & Cavalier, 1982).

Psychodynamic model. The oldest theory of psychopathology is Freud's psychodynamic model (Freud, 1966). According to this theory, all emotional disturbances are the result of unresolved intrapsychic conflict and imbalance between the three constructs of the mind: the id, ego, and superego.

People are driven by psychic energy or drives. In an emotionally healthy individual, the ego exercises executant control over the id and superego and satisfies certain drive states in a socially acceptable manner (Brenner, 1974). An important feature of the ego is its ability to distort reality by means of defense mechanisms in order to reduce anxiety (Robinson & Robinson, 1965).

According to this model, the psychopathology of the person with mental retardation is primarily a result of ego deficits (Balthazar & Stephens, 1975). The cognitive deficits of the person with mental retardation limit reality testing and result in inadequate ego development early in life (Konarski & Cavalier, 1982).

Complex defense mechanisms never develop, and the individual must rely on the more immature mechanisms that have developed. Thus, the individual with mental retardation is locked into rigid, stereotyped patterns of behavior. He becomes fixated at an early developmental level and fails to acquire socially adaptive behavior patterns.

A great deal has been written regarding the emotional disorders of persons with mental retardation, according to the psychodynamic model. (See Konarski & Cavalier, 1982, for an excellent discussion on the subject.) However, the theory remains merely speculative in the absence of empirical support.

Behavioral model. Another traditional theory of psychopathology that has been successfully applied to persons with mental retardation is behavior theory. This model finds its roots in the works of Thorndike (1911), Pavlov (1927), and Skinner (1938). It emphasizes: (a) explanations of human behavior according to learning principles established through empirical means and (b) evaluation of treatment techniques through scientific methodology (Agras, Kazdin, & Wilson, 1979). Behavior theory focuses on abnormal behavior itself rather than on unobservable, underlying causes. Modifying target behaviors is the primary goal of intervention.

According to this model, behavior is a function of its consequences. The behavioral repertoire of an individual develops through complex interactions between the individual and the environment. All behavior, including deviant behavior, is learned according to the same principles. Thus, the "primary areas of intervention are the conditions maintaining the presence or absence of the behavior" (Konarski & Cavalier, 1982; pp. 53-76).

According to Bijou (1966) there are four possible explanations for the deviant behavior of the person with mental retardation . First, physiological or anatomical abnormalities may alter stimulus or response function, with adverse affects on the stimulus-response relationship. Second, insufficient reinforcement from the environment may prevent the individual from acquiring a behavioral repertoire adequate for dealing with everyday tasks. Third, inappropriate punishment may modify adaptive behavior and increase avoidance behavior. Fourth, deviant response sets may develop as a result of contingent reinforcement. It is likely that all of these play a role in the psychopathology of persons with mental retardation.

Because of its stress on empirical procedures and scientific verification, the behavioral model has greatly contributed to the understanding and treatment of psychopathology in persons with mental retardation. Several behavior theory–based treatment packages that have proved successful in treating emotional disorders in persons with mental retardation will be discussed throughout this chapter. (For a more thorough discussion of behavioral theory as it relates to dual-diagnosis patients, see Konarski & Cavalier, 1982.)

Biodevelopmental model. A third model, which is primarily biological-developmental, has been discussed by Menolascino (1977). Timing of and reaction to intrinsic and/or extrinsic variables are related primarily to neuroanatomic, physiologic, and developmental stages. Thus, certain *critical* periods are emphasized as to their effects on emotional disorders. Factors receiving the greatest emphasis have included: (a) familial history, (b) genetics, (c) neurological organization, (d) sensory and motor systems, (e) cognitive capacities, (f) mother–child interactions, and (g) professional support systems. There are some data in the various biologically based approaches to psychopathology that support this theoretical model. However, such research is largely inferential and the theory is still in need of empirical support.

Social competency model. Zigler and Seitz (1978) have discussed psychopathology from an environmental perspective. Development is a life-long process that influences the way behavior is perceived and processed. However, the environment to which the individual is exposed undoubtedly plays an important role. Thus, the changing organism and the environment are seen as crucial variables. In addition, Zigler's theory, in contrast to previous developmental theories, emphasizes empirical verification.

Zigler's group (Achenbach & Zigler, 1968; Kohlberg & Zigler, 1967; Yando, Seitz, & Zigler, 1978) has argued that cognitive development is important in the learning process. This issue is even more significant with persons with mental retardation where certain intellectual aspects are delayed or do not develop at all.

Several important factors are emphasized in the cognitive developmental model. One is *self-image disparity*, or the difference between the individual's perception of him- or herself (real self) and his or her aspirations of how he or she should be (ideal self). Cognitive deficits drastically affect this image (Katz & Zigler, 1967; Philips & Zigler, 1980).

A second factor is conformity to culture (Kohlberg, 1966; Kohlberg & Zigler, 1967). Socialization can greatly affect the development of the individual. Sex-role adoption and life-style are two important areas in this category.

Several other factors can be incorporated into this approach, which Achenbach (1974) has termed developmental psychopathology. Perhaps the most heavily emphasized factor is *social competence*, which has been applied primarily to schizophrenia (Philips, Broverman, & Zigler, 1966; Zigler & Philips, 1961). The considerable overlap observed between the problems in individuals with mental retardation and schizophrenia is primarily adaptive (Matson, 1980). Marital status, IQ, number of years in school, type of living arrangement, and friendships are some of the variables used in evaluating social competence. Psychopathology and low social competence are highly correlated (Kolstoe & Schaffer, 1961; Zigler & Philips, 1960). However, studies examining the relationship of social competence to psychopathology in persons with mental retardation are still needed.

Learned helplessness model. One final model that has recently been applied to depression in persons with mental retardation is Seligman's (1975) learned helplessness theory (DeVellis, 1972; Floor & Rosen, 1975; Weisz, 1979). According to this model, repeated failure experiences result in increases in nonadaptive withdrawal behavior even in situations that should under normal circumstances be characterized by more adaptive behavior resulting in reinforcement. Initial studies have given some support to this theory (DeVellis, 1977; Raber & Weisz, 1981). Also, Zeaman and House (1963) found that children with mental retardation were unable to solve problems they could complete prior to introduction of a prolonged failure paradigm. Weisz (1982) has recently provided a more detailed review of this approach. However, people with depression and mental retardation constitute only a subpopulation of individuals with emotional disturbance and mental retardation. Thus, a more broad-based theory is needed.

Etiology

A discussion of these theoretical models brings to the surface several factors that are frequently cited in relation to psychopathology in persons with mental retardation. The strong association between low IQ and psychiatric disturbances is evident from prevalence studies. Several researchers have also uncovered specific biological, environmental, and personality correlates frequently seen in conjunction with emotional disorders in persons with mental retardation. The emphasis placed on various physiological, intrapsychic, and environmental factors may vary across psychotherapists according to theoretical positions. However, it seems reasonable to assume that all three variables play a role in emotional disturbances (Matson, 1984). In most cases, the precise relationship between psychopathology and associated variables is unclear. Still, certain biological factors, environmental factors, and other conditions have been documented in many studies as correlating highly with emotional disorders. Awareness of these might alert the psychotherapist to an increased likelihood of psychopathology in persons in which these variables are found.

Biological factors. Several authors have addressed biological correlates of psychological disturbances in persons with mental retardation. First, there is the matter of structural brain pathology. Most cases of severe and profound mental retardation are associated with structural brain abnormality (Crome & Stern, 1972). The relationship is less clear in the mild and moderate ranges. Yet, post mortem studies reviewed by Baumeister and MacLean (1979) have led to the conclusion that even mild mental retardation may be associated with central nervous system (CNS) insult. Reid (1985) notes that brain damage has effects on behavior, personality, affect, language, and sensory functioning to varying degrees depending on the site of damage and developmental period during which damage was sustained. Donaldson and Menolascino (1977) reported strong associations between CNS dysfunction and childhood psychoses in persons with mental retardation. Also, Rutter (1971) found psychiatric disorders to be more common in children with mental retardation plus neurological abnormalities than in children with mental retardation without such abnormalities.

Several studies have attributed specific behavior patterns to different genetically determined syndromes of retardation. However, the majority of these studies have proven inconclusive. Reid (1980) reported that persons with Down's syndrome are likely to show conduct disorders in childhood, yet for unknown reasons seem less vulnerable to early infantile autism. Previous studies pairing tuberous sclerosis with schizophrenia (Critchley & Earl, 1932), phenylketonuria with hyperkinesis, and the XYY chromosome pattern with aggression have not borne out under empirical investigation (Reid, 1985).

Epilepsy has also been investigated in relation to psychopathology in individuals with mental retardation. The prevalence of epilepsy is much greater in individuals with mental retardation than in the general population and increases dramatically with the severity of intellectual impairment (Corbett & Harris, 1974; Corbett, Harris, & Robinson, 1975). Eyman, Moore, Capes, and Zachofsky (1970), in a study of patients with mental retardation in three hospitals, reported psychiatric disorders as more common in patients with a history of seizures than in those without seizures. In the Isle of Wight studies, Rutter, Graham, and Yule (1970) found behavior disturbances in approximately one third of children with neuroepileptic conditions. Disturbances occurred in 58% of epileptic persons with mental retardation with seizures. In a recent review of relevant literature, Reid (1985) reported associations of rigidity and egocentricity, outbursts of rage, aggressiveness, schizophreniform psychosis, depression, and increased rates of suicide with epilepsy, especially temporal lobe epilepsy. However, no empirical data were referenced.

One final biological issue that has recently begun to receive attention is the association between sensory disorders and psychopathology (Lewis & MacLean, 1982). Sensory disorders frequently accompany mental retardation. Deafness has been associated with a greater risk for emotional disturbance in the general population (Freedman & Malkin, 1977; Rutter et al., 1970). The relationship between visual impairment and psychopathology is still not clear. Studies examining the association of sensory disorders and psychopathology in persons with mental retardation are still needed. In all of the above conditions, it is unclear whether the relationship between biological abnormalities and psychopathology is coincidental or causal.

Environmental factors. A second issue requiring further investigation is the relationship between psychopathology in persons with mental retardation and environmental conditions. It is reasonable to assume that environmental factors such as SES play a role in the emotional disorders of persons with retardation, due to studies with disturbed persons without retardation (Kisker, 1977). Factors such as parental attitudes, child-rearing, and cultural practices all play a role in social and emotional development. Zigler's social competency model is really the only theory that has attempted systematically to investigate the effects of life history on the emotional development of the individual with mental retardation (Zigler, Lamb, & Child, 1982). Zigler and his colleagues have attempted to identify a set of constructs (Balla & Zigler, 1979; Zigler, 1973) that explain motivational differences between persons with and without retardation. These constructs include positive and negative reaction tendencies, expectancies of failure and success, and reinforcer preference. These may affect the nature of the individual's relationship with his or her environment and thus influence social adjustment and adaptive functioning. Several authors have expressed the view, without referencing empirical data, that environmental factors such as parental love (Forbes, 1958) and expectancies by significant others (Donaldson & Menolascino, 1977) may play a role in behavioral disturbances. More research in this area is badly needed.

Personological factors. Closely related to environmental factors is the issue of personological variables. That personality variables are significantly interrelated with adaptive behavior and adjustment has been established by Penrose (1963). Yet, it remains to be seen whether there are personality constructs that predispose the person with mental retardation to emotional disorders (Lewis & MacLean, 1982). One personality variable that may be related to psychopathology is failure expectancy. A few studies have reported that persons with mental retardation have higher expectancies of failure (Cromwell, 1963). Failure expectancy can result in abnormal levels of avoidance behavior (Cromwell, 1963). It can also result in increased frustration (Viney, Clark, & Lord, 1973) and overdependency on others (Windle, 1962; Zigler, 1973).

Another closely related personality variable is Seligman's concept of learned helplessness. As stated earlier, repeated failure results in avoidance behavior, feelings of worthlessness, and decreases in adaptive behavior. Floor and Rosen (1975) were the first to describe increased failure and passivity as helplessness. They reported higher rates of helplessness in both institutionalized and noninstitutionalized subjects with mental retardation. Also, Zeaman and House (1963) found that children with mental retardation were unable to solve problems they could previously solve prior to the introduction of a prolonged failure paradigm.

Chess and Korn (1970) examined "temperament" in relation to emotional disorders in persons with mental retardation. The authors identified five dimensions of temperament: (a) rhythmicity, (b) approach-withdrawal, (c) adaptability, (d) intensity of reaction, and (e) quality of mood. Fifty-two children, all from middle-class families and living at home, were subjects for the study. Thirty-one of the children (60%) were judged to have psychiatric disorders by clinical examination. Five children showed the complete cluster of pathological temperament traits; all five of these proved to have behavior disorders. Of the 31 emotionally disturbed children, all but 12 fell into the maladaptive range on three or more of the five dimensions. The authors report that the risk of being diagnosed as emotionally disturbed may be greatest in children who show irregularities in bodily functions, withdrawal responses to new stimuli, nonadaptability, predominantly negative mood, and high intensity. The authors of this study failed to report reliability data and utilization of proper blind techniques.

Deinstitutionalization

A fourth and crucial issue to be considered in the emotional and social development of persons with mental retardation is deinstitutionalization. Institutionalization has generally been perceived as a debilitating force for persons with mental retardation (White & Wolfensberger, 1969). Thus, deinstitutionalization has become the recent trend of mental health facilities, in order to allow the individual to live as normal a life as possible. In light of this, it is important to address the difficulties encountered by the person leaving the institution.

The newly released outpatient encounters many new and more complex challenges due to the sudden lack of structure. He or she encounters a whole range of new stressors that may result in increases of emotional disorders. For example, in many instances there is resistence by community members to the individual with mental handicaps (Matson, 1984). Also, in a recent review of relevant studies, Emerson (1985) found reports that persons with retardation who live in the community still interact mainly with other persons with disabilities, experience loneliness as a considerable problem, and have little experience of everyday aspects of community living.

In addition, Rosen, Floor, and Baxter (1971) observed five major personality and behavior problems in discharged persons with mental retardation. These were:

(a) low self-esteem, (b) learned helplessness, (c) acquiescence, (d) socially inappropriate behavior, and (e) sexual inadequacies. Hence, it is quite probable that a large number of institutionalized persons with mental retardation are being discharged without the social skills necessary to cope with the new challenges of noninstitutionalized life. Thus, deinstitutionalization itself may in some cases contribute to psychopathology. Rosen et al. (1971) have stressed the importance of increasing the emphasis on socialization and interpersonal relationships *within* the institution to prepare inpatients adequately for the outside. Also, institutions should be structured to simulate the reinforcement contingencies available in the community.

Thus, in reviewing the literature, a host of conditions and factors have been reported to be associated with psychopathology in persons with mental retardation. Biological conditions such as structural brain abnormalities, genetic abnormalities, epilepsy, and sensory disorders may all play a role in emotional disturbances. It is also likely that external agents such as maternal nutrition, drugs, infections, and birth injury may lead to cerebral defect and play a role in psychopathology (Ollendick & Ollendick, 1982). Environmental and personological factors associated with behavior disorders have also been reported. All of these are worthy of further consideration. A greater understanding of etiological factors and correlates of emotional disturbances may be instrumental in designing comprehensive treatment packages. Such knowledge may also prove valuable in alerting the therapist to increased likelihood of emotional disorders in persons in whom these correlates are present. Again, it should be stressed that in most cases it is still unclear whether the relationship between these conditions and psychopathology in persons with mental retardation is causal or coincidental.

Assessment

The chapter by Prout and Strohmer in this volume will deal extensively with methods of assessing psychopathology in persons with mental retardation. However, assessment in dual-diagnosis patients is such a complicated task that it might be helpful to highlight some of the more important issues here. The difficulty in assessing psychopathology in persons with mental retardation is due primarily to the one outstanding aspect that separates this group from all others—cognitive deficits. It becomes increasingly difficult across ranges of mental retardation to determine which deviant behaviors are the result of intellectual impairment and which are due to emotional problems. Cognitive deficits often result in deviant behavior that may be easily confused with schizophrenia or other emotional disorders (Chess & Hassibi, 1970). Chronic emotional disorders coupled with long-term institutionalization may impair or alter thought processes and adaptive behavior, thus giving the impression of mental retardation. Sensory disorders, language deficits, and early infantile autism all compound the difficulties of assessment and diagnosis.

In many cases deviant behavior is noted in persons with mental retardation yet is considered to be a normal feature of mental retardation. Reiss, Levitan, and Szyszko (1982) investigated the phenomenon of "diagnostic overshadowing" or the tendency of clinicians to downplay the diagnostic significance of abnormal behaviors in the population with mental retardation that in nonretarded persons would be considered indicative of emotional disturbances. Thus, the emotional disturbances are "overshadowed" by the presence of the mentally retarded label. In one experiment (Reiss et al., 1982), 48 psychologists were divided into three groups. One group rated the phobia for an individual who was suggested to have mental retardation. One group rated the phobia for an individual who was suggested to have alcoholism. One group rated the phobia for an individual who was suggested to be of average intelligence. Results showed that psychologists tended to provide the single diagnosis of mental retardation or alcoholism in the first two groups. Also, these two groups recommended systematic desensitization as a treatment option less frequently than did the psychologists in the control group. In a second experiment, the authors showed that case descriptions were less likely to be rated as examples of schizophrenia, psychosis, an emotional disorder, or personality disorders if the individual was also suggested to have subnormal intelligence. In a second study (Reiss & Szyszko, 1983) diagnostic overshadowing by clinicians was reported to be unrelated to different ranges of clinical experience with persons with mental retardation. Alford and Locke (1984), in a study of 372 psychologists, also reported that the label of mental retardation resulted in: (a) ratings of less severity of emotional disorders, (b) first treatment choices that were more behavioral in nature, and (c) tendencies to focus on intellectual functioning for assessment.

The above studies suggest several things relevant to diagnostic assessment of emotional disorders in persons with mental retardation. First, the extreme variability of behaviors in this population suggests the need for precise, detailed descriptions of behavior and the strict following of definitional guidelines in diagnosis in order to avoid analogue errors. Second, diagnosis should depend on comprehensive assessment, involving the pooling of several different types of information from several settings.

It will be briefly noted that, despite the relative dearth of assessment studies in this field, initial studies have reported the utility of several different assessment methods. It has traditionally been assumed that, due to lack of sufficient introspective skills and language skills, many conventional techniques are not usable with persons with mental retardation. However, this may not be true for persons with mild or moderate mental retardation, who make up over 90% of this population (Ollendick & Ollendick, 1982). A few studies have reported the efficacy of the clinical interview (Ballinger, Armstrong, Presly, & Reid, 1975; Pilkington, 1972), self-report forms (Miller, Barrett, Hampe, & Noble, 1972; Ollendick, 1978), and other report forms (Guarnaccia & Weiss, 1974) in assessing emotional disturbances in persons with mental retardation. Also, Matson, Kazdin, and Senatore (1984) have developed the Psychopathology Instrument for Mentally Retarded Adults (PIMRA) to assist in the diagnosis of schizophrenia, depression, psychosexual disorders, adjustment disorders, anxiety, somatiform disorders, and personality problems. Initial data are promising. Utilization of these techniques in combination with behavioral observation should facilitate assessment and diagnosis.

Diagnosis

Two multiaxial diagnostic systems permit the documentation of intellectual level, emotional disorders, and other relevant data. The Multiaxial Classification of Child Psychiatric Disorders (Rutter et al., 1969) is the first. This system contains three axes. The first axis describes the clinical psychiatric syndrome. The second axis reports the individual's level of intellectual functioning. The third axis notes etiological data and other associated factors. This system was elaborated in 1975 and later was encompassed into the second multiaxial system, *DSM-III/DSM-III-R* (APA, 1980/1987). At present, a system for diagnosing psychopathology specifically in the population with mental retardation has not been devised. The existing system, the *DSM-III/DSM-III-R,* contains five axes. These include:

Axis I	Clinical syndromes, Conditions not attributable to a mental disorder that are a focus of attention and treatment, Additional Codes
Axis II	Personality disorders, Specific developmental disorders
Axis III	Physical disorders and conditions
Axis IV	Severity of psychosocial stressors
Axis V	Highest level of adaptive functioning of the past year

Thus, mental retardation and emotional disorders can coexist in *DSM-III/DSM-III-R* and are both entered under Axis I. The first three axes constitute the official diagnostic assessment. Axes IV and V provide supplemental information useful for planning treatment and predicting outcome.

Matson (1985) has recently proposed a Biosocial Theory of Psychopathology, a 3×3 factor model. This represents the beginnings of what is the most inclusive and holistic theory of psychopathology in persons with mental retardation to date. Matson emphasizes three major factors in the genesis of emotional disturbances (biological, social, and psychological developmental processes) along three dimensions of determinants of care (etiology, assessment and diagnosis, and treatment). Although originally discussed as a *theory* of psychopathology, biosocial theory will be discussed here due to its diagnostic utility.

First, the author defines several biological factors that are generally conceded to play a significant role in psychopathology and thus must be considered for diagnostic assessment. These include: (a) genetic factors; (b) developmental factors—the developmental stage during which symptoms are first manifested, the length of time symptoms are displayed, and the long-term effects of both acute and chronic disturbances. (It is noted that decreases in behavioral disturbances might take place more slowly in persons with mental retardation because intellectual deficits generally result in poorer ability to adjust and cope.); (c) biochemical findings; (d) physical impairments: and (e) neurophysical impairments.

Second, various social factors are discussed as they relate to psychopathology in persons with mental retardation. Major categories prevalent in the literature include social skills; family interactions; personality variables; self-help skills; prenatal, perinatal, and postnatal factors; normalization/deinstitutionalization; and work and school behavior. Inability to perform basic social skills can have profound effects on self-concept, personality, and emotional stability. Social skills deficits often prevent individuals with mental retardation from establishing beneficial relationships with others, forcing the individual into an isolated environment that can only exacerbate emotional disturbances.

Third, psychological and developmental processes are addressed. include several descriptors of thought and/or problem-solving abilities short- and long-term memory, cognitive development, perceptual and r and self-control.

Matson's biosocial theory (1985) is important for several r these, it represents a departure from frequent efforts to disprove Rather, it attempts to integrate the existing data and theories professionals. Furthermore, it emphasizes the importance c and continued empirical investigation for clarification and modification of the theory of psychopathology. Etiology, assessment, diagnosis, and treatment should be reconciled to dissolve the division between theoretical-academic camps and clinicians. By considering as many biological, social, and psychological variables as possible in diagnostic assessment, a holistic picture of psychopathology in the person with mental retardation is possible. Taking this broad range of factors into account should facilitate differential diagnosis and lead to more appropriate treatment packages. All of this adds up to more effective intervention with emotional disorders, which can affect the quality of life of the individual with mental retardation just as profoundly as physical deformities and cognitive deficits.

Treatment

Very few studies have attempted to assess the efficacy of treatment methods for the emotional disorders of individuals with mental retardation. In the following section, we will attempt to highlight important treatment issues relating to the three main models of intervention: pharmacological, dynamically oriented, and behaviorally oriented methods. The successful application of these three methods will be briefly discussed, as well as some general procedures for evaluating treatment efficacy.

Pharmacotherapy. Drugs are frequently prescribed to treat any of a number of behavioral disorders in individuals with mental retardation. In fact, several studies have reported that as many as 50% of institutionalized persons with mental retardation are receiving psychotropic medication (Lipman, 1970; Sprague & Baxley, 1978). Neuroleptics (also known as antipsychotics and major tranquilizers), which include phenothiazines and butyrophenones, are most frequently prescribed to treat certain problem behaviors such as abnormal aggressiveness and certain psychotic-like behaviors. Anxiolytics, antidepressants, and stimulants are also used with the mentally retarded to a much lesser degree (Sprague, 1977). Antiepileptics are probably prescribed to as many as 30% of all institutionalized persons with mental retardation (Davis, Cullari, & Breuning, 1982; Sprague, 1977) and are the most frequently used drugs after the antipsychotics.

Pharmacotherapy has been used to treat a variety of emotional disturbances in persons with mental retardation. Several methodologically sound studies have reported reductions of aggression, motor activity, and self-stimulation due to drug therapy with certain neuroleptics (Breuning, 1982; Ferguson & Breuning, 1982; Singh & Aman, 1981). Lithium may exert a nonspecific effect on irritability and aggression (Dale, 1980). Antiepileptics have proved largely successful in regulating seizure disorders in individuals with mental retardation (Gibbs et al., 1982).

However, the behaviors that have been successfully treated are limited, and the majority of drug studies suffer from methodological weaknesses (Aman & Singh, 1980; Sprague & Werry, 1971).

It is evident that pharmacotherapy can serve as a valuable and effective treatment option. However, it is crucial that the effectiveness of individual drugs must be thoroughly evaluated and weighed in light of their side effects and other treatment options *before* they are administered. Short-term and long-term side effects for many of these drugs have already been clearly documented. (See Breuning & Poling, 1982, for a review.) For example, antipsychotics have been shown to affect rates of operant responding in animals and humans (Breuning & Davidson, 1981; Breuning & Poling, 1982). Also, possible effects on memory and learning have been hypothesized (Wysocki, Fuqua, Davis, & Breuning, 1981). These findings make studies of drug efficacy crucial.

Breuning and Poling (1982), in a recent survey of the literature, have identified eight methodological criteria that should be met by drug studies. These are: (a) use of placebo control, (b) use of double blind, (c) standardized dosage of drugs, (d) standardized evaluations that include evidence of changes in specifically defined target behaviors, (e) random assignment of subjects to groups, (f) use of appropriate statistical analysis, (g) comparison of drug treatment with some alternate treatment, and (h) follow-up assessment of drug effects 12–16 weeks posttreatment. More studies designed according to these criteria would greatly contribute to the argument for drug therapy.

Psychotherapy. Psychotherapy has frequently been used to treat a variety of interpersonal problems in the population without retardation. However, psychotherapy with persons with mental retardation has often been overlooked as a treatment option, probably due to one of several assumptions. Sternlicht (1966) has suggested that it has often been assumed that persons with mental retardation lack the ability for insight and introspection necessary for treatment effectiveness. Another assumption has been that persons with mental retardation lack verbal skills necessary to benefit from dynamically oriented therapies (Gardner, 1971). Although this is probably true for the severe and profound ranges of mental retardation, it may not be so for mild ranges. Another problem is the unavailability of appropriately trained therapists (Lewis & MacLean, 1982). Most therapists are trained primarily in verbally dependent therapies.

In addition, studies evaluating the efficacy of psychotherapy have frequently suffered from many of the same methodological weaknesses found in pharmacological studies. Failures to define outcome variables, to use controls, and to report reliability of assessment instruments (Lewis & MacLean, 1982) have not served to enhance the argument for psychotherapy.

Nevertheless, data from studies with nonretarded populations suggest that psychotherapy could be a viable treatment option. In several cases dynamic psychotherapy (Freeman, 1936; Mundy, 1957; Sarbin, 1945) and group therapies (Cotzin, 1948; Fisher & Wolfson, 1953) have been described as successful. Psychotherapeutic techniques have emphasized expression and ventilation of emotions along with training in emotional control, catharsis, self-actualization, and rapport building. Reid (1985) has suggested that group therapy might be an appropriate setting in which to explore topics related to independent living such as finance, sexuality, and use of leisure time. Due to the increased prevalence of emotional disorders in the population who have mental retardation, it is important not to rule out any treatment options on the basis of unverified assumptions. Empirical research designed according to many of the same criteria mentioned above for drug studies is needed.

Behavioral therapy. The application of applied behavioral analysis to the emotional disorders of persons with mental retardation has had significant impact on treating dual-diagnosis patients and appears promising for the future. The success of behavioral treatment packages has been due largely to emphasis on empirical procedures and scientific methodologies. Operant procedures have been successfully applied to treating phobias (Matson, 1981; Peck, 1977), psychotic speech patterns (Kazdin, 1971; Stephens, Matson, Westmoreland, & Kulpal, 1981), depression (Matson, Dettling, & Senatore, 1981), temper outbursts (Harvey, Karan, Bhargava, & Morehouse, 1978), compulsive behavior (Cuvo, 1976; Foxx & Azrin, 1973), hyperactivity (Stoudenmire & Salter, 1975), and public masturbation (Lutzker, 1973). The types of designs most frequently used are : (a) ABA designs, (b) multiple-baseline designs, and (c) group designs with appropriate controls. Procedures utilized have included instructions, modeling, role playing, performance feedback, reinforcement, and aversive techniques.

Although initial behavioral treatment has appeared promising, several treatment issues must be considered in evaluating the overall effectiveness of such procedures. First, improvements in treatment sessions may fail to generalize to less-structured settings. In a review of the behavioral studies, Matson, DiLorenzo, and Andrasik (1983) found that over 50% of past studies reported no follow-up data. Second, do changes in target behaviors maintain and do they generalize to other problem behaviors? Third, the degree to which deviant collateral behaviors are induced by treatment must be considered in evaluating effectiveness. Fourth, sufficient detail about subjects is frequently not provided. Rarely is such information as adaptive behavior level, compliance to treatment, and descriptions of other behavior deficits and skills provided. Most of the above weaknesses are shared by pharmacological and dynamically oriented studies in this field. To assist in evaluating the efficacy of various operant studies, Matson et al. (1983) classify all existing studies according to sample size, classification of retardation, treatment strategy, target behaviors, setting, follow-up, and experimental design. Several of these studies will be discussed more fully in relation to specific disorders later in this chapter.

In relation to the three treatment models mentioned above, several criteria for improving experimental design were briefly discussed. There are also some general treatment considerations that apply to all three models. Donaldson and Menolascino (1977) have asserted a few basic principles necessary in a comprehensive treatment approach. They have emphasized the importance of periodic reevaluations of patients to allow shifts in treatment goals according to the needs of the individual. They also emphasize the importance of early diagnosis and intervention. Early establishment of treatment goals may assist families in establishing realistic expectations, thus avoiding unnecessary frustration. Also, the authors note that treatment should utilize active family participation when helpful. Finally, treatment should be coordinated with other services such as specialized medical care and special education.

Several authors have noted that nurses and other institutional staff might, if given extra training, be invaluable in initial detection of behavior disturbances (Hasan & Mooney, 1979; Reid, 1972).

Wherever possible, multiple assessment devices should be used for determining treatment effectiveness. Such procedures are particularly important in caring for emotionally disturbed persons with mental retardation, where the number and type of responses are so varied and complex. Structured clinical interviews (Chambers, Puig-Antich, & Tabrizi, 1978), rating scales such as the PIMRA (Matson et al., 1984), and direct observations (Shapiro & Barrett, 1982) may all be useful in assessing treatment efficacy.

Another evaluative approach to therapy that has appeared in several studies recently is social validation. Matson (1982c), in treating three obsessive-compulsive adults with mental retardation, had 15 community members blind to treatment conditions view tapes of baseline and treatment stages. Raters perceived statistically significant improvement in each of the patients that supplemented the quantitative changes in target behaviors. In a second study (Matson, Kazdin, & Esveldt-Dawson, 1980), two children with mental retardation with social skills deficits were matched according to age and sex with two children without retardation. Treatment was provided on behaviors where patients did not perform up to the average skills of the children without retardation. Treatment was continued until patients reached the mean performance of the normal children. Social validation is one useful method of attaining clinically and ecologically valid criteria for assessing treatment effectiveness.

Summary

Emotional disturbance in the population with mental retardation is a very serious problem that is becoming increasingly evident. Prevalence studies have almost unanimously supported the assertion that rates of mental illness are higher in persons with mental retardation than in the general population. Several theories of psychopathology in persons with mental retardation currently exist, yet they are for the most part in their formative stages. Also, initial studies have identified several biological, environmental, and personological correlates of mental illness in persons with mental retardation. The presence of these variables may alert the psychotherapist to the increased likelihood of emotional disturbances in a patient. In many cases these variables may predispose the patient to mental illness. This question is empirical and remains to be answered.

If the findings of various studies are to be integrated and compared, it is essential that a broad, flexible, unitary diagnostic system of psychopathology in persons with mental retardation be devised and adopted. An initial attempt at such a system is Matson's biosocial theory (1985). Strategies of intervention have only begun to be evaluated. A few methods of intervention that have proven effective for emotionally disturbed persons without retardation have also been successfully applied to psychopathology in the population with mental retardation. Many studies lack the empirical rigor to provide conclusive statements on treatment efficacy. Social validation promises to be an effective method for establishing clinically valid criteria for treatment evaluation. More scientifically sound studies in all of these areas are needed.

Specific Disorders

This section will focus on specific psychiatric illnesses. Anxiety disorders, affective disorders, psychoses, psychosexual disorders, personality disorders, and disorders of impulse control will be discussed. The topics of incidence, etiology, treatment, and presenting symptoms will be covered where possible. Subcategories of disorders will be discussed in accordance with *DSM–III/DSM–III–R*.

Anxiety Disorders

In the *Diagnostic and Statistical Manual-III* (APA, 1980), a very clear set of criteria exists for the differentiation of subtypes of anxiety disorders. In some cases anxiety is experienced by the individual as a result of attempts to master symptoms, as in confronting the feared object in a phobic disorder, or in resisting the obsession or compulsion of an obsessive-compulsive disorder. In panic disorders and generalized anxiety disorders, anxiety is the predominant disturbance.

DSM-III/DSM-III-R classifies three general categories of anxiety disorders. The first major category is phobic disorders. These include agoraphobia, with or without manic attacks, in which there is a marked fear of being alone or in places from which escape might be difficult or help not available; social phobia, which involves persistent, irrational fear of social situations; and simple phobias, which involves fear of and compelling desire to avoid other objects and situations not covered in the first two categories. The second major category is anxiety states, which include panic disorders, in which recurrent panic attacks occur unpredictably; the generalized anxiety disorder, persistent anxiety of at least one month's duration; and obsessive-compulsive disorders, in which there are recurrent obsessions and compulsions. The third and final category is post-traumatic stress disorders, in which anxiety symptoms develop following a psychologically traumatic event. Diagnosis of an Anxiety Disorder is not made if anxiety is due to another disorder, such as schizophrenia.

Behaviors that categorize the syndrome. The full range of anxiety disorders is seen in the population with mental retardation, yet diagnoses are infrequently made. It appears that much of the behavior now recognized as psychiatric disorders was formerly considered "expected behavior" in persons with mental retardation (Donaldson & Menolascino, 1977). Of the anxiety disorders, simple phobias are found most frequently among persons with mental retardation.

In a study of 53 adults with mental retardation, Novosel (1984) reported that phobias were by far the most frequent pathological condition. In this sample, fear of the dark was the most frequently reported phobia. Others included fear of traveling on public transportation systems, animals, going out alone, insects, and heights. Also, several patients had multiple phobias, with phobias occurring slightly more frequently in females. However, the small sample size must be considered. Types and degrees of phobias were not found to differ from those of persons without retardation. Sixty-five percent of Novosel's (1984) sample were short-stay patients. This suggests that a large number of persons with mental retardation who have phobias may be living in the community. This point magnifies the importance of treating these disorders because society is less likely than institutional staff to tolerate phobic behavior.

Several other studies have reported phobic behavior in persons with mental retardation. Peck (1977) treated 20 persons with mild mental retardation for fears of either rats or high places. Several studies have specifically noted socially oriented phobias in the population with mental retardation (Matson, 1981a,b).

The existence of obsessive-compulsive (O/C) behavior in persons with mental retardation has been a topic of debate for some years. Several professionals have asserted that the complexity of the psychoneurotic transactions of these disorders is beyond the capacity of all but the individual with the most mild mental retardation (Reid, 1985; Webster, 1970). Several authors, however, have reported cases of O/C behavior in persons with mental retardation, while cautioning against the tendency to confuse O/C behavior with stereotyped behavior (Matson, 1982c).

Cuvo (1976) reported the case of an institutionalized adult who ran in circles, up and down stairs, and paced the sidewalk—responses that had been occurring for approximately 40 years. Foxx and Azrin (1973) treated a case of repetitive walking. Matson and Stephens (1981) treated an institutionalized adult with mental retardation for excessive wall-patting and fondling of wall thermostats. Conflicting theories exist over whether compulsive rituals reduce (Carr, 1974), increase (Beech, 1974), or have no effect (Rachman, 1976) on anxiety levels.

Post-traumatic stress disorders are difficult to diagnose due to cognitive deficits and inabilities of many persons with mental retardation to relate feelings of anxiety. However, some cases of sudden or delayed anxiety reactions following a psychologically traumatic event have been observed (Ollendick & Ollendick, 1982).

Incidence. Surprisingly, only a few studies have examined the incidence of anxiety disorders in persons with mental retardation. In an early study, Penrose (1938) examined clinical and genetic data on 1,280 inpatients with mental retardation. He found that 132 individuals (10.2%) were "psychoneurotic," characterized by anxiety and nervous energy. Neuer (1947) reported that 39 cases out of 300 patients (13%) in a state institution were neurotic. Symptoms included restlessness, anxiety, and compulsions. In another inpatient study, Craft (1959) examined 324 patients with mental retardation and reported that 104 (33%) had personality disorders with prominent anxiety. Webster (1963) reported and described high rates of excessive fears, compulsive traits, and nervous mannerisms in 159 outpatient children with mental retardation. Exact rates were not reported. In a life span study of children with mental retardation born in a British city between 1951 and 1955, Richardson, Katz, Koller, McLaren, and Rubinstein (1979) found that 26% of 222 subjects displayed anxious behavior sometime within the first 22 years of life. In Novosel's (1984) study, mentioned above, 23 patients (43%) exhibited phobic behavior and 7 (13%) showed high levels of anxious behavior.

All of the above studies suffer from weaknesses. Most failed to distinguish between subtypes of anxiety disorders. Nevertheless, it seems safe to conclude that anxiety, at least in its general pervasive form (Ollendick & Ollendick, 1982) and as displayed in phobias, is more prevalent in the retarded than in the general population. Epidemiological investigations studying anxiety disorders in relation to sex differences and degree of retardation are still needed.

Etiology. In a recent review of relevant literature, Ollendick and Ollendick (1982) proposed four etiological explanations for anxiety disorders in persons with mental retardation. These include cerebral defect, psychodynamic views, learning theory, and experiential factors. Although these theories have already been discussed in relation to psychopathology in general, they will be briefly considered as contributing factors to anxiety disorders in persons with mental retardation.

As discussed previously, from the psychodynamic viewpoint, ego deficits that result from developmental delays can result in inability to progress effectively through psychosexual stages. The defective ego is unable to cope with the simultaneous demands of the id and superego. All of this contributes to heightened levels of anxiety in persons with mental retardation.

Anxiety has also been explained according to any of a number of learning theories. Anxiety may function as a conditioned response that is evoked by environmental, proprioceptive, or cognitive stimuli (Ollendick & Ollendick, 1982). Inability to discriminate between various stimuli (deficits in discriminative learning) in persons with mental retardation means that once anxiety has become a classically conditioned response to a stimulus, the probability is high that similar stimuli will elicit the anxiety response. According to social learning theory, anxiety responses and phobias can be modeled from parents and significant others. According to the response-reinforcement model (Lick & Katkin, 1976), consequences of anxiety reactions may serve as reinforcers that maintain anxiety reactions.

According to experiential models, repeated failure experiences of persons with mental retardation result in general expectancies of future failures, low expectancies and success, and increased levels of anxiety. Ollendick, Balla, and Zigler (1971) found that if a person were provided with sufficient opportunities to succeed, their situational expectancy of success was increased and their inferred level of anxiety was decreased.

Also, cerebral defects can slow developmental rates causing heightened anxiety in parents that may be subsequently modeled. Brain abnormalities may also affect memory, motivation, and the ability to discriminate between stimuli, thus affecting adaptive behavior and increasing anxiety. Most of these theories are merely speculative.

Treatment. Although more work is still needed in this area, several therapeutic approaches to treating anxiety disorders in persons with mental retardation have surfaced in the literature. Within certain limitations, the same methods of intervention found to be effective with persons without retardation have, when applied, proven successful with persons with retardation. Some of the more promising pharmacological and behavioral methods will be discussed briefly.

In general, two major types of drugs have been used to treat anxiety in the population with retardation. These are benzodiazepines, which include Valium® and Librium®, and beta-andrenergic blocking agents (Ollendick & Ollendick, 1982). Benzodiazepines have been effectively used in treating anxiety in subjects with and without mild mental retardation (Solomon & Hart, 1978). Beta-andrenergic blocking agents have been tested in persons without mental retardation (Tanna, Penningroth, & Woolson, 1977; Wheatley, 1969) and are reported to relieve somatic complaints associated with certain types of anxiety disorders. This suggests their possible utility especially in treating panic and pervasive anxiety states, which are characterized by heightened somatic complaints (Ollendick & Ollendick, 1982). However, it is important to weigh successful anxiety reduction against side effects. Dizziness, disorientation, and psychomotor retardation (side effects of benzodiazepines) may prove more debilitating than the anxiety disorders themselves (Ollendick & Ollendick, 1982). The decision to use drugs must in every individual case be based on clinical data and weighed against other treatment options.

Several studies have reported the efficacy of behavioral techniques in reducing anxiety levels of persons with mental retardation. Peck (1977) treated 20 persons with mental retardation for fears of high places or rats. Subjects were randomly assigned to (a) contact desensitization, (b) vicarious symbolic desensitization, (c) systematic desensitization, (d) placebo attention control, or (e) no treatment group. Although group sizes were small and variable, some tentative conclusions can be drawn. Contact desensitization was the most effective procedure; and, according to the author, the acting out of situations by the subjects contributed to positive results.

Matson (1981b) studied 24 adults with mild or moderate mental retardation who were paired by level and type of fear. One member of each pair was randomly assigned to a participant modeling group or a no-treatment group. Subjects were treated for fear of participating in community-based projects, such as going to the grocery store or to movie theaters. Improvements in anxiety levels were found after 3 months of treatment and at 4-month follow-up.

Matson (1981a) also treated fear of speaking to adults in three children with moderate mental retardation between 8 and 10 years of age. Subjects were matched according to age, sex, and level of mental retardation with persons who were judged to evidence normal levels of fear. Control children were assessed to establish criteria for treatment outcome. Subjects were treated with participant modeling in multiple-baseline fashion across subjects. Positive results were achieved and maintained at 6-month follow-up.

In a recent study, Calamari, Geist, and Shahbazian (1987) used multiple component relaxation training combined with auditory electromyographic (EMG) biofeedback, modeling, and reinforcement to teach relaxation skills to subjects. The procedure was effective in reducing the experimental group's EMG levels. Although the subjects were not suffering from maladaptive levels of anxiety, this study suggests that persons with mental retardation have the ability to master and benefit from relaxation training.

Other studies have successfully utilized behavior techniques to treat phobias of riding in a car (Mansdorf, 1976), acrophobia (Guralnick, 1973), and compulsive clothes and body checking (Matson, 1982c).

Affective Disorders

The diagnosis of affective disorders in persons with mental retardation has been influenced almost exclusively by trends in differential diagnosis of psychopathology in persons without mental retardation (Matson & Barrett, 1982). The essential feature of this group of disorders is a disturbance of affect, or mood. These disorders are dominated by extreme elation or depression, the latter being the most frequent subcategory, which influence the whole of psychic life.

Emil Kraeplin (1889) was the first person to formally classify depression. Kraeplin saw two separate types of this disorder: (a) persons with affective and psychomotor retardation (termed volitional inhibition) and (b) those who manifested agitation and apprehension as primary symptoms. Kraeplin's system emphasized the notion of a single endogenous causal factor.

In recent years, three diagnostic systems have emerged. The first, presented by Winokur (1973), identifies two types of depression, bipolar and unipolar. Bipolar disorder, with or without mania, is characterized by greater psychomotor retardation, higher genetic loading for affective disorders, and increased likelihood of postpartum affective episodes. Family studies of inpatients by Perris (1966) and studies of both hospital patients and outpatients by Winokur (1973) have supported the idea of two genetic subtypes of depression: bipolar (manic-depression) and unipolar (recurrent depression). The unipolar-bipolar system is also supported by psychological measures of sleep activity, clinical presentation, and spinal fluid level (3-methoxy-4-hydroxy-phenylaline).

The second diagnostic system, derived from factor–analytic studies, is described by Rosenthal and Klerman (1966) and Mendels and Cochran (1968) and emphasizes endogenous vs. reactive depression. Endogenous depression occurs in patients who tended to be older with a previous history of depressive episodes, with greater amounts of weight loss, early morning awakening, self-reproach and guilt, and lesser degrees of hysteria and inadequacy than in reactive depression. The relationship between exogenous/reactive and endogenous depression is unresolved.

The third classification scheme appears in *DSM-III/DSM-III-R* and is the system that will be emphasized in this chapter. This model favors the unipolar-bipolar binary system; however, additions were added to describe other types of depression. The division of affective disorders includes major affective disorders, in which there is a full affective syndrome; other specific affective disorders, in which there is only a partial affective syndrome of at least 2 years duration; and finally atypical affective disorders, which cannot be classified in either of the first two categories.

Major affective disorders include bipolar disorder and major depression, differing according to the presence (bipolar) or absence of manic episodes. Other specific affective disorders include cyclothymic disorder and dysthymic disorder. In the cyclothymic disorder, there are symptoms characteristic of both the major depressive and manic syndromes, but they are not of sufficient severity or duration to meet the criteria of major depressive disorder. In the dysthymic disorder (or depressive neurosis) symptoms are not of sufficient severity or duration to meet the criteria for major depressive disorder, and there is no history of manic episodes.

All of these systems were developed for persons of normal intelligence and have been adopted for use with individuals with mental retardation. Some diagnostic categories may have little or no utility for this population, particularly for persons with more serious impairment and mental retardation. In persons with severe and profound mental retardation, manifestations of depression may be markedly different, or this disorder may not occur at all.

Behaviors that categorize the syndrome. Diagnosis of depression in persons with mental retardation is not as straightforward as it is in persons of normal intelligence. Depression is often overlooked or not recognized in persons with mental retardation because withdrawal behavior and lowered activity levels make these persons less of a management problem (Hasan & Mooney, 1979). Also, manic episodes may simply be considered as acting out or temper tantrums because a certain amount of deviant behavior is frequently "expected" in the persons with mental retardation (Donaldson & Menolascino, 1977).

Depression may be characterized along several different dimensions. First, severity of behavior manifested may vary greatly from mild spells to psychotic reactions characterized by hallucinations and delusions. Second, an affective disorder may occur once or with recurrent episodes. Third, there is the unipolar-bipolar dimension. Fourth, depression may be diagnosed as a primary psychological disorder, changes in affect being the dominant syndrome, or as a secondary disorder, occurring during the course of some nonaffective disorder such as anxiety, neurosis, heart disease, etc. (Matson, 1982a). This tremendous amount of variability contributes to difficulties in diagnosis, because depression may be manifested differently with different degrees of retardation.

Two alternate views of depression in persons with mental retardation have been proposed. The first view is that persons with mental retardation do not express depression directly; it must be inferred from behaviors and symptoms "masking" the underlying depressive feelings (Carlson & Cantwell, 1980). Thus, delinquency, school phobia, and psychophysical complaints may all be signs of underlying depression (Glaser, 1967). This approach makes comparisons with population norms and statistical analysis of behaviors very difficult. It also may serve to increase the number of persons with mental retardation who are mistakenly diagnosed as depressed. For a fuller discussion of the problems of this approach, see Matson (1983b).

These authors have adopted the second view which holds that depression is manifested in persons with mental retardation along the same lines (same types of operationally defined behaviors) as in persons with normal intelligence. This approach leads to a more reliable and more conservative definition of depression. Only if rates of behavior are compared on normative bases can clinicians get away from diagnosis based on parent and clinical tolerance levels (Lefkowitz, 1980).

Having accepted this view, it still remains to define the behaviors that characterize affective disorders. Cytryn, McKnew, and Bunney (1980) compiled a list of behaviors by examining the criteria of depression as proposed by Kovacs and Beck (1977), and *DSM-III/DSM-III-R* (1980/1987). These four systems for assessing depression in children are among the most widely used. For a behavior to be added to the following list, it was included in at least three of the four systems. The behaviors derived from this procedure include dysphoria, sadness, hopelessness, sleep disturbance, psychomotor retardation, loss of pleasure, low self-esteem, decreased concentration, aggression, suicidal statements, disturbances in social or family behavior, loss of interest, somatic complaints, and loneliness. Duration of time for each of these behaviors varied from one week to several months, with one month seeming to approximate a mean length of behaviors' occurrence. This core group of symptoms represents a valuable starting point for diagnosing depression in persons with mental retardation.

Three studies have attempted to identify operationalized behaviors of adults with mental retardation. Schloss (1982) obtained eighteen 5-minute observations of nine depressed (according to *DSM-III/DSM-III-R* criteria) adults with mental retardation during social interaction situations. He reported that at least five differences in social behavior existed between depressed patients and the nondepressed control group: (a) other individuals were more likely to request action from depressed subjects than to make declarative statements; (b) depressed subjects were more likely to gain compliance by exhibiting negative affect; (c) the depressed subjects were more likely to risk requests by exhibiting negative affect; (d) other individuals were more likely to exhibit negative affect when interacting with depressed subjects; and (e) staff rather than peers were more likely to interact with depressed adults with mental retardation.

In the second study, Matson et al. (1981) found statements concerning self-worth, suicidal statements, and negative statements about present (as compared to past) to be target behaviors frequently exhibited during therapy sessions.

In the third study, Matson (1982b) treated depressed persons for abnormalities in number of words spoken, somatic complaints, irritability, grooming, aggression, self-statements, flat affect, eye contact, and speech latency.

Features suggesting a diagnosis of manic depression have also been reported. Sovner and Hurley (1982) listed periodic hyperactivity, withdrawal, sadness; response to lithium carbonate; and identification of family member suffering from depression or mania as characteristic symptoms of manic depression in persons with mental retardation. Reid (1985) also reported that affectively loaded delusions and hallucinations, ideas of guilt or failure leading to suicide or attempted suicide, diurnal variation of mood, and sleep disturbances are among behaviors that frequently characterize mania in persons with mental retardation.

The above data suggest several things. First, both types of major depressive disorders exist in persons with mental retardation and can be correctly diagnosed with careful observation of the patient. Second, clinical symptoms of depression and mania, as described by *DSM-III/DSM-III-R*, do occur in persons with mental retardation. Third, affective features become less typical and more difficult to diagnose as one moves into the lower ranges of retardation.

Incidence. In a number of survey studies, most of which were conducted in England, high rates of depression, particularly the more severe forms, have been noted in persons with mental retardation. In the Colchester survey of 1938 (Penrose, 1962), 24 out of 1,280 institutionalized persons with mental retardation were diagnosed as bipolar depressives. Similarly, Payne (1968) and Pollock (1945), who surveyed 216 and 444 hospitalized psychiatric patients, respectively, found that 2% of their samples were persons with mental retardation and bipolar depression. Neustadt (1928) found 14 cases of unipolar depression in 190 persons with mental retardation with emotional disorders. Herskovitz and Plesset (1941) found a high incidence of bipolar depression also, but none of their cases included persons with an IQ less than 50. Finally, Jacobsen (1983), in an epidemiological study of 38,000 presons with mental retardation, found that approximately 6–7% of these individuals were depressed. Similar rates have been found by other investigators (Duncan, Penrose, & Turnbull, 1936; Reid, 1972; Weaver, 1946).

Fluctuations in data may be due, at least in part, to the differing views on diagnosis, settings in which the patients were studied, degree of mental retardation of the subjects, and other population characteristics (Craft, 1959). Based on the majority of studies reported, it can be tentatively concluded that prevalence rates of affective disorders in persons with mental retardation approach rates evident in the nonretarded, with affective symptoms becoming less typical as one moves into the lower levels of mental retardation.

Etiology. Although several theories of depression have been proposed for the general population, etiology of affective disorders in the population with mental retardation remains relatively unstudied. The only two models of depression that have been applied to persons with mental retardation are the learned helplessness approach of Seligman (1975) and Lewinsohn's (1975) social learning theory.

As discussed previously in the section on etiology, Seligman has proposed that helplessness is a learned operant that is negatively reinforced and results when an animal repeatedly fails to terminate aversive stimuli. Learned helplessness manifests itself in motivation, cognition, and emotions. The data from several studies indicate that success and failure experiences influence general drive levels, resulting in differing expectancies of failure. This affects a wide variety of behavior differences between children with and without mental retardation (Butterfield & Zigler, 1965). Floor and Rosen (1975) proposed that rigid patterns of helplessness are learned in institutions and frequently continue to be exhibited even after release. DeVellis (1977) has extended Floor and Rosen's (1975) hypotheses to Seligman's learned helplessness model. A parallel theory has been proposed by Weisz (1979). A major problem with these hypotheses is that no studies have been conducted with persons who were actually diagnosed as depressed.

The second model, the social learning approach, builds on Harlow's (1958) work with rhesus monkeys. Characteristic patterns of behavior that are analogous to human depression have been induced in animals by depriving them of social contact (Berkson, 1967; Scott, Stewart, & DeGlett, 1973). According to this model, the isolation of persons with mental retardation in institutions, group homes, and nursing homes produces behaviors that closely approach Harlow's (1958) findings (Baumeister, 1978).

In addition, communication deficiencies pervasive in persons with mental retardation may increase this isolation and thus the likelihood of depression. This model has been espoused by Lewinsohn (1975) and is supported by studies conducted by Matson (1982a) and Schloss (1982). In these situations, adults with mild and moderate retardation and diagnosed as depressed have shown greater deficits in social behavior than those individuals with mental retardation for whom a diagnosis of depression was not given.

Certainly, more work in these areas is needed. Additionally, no biological data on the depression of persons with mental retardation are available, although several possible biological precipitants of depression have been postulated (Reid, 1985).

Treatment. Because few studies are available on the treatment of affective disorders with persons with mental retardation, this topic can be covered briefly. All of the studies have employed a case report or single-case experimental design, with three studies employing pharmacological methods and three employing behavior methods.

In the pharmacological studies, major tranquilizers (trifluoperazine and chlorpromazine) were used in two of the reports and lithium was used in the third. Rioth (1961) treated a 35-year-old Down's syndrome manic-depressive male with an IQ of 45. He administered trifluoperazine after imipramine, electroconvulsive shock therapy, and chlorpromazine had proven ineffective against delusions, hallucinations, withdrawal, and crying. Rioth (1961) reported major improvements after drug therapy, but no controlled method of evaluating outcome was utilized. The second study used chlorpromazine successfully to treat a psychotic-based depression in an 18-year-old girl with mild mental retardation (Adams, Kirowitz, & Ziskind, 1970). In the final drug study, Rivinus and Harmatz (1979) used lithium to treat a group of five institutionalized persons with mental retardation. After an initial 90-day baseline, each of the patients began a 1-year trial of lithium followed by a 90-day placebo period, then a second lithium trial of 1.5 years. The authors reported improvements during the lithium trials but not during the placebo period.

The methodological shortcomings of these studies were considerable. In the first two studies, the dosage given, the manner in which the drugs were administered, and criteria for determining depression were not described in adequate detail. Also, no systematic method of assessing treatment effectiveness was used. The third study represents an improvement with the use of the ABA design. The primary difficulty with this study was inadequate descriptions of the dependent variables, and failure to mention reliability data. These are serious weaknesses that limit the clinical utility of these studies.

Three behaviorally oriented studies have also been reported. In the first study, Matson et al. (1981) treated a 32-year-old male in the mild to borderline ranges of retardation. His depression was initially precipitated by his removal from a state institution. Upon discharge, having spent most of his life in an institutional setting, the patient became increasingly reclusive and depressed. An ABA experimental design was employed with a daily maintenance dosage of 100 mg of imipramine used throughout. Behaviors targeted for treatment included self-worth, suicide statements, and statements of past history. Each behavior was rapidly modified only when the behavior contingencies of instructions, modeling, performance feedback, and reinforcement were put into effect.

In a second study, Frame, Matson, Sonis, Fialkov, and Kazdin (1982) treated a 10-year-old boy diagnosed as depressed according to *DSM-III/DSM-III-R* criteria and multiple methods of assessment. Behaviors selected for intervention were inappropriate body position, lack of eye contact, poor speech, and bland affect. Treatment was evaluated in multiple-baseline fashion across behaviors and consisted of instructions, modeling, role playing, and feedback. Treatment produced marked changes in behaviors that were still maintained at a 12-week follow-up. In the third study, Matson (1982b) replicated these findings with four mild to moderately retarded adults with a larger number of target behaviors.

These studies, unlike the pharmacological studies, typically used systematic techniques for assessing treatment outcome. Also, target behaviors were operationally defined. All three studies indicated that behaviors characteristic of depression could be reliably identified and effectively treated using behavioral techniques.

Psychoses

Of the many types of psychopathology, psychoses were among the first to be identified in persons with mental retardation. Practically every major psychotic symptom found in persons without mental retardation has been reported in the population with mental retardation (Sarason & Gladwin, 1958). In past research, childhood psychoses have probably been the condition most frequently confused with mental retardation (Creak, 1963). In contrast to anxiety and affective disorders, a great amount has been written, most of it still anecdotal, on psychotic disorders in persons with mental retardation. However, the research has been so variable that a coherent picture of psychoses in individuals with mental retardation is difficult to construct. The sum of the research presents a very muddled picture of psychosis in the population with mental retardation for several reasons. First, earlier studies seldom made the distinction between subcategories of severe developmental and psychotic disorders (Romanczyk & Kistner, 1982). Second, the studies taken together lack uniform usage of terminology. Child psychosis, early infantile autism, autism, symbiotic psychosis, atypical development, and schizophrenic syndrome of childhood have frequently been used interchangeably by different authors (Rutter, 1965). Donaldson and Menolascino (1977) have noted that the word "autism" has been employed as a diagnosis, as a synonym for childhood schizophrenia, and as an abbreviation of early infantile autism; this imprecise usage contributes further to confusion. Furthermore, diagnosis has been complicated by different stresses in etiological factors and unwarranted expectations of homogeneity of etiology or pathogenesis in specific disorders (Beier, 1964). Individual differences in behavior and personality exist even in the severe levels of mental retardation (Sarason & Gladwin, 1958). This natural variability between individuals must be considered in the construction of diagnostic categories. Finally, the use of different diagnostic systems of psychopathology has further served to make cross comparisons of studies difficult. All of these problems point to the necessity of uniform usage of terms and a unitary system of diagnosis.

Several types of psychoses have been described. Due to limitations of space, this section will selectively discuss infantile autism and schizophrenia, the two psychotic disorders most frequently described in persons with mental retardation.

DSM-III/DSM-III-R has provided a classification of developmental disorders. The two major subcategories of these disorders are Early Infantile Autism and Childhood Onset Pervasive Developmental Disorder. These two disorders are distinguished primarily according to age of onset. The diagnostic criteria for infantile autism include:

1. onset before 30 months of age;
2. pervasive lack of responsiveness to other people;
3. gross deficits in language development;
4. if speech is present, peculiar speech patterns such as immediate and delayed echolalia, metaphorical language, pronomial reversal;
5. bizarre responses to various aspects of the environment, e.g., resistance to change, peculiar interest in or attachment to animate or inanimate objects;
6. absence of delusions, hallucinations, loosening of associations, and incoherence as in schizophrenia.

DSM-III/DSM-III-R notes that behavioral abnormalities similar to those seen in early infantile autism often occur in mental retardation. However, the full syndrome of infantile autism is rarely present. When both disorders are present, both diagnoses should be made.

According to *DSM-III/DSM-III-R*, schizophrenia involves disturbances in several different processes including: content and form of thought, perception, affect, sense of self, volition, relationship to the external world, and psychomotor behavior. Characteristic symptoms of the active phase of schizophrenia include delusions, hallucinations or marked loosening of associations, accompanied by deterioration from previous level of functioning. This disorder may also include a residual or prodromal phase that is characterized by social withdrawal, impairment in role functioning, peculiar behavior, impairment in personal hygiene, blunted or inappropriate affect, disturbances in communication, bizarre ideation, and unusual perceptual experiences. Diagnosis of schizophrenia requires that continuous signs of illness have lasted for at least 6 months. *DSM-III/DSM-III-R* also distinguishes between disorganized, paranoid, catatonic, undifferentiated, and residual types of schizophrenia.

Presenting symptoms. Behaviors that characterize infantile autism have been mentioned above. The most striking symptoms include failure to develop interpersonal relationships, speech and language deficits and oddities, and insistence on sameness. Self-help skills such as feeding, dressing, and toileting are frequently absent (Philips, 1966). During infancy, lack of eye contact and failure to cuddle are early indicators (Reid, 1985). Children have no interest in functional play (Menolascino, 1965a). Some cases later exhibit seizures (Menolascino & Eaton, 1972). Several autistic children exhibit "islets," or brief periods of normal functioning (Gillies, 1965; Reid, 1985). However, these appear to be unrelated to prognosis (Menolascino & Eaton, 1972).

Recent trends have placed increasing emphasis on the language components of the syndrome, such as echolalia and abnormalities in intonation and timing of speech. Barlow (1978) has reported that language is the single most important factor in prognosis. Also, Spreat, Roszkowski, Isett, and Alderter (1980), in a study to determine whether four psychotic subcategories could be distinguished according to epidemiological variables, found language development the primary distinguishing feature between autism and the three other disorders.

In addition, autistic children frequently show manneristic, stereotyped patterns of behavior. These may include finger-posturing, hand flapping, and rocking and twirling (Reid, 1985). Self-stimulatory and self-injurious behavior, such as hand biting and head banging, are also typical.

When Kanner (1943) first identified infantile autism, he and many others held that intelligence levels of these children were normal. It is now widely accepted that a large proportion, perhaps 70%, of autistic children have mental retardation.

Virtually all of the symptoms characteristic in schizophrenia in persons without retardation have been observed in persons with mental retardation. Also, symptoms of schizophrenia are frequently noticeably manifest in persons with mental retardation. Delusions and hallucinations are common (Doria, 1964; Wolfensburger, 1960). Altered affect responses, hallucinatory phenomena, bizarre rituals, and utilization of interpersonal distancing devices may all be exhibited by patients at various levels of retardation.

Sarason and Gladwin (1958) have described, in depth, signs of deterioration (e.g., speech fades, toilet habits are lost), signs of catatonia (including catalepsy, automatic obedience, and muscular catatonia), and signs of emotional dissociation (including mood variability and impulsiveness) in schizophrenic persons with mental retardation. From this, it is apparent that many symptoms of schizophrenia in persons with mental retardation are similar to those in schizophrenics without retardation, making dual diagnosis easier. Schizophrenia may occur and is diagnosable at all levels of retardation. Of course, diagnosis is more difficult in severe ranges due to speech deficits and general lower levels of intellectual functioning.

Incidence. The incidence of early infantile autism in the person with mental retardation is difficult to estimate. Available statistics are probably based on the more severely psychotic individuals (Sarason & Gladwin, 1958). Most researchers would, however, agree that infantile autism occurs more frequently in persons with retardation than in the general population. *DSM-III/DSM-III-R* rates this disorder as occurring only 2–4 times per 10,000 in the normal population. Russell and Tanguay (1981) examined 93 patients admitted to a psychiatric unit for emotionally disturbed, developmentally disabled adolescents. Five of these patients (5.4%) received a diagnosis of infantile autism.

Neuer (1947) examined the records of 300 consecutive admissions to a state school and found 11% of these to be psychotic. Webster (1970) estimated that 8% of his sample with mental retardation exhibited psychotic behavior.

Pollack (1967), in a literature review, estimated one third to one half of autistic children have mental retardation. Kolvin et al. (1971) found over 90% of a sample of autistic children to either have mental retardation or be untestable. Similarly, DeMyer et al. (1974) reported that 94% of their sample of autistic children had IQs below 70.

Incidence rates of schizophrenia are equally difficult to estimate. Penrose (1954) examined the records of 1,280 institutionalized persons with mental retardation and found that 3.7% were also diagnosed as schizophrenic. Angus (1948) reported that 28% of 150 admissions to the Devereaux School were schizophrenic. In a group of 616 children expected to have mental retardation, Menolascino (1965a) found 32 (5.2%) patients who displayed psychotic reactions. Of these, six (19.4%) were diagnosed as schizophrenic. In Russell and Tanguay's study (1981), mentioned above, 6.5% of their patients were diagnosed as schizophrenic. Finally, evaluating persons with mental retardation at a local community-based center, Menolascino and Swanson (1982) reported that 20.4% of 115 emotionally disturbed persons with mental retardation were schizophrenic.

Etiology. Many studies have reported the possible associations between infantile autism and organic brain damage (Bialer, 1970; Haracopos & Kelstrup, 1978; Menolascino & Eaton, 1977; Rutter, Graham, & Yule, 1970). Infantile autism has frequently been reported in association with specific organic brain syndromes such as rubella embryopathy (Chess, Fernandez, & Korn, 1978), infantile spasms (Rivkonen & Amnell, 1981; Kolvin et al., 1971), and Addison's disease (Money, Borrow, & Clarke, 1971). Influence of organic factors is further supported by frequent developments of epilepsy in autistic persons during adolescence (Deykind & MacMahon, 1979; Rutter, 1965). Pneumoencephalograms of selected children have shown a high incidence of enlargement of the left temporal horn, implying asymmetrical atrophic lesions of the brain as a possible factor (Barlow, 1987).

Others have focused on genetic factors (Minten, Campbell, Green, Jennings, & Samit, 1982). Ornitz (1978) has suggested that a specific genetic abnormality might result in a number of different pathological conditions. Thus, autism may have a single genetic mechanism involving several different brain systems. Romanczyk and Kistner (1982) have correctly noted that the association between autism and so many organic brain syndromes makes a single etiological factor unlikely. An exact neuropathological or biochemical mechanism remains to be identified.

Early studies suggested the possibility that autism was brought on by psychogenic factors (Esman, Kohn, & Nyman, 1959; Kanner, 1949). However, reports of behavioral disorders among parents of autistic children have typically failed to account for children's effects on parents (Bell, 1968; Romanczyk & Kistner, 1982). Empirical support for psychogenic factors is lacking (Rutter, 1965).

Biological causation of schizophrenia in persons with mental retardation has been suggested largely due to increased prevalence of neurological abnormalities, such as seizures and abnormal EEG records, in these persons. However there is little empirical evidence suggesting biological causation at present (Romanczyk & Kistner, 1982).

A different etiological factor suggested is that some individuals with mental retardation are born with a biological predisposition to schizophrenia which is brought on by traumatic stress, resulting from deficits in coping mechanisms. This theory also lacks direct empirical support.

Treatment. A great deal of work remains to be done in the area of treating psychoses in persons with mental retardation. The use of neuroleptics in treating schizophrenia and other types of psychotic behaviors has proven moderately successful (Breuning & Poling, 1982). However, more methodologically sound studies are needed.

Several psychotherapeutic techniques remain to be evaluated. Although it is likely that psychotic persons with more severe retardation will gain less from psychotherapy (Clarizio & McCoy, 1976), persons in the lesser ranges of retardation may benefit from the interactive processes between the client and therapist.

Behavioral approaches have been successfully employed in treating a wide variety of behavioral abnormalities associated with infantile autism and schizophrenia. Studies utilizing behavior techniques have reported success in treating incontinence and encopresis (Azrin & Foxx, 1971; Matson, 1977), absence of self-help skills (Touchette, 1978), language training (Lovaas, 1977), modification of psychotic speech patterns (Kazdin, 1971; Matson & Stephens, 1978; Stephens et al., 1981), aggression (Colletti, Kaplan, Brutuan, & Romanczyk, 1981; Foxx & Azrin, 1972), and self-injurious behavior (Carr, Newsom, & Binkoff, 1976). Procedures utilized have included positive reinforcement, overcorrection, differential reinforcement of other behaviors, time-out procedures, and various aversive techniques. (See Romanczyk & Kistner, 1982, for a more thorough review of the behavioral literature.) It is the authors' opinion that a combination of treatment methods would be most effective in treating psychotic behaviors.

Psychosexual Disorders

Very little appears in the literature on psychosexual disorders in the population with mental retardation. Of the many psychosexual disorders listed in *DSM-III/ DSM-III-R*, only a few of the paraphilias, namely exhibitionism, voyeurism, and pedophilia, have been reported to occur in persons with mental retardation. No studies were found dealing with gender identity disorders or psychosexual dysfunctions.

Prevalence. It was frequently believed at the beginning of this century that persons with mental retardation were much more at risk for becoming sex offenders. Some studies have corroborated this view. In an early study, Selling (1939) investigated the records of 551 individuals charged with indecent conduct from the Psychopathic Clinic of the Recorders Court of Michigan. Of these, 192 persons were charged with rape, attempted rape, or statutory rape. Approximately 51% of these had IQs below 70. Meyerowitz (1971) writes that almost one third of the criminal charges made against persons with mental retardation are charges of sex offenses. However, no reference is made to empirical data. Many recent studies have not supported these high rates. However, reasons for discrepancies in findings are not clear.

Mohr, Turner, and Jerry (1964), investigating a sample of pedophiles and exhibitionists at a forensic clinic in Toronto, found that only 4% of the pedophiles and 3% of the exhibitionists had IQs below 79. MacDonald (1973), in a review of the literature on the intellectual levels of exhibitionists, found rates of mental retardation varied in different studies from 2% (Taylor, 1947) to 16% (East, 1924). The majority of other studies indicate similar rates (Christie, Marshall, & Lanthier, 1977; MacDonald, 1973; Mohr et al., 1964). In general, data do not support an overrepresentation of persons with mental retardation among sex offenders.

Treatment. In a recent survey of the literature, Murphy, Coleman, and Abel (1983) reported that the vast majority of institutions for persons with mental retardation had no programs for sex offenders. Only three single-case design studies treating psychosexual disorders in persons with mental retardation were found. Lutzker (1973) treated an institutionalized male with profound retardation for exhibitionism. The method of intervention chosen was differential reinforcement of behaviors other than exhibitionism (which occurred 30% of the time during which observations were made). The procedure was effective within a few weeks. However, the study included no follow-up.

Cook, Shaw, and Blaylock (1978) successfully eliminated instances of public masturbation in a boy with severe mental retardation. Treatment consisted of squirting lemon juice into the subject's mouth contingent on initiation of masturbation.

Also, Murphy et al. (1983) reported a single-case treatment study of pedophilia. In this study, a 38-year-old male referred himself to treatment because of pedophilic urges. The patient had been successfully treated for the same condition 8 years prior with electrical aversion therapy while in prison. The subject was, upon his own request, treated with a series of 16 electrical aversion sessions over a 3-month period. The authors reported extinction of pedophilic behavior which was maintained at a 1-year follow-up.

A great amount of research has been published dealing with topics such as physical sexual maturation in persons with mental retardation, parental attitudes toward sex, and the sterilization controversy. However, systematic examination of the psychosexual disorders in persons with mental retardation is only beginning. It is quite evident from prevalence data that at least some paraphilic disorders are found in the population with mental retardation. Treatment studies in this area are sorely lacking. A few behavioral studies have reported success, and application of behavioral methods appears promising.

In a different light, several authors have hypothesized that many psychosexual disorders in persons with mental retardation may be due simply to ignorance and lack of training in appropriate sexual behavior (Craft & Craft, 1981; Mitchell, 1985). If this is true, a large part of treatment could take the form of prevention. Sex education programs for persons with mental retardation in institutions may be the first step in preventing abnormal sexual behavior later in life. Parents need to be made aware that their children with mental retardation develop physically in the same manner as do persons without retardation and have the same sexual urges and problems as do normal adolescents (Hall, 1974).

Social skills training has been successfully applied in treating a variety of disorders in persons with mental retardation (Matson & DiLorenzo, 1986) and may be useful for modifying problems such as inappropriate aggressive sexual behavior and overly affectionate behavior. Group therapy with male and female persons with retardation may assist in establishing appropriate sex-role behavior and gender identity. Sexual knowledge, exposure to the opposite sex in a structured setting, and social skills training may serve to prevent psychosexual disorders that result from lack of training. These techniques may also promote appropriate sexual behavior, possibly enhancing the individual's self-esteem and improving the overall quality of life.

Personality Disorders

Personality disorders are characterized by inflexible and maladaptive patterns of behavior that cause significant impairment in social and occupational functioning (*DSM-III/DSM-III-R*, 1980/87). They are generally recognizable by adolescence or slightly earlier and continue throughout most of adult life. Personality disorders are seldom diagnosed in the population with mental retardation, probably in part because they are not easily distinguishable from classic psychiatric disorders (Lewis & MacLean, 1982).

Menolascino and Swanson (1982) reported personality disorders in 38% of 165 individuals with mental retardation referred to a clinic for psychiatric diagnosis. Passive-depressive personalities, schizoid personalities, and emotionally unstable personalities were diagnosed most frequently.

Of all the personality disorders, only antisocial personality has received serious attention in the population with mental retardation. Antisocial personalities have been reported in several studies dealing with persons with mental retardation (Beier, 1964; Donaldson & Menolascino, 1977; Humphreys, 1940; Philips & Williams, 1975; Tarjan, 1948). In most studies it is reported that this disorder is overrepresented in the population with mental retardation, especially in mild and borderline cases. However, exact incidence rates are rarely given.

Antisocial personality is characterized by persistent violations of the rights of others and total disregard for social obligations. Lying, stealing, fighting, and resisting authority are early childhood signs. Aggressive or deviant sexual behavior is frequently noted. Antisocial disorder has been predominantly regarded as a male problem, and this is probably also true for the population with mental retardation (Reid, 1980). Severe mental retardation preempts the diagnosis of this disorder.

Personality disorders in general appear highly resistant to treatment. The more severe symptoms of antisocial personality may diminish with old age. Pharmacotherapy or behavioral techniques may be employed to reduce aggression. Only one study was found in which antisocial behavior was treated systematically in a sample of persons with mental retardation.

Burchard (1967) used a token reinforcement system to treat antisocial inpatients with retardation. The study consisted of two experiments employing a BAB design. In experiment I, in phase B of treatment, subjects were contingently reinforced with tokens for school and workshop performance. In phase A, subjects were noncontingently awarded tokens. Tokens could later be exchanged for food items, clothing, or recreational activities. School and workshop performance improved significantly during contingent reinforcement phases.

In the second experiment, effects of a punishing stimulus were investigated (response cost). During B phases, various antisocial behaviors (cheating, lying, stealing, fighting, etc.) resulted in time out and a loss of four tokens or seclusion and a loss of 15 tokens, depending on the seriousness of the offense. During phase A, response cost was not employed. Results showed that antisocial responses were not brought under complete control of experimental conditions. Although responses generally decreased during B phases, some overlap of behaviors occurred across phases, indicating that other uncontrolled variables were influencing responses.

Aggression and Disorders of Impulse Control

Virtually every study dealing with psychopathology in the population with mental retardation has commented to some degree on the high amount of aggressive behavior exhibited by this population. In a recent survey, Benson (1985) found that 30% of persons with mental retardation reporting to a health clinic were referred for self-control problems. However, studies have largely failed to discriminate between aggressive conduct disorders, intermittent explosive disorders, and isolated explosive disorders within the population with mental retardation; and it is unclear whether this distinction should be made. For this reason, aggression and disorders of impulse control will be discussed here together.

Several possible explanations for high rates of aggression in the population with mental retardation exist. Several studies have suggested heightened aggressive activity in persons without retardation and in animals can be related to biological factors such as hormone levels (Kreuz & Rose, 1972; Persky, Smith, & Basu, 1981), imbalances in neurotransmitters (Valzelli, 1981), and structural brain abnormalities (Mark & Ervin, 1970; Sweet, Ervin, & Mark, 1969).

Regarding the population with mental retardation, Talkington and Hall (1969) have adopted the frustration-aggression hypothesis of Dollard, Doob, Miller, Mowrer, and Sears (1939). According to this model, blocked drives produce frustrations which may result in aggression. Talkington and Hall (1969) suggested that factors related to the institutional setting, including minimum opportunity for privacy, control of individual freedom, and few available avenues for ventilation of hostility, may contribute to aggression in persons with mental retardation.

Talkington and Riley (1970) cross-matched 32 adults with retardation according to age, ability level, length of institutionalization, and number of aggressive incidents reported in prior 6-month period. One person from each pair was randomly assigned to a weight reduction diet program. The remaining person from each pair served as a control group. Aggressive incidents were operationally defined as an act of physical assault upon another resident or staff member. Over a 6-month period, the Diet group demonstrated significant increases in aggressive conduct as compared to the no-Diet group.

In a second study, Talkington, Hall, and Altman (1971) expanded the frustration-aggression hypothesis to a frustration-aggression-attention hypothesis. The authors suggested that attention received for engaging in aggressive acts may act as a social reinforcer which sustains aggressive behavior.

Several studies have reported successful methods of intervention. Two studies were found reporting successful use of punishment procedures to eliminate aggression in persons with mental retardation. Hamilton, Stephens, and Allen (1967) used a time-out procedure to reduce aggression and destructive behavior in five females with severe retardation. Harvey (1973) extinguished aggression, spitting, exhibitionism, self-mutilation, and some autistic behaviors by shooting a pressurized stream of water into the patient's face, using time-out procedures, and by electroshock.

Many other studies have reported success using behavioral techniques. In a single-case study, Pelechano and Vinagre (1976) used positive and negative social reinforcement to extinguish physical harm to peers by a 12-year-old female with retardation. Harvey et al. (1978), in another single-case study, reduced the frequency of temper outbursts in a 38-year-old epileptic, emotionally disturbed female with moderate mental retardation through relaxation training and cognitive behavior procedures.

Golden and Consorte (1982) used a cognitive behavioral approach, emphasizing self-control as opposed to control of external contingencies, to treat four adults with mild mental retardation with chronic anger problems. Therapy consisted of a combination of rational-emotive therapy, coping self-statements, relaxation training, biofeedback, coping imagery, behavioral rehearsal, and assertiveness training. The authors reported that violent behavior and destruction of property was totally eliminated in all four subjects over the course of a year. Follow-up data in two of the patients reported continued absence of aggression.

In recent studies, Benson and her colleagues (Benson, Rice, & Miranti, 1986;

Saylor, Benson, & Einhaus, 1985) have reported initial success in eliminating aggression in mild and moderately retarded adults through an Anger Management training program. As in Golden and Consorte's study (1982), emphasis was placed on self-control.

Pharmacotherapeutic studies have also reported moderate success in controlling aggression using haloperidol (Burk & Menolascino, 1968) and lithium carbonate (Dale, 1980; Elliot, 1986; Lion, Hill, & Madden, 1975).

In all of the above studies, lack of no-treatment controls makes interpretation of results difficult. Studies comparing the efficacy of various treatment techniques in reducing aggression in persons with mental retardation are badly needed.

Psychosomatic Illnesses

Only one study was found regarding psychosomatic illnesses in persons with mental retardation. Matson (1983a) treated three adults with mild mental retardation using multiple baseline design across types of behaviors and therapists. Treatment consisted of a combination of reinforcement, performance feedback, instructions, and modeling. Stomach ache, headache, and multiple body complaints were behaviors targeted for change. In addition, socially appropriate behaviors incompatible with target behaviors were assessed. Subjects were matched on age, sex, and intelligence level with persons who did not have this disorder in order to establish clinical significance in frequency of psychosomatic complaints. Also, baseline, treatment, and follow-up sessions were rated according to frequency of complaints by 10 adults from the community. Frequencies of target behaviors were decreased to near zero and were maintained at that level at follow-up. Also, subjects' performance on adaptive behavior improved and was rated in normal ranges of performance according to both social validation criteria.

Summary

In general, the study of the emotional disorders of persons with mental retardation is in its early stages. Still, initial progress has been made in several areas. High prevalence rates of psychiatric disorders in the population with mental retardation are fairly well documented, although it is difficult to determine these rates with any great specificity. Important pioneer work has been done addressing etiology, treatment, and theoretical models of psychopathology in persons with mental retardation. Regarding specific disorders, findings from early studies in anxiety disorders, affective disorders, and psychoses of individuals with mental retardation provide a valuable base from which to continue research. However, in all areas there is a great need for future research. A widely accepted diagnostic system of psychopathology in persons with mental retardation still does not exist. It remains to be seen whether many of the subcategories of disorders in *DSM-III/DSM-III-R* are appropriate for this population. Also, a great many treatment techniques that have proven successful in persons without retardation remain untested in the population with retardation. Substance abuse, somatiform disorders, personality disorders, and psychosexual disorders are all important areas that have received little or no attention in the literature.

In all areas, it is important to view psychopathology in relation to the complex life events that result from cognitive deficits and are unique to individuals with mental retardation. Continued emphasis on empirical procedures is vital. Although the research is incomplete, it evidences a growing concern for the emotional development of persons with mental retardation, an area that has been too long neglected. The outlook is hopeful.

References

Achenbach, T. M. (1974). *Developmental psychopathology*. New York: Ronald.

Achenbach, T. M., & Zigler, E. F. (1968). Cue-learning and problem learning strategies in normal and retarded children. *Child Development, 39*, 827-848.

Adams, G. L., Kirowitz, J., & Ziskind, E. (1970). Manic depressive psychosis, mental retardation, and chromosomal rearrangement. *Archives of General Psychiatry, 23*, 305-309.

Agras, W. S., Kazdin, A. E., & Wilson, G. (1979). *Behavior therapy: Toward an applied clinical science*. San Francisco: Freeman.

Akiskal, H. S., & McKinney, W. T. (1975). Depressive disorders: Toward a uniform hypothesis. *Science, 182*, 20-29.

Alford, J. D., & Locke, B. J. (1984). Clinical responses to psychopathology of mentally retarded persons. *American Journal of Mental Deficiency, 89*, 195-197.

Aman, M. G., & Singh, N. N. (1980). The usefulness of thioridazine in childhood disorders—Fact or folklore? *American Journal of Mental Deficiency, 84*, 195-197.

American Psychiatric Association. (1980). *Diagnostic and statistical manual of mental disorders* (3rd ed.). Washington, DC: Author.

American Psychiatric Association. (1987). *Diagnostic and statistical manual of mental disorders* (3rd ed., rev.). Washington, DC: Author.

Angus, L. R. (1948). Schizophrenia and schizoid conditions in students in a special school. *American Journal of Mental Deficiency, 53*, 227-238.

Azrin, N. H., & Foxx, R. M. (1971). A rapid method of toilet training the institutionalized retarded. *Journal of Applied Behavior Analysis, 4*, 88-89.

Balla, D., & Zigler, E. (1979). Personality development in retarded persons. In N. R. Ellis (Ed.), *Handbook of mental deficiency, psychological theory and research* (2nd ed., pp. 154-168). Hillsdale, NJ: Lawrence Erlbaum.

Ballinger, B. R., Armstrong, J., Presly, A. S., & Reid, A. H. (1975). Use of standardized psychiatric interview in mentally handicapped patients. *British Journal of Psychiatry, 127,* 540-545.

Balthazar, E., & Stevens, H. A. (1975). *The emotionally disturbed, mentally retarded: A historical and contemporary perspective.* Englewood Cliffs, NJ: Prentice-Hall.

Barlow, C. F. (1978). *Mental retardation and related disorders.* Philadelphia, PA: F. A. Davis Company.

Baumeister, A. A. (1978). Origins and control of stereotyped movements. In C. E. Meyers (Ed.), *Quality of life in severely and profoundly mentally retarded people: Research foundations for improvement* (pp. 353-384). Washington, DC: American Association on Mental Deficiency.

Baumeister, A. A., & MacLean, W. E., Jr. (1979). Brain damage and mental retardation. In N. R. Ellis (Ed.), *Handbook of mental deficiency* (2nd ed., pp. 197-236). Hillsdale, NJ: Lawrence Erlbaum.

Beech, R. (Ed.). (1974). *Obsessional states.* London: Methuen.

Beier, D. (1964). Behavioral disturbances in the mentally retarded. In H. A. Stevens & R. Heber (Eds.), *Mental retardation* (pp. 453-487). Chicago: University of Chicago Press.

Bell, R. Q. (1968). A reinterpretation of the effects in studies in socialization. *Psychological Review, 75,* 81-95.

Benson, B. (1985). Behavior disorders and mental retardation: Associations with age, sex, and level of functioning in an outpatient clinic sample. *Applied Research in Mental Retardation, 6,* 79-85.

Benson, B. A., Rice, C. J., & Miranti, S. V. (1986). Effects of anger management training with adults in group treatment. *Journal of Consulting and Clinical Psychology, 5,* 728-729.

Berkson, G. (1967). Abnormal stereotyped motor acts. In J. Zubin & H. F. Hunt (Eds.), *Comparative psychopathology: Animal and human* (pp. 76-94). New York: Grune & Stratton.

Bialer, I. (1970). Relationship of mental retardation to emotional disturbance and physical disability. In H. C. Haywood (Ed.), *Social-cultural aspects of mental retardation* (pp. 607-660). New York: Appleton-Century-Crofts.

Bijou, S. W. (1966). A functional analysis of retarded development. In N. R. Ellis (Ed.), *International review of research in mental retardation* (Vol. 1, 1-20). New York: Academic Press.

Brenner, C. (1974). *An elementary textbook of psychoanalysis* (rev. ed.). Garden City, NY: Anchor Books.

Breuning, S. E. (1982). An applied dose-response curve of thioridazine with the mentally retarded: Aggressive, self-stimulatory, intellectual, and workshop behaviors—A preliminary report. *Psychopharmacology Bulletin, 18,* 57-59.

Breuning, S. E., & Davidson, N. A. (1981). Effects of psychotropic drugs on the intelligence test performance of mentally retarded adults. *American Journal of Mental Deficiency, 85,* 575-577.

Breuning, S. E., & Poling, A. D. (1982). Pharmacotherapy. In J. L. Matson & R. P. Barrett (Eds.), *Psychopathology in the mentally retarded* (pp. 195-252). New York: Grune & Stratton.

Burchard, J. D. (1967). Systematic socialization: A programmed environment for the habilitation of antisocial retardates. *The Psychological Record, 17,* 461-476.

Burk, H. W., & Menolascino, F. J. (1968). Haloperidol in emotionally disturbed mentally retarded individuals. *American Journal of Psychiatry, 124,* 147-149.

Butterfield, E. L., & Zigler, E. (1965). The effects of success and failure on the discrimination learning of normal and retarded children. *Journal of Abnormal Psychology, 70,* 25-31.

Calamari, J. E., Geist, G. O., & Shahbazian, M. J. (1987). Evaluation of multiple component relaxation training with developmentally disabled persons. *Research in Developmental Disabilities, 8,* 51-70.

Carlson, G. A., & Cantwell, D. P. (1980). A survey of depressive symptoms, syndromes, and disorders in a child psychiatric population. *Journal of Child Psychology and Psychiatry, 21,* 19-25.

Carr, A. (1974). Compulsive neurosis. *Psychological Bulletin, 81,* 311-318.

Carr, E. G., Newsom, C. D., & Binkoff, J. A. (1976). Stimulus control of self-destructive behavior in a psychotic child. *Journal of Abnormal Child Psychology, 4,* 139-153.

Chambers, W., Puig-Antich, J., & Tabrizi, M. A. (1978). *The ongoing development of the Kiddie-SADS (Schedule for Affective Disorders & Schizophrenia for school age children).* Paper presented at the annual meeting of the American Academy of Child Psychiatry, San Diego, CA.

Chazan, M. (1964). The incidence and nature of maladjustment among children in schools for the educationally subnormal. *British Journal of Educational Psychology, 34,* 292-304.

Chess, S., Fernandez, P., & Korn, S. (1978). Behavioral consequences of congenital rubella. *Journal of Pediatrics, 93,* 699-703.

Chess, S., & Hassibi, M. (1979). Behavior deviations in mentally retarded children. *Journal of the American Academy of Child Psychiatry, 9,* 282-297.

Chess, S., & Korn, S. (1970). Temperament and behavior disorders in mentally retarded children. *Archives of General Psychiatry, 23,* 122-130.

Christie, M. M., Marshall, W. L., & Lanthier, R. D. (1977). *A descriptive study of incarcerated rapists and pedophiles.* Unpublished manuscript.

Clarizio, H. F., & McCoy, G. F. (1976). *Behavior disorders in children* (2nd ed.). New York: Cromwell.

Clouston, T. S. (1883). *Clinical lectures on mental diseases.* London: Churchill.

Colletti, G., Kaplan, J., Brutuan, L., & Romanczyk, R. G. (1981). *Enforced relaxation: Application to severe aggression and acting out behavior.* Paper presented at the Association for Behavior Analysis Eighth Annual Convention, Milwaukee, WI.

Cook, J. W., Shaw, J., & Blaylock, M. (1978). Use of contingent lemon juice to eliminate public masturbation by a severely retarded boy. *Behavior Research & Therapy, 16,* 131-134.

Corbett, J. A., & Harris, R. (1974). *Epilepsy in children with severe mental handicap* (Symposium No. 16). London: Institute for Research into Mental and Multiple Handicap.

Corbett, J. A., Harris, R., & Robinson, R. G. (1975). Epilepsy. In J. Wortis (Ed.), *Mental retardation and developmental disabilities* (Vol. VII, pp. 79-111). New York: Brunner/ Mazel.

Cotzin, M. (1948). Group therapy with mentally defective problem boys. *American Journal of Mental Deficiency, 53*, 268-283.

Craft, A., & Craft, M. (1981). Sexuality and mental handicap: A review. *British Journal of Psychiatry, 139*, 494-505.

Craft, M. (1959). Mental disorder in the defective: A psychiatric survey among inpatients. *American Journal of Mental Deficiency, 63*, 829-834.

Creak, E. M. (1963). Childhood psychosis: A review of 100 cases. *British Journal of Psychiatry, 109*, 84-89.

Critchley, M., & Earl, C. J. C. (1932). Tuberous sclerosis and allied conditions. *Brain, 55*, 311-346.

Crome, L., & Stern, J. (1972). *Pathology of mental retardation* (2nd ed.). Edinburgh: Churchill Livingstone.

Cromwell, R. L. (1963). A social learning approach to mental retardation. In N. R. Ellis (Ed.), *Handbook of mental deficiency, psychological theory and research* (pp. 41-91). New York: McGraw-Hill.

Cuvo, A. J. (1976). Decreasing repetitive behavior in an institutionalized mentally retarded resident. *Mental Retardation, 14*, 22-25.

Cytryn, L., McKnew, D. H., & Bunney, W. (1980). Diagnosis of depression in children: A reassessment. *American Journal of Psychiatry, 137*, 22-25.

Dale, P. G. (1980). Lithium therapy in aggressive mentally subnormal patients. *British Journal of Psychiatry, 137*, 469-474.

Davis, V. J., Cullari, S., & Breuning, S. E. (1982). Effects of phenytoin withdrawal on matching to sample and workshop performance of mentally retarded persons. *Journal of Nervous and Mental Disease, 169*, 718-725.

DeMyer, M. K., Barton, S., Alpern, G. D., Kimberlin, C., Allen, J.,Yang, E., & Steele, R. (1974). The measured intelligence of autistic children. *Journal of Autism and Childhood Schizophrenia, 4*, 42-60.

DeVellis, R. F. (1977). Learned helplessness in institutions. *Mental Retardation, 15*, 10-15.

Deykind, E. Y., & MacMahon, B. (1979). The increase of seizures among children with autistic symptoms. *American Journal of Psychiatry, 136*, 1310-1312.

Dewan, J. G. (1948). Intelligence and emotional stability. *American Journal of Psychiatry, 104*, 548-554.

Dollard, J., Doob, L., Miller, N., Mowrer, O., & Sears, R. (1939). *Frustration and aggression*. New Haven: Yale University Press.

Donaldson, J. Y., & Menolascino, F. J. (1977). Emotional disorders in the retarded. *International Journal of Mental Health, 6*, 73-95.

Doria, M. R. (1964). Episodios psicoticos en el debil mental [Psychotic episodes in the mental defective]. *Acta Psiquiatrica y Psicologica American Latina, 10,* 118-121.

Duncan, A. C., Penrose, L., & Turnbull, R. (1936). Mental deficiency and manic depressive insanity. *Journal of Mental Science, 82,* 635-641.

East, W. N. (1924). Observations on exhibitionism. *Lancet, 23,* 370-375.

Elliot, R. L. (1986). Lithium treatment and cognitive changes in two mentally retarded patients. *Journal of Nervous and Mental Disease, 174,* 689-692.

Emerson, E. B. (1985). Evaluating the impact of deinstitutionalization on the lives of mentally retarded people. *American Journal of Mental Deficiency, 90,* 277-288.

Esman, A. H., Kohn, M., & Nyman, L. (1959). The family of the "schizophrenic" child. *American Journal of Orthopsychiatry, 29,* 455-459.

Eyman, R. K., Moore, B. C., Capes, L., & Zachofsky, T. (1970). Maladaptive behavior of institutionalized retardates with seizures. *American Journal of Mental Deficiency, 74,* 651-659.

Ferguson, D. G., & Breuning, S. E. (1982). Antipsychotic and antianxiety drugs. In S. E. Breuning & A. D. Poling (Eds.), *Drugs and mental retardation* (pp. 121-193). Springfield, IL: Thomas.

Fernald, W. E. (1908). *The imbecile with criminal instincts.* Paper presented at the American Medico-Psychological Association, Cincinnati, OH.

Fisher, L. A., & Wolfson, J. N. (1953). Group therapy of mental defectives. *American Journal of Mental Deficiency, 57,* 463-476.

Floor, L., & Rosen, M. (1975). Investigating the phenomenon of helplessness in mentally retarded adults. *American Journal of Mental Deficiency, 79,* 565-572.

Forbes, L. M. (1958). Some psychiatric problems related to mental retardation. *American Journal of Mental Deficiency, 62,* 637-641.

Foxx, R. M., & Azrin, N. H. (1972). A method of eliminating aggressive-destructive behavior of retarded and brain damaged patients. *Behavior Research & Therapy, 10,* 15-27.

Foxx, R. M., & Azrin, N. H. (1973). The elimination of autistic self-stimulatory behavior by overcorrection. *Journal of Applied Behavior Analysis, 6,* 1-14.

Frame, C., Matson, J. L., Sonis, W. A., Fialkov, M. J., & Kazdin, A. E. (1982). Behavioral treatment of depression in a prepubertal child. *Journal of Behavior Therapy and Experimental Psychiatry, 13,* 239-243.

Freedman, R. D., & Malkin, F. F. (1977). A comparison of the psychosocial problems of deaf, visually impaired, and of non-handicapped children. *Developmental Medicine and Child Neurology, 19,* 111.

Freeman, M. (1936). Drawing as a psychotherapeutic medium. *American Journal of Mental Deficiency, 41,* 182-187.

Freud, S. (1966). *Complete introductory lectures on psychoanalysis.* New York: Norton.

Gardner, W. I. (1971). *Behavior modification and mental retardation.* Chicago: Aldine.

Gibbs, E. L., Gibbs, T. T., Gibbs, F. H., Gibbs, E. A., Dickman, S., & Hermann, B. P. (1982). Antiepileptic drugs. In S. E. Breuning & A. D. Poling (Eds.), *Drugs and mental retardation.* (268-329). Springfield, IL: Thomas.

Gillies, S. (1965). Some abilities of psychotic children and subnormal controls. *Journal of Mental Deficiency Research, 9*, 89-101.

Glaser, K. (1967). Masked depression in children and adolescents. *American Journal of Psychotherapy, 21*, 565-574.

Golden, W. L., & Consorte, J. (1982). Training mildly retarded individuals to control their anger through the use of cognitive-behavior therapy techniques. *Journal of Contemporary Psychotherapy, 13*, 182-187.

Guarnaccia, V. S., & Weiss, R. L. (1974). Factor structure of fears in the mentally retarded. *Journal of Clinical Psychology, 30*, 540-544.

Guralnick, M. J. (1973). Behavior therapy with an acrophobic mentally retarded young adult. *Journal of Behavior Therapy and Experimental Psychiatry, 4*, 263-265.

Hall, J. E. (1974). Sexual behavior. In J. Wortis (Ed.), *Mental retardation (and developmental disabilities): An annual review* (Vol. VI, pp. 178-212). New York: Brunner/Mazel.

Hamilton, J., Stephens, L., & Allen, P. (1967). Controlling aggression and destructive behavior in severely retarded institutionalized residents. *American Journal of Mental Deficiency, 71*, 852-856.

Haracopos, D., & Kelstrup, A. (1978). Psychotic behavior in children under the institutions for the mentally retarded in Denmark. *Journal of Autism and Childhood Schizophrenia, 8*, 1-11.

Harlow, H. F. (1958). The nature of love. *American Psychologist, 13*, 673-685.

Harvey, J. R., Karan, O. C., Bhargava, D., & Morehouse, N. (1978). Relaxation training and cognitive behavioral procedures to reduce violent temper outbursts in a moderately retarded woman. *Journal of Behavior Therapy & Experimental Psychiatry, 9*, 347-351.

Harvey, M. (1973). [Behavior modification technique for the "ineducable."] *Revue de Psychologie Apliquee, 23*, 151-183.

Hasan, M. K., & Mooney, R. P. (1979). Three cases of manic-depressive illness in mentally retarded adults. *American Journal of Psychiatry, 136*, 1061-1071.

Herskovitz, H. H., & Plesset, M. R. (1941). Psychoses in adult mental defectives. *Psychiatric Quarterly, 18*, 574-588.

Humphreys, E. J. (1940). Psychopathic personality among the mental defectives. *Psychiatric Quarterly, 14*, 231-247.

Hurd, H. M. (1888). Imbecility with insanity. *Journal of Insanity, 45*, 263-371.

Jacobson, J. W. (1983). Problem behavior and psychiatric impairment within a developmentally disabled population. I: Behavior frequency. *Applied Research in Mental Retardation, 3*, 121-140.

Kanner, L. (1943). Autistic disturbances of affective contact. *Nervous Child, 3*, 217-250.

Kanner, L. (1949). Problems of nosology and psychodynamics of early infantile autism. *American Journal of Orthopsychiatry, 19*, 416-426.

Katz, P., & Zigler, E. F. (1967). Self-image disparity: A developmental approach. *Journal of Personality and Social Psychology, 5*, 186-195.

Kazdin, A. E. (1971). The effect of response cost in suppressing behavior in a pre-psychotic retardate. *Journal of Behavior Therapy & Experimental Psychiatry, 2*, 137-140.

Kisker, G. W. (1977). *The disorganized personality* (3rd ed.). New York: McGraw-Hill.

Kohlberg, L. (1966). Sex differences in morality. In E. E. Maccoby (Ed.), *The development of sex differences* (pp. 97-124). Stanford, CA: Stanford University.

Kohlberg, L., & Zigler, E. F. (1967). The impact of cognitive maturity on the development of sex role attitudes in the years four to eight. *Genetic Psychology Monographs, 75*, 89-165.

Koller, H., Richardson, S. A., & Katz, M. (1983). Behavior disturbances since childhood among a five year birth cohort of all mentally retarded young adults in a city. *American Journal of Mental Deficiency, 87*, 386-395.

Kolstoe, O. P., & Schaffer, A. J. (1961). Employability prediction for mentally retarded adults: A methodological note. *American Journal of Mental Deficiency, 66* , 287-289.

Kolvin, I., Ounsted, C., Humphrey, M., McNay, A., Richardson, L. M., Garside, R. F., Kidd, J. S. H., & Roth, M. (1971). Six studies in the childhood psychoses. *British Journal of Psychiatry, 118*, 382-419.

Konarski, E. H., Jr., & Cavalier, A. R. (1982). Current models of psychopathology. In J. L. Matson & R. P. Barrett (Eds.), *Psychopathology in the mentally retarded* (pp. 53-76). New York: Grune & Stratton.

Kovacs, M., & Beck, A. T. (1977). An empirical-clinical approach toward a definition of childhood depression. In J. G. Schulterbrandt & A. Rasker (Eds.), *Depression in childhood: Diagnosis, treatment, and conceptual models* (pp. 1-25). New York: Raven Press.

Kraeplin, E. (1889). *Psychiatrie: Ein Lehrbuch fur Studierendeund Aertze* (3rd ed.). Leipzig: Barth.

Kreuz, L. E., & Rose, R. M. (1972). Assessment of aggressive behavior and plasma testosterone in a young criminal population. *Psychosomatic Medicine, 43*, 321-332.

Lefkowitz, M. M. (1980). Childhood depression: A reply to Costello. *Psychological Bulletin, 87*, 191-194.

Lewinsohn, P. M. (1975). The behavioral study and treatment of depression. In M. Hersen, R. M. Eisler, & P. M. Miller (Eds.), *Progress in behavior modification* (Vol. 1, pp. 19-59). New York: Academic Press.

Lewis, M. H., & MacLean, W. E., Jr. (1982). Issues in treating emotional disorders. In J. L. Matson & R. P. Barrett (Eds.), *Psychopathology in the mentally retarded* (pp.1-36). New York.

Lick, J. R., & Katkin, E. S. (1976). Assessment of anxiety and fear. In M. Hersen & A. S. Bellack (Eds.), *Behavioral assessment: A practical handbook* (pp. 175-206). New York: Pergamon Press.

Lion, J. R., Hill, J., & Madden, D. J. (1975). Lithium carbonate and aggression: A case report. *Diseases of the Nervous System, 36*, 97-98.

Lipman, R. S. (1970). The use of pharmacological agents in residential facilities for the retarded. In F. Menolascino (Ed.), *Psychiatric approaches to mental retardation* (pp. 387-398). New York: Basic Books.

Lovaas, O. I. (1977). *The autistic child–Language development through behavior modification*. New York: Irvington.

Lutzker, J. R. (1973). Reinforcer control of exhibitionism in a profoundly retarded adult. *Proceedings of the 81st Annual Convention of the American Psychological Association, 8,* 925-926.

MacDonald, J. M. (1973). *Indecent exposure.* Springfield, IL: Charles C. Thomas.

Mansdorf, I. J. (1976). Eliminating fear in a mentally retarded adult by behavioral hierarchies and operant techniques. *Journal of Behavior Therapy & Experimental Psychiatry, 7,* 189-190.

Mark, V. H., & Ervin, F. R. (1970). *Violence and the brain.* New York: Harper & Row.

Matson, J. L. (1977). Simple correction for treating an autistic boy's encopresis. *Psychological Reports, 41,* 802.

Matson, J. L. (1980). Behavior modification procedures for training chronically institutionalized schizophrenics. In M. Hersen, R. M. Eisler, & R. P. Miller (Eds.), *Progress in behavior modification* (pp. 127-154). New York: Academic Press.

Matson, J. L. (1981a). Assessment and treatment of clinical phobias in mentally retarded children. *Journal of Applied Behavior Analysis, 14,* 145-152.

Matson, J. L. (1981b). A controlled outcome study of phobias in mentally retarded adults. *Behavior Research and Therapy, 19,* 101-108.

Matson, J. L. (1982a). Depression in the mentally retarded: A review. *Education and Training in the Mentally Retarded,* April, 159-163.

Matson, J. L. (1982b). The behavioral treatment of depression in the mentally retarded. *Behavior Therapy, 13,* 209-218.

Matson, J. L. (1982c). Treatment of obsessive-compulsive behavior in mentally retarded adults. *Behavior Modification, 6,* 551-567.

Matson, J. L. (1983a). Behavioral treatment of psychosomatic complaints of mentally retarded adults. *American Journal of Mental Deficiency, 88,* 638-646.

Matson, J. L. (1983b). Depression in the mentally retarded: Toward a conceptual analysis of diagnosis. In M. Hersen, R. M. Eisler, & P. M. Miller (Eds.), *Progress in behavior modification* (pp. 58-74). New York: Academic Press.

Matson, J. L. (1984). Psychotherapy with persons who are mentally retarded. *Mental Retardation, 22,* 170-175.

Matson, J. L. (1985). Biosocial theory of psychopathology: A three by three factor model. *Applied Research in Mental Retardation, 6,* 199-227.

Matson, J. L., & Barrett, R. P. (1982). Affective disorders. In J. L. Matson & R. P. Barrett (Eds.), *Psychopathology in the mentally retarded* (pp. 121-146). New York: Grune & Stratton.

Matson, J. L., Dettling, J., & Senatore, V. (1981). Treating depression of a mentally retarded adult. *British Journal of Mental Subnormality, 16,* 86-88.

Matson, J. L., & DiLorenzo, T. M. (1986). Social skills training and mental handicap and organic impairment. In C. R. Hollin & P. Trower (Eds.), *Handbook of social skills training* (Vol. 2, pp. 67-90). Oxford: Pergamon Press.

Matson, J. L., DiLorenzo, T. M., & Andrasik, F. (1983). A review of behavior modification procedures for treating social skills deficits and psychiatric disorders of the mentally retarded. In J. L. Matson & F. Andrasik (Eds.), *Treatment issues and innovations in mental retardation* (pp. 112-197). New York: Plenum Press.

Matson, J. L., Kazdin, A. F., & Esveldt-Dawson, K. (1980). Training interpersonal skills among mentally retarded and socially dysfunctional children. *Behavior Research and Therapy, 18*, 419-427.

Matson, J. L., Kazdin, A. E., & Senatore, V. (1984). Psychometric properties of the psychopathology instrument for mentally retarded adults. *Applied Research in Mental Retardation, 5*, 81-89.

Matson, J. L., & Stephens, R. M. (1978). Increasing appropriate behavior of explosive chronic psychiatric patients with a social skills training package. *Behavior Modification, 2*, 61-75.

Matson, J. L., & Stephens, R. M. (1981). Overcorrection treatment of stereotyped behavior in chronic psychiatric patients. *Behavior Modification, 5*, 491-502.

Mendels, J., & Cochran, L. (1968). The nosology of depression: The endogenous-reactive concept. *American Journal of Psychiatry, 124*, 1-11.

Menolascino, F. J. (1965a). Psychoses of childhood: Experiences of a mentally retarded pilot project. *American Journal of Mental Deficiency, 70*, 83-92.

Menolascino, F. J. (1965b). Emotional disturbances and mental retardation. *American Journal of Mental Deficiency, 70*, 248-256.

Menolascino, F. J. (1977). *Challenges in mental retardation: Progressive ideology and services.* New York: Human Services Press.

Menolascino, F. J., & Eaton, L. (1972). Psychoses of childhood: A five year follow-up study of experiences in a mental retardation clinic. *American Journal of Mental Deficiency, 72*, 370-380.

Menolascino, F. J., & Swanson, D. A. (1982). Emotional disorders in the mentally retarded. *British Journal of Mental Subnormality, 28*, 46-55.

Meyerowitz, J. H. (1971). Sex and the mentally retarded. *Medical Aspects of Human Sexuality, 5*, 94-118.

Miller, L. C., Barrett, C. L., Hampe, E., & Noble, H. (1972). Factor structure of childhood fears. *Journal of Consulting and Clinical Psychology, 39*, 264-268.

Minton, J., Campbell, M., Green, W. H., Jennings, S., & Samit, C. (1982). Cognitive assessment of siblings of autistic children. *Journal of the American Academy of Child Psychiatry, 21*, 456-461.

Mitchell, L. J. (1985). *Behavioral intervention in the sexual problems of mentally handicapped individuals.* Springfield, IL: Charles C. Thomas.

Mohr, J. W., Turner, R. E., & Jerry, M. B. (1964). *Pedophilia and exhibitionism.* Toronto: University of Toronto Press.

Money, J., Borrow, N. A., & Clark, F. C. (1971). Autism and auto immune disease—A family study. *Journal of Autism and Childhood Schizophrenia 1*, 146-160.

Mundy, L. (1957). Therapy with physically and mentally handicapped children in a mental deficiency hospital. *Journal of Clinical Psychology, 13*, 3-9.

Murphy, W. D., Coleman, E. M., & Abel, G. G. (1983). Human sexuality in the mentally retarded. In J. L. Matson & F. Andrasik (Eds.), *Treatment issues and innovations in mental retardation* (pp. 581-643). New York: Plenum Press.

Neuer, H. (1947). The relationship between behavior disorders in children and the syndrome of mental deficiency. *American Journal of Mental Deficiency, 55*, 143-147.

Neustadt, R. (1928). *The episodic psychosis of the defective.* Berlin: Karger.

Novosel, S. (1984). Psychiatric disorders in adults admitted to a hospital for the mentally handicapped. *British Journal of Mental Subnormality, 30*, 54-58.

Ollendick, T. H. (1978). *The revised fear survey schedule for children.* Unpublished manuscript, Indiana State University.

Ollendick, T. H., Balla, D., & Zigler, E. F. (1971). Expectancy of success and the probability learning performance of retarded children. *Journal of Abnormal Psychology, 77*, 275-281.

Ollendick, T. H., & Ollendick, D. G. (1982). Anxiety disorders. In J. L. Matson & R. P. Barrett (Eds.), *Psychopathology in the mentally retarded* (pp. 77-120). New York: Grune & Stratton.

Ornitz, E. N. M. (1978). Biological homogeneity or heterogeneity? In M. Rutter & E. Schopler (Eds.), *Autism.* New York: Plenum Press.

Pavlov, I. P. (1927). *Conditioned reflexes* (G. V. Anrep, Ed. and Trans.). London: Oxford University Press.

Payne, R. (1968). The psychotic subnormal. *Journal of Mental Subnormality, 14*, 25-34.

Peck, C. L. (1977). Desensitization for the treatment of fear in the high level adult retardate. *Behavior Research & Therapy, 15*, 137-148.

Pelechano, V., & Vinagre, J. (1976). [Efficacy and differential effects of social reinforcement on the behavior modification of a mental retardate.] *Analisiy Modificacion de Conducta, 2*, 133-144.

Penrose, H. M. (1963). Mental disease among mental defectives. *American Journal of Psychiatry, 101*, 361-363.

Penrose, L. S. (1938). *A clinical and genetic study of 1,280 cases of mental defect* (Special Report No. 229). London: Medical Research Council.

Penrose, L. S. (1954). Observations on the aetiology of mongolism. *Lancet, 1*, 505-509.

Penrose, L. S. (1962). *The biology of mental defectives.* New York: Grune & Stratton.

Perris, C. (1966). A study of bipolar (manic-depressive) and unipolar (recurrent) depressive psychosis. *Acta Psychiatrica Scandinavica, 42*, 58-67.

Persky, H., Smith, K. D., & Basu, G. K. (1981). Relation of psychologic measures of aggression and hostility to testosterone production in man. *Psychosomatic Medicine, 33*, 265-277.

Philips, I. (1966). The emotional impact of mental retardation. In M. A. Esser (Ed.), *Prevalence and treatment of mental retardation* (pp. 111-124). New York: Basic Books.

Philips, I., & Williams, N. (1975). Psychopathology and mental retardation: A study of 100 mentally retarded children. I. Psychopathology. *American Journal of Psychiatry,*

132, 1265-1271.

Philips, L., Broverman, I. K., & Zigler, E. (1966). Social competence and psychiatric diagnosis. *Journal of Abnormal Psychology, 71*, 209-214.

Philips, P. A., & Zigler, E. F. (1980). Children's self-image disparity: Effects of age, socioeconomic status, ethnicity, and gender. *Journal of Personality and Social Psychology, 39*, 689-700.

Pilkington, T. L. (1972). Psychiatric needs of the subnormal. *British Journal of Mental Subnormality, 38*, 66-70.

Pollack, M. (1967). Mental subnormality and childhood schizophrenia. In J. Zubin & G. A. Jerris (Eds.), Psychopathology in mental development (pp. 460-471). New York: Grune & Stratton.

Pollock, H. M. (1944). Mental disease among mental defectives. *American Journal of Psychiatry, 101*, 361-363.

Pollock, H. M. (1945). Mental disease among mental defectives. *American Journal of Mental Deficiency, 49*, 477-480.

Raber, S. M., & Weisz, J. R. (1981). Teacher feedback to mentally retarded and nonretarded children. *American Journal of Mental Deficiency, 86*, 148-156.

Rachman, S. (1976). Obsessional compulsive checking. *Behavior Research and Therapy, 14*, 269-277.

Reid, A. H. (1972). Psychoses in adult mental defectives: I. Manic-depressive psychosis; II. Schizophrenic and paranoid psychosis. *British Journal of Psychiatry, 120*, 205-212 and 213-218.

Reid, A. H. (1980). Psychiatric disorders in mentally handicapped children: A clinical and follow-up study. *Journal of Mental Deficiency Research, 24*, 287-298.

Reid, A. H. (1985). Psychiatric disorders. In A. M. Clarke, A. D. B. Clarke, & J. M. Berg (Eds.), *Mental deficiency: The changing outlook* (pp. 291-325). New York: The Free Press.

Reiss, S., Levitan, G. W., & Szyszko, J. (1982). Emotional disturbance and mental retardation: Diagnostic overshadowing. *American Journal of Mental Deficiency, 86*, 567-574.

Reiss, S., & Szyszko, J. (1983). Diagnostic overshadowing and professional experience with mentally retarded persons. *American Journal of Mental Deficiency, 87*, 396-402.

Richardson, S. A., Katz, M., Koller, H., McLaren, L., & Rubinstein, B. (1979). Some characteristics of a population of mentally retarded young adults in a British city: A basis for eliminating some service needs. *Journal of Mental Deficiency Research, 23*, 273-283.

Rioth, A. (1961). I. Psychotic depression in a Mongoloid. *Journal of Mental Subnormality, 7*, 45-47.

Rivinus, T. M., & Harmatz, J. S. (1979). Diagnosis and lithium treatment of affective disorders in the retarded: Five case studies. *American Journal of Psychiatry, 136*, 551-554.

Rivkonen, R., & Amnell, G. (1981). Psychiatric disorders in children with earlier infantile spasms. *Developmental Medicine of Child Neurology, 23,* 747-760.

Robinson, H. B., & Robinson, N. M. (1965). *The mentally retarded child: A psychological approach.* New York: McGraw-Hill.

Romanczyk, R. G., & Kistner, J. A. (1982). Psychosis and mental retardation: Issues of coexistence. In J. L. Matson & R. P. Barrett (Eds.), *Psychopathology in the mentally retarded* (pp. 147-194). New York: Grune & Stratton.

Rosen, M., Clark, G. R., & Kivitz, M. S. (Eds.). (1976). *The history of mental retardation: Collected papers* (Vol. 1). Baltimore: University Park Press.

Rosen, M., Floor, L., & Baxter, D. (1971). The institutional personality. *British Journal of Mental Subnormality, 17,* 125-131.

Rosenthal, S. H., & Klerman, G. L. (1966). Content and consistency in the endogenous depressive pattern. *British Journal of Psychiatry, 112,* 471-484.

Russell, A. T., & Tanguay, P. E. (1981). Mental illness and mental retardation: Cause or coincidence? *American Journal of Mental Deficiency, 85,* 570-574.

Rutter, M. (1965). The influence of organic and emotional factors on the origins, nature, and outcome of child psychosis. *Developmental Medicine of Child Neurology, 7,* 518-528.

Rutter, M. (1971). Psychiatry. In J. Wortis (Ed.), *Mental retardation: An annual review* (Vol. 3, pp. 186-221). New York: Grune & Stratton.

Rutter, M., Graham, P., & Yule, W. (1970). *A neuropsychiatric study in childhood clinics in developmental medicine* (Nos. 35/36). London: SIMP/ Heinemann.

Rutter, M., Lebovici, S., Eisenberg, L., Sneznevskij, A. V., Sadoun, R., Brooks, E., & Lin, T. Y. (1969). A tri-axial classification of mental disorders in childhood. *Journal of Child Psychology and Psychiatry, 10,* 41-61.

Rutter, M., Tizard, J., & Whitmore, K. (Eds.). (1970). *Education, health, and behavior.* London: Longman.

Rutter, M., Tizard, J., Yule, W. Graham, Y., & Whitmore, K. (1976). Isle of Wight Studies. 1964-1974. *Psychological Medicine, 7,* 313-332.

Saenger, G. (1960). *Factors influencing the institutionalization of mentally retarded individuals in New York City.* A report to New York State Interdepartmental Health Resources Board.

Sarason, S. B., & Gladwin, T. (1958). The severely defective individual. *Journal of Nervous and Mental Disorders, 126,* 64-96.

Sarbin, T. R. (1945). Spontaneity training of the feebleminded. *Sociometry, 8,* 389-393.

Saylor, C. F., Benson, B. A., & Einhaus, L. (1985). Evaluation of an anger management program for aggressive boys in residential treatment. *Journal of Child and Adolescent Psychotherapy, 2,* 5-15.

Schloss, P, J. (1982). Verbal interaction patterns of depressed and non-depressed institutionalized mentally retarded adults. *Applied Research in Mental Retardation, 3,* 1-12.

Scott, J. P., Stewart, J. M., & DeGlett, V. J. (1973). Separation in infant dogs. Emotional responses and motivational consequences. In J. P. Scott & E. C. Senay (Eds.), *Separation and depression: Clinical and research aspects.* Washington, DC:

American Association for the Advancement of Science.

Seligman, M. E. P. (1975). *Helplessness: On depression, development and death.* San Francisco: Freeman.

Selling, L. S. (1939). Types of behavior manifested by feeble-minded sex offenders. *Proceedings from the American Association on Mental Deficiency, 44*, 178-186.

Shapiro, F., & Barrett, R. P. (1982). Behavioral assessment. In J. L. Matson & F. Andrasik (Eds.), *Treatment issues and innovations in mental retardation* (pp. 159-212). New York: Plenum.

Singh, N. N., & Aman, M. G. (1981). Effects of thioridazine dosage in the behavior of severely retarded persons. *American Journal of Mental Deficiency, 85*, 580-587.

Skinner, B. F. (1938). *The behavior of organisms: An experimental analysis.* New York: Appleton Century.

Solomon, K., & Hart, R. (1978). Pitfalls and prospects in clinical research in antianxiety drugs: Benzodiazepines and placebo—A research review. *The Journal of Clinical Psychiatry, 61*, 823-829.

Sovner, R., & Hurley, A. D. (1982). Diagnosing mania in the mentally retarded. *Psychiatric Aspects of Mental Retardation Newsletter, 1*, 10-12.

Sprague, R. C. (1977). Overview of psychopharmacology for the retarded in the United States. In P. Mittler (Ed.), *Research to practice in mental retardation—Biomedical aspects* (Vol. 3, pp. 191-198). Baltimore: University Park Press.

Sprague, R. C., & Baxley, G. B. (1978). Drugs for behavior management with comment on some legal aspects. In J. Wortis (Ed.), *Mental retardation* (Vol. 10, pp. 92-129). New York: Brunner/Mazel.

Sprague, R. C., & Werry, J. S. (1971). Methodology of psychopharmacological studies with the retarded. In N. R. Ellis (Ed.), *International review of research on mental retardation* (Vol. 5, pp. 148-220). New York: Academic Press.

Spreat, S., Roszkowski, M., Isett, R., & Alderter, R. (1980). Emotional disturbance in mental disturbance: An investigation of differential diagnosis. *Journal of Autism and Developmental Disorders, 10*, 361-367.

Stephens, R. M., Matson, J. L., Westmoreland, T., & Kulpal, J. (1973). Use of modeling in survival skill training with educable mentally retarded. *The Training School Bulletin, 20*, 63-68.

Stephens, R. M., Matson, J. L., Westmoreland, T., & Kulpal, J. (1981). Modification of psychotic speech with mentally retarded patients. *Journal of Mental Deficiency Research, 25*, 187-197.

Sternlicht, M. (1966). Psychotherapeutic procedures with the retarded. In N. R. Ellis (Ed.), *International review of research in mental retardation* (pp. 279-354). New York: Academic Press.

Stoudenmire, J., & Salter, L. (1975). Conditioning prosocial behaviors in a mentally retarded child without using instructions. *Journal of Behavior Therapy & Experimental Psychiatry, 6*, 39-42.

Sweet, W. H., Ervin, F., & Mark, V. H. (1969). The relationship of violent behavior to focal cerebral disease. In S. Garattini & E. B. Siggs (Eds.), *Aggressive behavior* (pp. 336-

352). New York: Wiley.

Syzmanski, L. S. (1977). Psychiatric diagnostic evaluation of mentally retarded individuals. *Journal of American Academy of Child Psychiatry, 16*, 67-87.

Talkington, L., Hall, S., & Altman, R. (1971). Communication deficits and aggression in the mentally retarded. *American Journal of Mental Deficiency, 2*, 235-237.

Talkington, L., & Riley, J. (1970). *Reduction diets and aggression in institutionalized mentally retarded* (Mental Retardation research series, No. 1). Austin, TX: Austin State School.

Talkington, L. W., & Hall, S. (1969). Hearing impairment and aggressiveness in a mentally retarded. *Perceptual and Motor Skills, 28*, 303-306.

Tanna, V. T., Penningroth, R. P., & Woolson, R. F. (1977). Propranolol in the treatment of anxiety neurosis. *Comprehensive Psychiatry, 18*, 319-326.

Tarjan, G. (1948). Current thinking regarding psychopaths. *American Journal of Mental Deficiency, 53*, 302-312.

Taylor, F. H. (1947). Observations on some cases of exhibitionism. *Journal of Mental Sciences, 93*, 631-638.

Thorndike, E. L. (1911). *Animal intelligence: Experimental studies.* New York: Macmillan.

Touchette, P. E. (1978). Mental retardation: An introduction to the analysis and remediation of behavior deficiency. In D. Marholin (Ed.), *Child behavior therapy* (pp. 187-213). New York: Gardner Press.

Valzelli, L. (1981). Aggression and violence: A biological essay of the distinction. In L. Valzelli & L. Morgese (Eds.), *Aggression and violence* (pp. 39-60). Milan: Edicioni Saint Vincent.

Viney, L. L., Clarke, A. M., & Lord, J. (1973). Resistence to extinction and frustration in retarded and nonretarded children. *American Journal of Mental Retardation, 78*, 308-315.

Weaver, T. R. (1946). The incidence of maladjustment among mental defectives in a military environment. *American Journal of Mental Deficiency, 51*, 238-246.

Webster, T. (1963). Problems of emotional development in young retarded children. *American Journal of Psychiatry, 120*, 37-43.

Webster, T. G. (1970). Unique aspects of emotional development in mentally retarded children. In F. J. Menolascino (Ed.), *Psychiatric approaches to mental retardation* (pp. 3-54). New York: Basic Books.

Weisz, J. R. (1979). Perceived control and learned helplessness in mentally retarded and nonretarded children. A developmental analysis. *Developmental Psychology, 15*, 311-319.

Weisz, J. R. (1982). Learned helplessness and the retarded child. In E. Zigler & D. Balla (Eds.), *Mental retardation: The developmental-difference controversy* (pp. 27-40). Hillsdale, NJ: Lawrence Erlbaum Associates.

Wheatley, D. (1969). Comparative effects of propranolol and chlordiazepoxide in anxiety states. *British Journal of Psychiatry, 115*, 1411-1412.

White, W. D., & Wolfensberger, W. (1969). The evolution of dehumanization in our institutions. *Mental Retardation, 7*, 5-9.

Windle, C. (1962). Prognosis of mental subnormals. *American Journal of Mental Deficiency, 66* (Monogr. Suppl.).

Winokur, G. (1973). The types of affective disorders. *Journal of Nervous and Mental Disease, 156*, 82-96.

Wolfensberger, W. (1960). Schizophrenia in mental retardates: Three hypotheses. *American Journal of Mental Deficiency, 64*, 704-706.

Wysocki, T., Fuqua, R. W., Davis, N. J., & Breuning, S. E. (1981). Effects of thioridazine (Mellaril) on titrating delayed matching-to-sample performance of mentally retarded adults. *American Journal of Mental Deficiency, 55*, 539-547.

Yando, R., Seitz, V., & Zigler, E. F. (1978). *Imitation: A developmental perspective.* Hillsdale, NJ: Lawrence Erlbaum Associates.

Zeaman, P., & House, B. J. (1963). An attentional theory of retardate discrimination learning. In N. R. Ellis (Ed.), *Handbook of mental deficiency* (pp. 159-223). New York: McGraw-Hill.

Zigler, E. (1973). The retarded child as a whole person. In D. K. Routh (Ed.), *The experimental psychology of mental retardation* (pp. 231-322). Chicago: Aldine.

Zigler, E., Lamb, M. E., & Child, I. L. (1982). *Socialization and personality development* (2nd ed.). New York: Oxford University Press.

Zigler, E., & Phillips, L. (1960). Social effectiveness and symptomatic behavior. *Journal of Abnormal and Social Psychology, 61*, 231-238.

Zigler, E., & Phillips, L. (1961). Social competence and outcome in psychiatric disorder. *Journal of Abnormal and Social Psychology, 63*, 264-271.

Zigler, E., & Seitz, V. (1978). Changing trends in socialization theory and research. *American Behavioral Scientist, 21*, 731-736.

3 ASSESSMENT IN COUNSELING AND PSYCHOTHERAPY

H. Thompson Prout and
Douglas C. Strohmer

Thorough assessment is often seen as a key ingredient in the development of successful interventions. The various theoretical models and approaches discussed later in this book differ in the amount of emphasis they place on assessment. For some approaches, assessment is ongoing throughout treatment and seen as significantly interfacing with the specific therapeutic techniques. With others, assessment is viewed as peripheral and even unimportant. Many of the issues raised in Chapters One and Two of this book would indicate that assessment of social-emotional functioning in persons with mental retardation is crucial to the planning and conduct of therapeutic interventions. This is likely to lead to more focused interventions and less likely to cause important concerns encountered by individual clients to be overlooked.

This chapter begins with a discussion of general issues in assessment for counseling and psychotherapy and presents an assessment-based model of intervention. This is followed by more specific discussions of the role of cognitive assessment in planning interventions, behavioral assessment, projective assessment, behavior rating assessment (including assessment of adaptive/maladaptive behavior), self-report methods, and modification of instruments intended for the general population for use with persons with mental retardation. The reader is also directed to the recent technical report by Aman (1991) that provides a critique of formal measures used to assess psychopathology and behavior problems in persons with mental retardation. This report is both an excellent source of sound psychometric reviews of available measures and an overview of the current status of research and development in this area. Discussions of assessment in vocational counseling and family interventions are included in two respective chapters.

The Purpose of Assessment in Counseling and Psychotherapy

One of the purposes of assessment involves treatment or intervention planning. Palmer (1970), in fact, has stated that "the essential purpose of a psychological assessment is to determine the nature and extent of the disturbance in order to select and formulate the model(s) of behavior change" (p. 5). Within this realm, there are a number of personality assessment activities that relate directly to the development of treatment programs. These general purposes can be viewed as essentially atheoretical. Among these purposes and activities are:

1. Establish a baseline. It is often necessary to establish the current status and/ or the extent or severity of the referral problem. This may be a quantitative evaluation (e.g., frequency of hitting), a rating of intensity or severity (e.g., mild vs. moderate anxiety), or a relative presence or absence of some clinical sign or symptom (e.g., signs of depressed mood revealed in a thematic procedure). These baseline figures permit the evaluation of treatment progress by determining how successful treatment has been and whether a change in the treatment approach is necessary.

2. Pinpoint treatment targets. This activity involves problem identification and definition resulting in an operationalization of intervention foci and directions. This allows the practitioner to set goals and/or objectives and to prioritize the most significant of the referral problems. The situational or general (i.e., across situations) nature of the problem may also be assessed here. This procedure could also reveal themes or content that should be pursued in therapy sessions. For example, a behavior therapist might specifically delineate target behaviors related to aggression, whereas a more dynamically oriented therapist might direct his or her client towards dealing with affective responses to significant others.

3. Assessment of developmental status. The nature of interventions with persons with mental retardation requires that treatment be appropriate for the developmental level of the client. This includes two aspects, designing treatments that are appropriate (a) for a client's cognitive and language levels (e.g., using language appropriate for a client with cognitive abilities in the 8-year-old range), and (b) consideration of the client's level of social-emotional development (e.g., level of social skill development). This latter aspect may also be a treatment target. Developmental assessment may also identify relative strengths or assets that clients can utilize during treatment.

4. Assess clients' views of the problem. This includes assessing clients' perceptions and understanding of the presenting problems. Here, practitioners are concerned with whether the individual acknowledges that a problem exists, and what views he or she has of the various factors relating to the problem. Related to this are clients' understanding of the treatment process and willingness (e.g., motivation) to cooperate with treatment. This may involve prognostic assessments of whether an individual is open to direct intervention.

5. Assess relevant environmental factors. This activity involves assessing school, family, peer, and community factors that may influence the treatment plan. This may reveal factors that need to be considered in treatment, yet may not be the target of direct intervention. For example, other residents in a group home may not be included in treatment, yet may play an important role when planning the content of individual sessions with the client. Conversely, an environmental assessment may indicate interventions besides those involving direct work with the client. Certainly, a comprehensive treatment plan might include individual counseling with the client, as well as consultation with residential, day program, or school staff or counseling with a client's family.

6. Select appropriate treatment strategy. The assessment process should yield data that will help select the therapeutic approaches that best address the client's specific problems. Practitioners should not expect that a single treatment approach will be appropriate for all, or even most, problems. The assessment process may also identify behavior patterns that have clearly identified and proved treatment strategies. For example, an identified anxiety disorder might respond well to relaxation procedures. (See Chapter 5.)

7. Evaluate efficacy. All of the activities discussed above represent clinical practices that could (and likely should) be conducted by all practitioners in their professional work. This last activity involves the use of assessment to evaluate intervention program efficacy and/or to conduct more basic research on the outcomes of specific interventions. The use of appropriate outcome measures and methodologies allows for the evaluation of specific techniques that are utilized to resolve specific problems.

A Model of Intervention

Current thinking among theorists in psychotherapy suggests that the therapeutic process should no longer be viewed as magical and directionless. Indeed, most, but not all, theories of psychotherapy ascribe to some relatively standard, albeit individualized, intervention procedure. This usually involves problem identification, problem definition, assessment, intervention goal setting, and various stages of therapeutic change. Behaviorally oriented practitioners are perhaps most identified with this systematic, active, problem-focused approach to psychotherapy.

A systematic, step-by-step view of the intervention process has been advocated by a number of professionals, including Gottman and Leiblum (1974), Brown and Brown (1977), and Prout (1985). These authors present flowcharts diagramming their decision-making models of intervention. These models, attempting to demystify the process that leads to change, view the counselor/therapist/mental health practitioner as the manager or agent of change. The therapeutic relationship, although still viewed as important, is not seen as the sole key to the change process. Instead, the activities of and decisions made by the practitioner and the client are deemed to be crucial to the overall process. These models emphasize the use of assessment data throughout the intervention process. Although these models are generally compatible with intervention approaches associated with behavior therapy, they are essentially atheoretical in nature. Thus, although ongoing assessment is dictated in both the problem assessment and evaluation phases, it could involve either direct behavioral observations or repeated administration of more traditional projective measures, two seemingly disparate approaches to assessment.

An assessment-based model of intervention is presented in Figure 3.1, primarily as a guide for the practitioner. Clearly, it does not outline an absolute procedure. There will undoubtedly be cases that do not fit completely within this model. Nonetheless, this model emphasizes the systematic, data-based planning and implementation of interventions consistent with the purposes of assessment previously discussed. Further, the role of assessment in designing individually based interventions is implicit in this model. That is, assessment dictates the choice of therapeutic strategy. Finally, assessment is seen as an ongoing process where the practitioner and client(s) receive feedback when goals have been met and when a change in strategy might be necessary. Thus, the "looping" nature of the model is a key element. This feature emphasizes a "let's go back and take another look" attitude when, for example, an initial assessment is not totally accurate and its reevaluation is necessary in order to change a therapeutic direction.

We are reminded of a case we dealt with that involved what appeared to be a relatively minor problem in a sheltered workshop setting. The initial referral concerns focused on work speed and tardiness. After the initial assessment, some general recommendations were formulated focusing on some supportive counseling with a rehabilitation counselor and a reward system for task completion and being on-time. The initial assessment had revealed no major individual psychopathology or other significant concerns. Within a short period of time, however, it was discovered that the individual had a very serious substance abuse problem and was

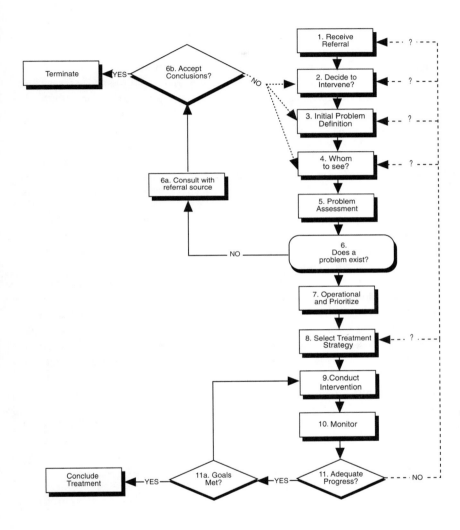

Figure 3.1. Assessment Based Therapeutic Intervention: A Model for Decision Making.

engaging in considerable inappropriate behaviors in the community. It appeared that at least some of the workshop problems were related to the substance abuse problem. Needless to say, it was necessary to "loop back" rather quickly, to reassess the new information presented, and to change direction. To continue solely with the original supportive and reward focus would have been ridiculous.

Below is a descriptive "walk through" of the flowchart presented in Figure 3.1. Again, this model is presented as a guide, and the steps are not seen as mutually exclusive or chronological. Some of the activities may occur concurrently and it may not be necessary to complete Step 2 before beginning Step 3.

Step 1. Receive referral. This simple first step is often overlooked in the assessment process. Indeed, information sometimes gathered at later stages in the assessment process could or should be obtained at this stage. For example, contrast the difference between receiving a note from a caseworker that says "Please see James Smith for counseling" versus a well-detailed referral form that allows you immediately to begin your problem analysis. Certainly the referral form or procedure should assist in making decisions about the types of information that will be collected during the more in-depth assessment procedures.

Step 2. Decide to intervene. This stage poses the question: "How was the decision made to refer the client for intervention?" and "Who made the decision?" Typically, clients with mental retardation do not refer themselves for treatment. Usually, someone in their environment has initiated the referral. Part of the process at this step is to assess the ownership of the "problem," that is, who views or has labeled the client's behavior as problematic? The motivations, expectations, and perceptions of those who might potentially be involved in the intervention are also assessed at this level. Any misperception or unclear information about the intervention process should be identified here.

The goal at this level, then, is to identify those who acknowledge that a problem exists; analyze perceptions, expectations, and motivations that may either hinder or facilitate treatment; and target attitudes that need modification before beginning the treatment program that focuses on the specific referral problems. This latter goal may involve pretherapy counseling or consultation for referred clients, referral sources, or both.

Step 3. Complete initial problem definition. This step represents an initial attempt at problem definition, which then generates a direction for more formal problem assessment. The referral information structures the preliminary priorities of the assessment package, and tentative operational definitions of referral concerns are developed. These initial priorities and definitions are the working hypotheses that will be adapted or validated during the problem assessment activities (e.g., Step 5), and they help determine who will participate in the assessment process (i.e., Step 4).

Step 4. Decide whom to see. The behavior of an individual with mental retardation may be significantly influenced by environmental factors. At this stage, practitioners decide from whom to obtain data during the assessment process (e.g., family? teachers? workshop supervisors? group home staff?) and what settings to evaluate relative to the occurrence of the referral problem(s) (e.g., home? school? specific settings? community?). A major goal here is to design an assessment package that will address the setting-general versus situation-specific aspects of referral concerns, to analyze discrepancies in perceptions of the "problem" among those in the environment, and to begin to identify individuals and behavior settings that might be involved in the intervention. Using the initial priorities and definitions developed in Step 3, the type of information needed from particular individuals can be determined.

Step 5. Complete problem assessment. At this point, a formal assessment of the referral concerns begins. Using the priorities developed in Step 3, the practitioner selects assessment techniques that will help to define problem areas further and/or confirm or disconfirm working hypotheses. As noted previously, this model is intended to be atheoretical and compatible with many assessment approaches. Thus, this step may involve the first significant differences among practitioners of varied theoretical persuasions. For example, assume that an initial screening has identified depression as a potential problem area for a client. Certainly depression can be assessed through a variety of modalities and techniques. Self-report inventories, behavior rating scales, structured clinical interviews, direct observation, incomplete sentence responses, thematic analysis of responses to projectives (e.g., Thematic Apperception Test), and *DSM-III-R* criteria might all be used. The use of several measures is consistent with the more reliable multimethod approaches (Gresham, 1983; Nay, 1979) to assess the clinical concept of depression. Thus, the same clinical question can be addressed in a variety of ways. Problem assessment also serves to establish a baseline that can be used as a reference and comparison point to evaluate the intervention program.

Step 6. Determine if a problem exists. This question represents the first major decision point in the assessment process as diagrammed in Figure 3.1. Based on the assessment data, the practitioner decides if a problem exists that warrants intervention. This must take into consideration the "social significance" of the problem, whether the problem is maladaptive, and whether the occurrence of the problem is not normative for the individual's level of functioning. If the data suggest that a genuine problem exists, then the planning and implementation of the intervention program (i.e., Step 7) should begin.

If the assessment data indicate that a problem of significant concern is not apparent, then the next step is to "loop back" and consult with the original referral sources (see Substep 6a). This, in effect, is also a therapeutic activity, as reassurances can be very comforting. The referral sources obviously may choose to accept or reject the practitioner's assessment conclusions of the situation (Substep 6b). If they accept the conclusion that a problem does not exist, the assessment process is completed and terminated. If they do not accept the assessment conclusions, it will be necessary (in lieu of a referral to another practitioner) to loop back into the initial assessment sequence. This may involve identifying and/or addressing other issues, involving other individuals in the assessment, reworking the initial priorities and definitions, and/or completing additional assessments. Significantly, the refusal of the referral sources to accept the conclusion of "no real problem" may itself become a treatment target.

Step 7. Operationalize and prioritize. The decision that a problem exists implicitly leads to the decision to intervene. Thus, at this point, the problem concerns related to a referral and problem assessment are put into an operational framework which is then prioritized. This activity will dictate the focus of intervention strategies, their chronological implementations (if they must be staggered), their interrelationships, and the process of monitoring treatment progress. For example, again using the example of depression, the practitioner may decide that this primary problem needs specific attention during the intervention program. The interventions planned, however, will obviously depend on the practitioner's therapeutic orientation; different orientations will focus on different aspects of this problem. For example, a behavior therapist might focus on increasing prosocial behaviors, a cognitive or rational-emotive therapist might concentrate on irrational self-statements, and a psychodynamically oriented therapist might attempt to resolve some past internal conflict. Although it is likely that some aspects of this operationalization were done during the planning of the problem assessment, actual treatment goals or objectives are set at this stage.

Step 8. Select treatment strategy. Based on the decisions in the previous steps, the practitioner selects and plans specific interventions to match the specific delineated problems. Again, within the limits of the practitioner's comfort and technical expertise with different approaches, this should be a thoughtful and systematic process. A wide variety of intervention options exist and blind adherence to one approach essentially negates much of the assessment process.

Step 9. Conduct intervention. At this step, specific intervention strategies are implemented. Thus, there may be several steps in the treatment process involving different behavioral settings and individuals at different points.

Step 10. Monitor. Using the data gathered in Step 5, the practitioner readministers all or part of the problem assessment package, comparing the new results with the baseline data. Monitoring essentially analyzes the progress being made toward the treatment goals. The implications of this data comparison are used for the decisions made at Step 11.

Step 11. Evaluate for adequate progress. It is best to conceive of Steps 9–11 within an ongoing and continually looping-back process that addresses the efficacy of the intervention program. Thus, the practitioner should be continually evaluating the implemented treatment strategies to assess their progress toward the treatment goals and, ultimately, the successful attainment of those goals. When adequate progress is observed, a decision to continue treatment as originally formulated is usually made. If the treatment goals and objectives have been met (Step 11a) and all parties agree with this evaluation, the assessment and treatment process is concluded. If adequate progress is lagging, the practitioner may loop back to several points in the process. Usually, a return to Step 8 to modify the treatment strategy and select another option is logical and appropriate. However, an entire reassessment and redefinition of the problem may be necessary. In the case cited above, the individual was originally referred for work problems and it was essentially necessary to disregard the entire initial assessment and start at the beginning by reframing the referral concerns.

In summary, a systematic approach to therapeutic intervention is advocated, irrespective of the practitioner's orientation. Further, this approach emphasizes an ongoing interface between assessment and intervention. This interface should allow for better selection of treatment strategies as well as for better monitoring of therapeutic progress.

The Role of Cognitive Assessment

Simply by the presence of a diagnosis of mental retardation or borderline intelligence, we can assume that there is a degree of cognitive limitation. However, it would be erroneous to assume that all persons with mental retardation, even within the same general level of functioning (e.g., mild) or with the same IQ score, have the same cognitive skills. Individuals with the same overall measured intelligence may bring different intellectual assets and weaknesses to counseling and psychotherapy. Palmer (1970) has written of the importance of assessing verbal intelligence in determining the appropriateness of psychotherapy with children. Similarly, with persons with mental retardation, the assessment of verbal abilities will be key in determining appropriateness for counseling and psychotherapy, as well as facilitating the initiation of interventions that are developmentally appropriate. Further, when modifying or adapting techniques, assessment of verbal ability will guide these adaptations.

Verbal intelligence is multifaceted and can be assessed in a variety of ways. For the purposes of assessing for psychotherapy or counseling, the aspects of receptive and expressive verbal abilities represent a useful clinical dichotomy. Receptive ability involves knowledge of vocabulary and understanding of spoken language (i.e., the individuals understand and comprehend what is said to them, although they may not necessarily be able to express themselves as clearly and coherently). In psychotherapy, a person with adequate receptive/understanding ability, but limited expressive abilities, may respond to a more directive, didactic therapeutic style as opposed to the more desirable client-therapist conversational interchanges. In fact, requiring these individuals to be conversational beyond their comfort levels may be counterproductive. These individuals may also respond better to nonverbal media. Individuals with adequate expressive skills, with assumed adequate comprehension, may be more likely to respond to more conversational therapeutic styles. Last, the assessment of verbal attention and memory may provide further data useful in planning interventions. Individuals with relative deficits in verbal memory and attention may require more repetition of issues discussed in counseling, may need more concrete memory aids to facilitate generalization, and may respond better to shorter, more frequent counseling sessions.

Most major instruments for assessing intelligence provide adequate sampling of verbal abilities. Utilizing the verbal portions or subtests on these measures will provide some information on the relative strengths and weaknesses in the verbal area. In evaluating this information, attention should be paid to the receptive/expressive dichotomy discussed above. For example, scores on the Wechsler verbal scales are primarily indicating levels of skills in the expressive area. Thus, the abilities of someone with adequate receptive verbal ability may be underestimated on these assessments. Practitioners may find that administration of only a few selected subtests may be helpful in planning counseling and psychotherapy.

Although the validity and utility of the concept of mental age has been debated, we have found this a useful tool in assessing clients for psychotherapy. Many instruments (e.g., the Wechsler Intelligence Scales for Children - III, the Cognitive Battery of the Woodcock-Johnson Psycho-Educational Battery—Revised) yield scores that can be transformed into age equivalents or test ages. These scores provide rough developmental markers for the individual's verbal ability level. Although the Wechsler Adult Intelligence Scales - Revised do not provide this, one can do rough conversions of verbal ability measures using the old *Mental Age = IQ/ 100 × 16 (Chronological Age)* formula—the age of 16 is used with adults for this computation. (Example: With a Verbal IQ of 70, an individual's estimated verbal level would be .70 × 16 = 11.2 years, for an estimated verbal ability age equivalent of around 11 years.) Some have found it useful to administer selected portions of children's scales to adults in order to obtain age equivalents to get a better picture of developmental levels.

More specific measures of language development may also be useful. The Peabody Picture Vocabulary Test—Revised is the most widely used instrument to assess receptive vocabulary skills. Conceptually, this instrument should be useful in obtaining an assessment of verbal abilities that would be useful in planning counseling. However, when compared to more general measures of intelligence, this instrument has been found to underestimate substantially the abilities of adults with mild mental retardation (Prout & Schwartz, 1984) and we cannot recommend its use with individuals with mental retardation. Other measures of language development (e.g., Test of Adolescent Language, Test of Language Development) may also be useful in therapeutic assessment. Again, some measures designed for use with children and adolescents might be used for assessing developmental levels with adults. Assessments by speech and language clinicians may also provide valuable information in this regard.

Behavioral Assessment

Behavioral assessment is the term used to describe a wide variety of assessment approaches that have certain core assumptions about human behavior, and the means for assessing and evaluating it. This approach is highly appropriate for use with clients with mental retardation, as many of the techniques employed do not require the client to be particularly verbally expressive or to have strong reading or writing abilities. From the behavioral assessment perspective, an individual's behavior can best be understood by focusing on the antecedents to a person's behavior, and on the consequences of the person's behavior. So, rather than attempting to identify certain person or trait variables (e.g., high or low self-concept) or intrapsychic processes (e.g., repression) that influence behavior, the behavioral approach to assessment looks for the situational determinants of an individual's behavior. This conceptual difference in approaching assessment also leads to differences in the ways in which the assessment suggests treatments for the problematic behaviors. Advocates of behavioral assessment (e.g., Bellack & Hersen, 1988) have long suggested that more traditional assessment approaches focus too extensively on abstract, unobservable phenomena that are too distinct from the client's actual world to be useful in understanding the client's world or in suggesting relevant ways in which client behavior might be changed. Behavioral assessment, on the other hand, is concerned with clearly observable aspects of the way a person interacts with his or her environment. This type of information can then easily be translated into behaviorally oriented treatment strategies designed to change relevant behaviors. A review of these strategies is presented in Chapter 5.

Less rigid advocates of any of the approaches to assessment might use behavioral approaches in conjunction with more traditional methods (e.g., Groth-

Marnat, 1990). A psychologist might assess the client's degree of low self-esteem using a personality test, while also employing a behavioral procedure designed to evaluate the actual client behaviors that may be related to low self-esteem. In other cases where traditional assessment methods are wholly inappropriate for use with a client, behavioral assessment methods may be the only means employed. The following sections suggest a variety of behavioral assessment approaches that are useful with clients with mental retardation. These sections are designed to provide an overview of behavioral assessment concepts, and those individuals wishing to go beyond them are referred to *Behavioral Assessment: A Practical Handbook* by Alan Bellack and Michel Hersen (1988).

Types of Behavioral Assessment

Although behavioral assessment has given rise to a large variety of approaches and techniques, behavioral assessment strategies can be organized into the general categories of behavioral interviewing, behavioral observation, cognitive-behavioral assessment, psychophysiological assessment, and self-report inventories. Only the general categories of behavioral interviewing, behavioral observation, and cognitive-behavioral assessment will be reviewed here. Self-report inventories are reviewed later in this chapter, and psychophysiological assessment is not within the general scope of this chapter.

Behavioral interviewing. Behaviorally oriented interviews focus on obtaining data concerning the relationship between the antecedents, behaviors, and consequences (ABC) that are related to the concerns of the client with mental retardation. Although the authors have found that it is possible to obtain useful data from the client, it is also quite common and generally recommended that an informant, such as a supervisor, teacher, or parent, be interviewed as well. In general the interview with the client is useful in obtaining a description of the client's concerns in his or her own words. The client interview is also useful in evaluating the client's social skills and general reaction to the stress and demands of an interview situation. Witt and Elliot (1983) provide an outline of what might occur in the behavioral interview. The level of depth, and the extent to which this data might be collected from an informant, will clearly depend on the client's abilities and reaction to the interview process.

1. Initially, provide the client with an overview of what needs to be accomplished and why a clear and detailed specification of the problem behavior is important. When the client with retardation is the informant, it is critical both that he or she understands the rationale, at a reasonable level, and also is at least to some extent invested in it.

2. Identify the target behavior(s) and articulate them in precise behavioral terms. Clear distinction must be made between inferences and actual behavior (e.g., anxiety or anger versus shouting or running away).

3. Identify the problem frequency, duration, and intensity ("How many times has it occurred today?" "How long has it been going on?" etc.).

4. Identify conditions in which the problem occurs in terms of its antecedents, behaviors, and consequences.

5. Identify the client's strengths.

6. Identify the procedures for measuring relevant behaviors. What will be recorded, who will record it, how will it be recorded, when and where will it be recorded?

7. When discussion regarding the above areas has been completed, summarize it for the client to ensure that it has been understood and is agreed upon.

Behavioral observation. The behavioral interview frequently is not sufficient to obtain the needed information from a client with mental retardation. In such cases it may be necessary to observe the client engaging in the targeted behaviors. This approach to assessment is a common one with clients with mental retardation, as a clear description of their concerns and their actual behaviors tends to be difficult to obtain. The most common, and frequently the most appropriate, method of observation is that done by a professional or a significant other in the client's life (e.g., teacher, parent, house parent, work supervisor). The following steps are commonly followed in setting up behavioral observation of this type:

1. Select target behavior(s) relevant to the issues of concern.

2. Establish a clear operational definition of the target behavior(s).

3. Decide when to observe.

4. Decide who will observe.

5. Decide on the observation format to be employed.

6. Begin recording, establish interrater reliability, and troubleshoot where needed.

The most frequent methods of observation employed are narrative recording, interval recording, and event recording. *Narrative recording* entails simply making anecdotal records of the behaviors that occur. This type of recording is frequently a precursor to more formal interval or event recording methods. *Interval recording* is a detailed recording of selected client behavior (antecedents, behavior, and consequences) during chosen intervals of time. For example, the client may be observed at the beginning of the school or work day, and again after the lunch break, concerning a problematic behavior that tends to occur at the beginning of a new activity. During these preselected times the observer records the antecedents and consequences for each instance of the targeted behavior. *Event recording* entails recording every instance of a behavior. Here the observer must be someone in the environment who will be with the client during a long span of the day. Behaviors such as aggression are commonly observed in this fashion with the observer noting duration and intensity. However, because the observer will not be able to collect data relating to antecedents and consequences, these critical aspects of the behavior are frequently not directly observed and must be reconstructed from memory (or not considered at all). *Self observations*, or self-monitoring, may also be used in those cases where clients are able to track their own behavior. Although such circumstances are likely to be limited, this approach is efficient and accurate in the right circumstances. Chapter 5 provides a detailed description of the use of behavioral self-monitoring as a treatment strategy.

Cognitive-behavioral assessment. Cognitive-behavioral assessment is a common approach which, although of less utility with clients with retardation, can be useful with certain individuals with mild retardation or borderline intelligence. The authors are quite familiar with the successful use of the monitoring and modification of a client's self-talk (Meichenbaum, 1986). In this approach an effort is made to assess the client's internal verbal behavior (i.e., self-talk). This may be done by asking the client to think aloud about a particular problem or incident, by observing the client's private speech (barely audible speech made while engaging in some task), or by engaging the client in a role play of a problematic situation and then sampling the client's thoughts at several intervals. A detailed description of the monitoring of self-talk and modification of self-talk is provided in Chapter Five.

Projective Assessment

The use of projectives has had a long and controversial history in professional psychology. The issue of the utility of projectives raises almost passionate opinions among professionals, whose views range from those proclaiming the total worthlessness of the instruments to those of advocates who claim projectives provide clinical perspectives not available through other assessment modalities. The traditional underpinnings of projectives are historically rooted in psychodynamic theory in which the understanding of the unconscious is of key importance (Lindzey, 1961). This view posits that the most significant aspects of personality and the resultant overt behavior are not observable to the clinician and in most cases are beyond the awareness of the individual. Thus, the individual is not able to report directly on these personality variables (Sundberg, 1977). The uncovering of these dynamics, most typically framed as sexual or aggressive instincts, forces, or drives with resulting conflicts, is the goal of assessment. Unfortunately, the psychometric analyses of instruments utilizing the traditional theoretical base has been disappointing (Anastasi, 1989). Generalizations about projectives are sometimes overstated in that a wide range of techniques fall in the projective category. The techniques include inkblot techniques (Rorschach), thematics (Thematic Apperception Test, Children's Apperception Test), drawings (Human Figure Drawings, House-Tree-Person, Kinetic Drawings-Family and School), and incomplete sentences.

The Rorschach and the Thematic Apperception Test (TAT) are two of the most widely used projective instruments, and applications for their use with persons with mental retardation have been described (Hurley & Sovner, 1982, 1985). Hurley and Sovner (1982) note that the Rorschach provides an assessment of intellectual functioning that is different from the information produced by an intelligence test. It can provide clinical information useful in helping to differentiate capacity and efficiency in cognitive function and to assess creativity and organizational ability. They assert that it provides a broader view of intellectual functioning and may detect atypical thought patterns. It may also help assess emotional functioning and affective responding and degree of emotional controls. Assessing the presence of active psychosis or possible organicity is described as a use of the Rorschach.

Hurley and Sovner (1985) advocate the use of the TAT with individuals with mild or moderate mental retardation. The individual's responses to the stories are assumed to be autobiographical with the respondent identifying with the main character depicted in the story. Hurley and Sovner offer some recommendations for modifying the instructions to deal with the lower and more concrete aspects of intellectual functioning of persons with mental retardation. They also suggest that the TAT may be used in counseling to facilitate responsiveness and provide a focus for discussion.

Prout and Ferber (1988) have offered an alternative view of projective assessment that is more consistent with behavioral assessment. They downplay the importance of unconscious variables and symbolic interpretation. Further, they favor projective instruments that are more rooted in real-life situations. For example, the TAT includes many stimulus pictures that do not depict real-life situations and, in some cases, depict very atypical, odd stimuli. The Roberts

Apperception Test for Children, on the other hand, is a thematic technique that utilizes a series of realistic drawings of children that tap such variables as school attitude, maternal support, fear, aggression release, etc. The alternative view advocates the use of more realistic stimuli designed to assess real-life issues, focusing on cognitive (content of thoughts) and affective variables. Thus, thematics such as the Roberts, incomplete sentence techniques, and family drawings of the individual's own family are seen as preferable to the more nebulous and less realistic stimuli in the Rorschach and TAT.

The alternative approach emphasizes a low-inference style of interpretation (Prout & Ferber, 1988). In this perspective, there is no symbolic interpretation or assessment of unconscious variables. Responses are taken at face value and interpreted directly. Techniques such as incomplete sentences and Kinetic Family Drawings are useful because the client is responding with his or her thoughts and feelings about various situations, or in the case of family drawings, views of his or her own family. Moderate levels of inference involve situations where the respondent is presumed to be projecting onto and identifying with a character in a story. These responses are taken more cautiously because the identification is only presumed and it cannot be verified whether the story related is actually reflective of the individual's current life situation and views about the situation. High-inference interpretation, which involves no real-life projection, with heavy symbolic and unconscious dynamics is given little credence.

One attempt to develop a projective for use with persons with mental retardation is the Sentence Completion Technique of the *Emotional Problems Scales (EPS)* (Strohmer & Prout, 1991) based on the alternative formulation of projectives described above. This instrument consists of 40 sentence stems that assess problems in nine empirically established problem areas: interpersonal relationships, psychological functioning, work/school, independence, sexuality, family, residential living and adjustment, behavior, and health. There is no formal scoring system and the instrument is designed more as a "technique" for obtaining client views about different areas as opposed to a psychometrically based "test." This technique is intended for use with other instruments in a multifaceted assessment and may generate hypotheses for further targeted assessment. It is not intended for a primary role in differential diagnosis. Item stems are read to the individual with the examiner recording responses. Interpretation, again, emphasizes the low-inference, direct assessment of responses.

Self-Report and Behavior Rating Approaches

The professional wishing to assess social-emotional functioning of persons with mental retardation has essentially two avenues to follow. The first involves use of traditional standardized or structured techniques or instruments designed primarily for use with nonretarded populations. Obviously, the utilization of these techniques often requires modification of the standardized procedures (e.g., reading and rewording a self-report inventory) and may violate standardization, thus making interpretation difficult. Structured diagnostic interviews, projectives, self-report inventories, and behavior rating scales all could be modified for use with persons with mental retardation. However, normative comparisons on the meaning of responses in modified administrations may limit their applicability. Behavior observation techniques, which tend to be less affected by bias, also have significant applicability.

The second approach lies in the use of the few measures available that are specifically designed to assess behavior and personality in the population with mental retardation. Scales of adaptive behavior often include a measure of maladaptive behavior. The *Inventory for Client and Agency Planning* and the *AAMD Adaptive Behavior Scales* both include informant-based assessment of maladaptive behavior. Recently, there have been several measures introduced that are specifically designed to assess social-emotional problems for individuals with mild mental retardation and borderline intelligence. Measures developed by Johnny Matson and Steven Reiss focus largely on assessment of psychiatrically relevant variables. Matson's *Psychopathology Instrument for Mentally Retarded Adults (PIMRA)* includes a structured interview format and rating-by-others form, whereas the *Reiss Screen* asks informants to rate the significance of symptoms/problems (i.e., "no problem" to "major problem"). Both instruments cluster into summary scores for different diagnostic areas. Michael Aman has developed the *Aberrant Behavior Checklist,* which largely focuses on problems in relatively lower functioning persons with mental retardation.

The following sections review the PIMRA, the Reiss Screen, and the Strohmer and Prout's Emotional Problems Scales as three assessment tools that target social or emotional concerns of the population of individuals with mild retardation and borderline intelligence.

PIMRA

The Psychopathology Inventory for Mentally Retarded Adults (PIMRA) (Matson, 1988) is a checklist of psychopathological behavior intended for use with people who are dually diagnosed (with both mental retardation and mental illness). It consists of two structured interviews: "Ratings-by-Others," which is completed with a significant other in the client's life (e.g., parent, teacher, caretaker or work supervisor); and the Self-Report Scales, which is completed with the client with mental retardation. The item content of the PIMRA is based on the *Diagnostic and*

Statistical Manual, Third Edition (*DSM-III*), of the American Psychiatric Association. The inventory is orally administered. The inventory produces eight clinical scales and a total score. The clinical scales are Schizophrenia, Affective Disorder, Psychosexual Disorder, Adjustment Disorder, Anxiety Disorder, Somatoform Disorder, Personality Disorder, Inappropriate Adjustment, and Total Score (a summation of pathological indicators). Some sample items and their scales are:

Self-Report

"Do you smile even when you are sad?" (*Inappropriate Adjustment*)

"Do you enjoy things that are funny?" (*Personality Disorder*)

"Have you ever tried to force someone else to take off their clothes?" (*Psychosexual Disorder*)

Ratings-by-Others

"Adjusts easily to new situations." (*Inappropriate Adjustment*)

"Indifferent to praise or criticism or to the feelings of others." (*Personality Disorder*)

"Typically wears clothes of the opposite sex." (*Personality Disorder*)

Piloting subjects for the PIMRA were 209 adults with mental retardation (115 females and 94 males, ages 17–54). Interpretation is primarily done using the clinician's clinical judgment, but a "four-item" rule of thumb (presence of at least four symptoms consistent with a category) is suggested as a guide to diagnosis.

Reliability and validity studies were conducted in the process of norming the PIMRA. In terms of reliability, assessment of internal consistency of the PIMRA total score through coefficient alpha yielded an internal consistency estimate of .83. The manual does not report internal consistency estimates for the individual scales. Test-retest reliabilities on the PIMRA clinical scales averaged .575 for the Self-Report Scales and .78 for the Ratings-by-Others scale. Validity data, although somewhat limited, show a relationship between total score and clinical diagnosis, the affective disorder scale and the Beck Depression Inventory, the Zung, and the Social Performance Survey Schedule.

Reiss Screen

The Reiss Screen (Reiss, 1988) is a 38-item rating scale that is designed for use with adolescents and adults who have mental retardation. It provides ratings on 38 symptoms. The minimum age for use is 12 years. The scale is completed by caretakers, teachers, service providers, or other professionals who know the client "reasonably well." Problem behaviors are rated from *no problem* (e.g., does not apply or exist with sufficient frequency to be a problem in the person's life), to *problem* (e.g., the behavior occurs often or causes a significant degree of suffering and discomfort), to *major problem* (e.g., the behavior causes a great deal of discomfort, has a very high frequency, causes placement in a restrictive environment). Once familiar with the scale, completion time is approximately 20 minutes. The Reiss Screen produces *eight* clinical scales: Aggressive Behavior, Autism, Psychosis, Depression (B–Behavioral Signs), Depression (P–Physical Signs), Dependent Personality Disorder, Paranoia, and Avoidant Personality. Some sample items and their scales are:

Feels nervous or tense. Examples: nervous, panicky, trembly (shaky), apprehensive, worried. (*Depression B*)

Self-stimulatory behavior. Repetitive movements that are performed frequently and appear to be nonfunctional. Examples: body-rocking, object twirling, head-rocking. (*Autism*)

Overly sensitive. Excessive or inappropriate reactions to criticism. Examples: reacts to failure by crying, withdraws when criticized, quits easily. (*Paranoia*)

The content of the eight clinical scales is based on a factor analysis using a varimax rotation. In addition to the eight clinical scales the Reiss Screen has six special symptom ratings that are not part of the any of the clinical scales. These items are: drug and alcohol, self-injury, stealing, overactive, sexual problem, and suicidal tendencies. These items follow the same format as the scale items.

Norms for the Reiss Screen were based on a sample of 205 individuals with mental retardation living in the Chicago, Illinois, area. Additional samples were collected for different aspects (e.g., validity, factor structure) of test development. Interpretation is based on cutoff scores for each of the scales and the total score. Cutoff scores are based on the distribution of scores in the Chicago sample (e.g., 2 standard deviations above the mean for the clinical scales). Cutoff scores were established on nonstatistical grounds for the total scores and special scales. No descriptive interpretive data are provided in the manual.

Reliability and validity studies were conducted in the process of norming the Reiss Screen. In terms of reliability, assessment of internal consistency of the individual subscales through coefficient alpha indicated adequate reliability. The Reiss Screen clinical scales range from .58 to .84, and average above .70. Interrater reliabilities range from .61 to .84 and averaged above .75.

The clinical scales on the Reiss Screen were developed via factor analysis; a statistically significant relationship exists between psychiatric diagnosis and the Reiss Screen scales and total scores. Concurrent validity was found between an early version of the Reiss Screen (the CHEMRA) and the "Rating by Others" version of the PIMRA. These data are reported only for the total scores on both tests. Similarly, concurrent validity was found (.78) between the Reiss Screen and Part II of the AAMR Adaptive Behavior Scales (ABS), which assess maladaptive behavior. Again these data included only total scores.

Emotional Problems Scales

The Emotional Problems Scales (EPS) are a conjointly normed set of instruments that tap both others' perceptions of the individual and the individual's self-report. The EPS consists of the Self-Report Inventory (SRI) (Prout & Strohmer, 1991), the Behavior Rating Scales (BRS) (Strohmer & Prout, 1991), the Sentence Completion Technique (SCT) (Strohmer & Prout, 1991), and the Personal Problem Checklist (Prout & Strohmer, 1993).

The Self-Report Inventory (SRI) is a 147-item self-report instrument that is administered to adolescents and adults (14 years and up) with IQs in the 55–83 range. All words on the scale are at the 4th-grade reading level or below and the inventory is orally administered, with the individual marking a "Yes" or "No" response to items. Typical administration time is 30 minutes. Data indicate that over 90% of adolescents and adults in this IQ range are able to complete this measure. The inventory produces six clinical scales and two validity scales. The clinical scales are Depression, Low Self-Esteem, Anxiety, Thought/Behavior Disorder, Impulse Control, and Total Pathology (a summation of pathological indicators). The validity scales are Positive Impression and Response Set indicators. Some sample items and their scales include:

I find it hard to wait for things. (*Impulse Control*)

I am a nervous person. (*Anxiety*)

People like to be with me. (*Low Self-Esteem*)

Evil forces control me. (*Thought/Behavior Disorder*)

The future looks good for me. (*Depression*)

The Self-Report Inventory (SRI) was conjointly normed with the Behavior Rating Scales (BRS) in seven states and Canada. Norming subjects were drawn from public schools, special schools, day treatment programs, sheltered workshops, supervised employment settings, developmental centers, and other rehabilitation settings. Norms for the SRI are based on 708 primarily community-based individuals. Interpretive and descriptive statements are empirically based and include clinical descriptions that summarize scale content and statements that reflect other relevant clinical correlates.

Reliability and validity studies were conducted in the process of norming the SRI. In terms of reliability, assessment of internal consistency of the individual subscales through coefficient alpha indicated very adequate reliability. Internal consistency for the SRI clinical scales ranges from .81 to .96. A comparison sample of over 200 college students who completed the SRI yielded somewhat higher alphas. Test-retest reliabilities on the SRI clinical scales averaged .85 in one study, and in a study using individuals at the lower end of the mild range of mental retardation averaged .80.

Validity data include significant correlations with clinical diagnosis, involvement with behavior plans, use of psychotropic medications, level of independent living, vocational placement, vocational performance, and other counselor ratings of adjustment. Additionally, significant correlations with other self-report measures have been found for the SRI (i.e., SRI Depression Scale with the Beck Depression Inventory). Similar results have been found in the comparison sample of college students. Computer scoring and interpretive software are available. An incomplete sentence technique to complement assessment has also been developed.

The Behavior Rating Scales (BRS) is a 135-item behavior rating scale that is part of the Emotional Problems Scales (EPS). It is completed by someone who is familiar with the individual, typically a rehabilitation counselor, teacher, work supervisor, social worker, psychologist, etc. Problem behaviors are rated from 0 to 3, from *never* observed or reported to *often* observed or reported. Once familiar with the scale, completion time is approximately 15 minutes. The BRS produces 12 clinical scales and 2 more global factors: Anxiety, Depression, Withdrawal, Low Self-Esteem, Somatic Concerns, Thought/Behavior Disorder, Physical Aggression, Non-Compliance, Distractibility, Hyperactivity, Verbal Aggression, and Sexual Maladjustment. The factors are Internalizing Disorder and Externalizing Disorder. Some sample items and their scales are:

Displays or talks about fears. (*Anxiety*)

Thinking appears mixed up or confused. (*Thought/Behavior Disorder*)

Appears gloomy, unhappy. (*Depression*)

Displays little respect for authority. (*Noncompliance*)

The BRS was conjointly normed with the Self-Report Inventory (SRI) in seven states and Canada. Norming subjects were drawn from public schools, special schools, day treatment programs, sheltered workshops, supervised employment settings, developmental centers, and other rehabilitation settings. Norms for the BRS are based on 673 primarily community-based individuals. Interpretive and descriptive statements are empirically based and include clinical descriptions that summarize scale content and statements that reflect other relevant clinical corre-lates.

Reliability and validity studies were conducted in the process of norming the BRS. In terms of reliability, assessment of internal consistency of the individual subscales through coefficient alpha indicated good reliability. The BRS clinical scales range from .90 to .97. Interrater reliabilities at the same setting averaged .84, while reliabilities *across settings* averaged .79.

Validity data include significant correlations with clinical diagnosis, involve-ment with behavior plans, use of psychotropic medications, level of independent living, vocational placement, vocational performance, and other counselor ratings of adjustment. The BRS has also been shown to be significantly related to other rating scale variables in a school-age sample, as well as with scales of maladaptive behavior in the more general population of persons with mental retardation. An extension of the rating scale is being developed for the population with moderate and severe retardation. Computer scoring and interpretive software are available.

Summary

In using assessment of any type with clients who have mental retardation or borderline intelligence, it seems clear that the key is using an assessment plan that is derived to answer the critical questions driving the assessment and, perhaps even more critical, tailored to address the unique needs and abilities of the individual. We strongly advocate a client-centered approach to assessment in which the client is made part of the process from the development of the question and assessment plan to the real-world interpretation of the data. Awareness of, and where necessary assessment of, cognitive abilities will be critical. Behavioral, projective, and self-report methods can all be appropriate in assessment, as long as the ultimate goal of the use of the information guides the selection of assessment methods. The recent publication of instruments developed for, and normed on, individuals with mental retardation is an important new aspect that should have a positive impact on counseling and psychotherapy with these groups.

References

Aman, M. G. (1991). *Assessing psychopathology and behavior problems in persons with mental retardation: A review of available instruments.* Rockville, MD: U. S. Department of Health and Human Services.

Anastasi, A. (1989). *Psychological testing* (6th ed.). New York: Macmillan.

Bellack, A. S., & Hersen, M. (Eds.). (1988). *Behavioral assessment: A practical handbook* (3rd ed.). New York: Pergamon Press.

Brown, J. H., & Brown, C. S. (1977). *Systematic counseling.* Champaign, IL: Research Press.

Gottman, J. M., & Leiblum, S. R. (1974). *How to do psychotherapy and how to evaluate it.* New York: Holt, Rinehart, & Winston.

Gresham, F. (1983). Multitrait-multimethod approach to multifactored assessment: Theoretical rationale and practical application. *School Psychology Review, 12,* 26-34.

Groth-Marnat, G. (1990). *Handbook of psychological assessment* (2nd ed.). New York: John Wiley & Sons.

Hurley, A. D., & Sovner, R. (1982). Use of the Rorschach technique with mentally retarded patients. *Psychiatric Aspects of Mental Retardation, 1,* 5-8.

Hurley, A. D., & Sovner, R. (1985). The use of the Thematic Apperception Test in mentally retarded persons. *Psychiatric Aspects of Mental Retardation, 4,* 9-12.

Lindzey, G. (1961). *Projective techniques and cross-cultural research.* New York: Appleton-Century-Crofts.

Matson, J. L. (1988). *The Psychopathology Instrument for Mentally Retarded Adults (PIMRA).* Orland Park, IL: International Diagnostic Systems.

Meichenbaum, D. (1986). Cognitive-behavior modification. In F. H. Kanfer & A. P. Goldstein (Eds.), *Helping people change: A textbook of methods* (3rd ed., pp. 346-380). New York: Pergamon Press.

Nay, W. R. (1979). *Multimethod clinical assessment.* New York: Gardner Press.

Palmer, J. O. (1970). *The psychological assessment of children.* New York: John Wiley & Sons.

Prout, H. T. (1985). Personality assessment and individual therapeutic intervention. In H. M. Knoff (Ed.), *The psychological assessment of child and adolescent personality* (pp. 609-632). New York: Guilford.

Prout, H. T., & Ferber, S. M. (1988). Analogue assessment: Traditional personality assessment measures in behavioral assessment. In E. S. Shapiro & T. R. Kratochwill (Eds.), *Behavioral assessment in schools* (pp. 322-350). New York: Guilford.

Prout, H. T., & Schwartz, J. F. (1984). Validity of the Peabody Picture Vocabulary Test–Revised with mentally retarded adults. *Journal of Clinical Psychology, 40,* 584-587.

Prout, H. T., & Strohmer, D.C. (1991). *Emotional Problems Scales: The Self–Report Inventory.* Tampa, FL: Psychological Assessment Resources.

Prout, H. T., & Strohmer, D. C. (1993). *Emotional Problems Scales: Personal Problem Checklist.* Tampa, FL: Psychological Assessment Resources.

Reiss, S. (1988). *Reiss Screen for Adaptive Behavior.* Orland Park, IL: International Diagnostic Systems.

Strohmer, D. C., & Prout, H. T. (1991). *Emotional Problems Scales: The Behavior Rating Scales.* Tampa, FL: Psychological Assessment Resources.

Strohmer, D. C., & Prout, H. T. (1991). *Sentence completion technique/Emotional Problems Scales.* Odessa, FL: Psychological Assessment Resources.

Sundberg, N. D. (1977). *Assessment of persons.* Englewood Cliffs, NJ: Prentice-Hall.

Witt, J. C., & Elliot, S. N. (1983). Assessment in behavioral consultation: The initial interview. *School Psychology Review, 12,* 42-49.

4 INDIVIDUAL COUNSELING APPROACHES

H. Thompson Prout and Randy L. Cale

The application of individual counseling and psychotherapeutic techniques with persons with mental retardation has received surprisingly little attention in the professional literature. Nuffield (1983), in his review, notes that group techniques have received significantly more attention than individual techniques. Further, much of the available literature has emphasized behavioral approaches as opposed to the more traditional verbally oriented psychotherapies. Thus, there is essentially a lack of both a research base on individual approaches as well as a clinical literature detailing practitioner approaches, techniques, and issues. As will be seen in our review, much of the "clinical research" on individual approaches is dated and case study–based.

The purpose of this chapter is to summarize the status of individual approaches and to bring together a variety of viewpoints that would be helpful in conducting individual counseling and psychotherapy with persons with mental retardation. As will be seen, some of our presentation involves suppositions based on our clinical experiences and work with persons with mental retardation. We will also highlight those general issues in counseling and psychotherapy that appear most salient for the population with mental retardation. As will be seen later in this chapter in our discussion of efficacy issues, the research base in this area is of limited value in generalizing to clinical populations. Additionally, much of our discussion will have relevance for other approaches that are discussed in the later chapters.

We begin with a discussion of therapeutic factors in counseling and therapeutic interventions, followed by an overview of a variety of theoretical approaches, techniques, and developmental adaptations. Discussion of individual crisis intervention approaches will be followed by a review of outcome research. We conclude with two brief case studies that demonstrate the application of two different theoretical approaches.

Therapeutic Factors in Counseling Persons with Mental Retardation

Numerous authors have addressed the therapeutic factors that influence psychotherapy (Bergin & Lambert, 1978; Frank, 1973; Garfield, 1978; Garfield & Bergin, 1986; Strupp, 1978). These writings reflect a trend toward deemphasizing theory while concomitantly increasing attention to shared therapeutic ingredients. The intention of this discussion is not to review this information, but rather to borrow from their conceptual models and focus on the factors germane to successful counseling of persons with mental retardation. These factors are often considered to be "nonspecific" counselor variables. The major areas of emphasis will be counselor beliefs, counselor knowledge, and counselor behavior.

Although research from the general psychotherapy literature has examined a wide range of counselor factors that influence therapy, there is no research to support the prepotence of any particular set of counselor variables when counseling individuals with mental retardation. Although factors such as counselors' personal qualities, experience, or demographic background are influential, we suspect these are secondary to the beliefs, assumptions, and knowledge the counselor possesses; thus, our focus will be on those issues.

Counselor Assumptions and Belief System

Regardless of theoretical orientation, counselors operate with a range of assumptions and beliefs about their clients. The therapist's view and perception of the client influences and establishes expectations, goals, and behavior as well as the level of energy and commitment to the therapeutic process. Many of the assumptions and beliefs that will be discussed may seem to be "obvious" requisites for therapy; however, too often counselors fail to examine the assumptions that form the basis for their behavior as therapists. This is particularly problematic with populations requiring special attention due to some set of deficits or differences. Generalizations tend to center around these deficits or differences—whether real or perceived—and form the expectations for behavior. Our belief systems often are translated into our own "therapeutic" behavior. A number of counselor beliefs are basic to the therapeutic process.

Assumption/Belief #1. Individuals with mental retardation are persons who experience the full breadth of human emotion, with the same intensity and unique appreciation as you or I.

It is only in recent years that mental health professionals have begun to recognize that mental retardation does not imply emotional retardation. Unfortunately the assumptions of many professionals have supported this view of a restricted emotional experience for persons with mental retardation. However, current literature provides considerable support for the existence in the population of persons with mental retardation of the same types of emotional illnesses as occur in people without cognitive impairment. Further, there is no evidence that the neuroanatomical structures responsible for some cognitive dysfunction in mental retardation limit the range of emotional responses. Cognitive dysfunction may moderate emotional response, but not negate the expression of emotion. As cited earlier in this book, empirical evidence supports the contention that this population is capable of experiencing the full spectrum of emotion. With this firmly established in the therapist's belief system, the therapist can remain open and flexible in exploring the range of emotion. In particular, such a belief allows the counselor to consider generating new emotional responses, rather than exclusively attempting to reduce undesirable responses.

Assumption/Belief #2. Verbal psychotherapy is an efficacious form of treatment for persons with mental retardation.

This may prove to be one of the most difficult beliefs to instill in the general psychotherapeutic community. Such a belief has been antithetical to the teachings of many prominent theoreticians. Early Freudian writings limited the application of psychoanalysis to individuals who were "educable" (but not in the sense associated with the term educable mental retardation). Similarly, Rogers (1951) strongly dissuaded his readers from working with individuals lacking full cognitive resources. As recently as the mid-1960s, Gardner (1967) suggested that psychotherapy is not generally efficacious or financially cost-effective, and that professional time would be wasted if spent researching the efficacy of psychotherapy with this population. The extent of the impact of such viewpoints is unknown, but clearly detrimental. Ironically, there is no research to support this position, and the limited data that do exist are suggestive of beneficial outcomes with both individual and group therapy.

Our emphasis here is on the beliefs we view as essential for successfully conducting psychotherapy. In order for psychotherapy to have the opportunity to be effective, the counselor must believe in the value of his or her efforts and in the outcomes that are established as objectives. Higginbotham, West, and Forsyth (1988), in their review, have highlighted the importance of therapist expectancy on outcome. Although these authors did not review studies with populations with mental retardation, they clearly attest to the importance of the therapist's beliefs in attaining positive outcomes. When counselors expect success with their clients, they are not only more likely to experience success, they will engage more clients in the process and effectuate change in a greater number of clients. Translated practically, counselors who do not expect persons with mental retardation to benefit from therapy or who expect minimal positive outcome are likely to have little success with this population.

Assumption/Belief #3. Counseling with persons with mental retardation can be interesting, stimulating, and challenging.

An unfortunate misconception in the therapeutic community is that individual therapy with this population is boring and lacks stimulation. This most frequently seems based on the experiences of therapists who work with a limited number of cases on a trial basis. Although we readily acknowledge that working with this population may require some adjustments, such changes can be the source of growth for the counselor. Rather than viewing this as a client deficiency, the therapist is better served by examining his or her own behavior. Expectations that the client join the counselor's "model of the world" will lead to failure and frustration. When the therapist is willing to challenge her- or himself and find ways to meet the client in her or his world, the process can become interesting and stimulating. The rewards to the therapist will be tremendous as he or she learns to become flexible and more versatile in the skills of relating to people.

Counselor Knowledge of Mental Retardation

In this book, it is postulated that meaningful psychotherapy can be conducted with individuals functioning above the 6-year-old level of cognitive development. This suggests a wide range of intellectual capacity for clients seen in therapy, and the importance of understanding how different levels of cognitive development will affect the therapeutic process. Our emphasis here is on a functional explanation of the ways in which language, cognition, and behavior vary with cognitive development.

A classic controversy in mental retardation involves the developmental versus defect approach to the etiology of intellectual impairment. Although this may appear marginally related to the current topic, the assumptions that therapists make regarding etiology can have a profound influence on how behavior is interpreted and what is attempted in therapy. The developmental approach emphasizes the distinction between mental retardation that is due to physiological processes that are abnormal, and retardation that has no known physiological cause. Individuals who fall within the latter group comprise the majority of all persons with mental retardation and have been historically referred to as having "cultural-familial" retardation. In this group, mental retardation is not viewed as pathological but rather the product of a developmental process that is delayed (Zigler, 1969). According to this approach, the cognitive development of those with mild, nonpathological retardation differs from normal-intelligence individuals only in terms of rate and upper limit achieved. Therefore, with this orientation many of the stage theories of cognitive development offer valid models for discussing mental retardation. Contrast this with the defect approach, which essentially hypothesizes a physiological or structural defect in all cases of mental retardation. Defect-oriented theorists have offered a variety of explanations that focus on neurological, anatomical, and other cognitive-deficit models. This controversy is emphasized due to the differences in the way counselors interpret the functioning of their clients. If intellectual limitations are viewed as defects of some structure or system, theories of normal cognitive development are of limited value. It is assumed that development is altered by these dysfunctional components and that the resultant cognitive product may not resemble that found in normal development. Such models also minimize the importance of other factors in the intellectual product.

A developmental position, on the other hand, offers therapists a powerful heuristic model, regardless of the strong status of the research data. Theories of normal cognitive development can be applied with great utility to the therapeutic process. In addition, the model "opens the door" to the role of motivational, environmental, and emotional factors in the development of mild, nonpathological retardation. We obviously advocate the developmental position as the counselor knowledge and philosophical base. It is within this model that we find value in utilizing Piagetian theory to examine the language and behavior of the mentally retarded client in therapy. As discussed in Chapter One, this theory has considerable applicability in conducting therapy with persons with mental retardation. For example, with clients functioning between the mental ages of approximately 7 and 11 years, their cognitive development is marked by the capacity to conduct logical *concrete* operations. When individuals enter this stage, they become open to reasoning. Behavior can be changed or directed by cognitive processes, which suggests that impulses begin to experience control by cognitive operations. Clients operating at earlier stages of cognitive development lack the capacity to utilize logical reasoning and thus are unlikely to benefit from verbal therapy. However, clients in the concrete stage are able to classify similar events and activities into groups, allowing the counselor to point out shared features of problematic situations and educate the client about strategies for problem solving. Complicating the counselor's efforts is a distinct "present" orientation and focus on the current problem. The normal markers for the passage of time do not seem to be integrated into memory; thus, recall of past events is without a sense of order, regularity, and understanding of the causal relationships between events. This implies the need for a strong present orientation on the part of the counselor and for addressing problems as they occur. Change will be maximized by capitalizing on effective problem solving of current difficulties and coupling these efforts with strategies to engender long-term learning. In addition, because time is not demonstrated for the client, events will be more difficult to retrieve when utilizing traditional markers. The counselor may find it helpful to exaggerate normal markers or provide novel anchors that help the client to recall how he or she solved a similar problem in the past. It should be emphasized again that there are limits of logical concrete operations. These clients may have great difficulty comprehending similarities or differences between experiences.

What is of importance to the counselor is that most clients with mild mental retardation to borderline intelligence can effectively benefit from strategies utilized in verbal psychotherapy. With a basic understanding of cognitive development, the counselor can modify his or her behavior to accommodate clients' cognitive capacities. This knowledge also alters the therapist's expectations. It is to be anticipated that clients with mental retardation will, to varying degrees, require greater time to process information, will make more errors in logic, will have problems with concepts of time, and will have difficulty with high levels of complexity. They will, however, be able to learn new behaviors, understand logical reasoning, and use cognition to control impulses. In many ways, *the parameters of verbal psychotherapy are limited more by lack of counselor flexibility and ingenuity, rather than by any inherent intellectual deficit of this population.*

Within-session counselor behavior. Counselor behavior during therapy is clearly influenced by a range of factors including counselor training, experience, and assumptions, as well as the reciprocal interaction with the client. Thus, although discussing within-session counselor behavior does not represent an isolation of factors, it is unique in that the focus is on strategic behavior. This discussion is offered with the hope of encouraging therapist flexibility during counseling, a requisite skill for psychotherapy with persons with mental retardation.

One of the obvious requisites for conducting verbal psychotherapy is the verbal exchange of information—information that allows the counselor to construct a model of the client's world and a means by which to influence it. In order for the counselor to construct such a model, the client must be able to relate his or her internal processes. Frequently clients with mental retardation have difficulty with this due to limited opportunities to express the perceptions of the world they experience. It is more common for these clients to be "talked to" rather than "listened to." With limited opportunity to develop verbal proficiency, many persons with mental retardation are ill equipped for the conversational nature of verbal psychotherapy. As previously pointed out, this is not due to cognitive deficiencies and is a skill that can be acquired with practice. Much of the following discussion accentuates techniques we have found helpful in developing the conversational skills necessary for therapy.

However, although the ostensible objective of many of these suggestions is for generating the necessary verbal contents of therapy, we recognize and will emphasize the important contributions to developing and maintaining the therapeutic alliance. Regardless of theoretical orientation, it is generally acknowledged that leverage for therapeutic change is founded upon the quality of the therapeutic alliance between counselor and client (Goldstein & Myers, 1986). Although clinicians from various theoretical orientations utilize the therapeutic relationship differently, this need for a positive working alliance is increasingly emphasized by a range of therapists. When working with persons with mental retardation, the therapeutic relationship is no less critical. Many of the suggestions that follow are designed to foster rapport and develop a solid therapeutic alliance.

Conducting therapy with persons with mental retardation may require changes in activity level. The present view is that it seems to make little sense to begin discussing emotion or beliefs when the client is unable to explain such concrete experiences as his or her hobbies or why he or she likes music. It is at this point that an increase in therapist activity may become helpful, and this is usually accomplished through one of two means.

First, the therapist may want to break with traditional roles and leave the office to participate in the client's world for one or more sessions. The act of generating shared experiences can serve a host of valuable functions that help to establish rapport. Such behavior engenders trust, establishes the counselor's integrity as a concerned person, and provides unlimited stimuli for building conversational skills. The counselor is provided with the information necessary to guide probes and elaborate on the client's perceptions. Such experiences can also provide the foundation for discussing emotion, by beginning with descriptions of very specific, shared experiences.

Although it is generally accepted that one of the best ways to learn is to teach, we seldom allow our clients this opportunity. When the therapist participates with the client in some aspect of the client's world, however, there exists a unique opportunity to allow our clients to teach us. And we can guide this teaching through questions that probe internal representations of visual, auditory, kinesthetic, olfactory, and gustatory modalities, as well as the emotional and cognitive processing of this information. Throughout this process the client is verbalizing and extending his or her perceptions of the world. Again, the impact of such efforts extends well beyond the actual teaching of conversational skills as the counselor is communicating the value of the client's perceptions, the willingness to listen, and concern for the relationship. Each of these helps to establish a strong therapeutic alliance.

As an example, the initial interview with Ron, a client at a vocational workshop, reveals a strong commitment to work. He seldom has problems at work, but when he does they are violent and harsh. The counselor sets up an appointment so that Ron can teach her about his work. Upon visiting, the counselor is taught by Ron, not the supervisor. In addition, the counselor is given the opportunity to perform the job. During the process the counselor is noting the various stimuli impacting upon the client. At the next session the counselor is equipped to explore the client's perceptions in greater detail and with greater accuracy.

A second area where changes are helpful is with counselor verbal activity, not typically found in interactions with persons with mental retardation. We are not endorsing the firing of a barrage of questions to which the client responds with single-word responses. Due to the limited verbal proficiency of most clients with mental retardation, the counselor will need to guide the conversation. Several strategies for doing this are discussed below.

The first of these strategies is quite simple and straightforward. Although counselors are well trained in reflecting statements back to clients and then "leading" (perhaps in different directions depending on orientation), therapy with persons with mental retardation will require a greater number of reflecting or pacing comments, as well as more specific leading comments. Such leading comments are one of the ways in which we gradually increase awareness of the processes that govern behavior.

One pattern we have found frequently with persons with mental retardation is that identified by Bandler and Grinder (1976) and termed *nominalization*. This is a cognitive process whereby experiences are simplified by representing active, dynamic experience with words usually associated with static, more concrete experience. The outcome of this is that much of the process that goes into an experience is not available; and, if critical information is deleted, there is less likelihood of influencing and changing the process. In effect, the client leaves out much of the emotional/cognitive and descriptive aspects of the experience that are appropriate targets for change. The task of the counselor is to clarify or lead the client to describe the experience in a manner in which parts of the process and a larger range of the experience are routinely identified, and thus open to influence. Questioning by the therapist challenges the communication offered by the client in a predictable and consistent manner. For example, the statement "I get mad" is a status description of the outcome of a set of experiences; the counselor simply paces, leads, and clarifies the experiences by stating "and so you feel mad about what?" The client is not allowed to simplify the experience, and further probing identifies the *specific* situations or events for which some control and intervention are available. Although we all exhibit such patterns, persons with mental retardation seem particularly prone to this, yet seem to benefit from this ongoing clarification process.

In a similar vein, the cognitive representations of experience are often lacking important information. Although each of us has preferred ways of storing experience (Bandler & Grinder, 1976), we find persons with mental retardation to be strongly biased toward a single representational system. For example, a client may see the world and represent the world in visual terms only and have great difficulty recalling what was said or what he or she felt. This provides an ongoing opportunity for the counselor to expand the client's experience by probing and accentuating all of the parameters of experience. There are other applications of the concepts of representational systems but these are not unique to working with persons with mental retardation. Interested readers are referred to Bandler and Grinder (1976).

Another strategy for altering verbal activity is to be willing to role-model appropriate discussion more actively. Persons with mental retardation are frequently asked to suppress emotion, discussions of sex and family, as well as spontaneous behavior. The counselor offers the rare opportunity to interact with a non–mentally retarded adult without the encumbrances of a caretaking relationship. One of the counselor tasks is to demonstrate the differences in the nature of the therapeutic relationship. The counselor can discuss his or her feelings about real-life issues, and model ways to open up to emotion and experience. With shared experiences, the counselor can contrast his or her experience with that of the client to demonstrate how people view experiences differently. This is a strategy that serves multiple teaching and relationship functions, through the pure act of modeling behavior and by the values communicated when the therapist shares openly with the client.

As a closing comment in regard to verbal activity, we need to remind ourselves constantly that many clients are better at reflection activities than we are. Although head nods and smiles are superficial and quickly identified, the resiliency of these patterns will most certainly outlast our capacity to monitor for them. The concern is not so much that we get an affirmative response to an occasional comment the client doesn't understand, but rather that the pattern interferes in an ongoing manner with the client's capacity to absorb. These patterns need to be recognized and interrupted regularly. Communications are easily monitored for comprehension by asking the client to repeat in his or her own words what was said (an old strategy applied by professors to the head-nodding masses of statistics students). A superior strategy would be behavioral observation to assess if a particular behavioral sequence was followed. Irregardless of the counselor's suspicions, it is advisable to establish a regular pattern of checking the accuracy of client comprehension, keeping in mind that the client can only derive value if the meaning is understood.

Last, the within-session activities need to interface with other aspects of clients' lives. Because the vast majority of clients are involved in some form of structured educational or vocational program, or receive residential support services, the clinician is afforded an additional clinical tool. Such agencies are interested in the growth and development of the client, and it remains incumbent on the therapist to enlist their assistance. There are numerous behavioral strategies that could be implemented to enhance the attainment of the goals of psychotherapy. In addition, open communication with such facilities provides the therapist with a rich source of data to monitor the behavioral impact of therapy. Although this chapter is clearly not the context for a discussion of behavioral strategies, the clinician is reminded to utilize all the potential supports available. We have found concomitant behavioral programming to be a tremendous adjunct to behavioral change.

Approaches and Developmental Adaptations

Rational-Emotive Therapy (RET)

Rational-emotive therapy (Ellis, 1962, 1973, 1989) is a cognitively oriented therapy that focuses on the effects of thoughts or cognitions on emotions and behavior. It is similar to Beck's (Beck, Rush, Shaw, & Emery, 1979; Beck & Weishaar, 1989) cognitive therapy and Maultsby's (1975) rational behavior therapy, which are not discussed in this chapter. The common thread in these cognitive therapies is the focus on cognitions and their resulting effects on emotions and behavior. Irrational beliefs, inaccurate perceptions, and other faulty cognitions lead to disturbed emotions. Rational beliefs and accurate perceptions of events prevent disturbed emotions and deintensify emotional reactions.

Rational-emotive therapy utilizes an A-B-C model to understand an individual's problems and to plan and conduct interventions. In this model, "A" stands for the

Activating Event, the situation to which the person is reacting. "B" stands for Belief or cognitions the person has about the event, and "C" stands for the Consequences, both emotional and behavioral. In RET, much of the assessment focus is on the beliefs and cognitions, with relatively little emphasis on the actual event or the resulting emotions. Rational-emotive therapists believe that irrational beliefs (e.g., "I must be successful in everything I attempt") lead to disturbed emotions out of proportion to the event. Disturbed emotions can be moderated through changing the belief system or cognitions. The primary therapeutic tool is Disputation, which is added to the model (i.e., A-B-C-D). Disputation involves a variety of activities that guide the client through a challenge of the irrational beliefs, misperceptions, and faulty cognitions with a goal of replacing the troublesome cognition with a more accurate or rational cognition. The rational cognition will result in better emotional functioning, which also reinforces the more rational cognition. Disputation activities may include philosophical, logical, or intellectual challenging of the irrational belief, homework (behavioral) activities to disprove the irrational belief, guiding the client through "objective" examination of his or her situation and responses, and direct teaching of new beliefs or cognitions.

In practice, RET is an active and conversational approach and begins with the therapist assessing the individual's problem in the A-B-C model. This is often viewed as a diagnostic interview to elicit as much information as possible about the components, but in particular the individual's thoughts, language, and cognitions (i.e., "B"). Once the therapist has "diagnosed" the problem in the A-B-C format, the therapist utilizes the variety of disputation techniques to alter the "B." Although there may be some continued discussion of the "A" and "C" components, the emphasis is clearly on the cognitive and belief aspects.

In developmentally adapting RET for use with persons with mental retardation, it is useful to examine what results in positive mental health in RET theory. Ellis (1973) and Beck and his colleagues (Beck et al., 1979) note that emotionally healthy individuals have good cognitive problem-solving skills, use less extreme language in describing situations (e.g., "horrible" vs. "uncomfortable"), have more flexible and probabilistic with mental retardation thinking, and are less prone to see the world in black/white, absolutistic, concrete terms. This view of what promotes emotional health may place the cognitively limited person with mental retardation "at risk" for emotional disturbance. With nonretarded persons, good problem-solving skills may circumvent negative emotions in unpleasant situations. The person with mental retardation who lacks these problem-solving skills may be more likely to become disturbed.

At the beginning of RET, the initial task of assessing the person with mental retardation's problem in an A-B-C format may be to necessitate teaching the individual some emotional language as well as how to identify his or her thoughts. Language limitations may somewhat complicate this task. Further, we have found that some persons with mental retardation have difficulty with the distinction between thoughts and feelings. For example, when asked how they *feel* about some event, some might respond with "I *thought* it was a rotten thing to happen." The assessment phase may need to be made more concrete for the person with mental retardation to elicit all the components. Role-playing, use of visual materials (cartoons, pictures), and arranging structured situations help identify the significant aspects of problems (Grieger & Boyd, 1989). The person with mental retardation may have difficulty describing the events, thoughts, and feelings surrounding an altercation with a co-worker. However, role playing the situation or interviewing the person in the setting may result in a better description of the A-B-C components.

Once the A-B-C components have been assessed, the therapist can proceed to the disputation phase. In therapy with nonretarded adults, there is a phase called "Rational-Emotive Insight" in which it is demonstrated to the client that the irrational beliefs are indeed causing the emotional disturbance. Grieger and Boyd (1989), describing applications with children, feel that this phase requires considerable conceptual ability about behavioral and emotional alternatives and thus is beyond the capability of most children. This would also apply to most persons with mental retardation. We concur, and feel the acceptance and understanding of the emotion–cognition link is not essential for therapeutic progress. This may account for most therapeutic progress with persons with mental retardation being "inelegant" or largely situationally based. (See Chapter One for a discussion "elegant" vs. "inelegant" change.) Again, we feel most goals will focus on resolving emotional difficulties around specific situations. Thus, the RET therapist would move directly to the disputation phase.

The disputation phase works directly on changing the cognitions about the specific situation. It may involve disputation or any technique that replaces a maladaptive cognition with a more adaptive one. With clients with mental retardation, disputation will be more concrete and behavioral, with less reliance on philosophical, logical, or intellectual disputation. This may involve direct teaching of alternative cognitions or language. This may also involve rational self-talk or teaching verbal self-instruction (Grieger & Boyd, 1989). As one would teach a social skill, the client with mental retardation can be taught to talk through a problem and to assess his or her own cognitions while in the situation. This may require the therapist to model how he or she would self-talk by talking out loud about how he or she might be thinking in the situation. As mentioned, role playing can be used as an assessment technique, but it also can be used therapeutically. Grieger and Boyd (1989) also recommend homework assignments to carry out tasks outside of therapy. This may require parents or staff who work with the client to facilitate the completion of these activities. We do not recommend written assignments for persons with mental retardation. Structured situations where the client can try out and utilize the disputation techniques are helpful. In conjunction with individual therapy, it may be helpful to train those who work with the individual in some aspects of the RET approach so that they may instruct and/or cue the individual to use the disputational techniques. Finally, if the disputational techniques have been helpful, it is useful to show the client that changing his or her thoughts did result in a more moderate emotional response. Ideally, this might yield generalization of the cognitive skills (i.e., elegant change), but is more likely to reinforce the person with mental retardation's use of the disputational or cognition-changing technique in the specific situation.

Person-Centered Therapy

Person-centered therapy was developed by Carl Rogers and has been known historically as client-centered therapy or nondirective therapy. Rogerian therapy or counseling is based on the assumption that given an appropriate therapeutic climate, individuals will move in growth-producing and emotionally healthy directions in their lives (Moore, 1989). Rogerians believe individuals will strive toward self-fulfillment and self-actualization. The theory is considered a self-theory or a phenomenological viewpoint, with a here-and-now, present focus. This viewpoint holds that individuals are the center of an ever-changing world and that the events and behavior in the world are interpreted from one's internal frame of reference. The sense of self or self-concept is the key to positive mental health. Problems occur when an individual becomes incongruent—an imbalance between a self-view and what an individual believes he or she should be, often based on interactions within the environment. The goal of therapy is both an enhanced and more congruent view of the self.

In practice, person-centered therapy places considerable emphasis on client–therapist relationships and expression of affect. Rogers (1957), in his classic essay, outlined the "necessary and sufficient" or core conditions for therapeutic change. Rogers argued that if these conditions were met, it would establish an optimal climate for client self-examination which would lead to therapeutic change. Briefly, the core conditions included client-therapist psychological contact, client incongruence, therapist congruence, the therapist's unconditional positive regard for the client, and therapist empathy (Raskin & Rogers, 1989). Although the sufficiency of the core conditions has been debated, the importance of the therapeutic climate and relationship has remained key to person-centered approaches. Boy and Pine

(1982) have expanded on the basic model to include more specifics on the relationship and the skills of the counselor. The Boy and Pine expansion and refinement is a good representation of the current elements of the person-centered approach.

In person-centered therapy, the counselor essentially is viewed as a facilitator to encourage the client's affective expression. The various techniques include active listening, accurate empathic responding, restatement, indirect leads, use of open-ended questions, acceptance, reflection, mild confrontation, clarification, and summarization (Moore, 1989). The base of application of the theory is that the client leads the direction of the session by providing the content, while the therapist objectively, empathically, and nonjudgmentally guides the client in this examination by encouraging expression.

The person-centered viewpoint has much to offer, both philosophically and clinically, for those who work with clients with mental retardation. The emphasis on worth of the individual and the unconditional positive regard have impact on counselor behavior. The beliefs we outlined earlier are very consistent with person-centered viewpoints. Clearly the more positive the regard we have for our clients with mental retardation, the greater our efforts in working with them. We again emphasize that counselor behavior is influenced by belief systems.

As discussed earlier, many clients with mental retardation may be unaccustomed to having someone present him- or herself as an active and concerned listener. They may be more accustomed to being "talked at" instead of "talked to." The person-centered counselor's initial task may be first to "socialize" the client to this new kind of relationship. Because so many of the client's relationships with persons without retardation may be in superior-inferior status (e.g., work supervisor-employee), he or she may be fearful about expressions of affect and their consequences. In effect, trust and relationship building are of prime initial concern.

The techniques used with persons with mental retardation will be very similar to techniques used with persons without retardation. There are, however, several adaptations that will enhance the effectiveness with language-limited persons with mental retardation. The counselor may find it necessary to be somewhat more directive initially in order to get the client with mental retardation focused and expressing content relative to personal issues. Just as play is used with children to enhance expression, the counselor may utilize a range of materials and media to encourage expression. Play materials will be appropriate for children with mental retardation, but other materials should be developmentally appropriate for the age of the client. In selecting materials, normalization issues should be considered, as discussed in Chapter One. Drawing pictures of social relationships, games, etc., may be helpful in this regard.

The other modification of techniques essentially involves the use of language appropriate for the client's developmental level. The counselor's responses to the client's expressed concerns must be in language understandable for the client. We once heard a tape of a nondirective counselor working in a sheltered workshop setting. The client, who has mild retardation, had just described a problem at his home. The counselor, attempting to empathize, responded, "That must have been disconcerting for you." The client had no idea what "disconcerting" meant, and this disrupted the conversation that followed. Thus, feedback, reflection, and other counselor leads need to be in simple language.

Last, the "nondirective" counselor may also need to be more directive to keep clients with mental retardation discussing relevant issues. It may be necessary to redirect clients back to topics or even to suggest topics. Once the client has become focused, the counselor can resume a more nondirective posture.

Reality Therapy

Reality therapy (Glasser, 1965, 1981) is an approach that focuses on one's "identity" as a major contributor to all behavior and emotions. According to this theoretical approach, all individuals have a basic, intrinsic drive toward achieving a distinct and unique identity. It is interesting to note that the roots of reality therapy are based in Glasser's work with adolescents. Thus, some of the similarities between the adolescent and the adult with mental retardation discussed in Chapter One may make reality therapy a viable option for working with the adult with mental retardation. Individuals who develop "success" identities have fulfilled their basic needs of love (being loved), power (importance, worth), fun (enjoyment, learning), and freedom (independence, choice) (Fuller & Fuller, 1989). Problems stem from the development of a "failure" identity. These individuals believe that they are worthless, no good, and have little chance to succeed. They often have given up and assume that they will fail. Thus, they put forth little effort to change their situation and, in many cases, may act to reinforce the failure self-view. Behaviorally, the failure identity may express itself with a variety of behaviors ranging from withdrawal to acting out.

The general goals of reality therapy concern values, concepts of individual responsibility, and self-acceptance and understanding (Fuller & Fuller, 1989). Little emphasis is placed on past behavior and the personal historical antecedents of the client's current situation. Changed or improved behavior is viewed as important, but secondary to a changed view of oneself. However, behavior change is viewed as key to changing this self-view. Changing behavior demonstrates to oneself that one is not worthless or a failure; it reinforces or builds a more positive self-view. Continued behavior change results in movement toward a success identity. As one builds a more positive identity, the individual begins to act in a more responsible and self-enhancing manner. Thus, the overall goal is one of enhanced self-image. It is a verbally active and conversational psychotherapy that may include negotiation and agreement/disagreement between client and therapist. Therapy is overtly quite behavioral. Initially, the counselor must develop a relationship with the client that communicates both caring and a belief in the potential for individual change. The focus in therapy is on the client's current behavior patterns that are creating problems for him or her. The emphasis is on "what" the client is doing, not the "why" (Fuller & Fuller, 1989). The examination of current behavior is to demonstrate that the present patterns are ineffective and causing problems for the client and to reinforce the idea of the need for changed behavior. Some of this examination of behavior can result in the highlighting of contingent relationships between behavior and negative outcomes. This also aids the client in making a value judgment relative to the helpfulness of the behavior.

Once the client has accepted the notion of the need for behavioral change, the major therapeutic task is developing a plan for behavior change. The client and counselor mutually work out a plan for changed behavior. The counselor encourages the client to accept the responsibility for the plan and to make a commitment to it. In subsequent sessions, the previous plans are reviewed and evaluated and new plans are developed. On review of plans, the counselor accepts no excuses for a plan that doesn't work yet is not punitive. The focus is on development of a new plan to address the behavior.

With clients with mental retardation the same basic "planning for change" strategies are applied as would be with an adult or non–cognitively limited child or adolescent. In addition, much of the practice of reality therapy is similar to behavioral contracting strategies, also discussed in this volume. The major difference between "change plans" and contracting lies in the specification of consequences, with reality therapy having more emphasis on the client's judgment of success in meeting the agreement of the plan. Fuller and Fuller (1989) describe a series of critical components in making plans with child and adolescent populations. These developmental adaptations would appear to be equally applicable in working with clients with mental retardation:

1. A plan must be small and manageable, considering both the time aspects and the specifics of the behavior. Plans too large reinforce failure, whereas initial successes contribute to changing self-view.

2. Plans need to be specific, detailed, and definite. The counselor and client should detail the "whats, wheres, hows, how oftens, with whom, and how manys" of the plan.

3. The plan should be reasonable, make sense, and client and counselor should both see value in doing it.

4. Plans should be stated positively, describing what the client is *going to do*, rather than what he or she won't do.

5. The plan should begin as soon as possible. Immediacy of beginning a plan will raise the chances of success.

6. Plans should be repetitive so that the new behaviors can be practiced each day. This enhances learning and helps establish new daily patterns of behavior.

Reality therapy has the positive aspect of attacking two areas. First, the improved behavior will often be seen positively by those working with the client who has mental retardation. As noted, many clients are referred for inappropriate behavior. The referral agents are obviously desirous of some kind of behavior change. Second, the emphasis on improved self-view is important. Low self-esteem and self-defeating attitudes are often seen in persons with mental retardation. Improvements in this area would obviously be beneficial.

Finally, because the major therapeutic activity revolves around the development of plans, it is important that the plans themselves are developmentally appropriate. This encompasses the language used to describe the plan, the complexity of the tasks, the number of the options in the plan, and the memory/learning demands included. In general, plans should be kept simple, workable, and straightforward.

Psychoanalytic/Psychodynamic Approaches

The psychoanalytic approaches to psychotherapy and counseling are perhaps the best known of all the therapeutic approaches because of their historical base in psychology, psychiatry, and clinical social work. Although still utilized, the psychoanalytically based approaches have also been the most widely criticized due to lack of demonstrated efficacy and empirical base, poor operational definitions of constructs, and lengthy treatment process. We will use the terms "psychoanalytic" and "psychodynamic" interchangeably, although they include a relatively wide range of theoretical and modality viewpoints. The cornerstones of these approaches are emphases on unconscious forces in mental life, psychic drives, psychological phases of development, internal conflict in the development of psychological difficulties, and the importance of past psychosocial experiences in current functioning. It is viewed as crucial in the therapeutic process to develop "insight" about these unconscious forces, drives, stages of development, conflicts, and the role of prior life experiences in one's psychological makeup (Arlow, 1989). The basic process of therapy relies heavily on the client–therapist relationship in which transference is a major issue. In transference, the client responds to the therapist in a manner similar to that which they would use with other important or significant persons in their lives. The client utilizes the therapist to work through the emotions and issues associated with these significant others. Psychoanalytically oriented therapies tend to be long term and relatively nondirective, with the content often focused on the past. The therapist's role could be categorized as reflective and interpretive, helping the client to recognize and uncover conflicts and move toward insight-based resolutions. With children, expressive enhancing modalities such as play are often used.

Szymanski (1980) offers a useful adaptation of psychodynamically oriented therapy for use with persons with mental retardation, although he borrows from other theoretical frameworks in his formulation. Szymanski's adaptation essentially utilizes the same approach as conducting psychodynamic therapy with a person without retardation. However, he offers a number of considerations in working with persons with mental retardation. Goals tend to be focused on self-image issues with exploration of the individual's understanding and feelings about the disability, frustration tolerance, and avenues of expression of affect. The therapist needs to be more directive in style with verbal language kept brief, concrete, clear, and at the client's level of understanding. Nonverbal techniques such as play may be useful.

Therapy is organized around initial, middle, and termination phases. In the initial phase, the focus is on establishing some awareness of the reason the individual has entered into therapy. Empathy and support are emphasized to build rapport and to develop the base for building a therapeutic alliance. The middle phase represents the phase in which the bulk of the therapeutic work is done. The therapist serves as a model for identification by showing how he or she would respond in various situations, a concept referred to as "auxiliary ego." Szymanski (1980) feels that it is necessary for the client to deal with developmental problems or deficits and that the client affectively come to terms with his or her retardation. This results in ego strengthening and ultimately promotes independence in the individual. The termination phase continues on building ego strength and preparing the client for termination. The idea of termination should be mentioned throughout the therapy process. Termination itself must be handled sensitively so that the client does not perceive it as rejection. Szymanksi feels that many persons with mental retardation have experienced considerable familial and societal rejection, and it is important that termination be distinguished from that. The processes of transference and countertransference may be especially important in the alliance between therapist and the client with mental retardation.

Other Approaches

There has been relatively little done in the development of specific approaches in therapeutic work with persons with mental retardation. Two less well-known intervention approaches have attempted to develop techniques more specifically aimed at the population with mental retardation. They are *pretherapy* (Prouty, 1976) and *affect abilities training* (Corcoran, 1982).

Pretherapy, as described by Prouty (1976, 1986), is directed at more disturbed and/or regressed clientele and has been utilized with persons with or without mental retardation who have psychosis, including those whose behavioral difficulties have an organic base. As the term "pretherapy" implies, the goal of this intervention is to develop basic reality contact and to make the client more open to other interventions and psychosocial relationships. In the disturbed state, the client has little or no contact with reality and cannot participate in any traditional therapeutic relationship. Further, in most cases where pretherapy is applicable, the client is not capable of engaging in routine, normal, day-to-day social interactions and relationships. It assumes that the client is deficient in the ability to experience and to communicate (Hinterkopf, Prouty, & Brunswick, 1979). The core of therapy focuses on the reflecting and experiencing process. Clients for whom pretherapy is appropriate have a deficit in reality contact that is defined as a low-level awareness of self, others, and the environment and related low levels of affective responding. The therapist's main role involves a series of six reflecting or experientializing activities:

1. *Situational reflecting*: This reflection is oriented toward the environment, situations, or milieux. The therapist may simply describe the client's activity or the aspects of the situation (e.g., "We are sitting in this room" "You are listening to music").

2. *Body reflections*: This can involve either verbalizing or experientializing the client's body position (e.g., "You are slumping in the chair") or literally reflecting the client's body position (i.e., the client is slumped, the therapist also slumps in a similar position).

3. *Reflection of facial expression*: The therapist makes an interpretation of the client's facial expression and reflects that interpretation to the client (e.g., "You look sad"). Again, this may involve literal reflection of the facial expression.

4. *Word for word and sound reflections*: When the client emits an only partially understandable verbalization, this is reflected back in a questioning or slightly restated form. For example, if the client says, "Bob goes to store!" the therapist might respond, "Bob goes to the store?" If the client says, "I have TV," the therapist might respond, "You have a TV." Some sounds, although incomprehensible, may imply some affect and can be reflected in a manner similar to facial reflections (e.g.,

"You sound angry").

5. *Reiterative principle*: The concept of this principle indicates the slow, careful repetition of the reflections described previously to maximize the effect of reflecting and experiencing. It may be necessary to repeat the same reflection several times and across several sessions before an observable effect is noted in client's behavior.

6. *Primary process reflections*: When a client is hallucinating or delusional, the literal content of the psychotic process is reflected without interpretation.

The situational and body reflections have a goal of making the client aware of being the locus of his or her own experience, whereas the facial and word/sound reflections aim to make the client more in touch with affect and to increase the range of affect. Obviously, the pretherapy approach is limited to a certain type of client with mental retardation, the client in a highly disturbed, regressed condition. Prouty (1976, 1986) indicates that this approach has been helpful in reducing the intensity of the experiential aspect of the disturbed behavior.

Affect abilities training (AAT) (Corcoran, 1982) is described as being applicable with persons in the 30 to 70 IQ range. Its goal is to develop those emotional behaviors that are socially and individually valued and to decrease those emotions and related behaviors that are counterproductive to adjustment. It assumes that with increased ability to understand and express emotions, there will be a decrease in personal frustrations and concomitant changes in a variety of adaptive behaviors.

The counselor utilizing this approach will use a variety of words, touches, gestures, and postures in a four-stage model to produce changes in the ability to express and understand emotions. More than a therapeutic model, it emphasizes a skill acquisition approach that places minimal demands on verbal comprehension and abstract reasoning. Rather, it makes heavy use of situational components of the individual's life, concrete materials, and practical exercises.

Stage I—Facilitating reality contact. The initial phase, similar to pretherapy, emphasizes intensifying reality contact and utilizes many of the same situational and body reflections described by Prouty (1976). It may also involve planned experiences that encourage the individual to use a variety of senses (visual, auditory, kinesthetic, and tactile). The primary goal at this stage is to sharpen the individual's attending, concentrating, thinking, and experiencing skills.

Stage II—Becoming aware of emotional states. At this stage, the counselor/ therapist helps the individual identify and label four primary feelings, discriminate among these four feelings, and develop socially acceptable emotional expression. The four feelings are happiness, sadness, anger, and fear. Initially, clients focus on facial and body aspects of the affective states. Depending on functioning level, clients will focus on the different cues that indicate different emotional states. The specific emotional training teaches clients to recognize the different emotions in others and themselves. This is accomplished by reflection, questioning the client about his or her own emotional responses, and more direct instruction and concrete exercises.

Stage III—Antecedents and consequences. Borrowing from the behavioral ABC format (A = antecedent, B = behavior, C = consequence), the therapeutic process focuses on helping the client understand the link between antecedents and the consequences of emotions. The emphasis is on the emotional consequences and the clear links among the ABC components. Presented with concrete examples (e.g., photographs, cartoon sequences), the client is asked questions about the situations in terms of how the person is feeling, what happened before the feeling, and what happened after the feeling. Role playing may be helpful at this stage.

Stage IV—Real-life situations. The culmination of AAT is in helping the person deal with real-life situations. At this stage, the client will have more understanding of his or her own emotional behavior and will be ready to translate his or her training to practical situations. The techniques used in the first three stages are used in helping the client understand actual situations he or she encounters. The process continues to be concrete, simple, and repetitive, with the counselor using reflection and questioning to help the client understand his or her emotional reactions in various situations. Ultimately, the client is steered toward acceptable alternative emotional reactions versus the previously nonadaptive emotional behaviors.

Although Corcoran (1982) describes AAT as being as much an "attitude" as an approach, it appears to have broader applicability than the pretherapy approach. Even though there is some overlap and both emphasize awareness aspects, AAT would appear to have applicability with less-disturbed populations. AAT provides a logical structure for affective interventions. Further, AAT would appear to complement some of the more general therapeutic approaches described above— AAT might be useful in making some clients more prepared to deal with other therapeutic modes.

Crisis Intervention Counseling

Crisis intervention counseling is generally considered to be a logical extension of brief forms of psychotherapy. The therapeutic contact may run from 2 to 6 weeks, with a primary therapeutic goal of attaining resolution of the current crisis and a return to the previous level of functioning. A more global goal would be some change in behavior that results in the improvement in psychosocial functioning.

Crisis intervention strategies as set forth in this book will represent a confluence of traditional crisis intervention theory, systems theory, behavioral methods, and clinical experience. The life situation of persons with mild mental retardation is decidedly different from that of most people. The model presented attempts to take these unique issues into consideration.

Definitional Clarity

There are a number of terms that have been used to describe similar psychotherapeutic interventions applied in time-limited situations. These include brief psychotherapy, emergency psychotherapy, and crisis intervention. Although the focus of this discussion is on crisis intervention strategies, a brief review of each of these approaches will help to clarify the concepts to be discussed.

Brief psychotherapy is typically viewed as having its roots in psychoanalytic theory (Bellak & Small, 1978). As a treatment method it evolved from the increased demand for mental health services to be provided on a community basis. This was primarily the result of two related contemporaneous events: (a) President Kennedy's Community Mental Health Act, which helped create community mental health centers across the country, and (b) the concomitant emptying of psychiatric hospitals, where the traditional forms of psychoanalytic psychotherapy were impractical for the volume of clients and particularly ill-equipped to deal with short-term problem resolution.

The focus of brief psychotherapy is limited to the amelioration of specific symptoms. It is a more directive approach with emphasis on the conceptualization of problem intervention from a psychodynamic perspective (Bellak & Small, 1978). The reconstruction of personality is not primary, though the possibility of movement to a higher level of functioning is acknowledged. The typical psychoanalytic tools of interpretation, free association, and analysis of transference are utilized, but in highly modified forms (Aguilerre & Messick, 1974). Bellack and Small (1978) emphasize that positive transference is encouraged and necessary to accomplish goals in short periods of time; however, negative transference feelings are not analyzed. The evaluation of the patient is of supreme importance because the intervention will be highly focused and has as its goal the stability of psychodynamic forces.

Emergency psychotherapy is a term utilized by Bellak and Small (1978) to refer to the application of brief psychotherapy to special situations of crisis and exigency. The essential difference seems to be the urgency and immediacy of the problem that dictates the use of emergency psychotherapy. However, conceptually and operationally the authors make no distinctions between these terms.

The application of brief and emergency psychotherapy, as defined above, seems to have limited utility to the crises experienced by persons with mental retardation. Psychodynamic strategies have seldom been applied in working with persons with mental retardation, due in large part to the widespread belief among analytic therapists that mentally "deficient" individuals could not benefit from psychotherapy (Hayes, 1977). In a more pragmatic vein, although several of the therapeutic processes appear appropriate for work with persons with mental retardation (i.e., reassurance, support, increasing self-esteem), one of the primary therapeutic tools remains that of interpretation and imparting insight (Bellak & Small, 1978). With cognitively limited individuals experiencing crises, we argue that a more eclectic, problem-solving model, resembling crisis intervention models, offers greater utility when working with persons with mental retardation.

Crisis Intervention

In certain respects the descriptions of crisis intervention and brief and emergency psychotherapy appear similar. Both encompass short-term therapeutic interventions where the focus is on the immediate crisis and the goal is restoration to at least the premorbid level of functioning. Both provide direction, goal orientation, and high levels of support. However, the critical distinction lies in the conceptual model and the strategies this model suggests for intervention.

The following crisis intervention model incorporates cognitive, behavioral, and systemic principles that the authors have found helpful in dealing with such situations.

The first phase of crisis intervention consists of completing a thorough, focused assessment. Often time does not permit an extensive review of the client's history and background, and examination of individual dynamics. However, when working with persons with mental retardation, the professional frequently has ongoing contact with the client and may be fortunate in having an understanding of the client's history and psychological profile. Such data are not critical for planning the intervention. Due to time constraints the data to be collected must be germane to resolution of the crisis and should cover the following areas.

A) *What is the precipitating event?*

It may be necessary to utilize a variety of resources to obtain this information, as the client may have difficulty specifying the antecedent. If a clear precipitant cannot be identified, the clinician may need to examine carefully possible systemic changes, particularly in the client's support system or environmental structure. For example, in a residential or vocational setting there may have been a change in staff scheduling or assignments 2 weeks prior to the crisis.

Although a moderate percentage of crises will have clearly identifiable precipitants, many will appear without one. It is of importance to remain cognizant that many individuals with mental retardation are products of structured lives. For certain clients, it may take only minor changes in that structure to precipitate a problem. It is therefore imperative that the assessment include an examination of possible systemic changes, particularly those involving support and structure.

B) *How much has the crisis affected the client's life?*

With the adult with mental retardation, crises often carry with them the potential to undermine placements—both vocational and residential. It is often extremely important to determine the extent to which a placement has been put in jeopardy, as future adjustment may hinge on continued placement.

C) *What are the support systems and how strong are they?*

The clients are frequently supported by both vocational and residential programs and, in addition, have family and other social support networks. These systems are important in both protecting the client and assisting in the recovery.

D) *What coping strategies does the client typically use and why have these failed?*

Clients will be able to answer this question through recall of examples more readily than by direct questioning. The therapist will attempt to determine how the client usually deals with problems.

E) *What is the risk of danger to self and others?*

For the professional engaged in crisis intervention work, there is need to be competent in assessing suicide potential and the probability of aggressive, assaultive, or homicidal behavior. With populations of persons with mental retardation, such assessments may become more difficult with clients who are language impaired or more limited in verbal skills. In particular, separating ideation from intent seems a difficult task during times of crisis for persons with mental retardation. An additional difficulty is often the compounding problem of low impulse control. Thus, such individuals may act impulsively to harm themselves or others when anxiety is aroused.

When planning the intervention, the professional will frequently be working with clients who are aided by two or more human service agencies. Too often plans are generated without consultation with these agencies. In such cases the plans at best may require revision; at worst, the effort to remediate the crisis is conducted without optimum support, with possible jeopardy to the success of the plan. Whenever possible, consultation in the planning phases will enhance the likelihood of setting support and follow-through from allied agencies.

Interventions will be most effective when both individual and systemic issues are addressed. Although these issues are separated for purposes of discussion, recognition of the dynamic interdependence of the two is essential to planning and conducting crisis interventions. The individual will be more capable at times of assessing systemic problems, while the systemic supports may provide the most accurate information on level of functioning, history, and previous successful interventions. Utilizing the resources of both will maximize efficacy.

Individual Crisis Intervention

When working with a client in crisis, the focus of the individual therapeutic intervention is in three main areas: cognitive awareness, emotional catharsis, and coping. Cognitive awareness refers to assisting the client in understanding the relationship between precipitating events and current emotional status. During this process the counselor should be able to determine the subjective meaning of the precipitating events to the client. Communicating this understanding to the client in the form of reflective responses will help to establish rapport. However, it is most critical that the relationship between stressor and crisis be made clear and the meaning of this relationship established. This awareness alone assists in clarifying the confusion often experienced by individuals in crisis. In addition, this information is requisite to several of the cognitive interventions discussed below.

The opportunity for emotional catharsis is the second area of focus fundamental to working with clients in crisis. However, as Levitas and Gibson (1989) point out, few clients with mental retardation are allowed opportunities for emotional expression. Pain, sadness, and guilt are rarely expressed, and by adolescence, individuals with mental retardation seldom cry. This lack of emotional expression results in denial and suppression. When a crisis evolves, the individual will be ill equipped to label and appropriately discuss pain and sadness. Instead what is frequently seen is anger and disruptive behavior. One of the counselor's tasks in crisis counseling is to recognize this process and explore the emotional experience such that accurate labels can be attached, and a catharsis of the emotion becomes available to the client. These experiences alone can teach the client appropriate methods of releasing emotion and thus circumvent future crisis. It is also noted that excellent opportunities for reframing exist following shared cathartic experiences as the counselor will have both rapport and a good sense of the meaning of events.

The development of coping strategies may occur over one to several sessions and is predicated on understanding the crisis. It is also of value to allow ventilation of strong emotion, as previously discussed. However, the importance of having an accurate understanding of the precipitating events cannot be overstated. With a time-limited intervention emphasizing immediate restoration of functioning, the problem-solving efforts are *highly* focused and in one of two general directions. First, once the precipitating events are identified, efforts are made to attack the stressor directly. At times there are mistakes that can be corrected or events that can be dealt with most effectively through direct confrontation. Several authors emphasize that such direct action to reduce or eliminate precipitating stressors is highly preferable to tolerating them (Matheny, Aycock, Pugh, Curlette, & Cannella, 1986; Tache & Selye, 1978). Efforts to effectuate change of the precipitant will require the application of problem-solving strategies. These include problem definition, client education about the problem, developing alternatives, and selecting the strategy (which becomes modifiable in the event of an unsuccessful outcome). It should be noted that reasonable alternatives may *not* be available for directly confronting the stressors. In this event efforts then shift toward strategies that assist the client to tolerate the stressor.

Matheny and his colleagues (Matheny et al., 1986) discuss several strategies for tolerating stressors. One of the more powerful strategies reviewed is cognitive restructuring or reframing. This intervention focuses on the meaning of the stressor to the client, as often there exists a cognitive set that "creates" subjective emotional pain. Often the meaning of the precipitating event can be altered by searching for ways in which the event could be seen in a more positive light. There may be another aspect or perspective that is not readily apparent, but when offered to the client, changes the meaning of the stressor. Before proceeding with attempts to reframe, it is essential that the therapist have a thorough understanding of the meaning of the precipitant to the client. When working in this field it is also important that the therapist generate and present the reframe in a clear, straightforward manner—not leaving gaps for the client to fill. Such restructuring may need to be repeated on several occasions and feedback solicited from the client. At times a slight change in meaning can reduce the emotional impact and create a situation more amenable to problem-solving strategies.

Matheny and his colleagues also review the use of denial as a tolerating strategy (Matheny et al., 1986). Recent literature has suggested that in times of crises it may be useful to deny the seriousness of a difficult situation (Lazarus, 1981). This strategy is mentioned as a tool; however, its utility and value are limited. Perhaps in highly select situations where the stressor is clearly overwhelming, denial may be of value.

The reduction of physiological arousal is also of value in tolerating stress. This can be accomplished in a variety of ways which can be discussed with clients. These include exercise, muscle relaxation, breathing exercises, diversions, and entertainment. All of the aforementioned approaches reduce arousal; however, the value is clearly palliative and has no direct bearing on the ongoing influence of the precipitant. In other words, without some cognitive shifting in the perceptions of the stressor, the crisis will persist.

Clients can also be medicated to reduce arousal. In situations of disruptive behavior, sedative medications may be of value. However, the lessons taught by repeated use of medicated responses to crises are both damaging and potentially addictive. No learning occurs that better prepares the client for the next crisis. Rather, he or she learns that he or she is emotionally unequipped to handle such situations.

In times of crisis, social support can be an asset in tolerating emotional pain. Friends, relatives, and professional staff provide the opportunity to cathart, but also allow the unstable client to experience stability—even in a state of emotional disarray. The source of emotional strength derived from solid social relationships is not well delineated and remains a difficult construct to research. It is also generally considered to be of greater value as a preventative coping resource, although studies support its value as a tolerating resource during periods of stress (Matheny et al., 1986).

System Supports

Although the focus of this chapter is on individual psychotherapeutic interventions, our discussion of crisis intervention would be incomplete without a review of systemic interventions. This is particularly important in working with persons with mental retardation because a majority of our clients are supported residentially or vocationally by institutions or agencies. These agencies offer the potential for an umbrella of support in times of crisis; however, the difficulty may be one of generating and coordinating efforts of support.

The first issue for any system sharing responsibility for the client in crisis is safety—of both the client and others. The initial assessment of the client must indicate potential for either suicidal and homicidal behavior. Whenever risk is present, the counselor is obligated to monitor ideation and to utilize institutional resources to protect all parties. If safety cannot be reasonably assured, then transfer to a more secure setting is in order.

Depending on client input, the counselor may or may not have a clear understanding of the precipitant. If the client is unable to identify the source, often the crisis represents the culmination of a series of escalating problems. There may have been signs of increasing anxiety, withdrawal, or acting out behavior. In our experience with this sort of crisis, the problem is frequently a breakdown in the systemic supports. Often these appear minor, but to the client such changes may represent major adjustments for which they have no support. These may be roommate changes, schedule alterations, a friend who has forgotten to write, and so forth. However, a commonly overlooked precipitant is the normal ebb and flow of staff energy and commitment. Certain "high need" clients demand more attention, and when staff energy drops, so do reinforcement schedules (both formal and informal). This issue is raised because the source of the problem can be easily overlooked. With proper identification, however, the solution is readily available.

In situations where no apparent breakdown in systemic supports has occurred, the availability of structured environments can complement efforts in therapy. The system changes that are suggested will be integrated into the client's routine smoothly if plans are fully discussed with the client. Several relatively simple guidelines appear helpful. First, an increase in environmental structure is more therapeutic than a decrease in structure. The specific activities should be low pressure but steady, in order that time is limited for ruminative behavior. Second, social support can be increased, with greater opportunity for client catharsis and staff reinforcement. Third, at times a transfer to a more structured program with new personnel is therapeutic to both client and staff. The client is occupied by learning the rules of the new system and receives support from unbiased staff, while regular staff receive a break.

The final issue that seems universally neglected by agencies that work with persons with mental retardation is the obvious lack of "planning for crises." Individuals with mental retardation present with more crises than other populations; however, this fact goes unnoticed. There remains a decided risk for return to crisis, and it is this event for which the counselor should prepare the client. As the client recovers, the therapist can emphasize how the client is coping and discuss the need to utilize those skills in future crises. Staff and parents can also be informed of early signs. Furthermore, preventative coping strategies can be taught to the client, such as how to avoid stressors, how to develop coping resources, social skill training, and time management skills. Coupled with this training can be the development of an explicit plan that goes into effect when early warning signals are present.

Efficacy of Individual Psychotherapy with Persons with Mental Retardation

As evidenced by the subheading, the purpose of this section is to review the empirical literature on the effectiveness of psychotherapy with persons with mental retardation. Such a review would normally consist of dissecting the topic area into major groupings that share theoretical, conceptual, or methodological similarities. Following this, certain criteria are usually established for acceptable research, and then the individual studies are examined for conceptual, methodological, and statistical rigor. Conclusions are usually drawn by tabulating supportive and nonsupportive evidence of the studies judged to be of acceptable quality.

Such a review cannot be done with the current status of both the quality and quantity of research that examines psychotherapy with this population. Complaints about the paucity of good research in this area are not new, and a number of reviewers have drawn attention to this over the last several decades (Bialer, 1967; Lott, 1970; Nuffield, 1983; Sternlicht, 1965). Unfortunately, the number of requests for research continue to be greater than the number of rigorous research studies.

This situation dictates several changes in the content and objectives of this review. The various approaches to individual psychotherapy will not be reviewed independently, as there is insufficient information to determine precisely what is going on in therapy for most of the studies. No standards are established for acceptable research, because even minimally acceptable standards for experimental research would omit the bulk of the studies available. Furthermore, the studies discussed will not be rigorously examined on the basis of conceptual and methodological quality, as the entire review would be consumed by criticism.

Instead this review will cover most of the available literature that has attempted to evaluate any form of individual psychotherapy. The objective is to acquaint the reader with what has been done and to focus upon tentative conclusions which, while lacking experimental rigor, point optimistically to the value of therapy. In the past the term "psychotherapy" has been used liberally by writers in this field, encompassing everything from psychodrama, music therapy, occupational therapy, milieu therapy, group counseling, nondirective and directive psychotherapy, and analytically oriented psychotherapy. The focus of this review will be on interventions that are conceptually based in a psychological model.

Before proceeding it is important to note that many of the studies reviewed are somewhat antiquated, having been conducted prior to 1960. During that era it was generally accepted that limited intelligence had such a profound impact on social awareness and personal insight that the person with mental retardation was limited in his or her capacity to experience mental and/or emotional distress. Morgan (1950) emphasized that persons with mental retardation were less likely to suffer from mental conflict, and those that are experienced are "out in the open." He further states that the conflicts are between impulses and society. If the impulses are stronger, the person becomes a criminal. If social pressures are stronger, he or she remains moral. Morgan notes, however, that mental conflict is between "ideals" and "reality," which requires intelligence. And, according to Morgan, this is a process persons with mental retardation do not experience.

The reader is reminded of this set of beliefs in order to provide the context for these early studies. Mainstream psychology and mental health professionals did not view these individuals as having the capacity for either emotional distress or emotional healing through therapy. This perspective was unfortunately supported by an early study in which the results of psychotherapy with 400 children revealed a consistent trend (Healy & Bronner, 1936). The authors found a strong relationship between IQ and treatment outcome, with approximately 66% of the children with IQs between 70–79 identified as treatment failures, 23% of those with IQs between 80–90 considered failures, and only 10% of those with IQs over 110 noted as treatment failures. Although the study emphasized caution in the interpretation of the findings, the writers concluded nonetheless that psychotherapy seemed inappropriate for the individual with mental retardation.

These findings contrast with a similar study by Glassman (1943). Traditional psychotherapy was utilized with two groups of children, one group with IQs between 80 and 90, and another group with IQs greater than 110. In addition, a no treatment control group was used, and all groups were matched on age, sex, economic status, and home situation. Outcome was evaluated by comparing therapists' ratings and parental evaluations (when available). Results indicated that the children with mild cognitive deficits benefited as much from psychotherapy as did the "normal" children.

An additional study by Cooley (1945) also compared the outcome of psychotherapy between children with and without mental retardation. The cases were matched for sex, age, and economic status. The IQ range for group one was 47–85, whereas all members of group two attained IQs greater than 115. Results indicated no significant differences between groups on a rating of adjustment at the close of therapy, and no need for differential amounts of therapeutic contact. Each group seemed to benefit equally well from the same amount of treatment.

The studies by Glassman (1943) and Cooley (1945) are the best examples of the older experimental research in this area. Control groups were utilized and attempts were made to match subjects. Unfortunately the precise nature of the psychotherapy treatment is unknown, and although outcome measures were not objective, the findings are suggestive of a positive response to individual therapy.

It is also out of this context that much of the initial research focused on change in IQ as an outcome variable in therapy. The term "pseudoretardation" evolved as a disorder of limited intelligence produced by extreme emotional distress. Hypothetically, personality patterns could be modified by psychotherapy, which would result in a concomitant increase in IQ. This "discovery" of emotional distress in the persons with mental retardation led to an unfortunate association between potential for improvement in IQ. The enticement of curing mental retardation led to a research focus on using psychotherapy to increase IQ. Some rather astounding results reported by Schmidt (1948) seemed to support this notion. In a well-controlled environment that included teaching, support, and psychotherapy, the author demonstrated an average IQ gain of 40.7 points over a 5-year period.

Although her methods were challenged (e.g., Kirk, 1948), other authors were reporting improvements in IQ. In a case study by Chidester and Menninger (1936), the IQs of several children increased between 10 and 34 points during treatment. Axline (1949) reports the case of a 5-year-old boy whose IQ was increased from 68 to 96 following 1 year of play therapy. Similar results were reported by Dichter (1962), who obtained improvement in both IQ and emotional difficulties following treatment by play therapy.

Two issues are of importance when discussing these studies. First, these findings are plagued with methodological problems, some of which are unique to the measurement of IQ in children. Results from IQ assessments vary greatly with young children, with wide fluctuation during periods of early development.

More germane to this discussion is the second issue; if these results are accepted as valid, it is assumed that an intellectual impairment exists secondary to an emotional disturbance (Bialer, 1967). The client does not have mental retardation, but rather is responding as if mental retardation is present. This has implications for diagnosis and treatment that are beyond the scope of this chapter.

However, such a perspective also tends to take the focus off areas where psychotherapy is likely to be effective. Although some of the studies to be reviewed noted changes in IQ, our emphasis will be on the psychosocial outcomes of therapy, as these are more consistent with the broad objectives of conducting psychotherapy with persons with mental retardation. It is also the area where the impact of therapy has been most effective, as might be expected. The following discussion will focus on those studies that examine the influence of psychotherapy on these psychosocial dimensions. An example of an early report that examined the influence of individual psychotherapy is that published by Thorne (1948), based on his work at Brandon State School in Vermont. The author initiated attempts to establish an accepting, therapeutic atmosphere in an institution for individuals with mental retardation. As part of the treatment program, clients were offered individual and group therapy, play therapy, psychodrama, and occupational therapy. Although the author does not identify the relative proportion of time involved in the various therapies, there is an emphasis on the importance of ongoing counseling and psychotherapy. Clients were taught to utilize the therapist as a resource when they encountered problems, and apparently the institution maintained an open door policy that allowed clients to problem-solve current difficulties. Although the author referred to the subjects as children, they ranged from young children to middle-aged adults. Outcome criteria were not objectively quantified; however, the author subjectively evaluated the status of 68 clients after 2 years of therapy and rated 45 as improved, 16 as unchanged, and 7 as worse. Few definitive conclusions can be drawn from this study, but it nonetheless remains an excellent example of the type of research findings available. The conclusions are supportive of the efficacy of individual therapies; however, multiple ill-defined interventions and the absence of experimental methodology leave us with only the clinical impressions of the author, who believed many of his clients improved.

In a study that combined play therapy with individual psychotherapy, Mundy (1957) reported the results of working with 23 multiply handicapped children. Children were seen over a period of 9 to 12 months, with 15 of the 23 demonstrating progress in social interactions and language development. Treatment was undertaken with the assumption that emotional understanding was more significant than intellectual comprehension. Some interpretations were offered, but these remained simple and direct. The emphasis was placed on experience rather than verbalization of process. Again, there are no objective criteria for evaluation and controls are lacking; however, the evidence is supportive.

Heiser (1954) reported on a program that provided individual psychotherapy to 14 clients with mental retardation, ranging in age from 8 to 32. The median IQ was 67, and behavioral outbursts were the predominant presenting concern. Therapy was provided by six different therapists and no attempt was made to assess similarity in therapeutic styles. The type of intervention strategy and length of treatment were determined on an individual basis, with the therapist choosing between supportive problem-solving therapy and more interpretive therapy. The author found 12 of 14 clients improved following a maximum of 58 individual sessions. The only objective outcome data reported were IQ scores, which indicated a mean change of an additional 3 points.

In a descriptive study, Hayes (1977) compared the effectiveness of psychoanalytically oriented psychotherapy with children with and without mental retardation in roughly matched groups of 20. The children with mental retardation ranged in age from 7 to 18 with most falling in the mild mental retardation range. Treatment lasted from 8 to 48 months, with the mode in the 18- to 24-month range. Although treatments were individualized for all subjects and the full range of psychoanalytic modalities were utilized, attempts were made to make the treatments equivalent. In each group, 15 of the subjects with mental retardation were globally rated as showing at least some improvement, whereas 14 of the subjects without retardation showed the same level of improvement. In fact, data regarding length of treatment, utilization of combinations of services (e.g., parent counseling along with child counseling), and other more psychoanalytically oriented outcome measures were relatively similar for both groups. Hayes concluded that the overall nature of treatment and outcome between the children with and without mental retardation were essentially similar. He concluded that there are children with mental retardation who can benefit from psychoanalytically oriented psychotherapy, and the views that they are "untreatable" are unfounded.

Although the studies reported are lacking in experimental rigor, there appears to be a gradual, steady buildup of clinical support in these group studies. Other studies have been primarily case studies with both children and adults. These are presented to illustrate further the base of clinical support for the efficacy of individual psychotherapy.

Glass (1957) reported a case study of a 12-year-old boy with behavior problems at home and at school. IQ scores ranged from 60–78, and the boy was also epileptic. He had a history of aggression and property destruction, and was treated with individual therapy that the author termed "relationship therapy." There is little information about what occurred during therapy, except that there were no interpretations or clarifications of feelings as found in traditional psychotherapy. As is frequently the case, the reader is left to determine what happened in therapy by omitting processes that did not occur and then developing a concept of the therapeutic procedure by combining the remaining options, perhaps best described as description by omission, rather than commission. Regardless of our disappointment with not knowing what went on in therapy, the author noted an improvement in behavior.

Further support is obtained from Friedman (1961), who reports the case of a child with IQ scores ranging from 51 to 72 who received individual psychotherapy. Therapy consisted of an initial 6-month period of highly permissive play and reinforcement from the therapist. As behavior began to improve, the child became more verbally interactive and therapy shifted toward intensive interviews. The author noted considerable transference which was utilized during the later part of therapy. Behavioral outbursts, which had been extreme at times, were reduced to the point that the client returned to the community with adequate adjustment. The therapist did maintain extended contact with the client following his release.

In a similar case study, Dichter (1962) utilized highly permissive play therapy that transitioned into more verbally oriented therapy. The client was a 10-year-old boy with an IQ of 72 and a history of emotional difficulties. Improvement was measured only by clinical judgment, with the author focusing on behavioral improvement, as well as increased social skills and self-esteem.

In a more recent discussion, Bernstein (1985) reports on three cases of psychotherapy, two of which were adolescent females and one an adult male. Measured IQs ranged from 55 to 67, and presenting problems were not unlike those found in a typical mental health clinic. In each case the author described a form of verbal psychotherapy that involved exploration of feelings, problem solving, direction, and support. The author emphasized the importance of certain process variables, such as establishing a trusting relationship and actively seeking resolutions to problems. No objective outcome data were offered, but in each case the presenting problem was resolved and the clients adjusted to their current life situation without further incident.

Gloria: A Rational-Emotive Case Study

Gloria was a 19-year-old student with mild mental retardation enrolled in a vocational training program. Although she was doing well in her training program and had the requisite skills to advance into competitive employment, she had presented significant problems with controlling her temper and at times became physically aggressive toward other students. The physical aggression had placed her at risk for being terminated from her training program. She had recently completed a 10-week group for persons with anger problems, but there was no noticeable change in her outbursts or aggressive behavior. This group had focused largely on the affective aspects of anger using a nondirective "exploring" mode.

The initial task with Gloria was to put the anger outbursts into an A-B-C format. After some interviewing and a week-long period where Gloria kept track of her outbursts, it was determined that the outbursts occurred at work and in the community when someone called her a name. The word "bitch" seemed to be particularly problematic for her. Thus, the "A" was being called a name ("Gloria, you're a bitch") and the "C" was an anger response. At this point, the therapist role-played a work situation with Gloria in which a minor dispute ended with the therapist calling Gloria a "bitch." Based on the role-play, Gloria was able to describe a number of cognitive aspects of her reaction. She equated the word "bitch" with "slut" or "whore" and automatically assumed that she was being described in this manner. She also stated that it was awful and horrible to be called names and that it should never happen.

The disputation phase focused on all these cognitive aspects. First, the accuracy of her assessment of the meaning of the word "bitch" was addressed. The therapist directly disagreed with her definition and offered a more commonly accepted definition. Although Gloria didn't like the other definition, she found it more palatable than the sexually oriented definition. Gloria was also taught to say to her self, "What do they mean?" when someone used the word. This served two purposes. First, it slowed her down to assess the situation so she would not instantly lose her temper, and second, it forced her to evaluate the situation. In almost all cases, she found herself using the alternative definition provided by the therapist. The therapy also used additional role plays in which she practiced using the technique. This also desensitized her to the word "bitch." In fact, she reacted with laughter when called a name in the role plays. The therapy also addressed the cognitive belief that it was awful to be called a name and that it shouldn't ever happen. After some discussion, she was able to agree that it was not fun being called a name, but it wasn't awful or horrible. The therapist also asked Gloria to keep track (by counting) of every time she heard someone else called a name in her workshop setting. When she brought back a tally of 74 "name-calls" for one week, she became somewhat more convinced that being called a name was inevitable and she gave up the belief that it shouldn't ever happen. She obviously still didn't like being called a name, but reacted much more moderately. This RET intervention spanned a total of seven sessions. Follow-up indicated that the outbursts has been completely eliminated. Further, Gloria reported that she was able to use her "new thinking" in other situations.

Robert: A Person-Centered Case Study

Robert, a 41-year-old male with mild mental retardation, was living in large group home and working in a supervised setting, primarily in food service activities. He had lived in this residence for almost 15 years and had worked at the same job for the last 7 years, with generally positive adjustment in both settings. Recently, staff at both the residence and at his work noticed significant changes in his behavior. He was becoming increasingly withdrawn and was almost nonverbal, responding with one-word or very brief answers. He rarely smiled and in general appeared depressed. At work, he was reluctant to try any new tasks and avoided contact with staff and other co-workers. His behavior change coincided with an announcement that the large group home would be closing in favor of several smaller residences. This announcement had been greeted positively by most other clients in the residence, but apparently had been the precipitant for Robert's unhappiness. Attempts at reducing his withdrawal with a behavior plan had not been successful.

The meetings with Robert were held away from the residence. At the beginning of the first session, Robert totally avoided eye contact as the counselor explained that some people at the house (group home) were concerned that he didn't seem very happy lately. The counselor also explained that what they talked about was up to Robert and that it was his choice whether he came back. Robert continued to avoid eye contact and sat slumped in his chair occasionally sighing and clenching his fists. After several minutes, the counselor reflected on what appeared to be anger on Robert's part ("It seems as if you are feeling angry about something"). At this, Robert looked up briefly at the counselor, averted his eyes again, and mumbled "moving." The counselor responded: " You're concerned about moving from the group home." Robert nodded and then said that he couldn't stop thinking about the move, with the counselor responding that a big move like that must be "scary." The remainder of the initial session focused on the affective reactions that Robert was experiencing in anticipation of the move. At the end of the session, the counselor reiterated a desire to meet with Robert again, but that it was Robert's choice to return.

At the next session, Robert was more spontaneous and indicated that he really needed someone to talk to about the move. Through a series of indirect leads (e.g., "There's going to be a lot of changes in your life"), empathic reflections ("You're feeling sad about not living with some of your friends"), and restatement ("You're not sure what living in a smaller house is going to be like"), two major issues were apparent in Robert's case. First, he was experiencing a range of emotions (anger, sadness) about having to leave his home and some of his friends. Second, he was very anxious about the adjustment and his acceptance by people in the new residence ("You're afraid that they won't like you there"). Much of the discussion centered on Robert's view of himself and his worthiness. It became clear that because of his long tenure and comfort level in the old residence and work setting, his personal adjustment had not been challenged by changes and he had given little thought to his acceptance by others. The move prompted a difficult self-examination.

Robert and the counselor met for a total of 14 sessions. The focus continued to be on the affective reactions and the self-examination that related to the move and life changes. Robert continued to be more open and clearly looked forward to his meetings with the counselor. Robert was able to articulate his "worries," with the counselor primarily reflecting and restating the concerns. The sessions continued during and several weeks after the move, when Robert pronounced himself "OK" and not needing to come to counseling anymore. Reports from the residence and work program substantiated the improvement, with decreased withdrawal and staff notations that the "old Robert" had returned.

References

Aguilerre, D. C., & Messick, J. M. (1974). *Crisis intervention: Theory and methodology.* St. Louis, MO: Mosby.

Arlow, J. A. (1989). Psychoanalysis. In R. J. Corsini & D. Wedding (Eds.), *Current psychotherapies* (4th ed., pp. 19-64). Itasca, IL: F. E. Peacock.

Axline, V. M. (1949). Mental deficiency: Symptom or disease? *Journal of Consulting Psychology, 13*, 313-327.

Bandler, R., & Grinder, J. (1976). *The structure of magic: A book about communication* (Vol. 2). Palo Alto, CA: Science and Behavior Books.

Beck, A. T., Rush, A. J., Shaw, B. F., & Emery, G. (1979). *Cognitive therapy of depression.* New York: Guilford Press.

Beck, A. T., & Weishaar, M. E. (1989). Cognitive therapy. In R. J. Corsini & D. Wedding (Eds.), *Current psychotherapies* (4th ed., pp. 285-322). Itasca, IL: F. E. Peacock.

Bellak, L., & Small, L. (1978). *Emergency psychotherapy and brief psychotherapy* (2nd ed.). New York: Grune & Stratton.

Bergin, A. E., & Lambert, M. J. (1978). The evaluation of therapeutic outcomes. In S. L. Garfield & A. E. Bergin (Eds.), *Handbook of psychotherapy and behavior change: An empirical analysis* (2nd ed., pp. 139-189). New York: Wiley.

Bernstein, N. R. (1985). Psychotherapy of the mentally retarded adolescent. In S. C. Feinstein (Ed.), *Adolescent psychiatry* (pp. 406-413). Chicago: University of Chicago Press.

Bialer, I. (1967). Psychotherapy and other adjustment techniques with the mentally retarded. In A. A. Baumeister (Ed.), *Mental retardation: Appraisal, education, and rehabilitation* (pp. 178-202). Chicago, IL: Aldine.

Boy, A. V., & Pine, G. J. (1982). *Client-centered counseling: A renewal.* Boston: Allyn & Bacon.

Chidester, L., & Menninger, K. A. (1936). The application of psychoanalytic methods to the study of mental retardation. *American Journal of Orthopsychiatry, 6,* 616-625.

Cooley, J. M. (1936). The relative amenability of dull and bright children to child guidance. *Smith College Studies in Social Work, 16,* 26-43.

Corcoran, J. R. (1982). Affect Abilities Training—A competency based method for counseling persons with mental retardation. *Journal of Career Education, 8,* 301-311.

Dichter, A. (1962). Psychotherapy for the mentally retarded. *Pathways in Child Guidance, 4,* 11-12.

Ellis, A. (1962). *Reason and emotion in psychotherapy.* New York: Lyle Stewart and Citadel Press.

Ellis, A. (1973). *Humanistic psychotherapy: The rational-emotive approach.* New York: Julian Press and McGraw-Hill Paperbacks.

Ellis, A. (1989). Rational-emotive therapy. In R. J. Corsini & D. Wedding (Eds.), *Current psychotherapies* (4th ed., pp. 197-240). Itasca, IL: F. E. Peacock.

Frank, J. D. (1973). *Persuasion and healing: A comparative study of psychotherapy.* Baltimore, MD: Johns Hopkins University Press.

Friedman, E. (1961). Individual therapy with a "defective delinquent." *Journal of Clinical Psychology, 17,* 229-232.

Fuller, G. B., & Fuller, D. L. (1989). Reality therapy approaches. In D. T. Brown & H. T. Prout (Eds.), *Counseling and psychotherapy with children and adolescents: Theory and practice for school and clinic settings* (2nd ed., pp. 363-428). Brandon, VT: Clinical Psychology Publishing.

Gardner, W. I. (1967). What should be the psychologist's role? *Mental Retardation, 5,* 29-31.

Garfield, S. L. (1978). Research on client variables in psychotherapy. In S. L. Garfield &

A. E. Bergin (Eds.), *Handbook of psychotherapy and behavior change: An empirical analysis* (2nd ed., pp. 191-232). New York: Wiley

Garfield, S. L., & Bergin, A. E. (1986). *Handbook of psychotherapy and behavior change* (3rd ed.). New York: Wiley.

Glass, H. L. (1957). Psychotherapy with the mentally retarded. A case history. *Training School Bulletin, 54*, 32-34.

Glasser, W. (1965). *Reality therapy.* New York: Harper & Row.

Glasser, W. (1981). *Stations of the mind.* New York: Harper & Row.

Glassman, L. (1943). Is dull normal intelligence a contraindication for psychotherapy. *Smith College Studies in Social Work, 13*, 275-298.

Goldstein, A. P., & Myers, C. R. (1986). Relationship enhancement methods. In F. H. Kanfer & A. P. Goldstein (Eds.), *Helping people change* (3rd ed., pp. 19-65). New York: Pergamon.

Grieger, R. M., & Boyd, J. D. (1989). Rational-emotive approaches. In D. T. Brown & H. T. Prout (Eds.), *Counseling and psychotherapy with children and adolescents: Theory and practice for school and clinic settings* (2nd ed., pp. 303-362). Brandon, VT: Clinical Psychology Publishing.

Hayes, M. (1977). The responsiveness of mentally retarded children to psychotherapy. *Smith College Studies in Social Work, 47,* 112-153.

Healy, W., & Bronner, A. F. (1936). *Treatment and what happened afterwards.* Boston: Judge Baker Guidance Center.

Heiser, K. F. (1954). Psychotherapy in a residential school for mentally retarded children. *Training School Bulletin, 50*, 211-218.

Higginbotham, N., West, J., & Forsyth, S. (1988). *Psychotherapy and behavior change.* New York: Pergamon.

Hinterkopf, E., Prouty, G., & Brunswick, L. (1979). A pilot study of pretherapy method applied to chronic schizophrenic patients. *Psychosocial Rehabilitation Journal, 3*, 11-19.

Kirk, S. (1948). An evaluation of the study of Bernadine G. Schmidt. *Journal of Exceptional Children, 15*, 34-40.

Lazarus, A. A. (1981). *The practice of multimodal therapy.* New York: McGraw-Hill.

Levitas, A. S., & Gibson, S. F. (1989). Psychotherapy with mildly and moderately retarded patients. In F. J. Menolascino & R. Fletcher (Eds.), *Mental retardation and mental illness: Assessment, treatment, and service delivery for the dually diagnosed* (pp. 96-122). Lexington, MA: Lexington Books.

Lott, G. (1970). Psychotherapy of the mentally retarded: Values and cautions. In F. J. Menolascino (Ed.), *Psychiatric approaches to mental retardation* (pp. 227-250). New York: Basic Books.

Matheny, K. B., Aycock, D. W., Pugh, J. L., Curlette, W. L., & Cannella, K. A. S. (1986). Stress coping: A qualitative and quantitative synthesis with implications for treatment. *Counseling Psychologist, 14*, 499-549.

Maultsby, M. C. (1975). Rational behavior therapy for acting out adolescents. *Social Casework, 56,* 35-43.

Moore, H. B. (1989). Person-centered approaches. In D. T. Brown & H. T. Prout (Eds.), *Counseling and psychotherapy with children and adolescents: Theory and practice for school and clinic settings* (2nd ed., pp. 167-232). Brandon, VT: Clinical Psychology Publishing.

Morgan, J. J. B. (1950). *The psychology of the unadjusted school child.* New York: MacMillan.

Mundy, L. (1957). Therapy with physically and mentally handicapped children. *Journal of Clinical Psychology, 13*, 321-327.

Nuffield, E. J. (1983). Psychotherapy. In J. L. Matson & J. A. Mulick (Eds.), *Handbook of mental retardation* (pp. 351-368). New York: Pergamon.

Prouty, G. (1976). Pre-therapy—A method of treating pre-expressive psychotic and retarded patients. *Psychotherapy: Theory, Research, and Practice, 13*, 290-294.

Prouty, G. (1986). The pre-symbolic structure and therapeutic transformation of hallucinations. In M. Wolpin, J. E. Shorr, & L. Krueger (Eds.), *Imagery* (Vol. 4), pp. 99-106.

Raskin, N. J., & Rogers, C. R. (1989). Person-centered therapy. In R. J. Corsini & D. Wedding (Eds.), *Current psychotherapies* (4th ed. pp. 155-196). Itasca, IL: F. E. Peacock.

Rogers, C. R. (1951). *Client-centered therapy.* Boston: Houghton-Mifflin.

Rogers, C. R. (1957). The necessary and sufficient conditions of therapeutic personality change. *Journal of Consulting Psychology, 21*, 95-103.

Schmidt, B. G. (1948). Changes in personal, social, and intellectual behavior of children originally classified as feebleminded. *Psychological Monographs, 60*, No. 5. Washington, DC: American Psychological Association.

Sternlicht, M. (1965). Psychotherapeutic techniques useful with the mentally retarded: A review and critique. *Psychiatric Quarterly, 39*, 84-90.

Strupp, H. H. (1978). Psychotherapy research and practice: An overview. In S. L. Garfield & A. E. Bergin (Eds.), *Handbook of psychotherapy and behavior change: An empirical analysis* (2nd ed., pp. 3-22). New York: Wiley.

Szymanski, L. S. (1980). Individual psychotherapy with retarded persons. In L. S. Szymanski & P. S. Tanguay (Eds.), *Emotional disorders of mentally retarded persons* (pp. 131-148). Baltimore, MD: University Park Press.

Tache, J., & Selye, H. (1978). On stress and coping mechanisms. In C. Spielberger & I. Sarason (Eds.), *Stress and anxiety* (Vol. 5, pp. 3-24). Washington, DC: Hemisphere.

Thorne, F. C. (1948). Counseling and psychotherapy with mental defectives. *American Journal of Mental Deficiency, 52*, 263-271.

Zigler, E. (1969). Developmental versus difference theories of mental retardation and the problem of maturation. *American Journal of Mental Deficiency, 73*, 536-556.

5 INDIVIDUAL BEHAVIORAL COUNSELING APPROACHES

Douglas C. Strohmer and Paul M. Spengler

Only recently, and relatively late in the historical development of systems of counseling and psychotherapy, have *behavioral counseling* approaches been considered with persons with mild mental retardation or borderline intelligence (cf. Reiss, Levitan, & McNally, 1982). A recent review of the counseling and mental retardation literature suggests that the use of behavioral counseling approaches with persons with low intelligence began substantially later than these techniques were actually developed. By contrast, other therapeutic approaches, including psycho-analytic (e.g., Ackerman & Menninger, 1936; Chidester & Menninger, 1936) and client-centered therapy (e.g., Neham, 1951), were attempted with persons of low intelligence around the time these techniques initially appeared in the literature. In fact, the treatment of emotional and behavioral problems in this population has been characterized by the dominant use, particularly over the last several decades, of operant behavioral procedures that modify environmental antecedents and contin-gencies with the goal of decreasing maladaptive or unwanted behaviors. (See Bornstein, Bach, & Anton, 1982.) The central premise underlying this chapter is that viewing persons with mild mental retardation or borderline intelligence from a positive *skills enhancement* or *training* perspective, as characterizes the compre-hensive behavioral counseling approach we present in this chapter, is long overdue.

In this chapter we discuss the use of individual behavioral counseling ap-proaches with individuals with mild retardation or borderline intelligence. First, a structured approach for the use of behavioral counseling techniques is suggested, then each approach is reviewed both in terms of research and application. Behavioral counseling techniques reviewed in this section are: behavioral contracting, self-monitoring, modeling, relaxation training, systematic desensitization, behavior rehearsal, and cognitive-behavior modification.

In order to use one or more of the behavioral counseling approaches described in this chapter effectively, counselors should be certain that their clients understand the nature of both counseling in general and the role of specific techniques in their counseling. It is important to ensure that clients have a good understanding of what to expect from counseling. The following section reviews issues related to educating clients as to the rules, roles, and expectations of counseling.

Providing a Systematic Structure for Counseling

Although providing clients with an understanding of the structure of counseling is thought to be an important factor contributing to effectiveness with all types of clients (e.g., Stewart, Winborn, Johnson, Burks, & Engelkes, 1978), it is even more critically important in counseling with individuals who are cognitively limited (Hurley & Hurley, 1986). Structure provides clients with a realistic understanding about the counselor and counseling and gives them some idea of what is involved in the counseling methods to be used.

Not unlike many clients with normal intelligence, individuals with mental retardation may come to counseling with preconceived notions about what will happen in counseling and what they are expected to do. Some clients may come to counseling with the idea that they are "in trouble," whereas others may come thinking that the counselor is a "miracle worker" (Nay, 1984). Additionally, individuals with mental retardation are frequently accustomed to dependency relationships in which their important decisions are made by others, rather than by themselves—not in consultation with another, as is the situation in counseling. In any case, unless these issues are addressed in the early stages of counseling, clients are likely to be less open and honest about their concerns and may not understand the need to be active participants.

Clients in general, and in particular clients with lower intelligence, need to have their question agenda addressed before beginning counseling. Issues of confidentiality, expectations, responsibilities, and the general process of counseling are likely to be misunderstood. This is typically true even if a client has seen a counselor previously, because the choice of methods among counselors varies considerably. Finally, providing clients with a solid understanding of counseling is even more important because of the growing recognition of "clients' right to know" (e.g., Hansen, Stevic, & Warner, 1986).

Several areas for education or structuring are important to consider. Stewart et al. (1978) proposed a framework that is useful in helping counselors to educate clients about counseling. They suggested that counselors must educate clients in four areas: the purpose of counseling, the responsibilities of the client and the counselor, the focus of counseling, and the limits of counseling. These areas, and their application to individuals with mild retardation or borderline intelligence, are discussed below.

Explaining the Purpose of Counseling

First, it is important that the client understand the purpose of counseling. If the client has misconceptions or unrealistic expectations about counseling, then success in addressing concerns will be difficult to achieve. Some clients may be accustomed to counselors who are authority figures or disciplinarians. Others may think of counselors as "shrinks" who deal only with "sick people." Thus it is important that counselors communicate to clients that the counseling situation is one in which they can address their problems and try to solve them. They must understand that it is not uncommon to experience problems and to need help dealing with them. Counseling can be described as a learning situation, where clients will learn—with the counselor's help—to cope with, or handle, their problems. It is important that clients understand that the counselor is not going to solve their problems for them, but rather will help them to learn to solve their own problems.

Explaining the Responsibilities of the Client and the Counselor

The counselor should explain the nature of his or her intended role with the client. Although the specifics may vary from counseling setting to counseling setting, the counselor's general responsibilities are to listen to the client's concerns and problems, and to help the client learn to handle them effectively. Counselors are not responsible for solving problems; rather, they try to help people come to their own solutions. Counselors provide someone to talk to about problems, and a safe environment to try out new solutions.

Clients' responsibilities are to talk about concerns and problems as openly and honestly as they can. They should also understand that counseling might involve them trying out new ways of thinking and behaving. Their ultimate responsibility is to learn to handle their own problems with the help of their counselor. It must be clear that the counselee is the one who makes life decisions and choices in counseling.

Explaining the Focus of Counseling

Behaviorally oriented counseling is, by nature of the techniques selected, goal oriented, and clients should understand this. The counselor should explain that counseling will focus on one concern at a time. By prioritizing concerns, it is possible to select the most important or sequentially logical concern to address, and then to select techniques to address that concern. Clients should be aware both of the direction of counseling and of the reason for selecting a particular treatment.

Explaining the Limits of Counseling

It is essential that clients understand the nature of the limits of their relationship with their counselor. The counselor should be clear in communicating the types of concerns that he or she is able or willing to address. If there is a limit in terms of the number of sessions or time period that services will be available, clients should know this from the beginning. A critical component of educating clients about the limits of counseling concerns the confidentiality of information. Clients should be clear about confidentiality, and counselors should be absolutely certain that their clients grasp the concept.

Once clients are clear about the nature, limits, goals, and responsibilities of counseling, their concerns can be detailed, goals set, and appropriate behavioral counseling approaches selected to meet the goals. The following sections review a variety of behavioral counseling techniques useful in counseling with individuals with mild mental retardation or borderline intelligence.

Behavioral Counseling Techniques: Research and Application

The following sections review in detail a number of behavioral counseling techniques. Some are commonly used with individuals with mental retardation. Although others are less commonly used, they are presented here as useful to and appropriate for the concerns presented by clients with mental retardation. Each technique will be considered from four perspectives: a definition of the technique, general research concerning the technique, research specific to use of the technique with special population clients, and the specific steps used in applying the technique in counseling. Although these approaches are discussed individually, it is quite common and very appropriate to use them in combinations, as the individual counseling situation dictates.

Behavioral Contracting

Definition: Behavioral contracting is a technique which uses a written statement of specific actions that the client agrees to undertake and which establishes both positive and negative consequences for fulfillment and nonfulfillment of the agreement (e.g., Kanfer & Gaelick, 1986). Behavior contracts structure the counselor's activities with clients by making each of the necessary elements of the behavior change process so clear and explicit that they may be written into an agreement that is understandable and acceptable to everyone involved. (Strohmer, 1987)

It is important to note in this definition that the term "contract" is used in a business sense. Just as business contracts are negotiated, so too are behavior contracts. Business contracts, and behavior contracts, imply an agreement that benefits all parties to the agreement. Similarly all effective behavior contracts are negotiated, with give and take on both sides. Contracts are frequently used with other behavioral counseling techniques and can provide a very tangible motivator in a variety of situations.

General Research: Behavioral contracts have been found to be useful in a variety of settings, and with a variety of problems. Reports of successful contract use are available in cases of addictive behaviors (Bigelow, Sticker, Leibson, & Griffiths, 1976; Boudin, 1972), weight control (Jeffery, Gerber, Rosenthal, & Lindquist, 1983), excessive smoking (Spring, Sipich, Trimble, & Goeckner, 1978), marital discord (Jacobson, 1977), and other problem behaviors. Contracts have a variety of positive features that make them effective with individuals needing to make behavior changes. They clarify expectations and consequences (both positive and negative), provide explicit criteria for successful behavior changes, and, perhaps most important, are developed in conjunction with the client, thus enhancing involvement and investment.

Special Population Research: Behavior contracting is also often used with a variety of special population groups. Although commonly used in the experience of the authors, little research examining its effectiveness is reported. We have heard reports of the effective use of behavior contracts with EMR students to improve performance in reading and arithmetic. Student performance significantly increased in both areas when a contract was implemented calling for rewards of sightseeing and picnicking, contingent on school performance.

Behavioral contracting has also been used successfully, in combination with other procedures (e.g., self-monitoring), to treat obese individuals with mental retardation. Similarly, Radler, Hudson, and Boag (1982b) found contracts effective in the treatment of enuresis as a supplement to a more traditional behavior modification approach (i.e., the bell and pad procedure) with adults with mental retardation (For review, see Rotatori, Switzky, & Fox, 1981a,b.)

Despite the paucity of research noted concerning behavior contracts with clients with mental retardation or borderline intelligence, the technique has a variety of features that make it highly appropriate for this group. Foremost among the factors is the explicitness with which expectations are presented to the client. This, coupled with clear communication of consequences, makes contracting a technique that fits well with the needs and limitations of clients with mental retardation or borderline intelligence.

Implementing Behavior Contracts: The following steps detail the procedure for effectively implementing behavior contracts. Following the steps, an example is provided for further clarification.

Step 1. Select one or two behaviors that you and your client want to work on first. It is important that the client understand the significance of increasing or decreasing the behaviors you have in mind. For example, an individual who is assaultive when he or she wants to get out of work might be taught to see how this impacts both on others and on how others react to him or her. In such a circumstance an individual may be motivated to learn more appropriate behaviors and then join the counselor in a mutual problem-solving effort.

Step 2. Describe the behaviors so that they may be observed and counted. Behaviors addressed by behavior contracts must be objective behaviors (i.e., those that are measurable and observable). An important distinction must be drawn between inferences (conclusions drawn from observed behaviors) and the actual behaviors themselves. For example, one might make an inference of anger when one's client yells at another individual. Contracts can deal only with the actual behavior (yelling), and not the inference (anger).

Step 3. Identify rewards that will help provide the motivation to do well. The counselor should help the client develop a list of possible rewards that might result from successful completion of the contract. The client should take the lead in developing the reward(s), to the extent he or she is able. The more clients feel that they have selected their reward, the more invested they will be in the contract, thus creating a higher probability for success.

Step 4. Negotiate and write the contract. Do it so that everyone can agree to it and understand it. Perhaps the most critical aspect of effective contracting is the point at which the negotiation with the client takes place. In order for a true contract to be derived, and the benefits of client interest and involvement to be tapped, the counselor must be prepared to negotiate an agreement with the client. A contract should spell out the behaviors the client needs to change and the benefits that will accrue if he or she does change the behavior. The client must feel that he or she was part of the contracting process. The more the counselor can engage the client in the negotiation process, the greater the chance for successful behavior change. In fact, this may be even more important for individuals with mental retardation, who often feel that they have little control over their environment. Contracts are mutual agreements between the client and the counselor. There must not be threats, or simply statements of policy. Negotiate a positive consequence, a bonus for exceptional performance, a negative consequence, and a penalty for very poor behavior.

Step 5. Set reasonable goals and time limits. The contracting process might best be thought of as sequential (i.e., made up of a number of small steps). It is generally better to have behavior contracts of short duration, calling for modest behavior change. Contracts of this type require frequent updating, but have the advantage of early and frequent client (and counselor) success. Kanfer and Gaelick (1986) state that the success of this type of contracting lies in the fact that "the client is not faced with the overwhelming task of eliminating the undesirable behavior all at once" (p. 173).

Step 6. Contracts should be treated very formally. They should always be in writing, and signed by all relevant individuals. This is critical even if the individual is unable to read. With careful review of the contract with the counselor, the client will understand the meaning—if not the specific wording—of the contract. Signed copies of the contract should be given to all parties. In other words, the behavior contract should be taken *very* seriously. Having a public commitment to the contract, with friends, co-workers, supervisors, or counselors, can help with motivation.

Step 7. Have the client carry his or her copy of the contract at all times. The simple act of carrying the contract is an important reminder of the individual's agreement. If an individual is unable to carry the contract (e.g., his or her job is too dirty or wet), he or she might post it inside his or her locker. Ask that the client review it daily at first, and very frequently (e.g., once a week) after the client understands the contract well. Discuss his or her progress in counseling.

Step 8. Collect data. Locate people who can help you keep track of the behaviors being performed and who can give out the rewards. As the contract progresses, we have found that it is important to increase the individual's control over his or her reinforcers. This enhances the intrinsic (versus extrinsic) aspect of the individual's behavior change. That is, the client will see the change as something done because he or she wanted to do it, rather than because some external contingency forced him or her to do it.

Step 9. Troubleshoot the system if the data do not show improvement. Continue to monitor, troubleshoot, and rewrite until there is improvement in the behaviors that were troublesome.

Step 10. Rewrite the contract frequently. Contracts lose their effectiveness quickly, and so should not be considered "long term." Contracts are fluid and are not longstanding agreements. We have often observed that staff members are reluctant to make frequent changes in the client's contract, preferring to wait for quarterly or even annual reviews to make changes. Such long periods of time are countertherapeutic and mitigate against effective use of contracts.

Step 11. Select another behavior to work on. Behavior contracting assumes a prioritization of client concerns, and so once a behavior is addressed successfully, in most cases another behavior will be selected for attention.

Step 12. Fade behavior contracts. When the client's goals have been met it is time to fade the extrinsic control of the contract. We have often found it useful to suggest that the individual consider the end of contracts as a "graduation" of sorts, helping the individual take pride in his or her accomplishments.

Special Considerations: Critical to the application of all of the above material is that the behavioral contract be just that, a contract. Frequently the authors have observed that individual clients sign behavioral agreements, or statements of policy, which do not meet many of the criteria for a successful contract. Often, a statement of agency rules, and a statement that the individual understands the rules and the consequences for not following them, is considered a contract. Such a written agreement might be important in certain settings but is by no means a behavioral contract. Contracting, first and foremost, involves negotiation. Second, a behavioral contract stresses both the incentive and the penalty. So, although it seems reasonable that certain settings may require individuals to sign a statement of understanding, it seems equally unreasonable to expect such an agreement to have the positive behavior change associated with behavior contracts. It is important to remember that the central ingredient to this type of behavioral counseling is that the client feel in control. The client must feel internally motivated. Behavior contracts developed and carried out in this way are effective in accomplishing this result.

Self-Monitoring

Definition: *Behavioral self-monitoring is a self-management technique in which individuals observe and record their own behaviors. It is an*

Behavior Contract—Example

Effective Date: July 27, 1993

Problem Behaviors:

In this contract verbal abuse is defined as any verbally aggressive action directed toward co-workers or staff (yelling, cursing, name-calling, arguing with supervisor or fellow workers).

In this contract noncompliance is defined as not following a supervisor's instructions on the first request.

Agreement: We, the undersigned parties, agree to perform the following behaviors:

If Nancy works for 4 of 5 days without any verbal abuse or unwillingness to follow directions, for 4 consecutive weeks,

Then, "her counselor" agrees to arrange for Nancy to have an interview with the food service supervisor to talk about working in the kitchen.

Bonus: For every week that Nancy has a perfect week she will earn the opportunity to have her Monday coffee with her counselor.

Penalty: If Nancy has 3 days in 1 week in which she exhibits either verbal abuse to others or unwillingness to follow her supervisor's directions, she will lose her bus privileges for the following week.

Nancy

"Counselor"

"Supervisor"

operation that closely parallels the measurement of behavior in situations where clients are under the continuous observation of their counselor or work supervisor. The very act of self-monitoring has frequently been shown to have a reactive effect in treatment, i.e., the effect of reducing (or under some circumstances increasing) the frequency of the observed or target behavior. Self-monitoring generally involves the use of some form of monitoring device, such as a checklist, graph, or wrist counter.

Although behavioral self-monitoring is frequently used in behavioral assessment as a means of obtaining data useful in making diagnostic and prognostic statements about clients, it is not intended for use in this way as discussed here. Here the oft-noted effect that observing one's own behavior results in bringing this behavior to the individual's immediate attention, and thus frequently results in behavior changes, is our sole intent in discussing the self-monitoring approach.

General Research: Behavioral self-monitoring has proven to be a useful procedure with clients in general. Reduction in targeted behaviors has been noted in studies examining the use of self-monitoring strategies with obese patients (Romanczyk, 1974), with smokers (Abrams & Wilson, 1979), with students having study problems (Johnson & White, 1971), and with agoraphobics (Emmelkamp, 1974). On the other hand, other investigators have failed in efforts to replicate certain of these findings. Kanfer and Gaelick (1986) suggest that the therapeutic benefits of self-monitoring appear to result from a complex interaction of a variety of variables. Factors such as the valance of the target behavior, the client's motivation, the number and kinds of behavior being monitored, and the extent to which feedback and reinforcement are used all appear to influence effectiveness. Still, most critical to all behavior change accomplished with self-monitoring is that it triggers the client's *self-regulatory* processes. By enhancing individuals' level of self-awareness, their ability to self-regulate should increase. Of course this self-regulation can only take effect when individuals are motivated and, most important, possess the requisite skills to modify their old behavior and engage in new behaviors. Recent findings suggest that self-monitoring is useful with clients with mental retardation, as well (Cole & Gardner, 1984). These findings are reviewed below.

Special Population Research: Cole and Gardner (1984) report in their review of this area of research that the reactivity of self-monitoring as a treatment strategy with individuals with mild to severe retardation has been extensively demonstrated. (For further discussion, see Litrownski & Freitas, 1980; Litrownski, Freitas, & Franzini, 1978.) It is interesting to note that the evidence suggests the accuracy of the individual's self-monitoring, or self-recording, does not appear to be related to the effectiveness of self-monitoring as a treatment strategy. Zegiob, Klukas, and Junginger (1978) found that the accuracy of self-recording with adolescents with retardation attempting to reduce socially undesirable behavior was not related to the actual reduction in the behavior being addressed in treatment, although self-monitoring did appear to have a positive (reactive) effect. So although research suggests that many individuals with mental retardation may be capable of accurate self-monitoring (Nelson, Lipinski, & Black, 1976), the inability of a given individual with mental retardation or borderline intelligence to self-monitor accurately does not preclude the possibility of benefiting from self-monitoring as a treatment strategy.

The effectiveness of self-monitoring as a treatment approach has been demonstrated in a variety of areas with individuals with mental retardation. A number of researchers have found self-monitoring to be effective in weight loss programs with individuals with mental retardation. It should also be noted that not unlike individuals who are not retarded, clients in the studies to be reviewed had a tendency to regain the weight they lost. Rotatori et al. (1981 a,b) reviewed 11 studies in which self-monitoring was used, sometimes in combination with other treatment approaches, to help children, adolescents, and adults with severe to mild mental retardation lose weight. Weight loss in these studies ranged from an average weight loss of 3.7 pounds for seven children with mild to moderate mental retardation (Rotatori, Parrish, & Freagon, 1979) to 38 pounds in 33 weeks with an adult with mild retardation (Joachim, 1977, cited in Rotatori et al., 1979). The most common approach to self-monitoring in these studies was to have the individual monitor food intake and weight, and in several cases engage in energy expenditure. Some studies combined these approaches with stimulus control and external reinforcement procedures. All of the studies reviewed by Rotatori et al. (1981 a,b) reported significant weight loss. However, as mentioned earlier, maintenance is perhaps the most critical and problematic variable, at least when using self-recording procedures for weight loss (cf. Jackson & Patterson, 1980). It seems clear that regardless of the approach used to help the individual with retardation lose weight, helping him or her to learn new ways of eating and thinking about food intake will be the key to maintenance of weight loss. This remains the primary challenge in this area.

Zohn and Bornstein (1980) report the successful use of self-monitoring to increase work productivity in a sheltered workshop setting. In this research four individuals with moderate retardation were taught to self-monitor their work output (number of hospital kits assembled). Not only was there a moderate increase in work productivity, there was an even more dramatic increase in the quality of the work performed and in the amount of "on-task behavior." It is also interesting to note that the accuracy of self-monitoring performed by these individuals was high, despite the fact that they were functioning at the moderate level of mental retardation.

Other researchers have used self-monitoring to reduce disruptive self-verbalizations of an adult with mental retardation in a vocational skills training setting (Gardner, Cole, & Cole, 1983), to teach subjects with borderline intelligence to count the number of homework (math) problems they finished each night (Mahoney & Mahoney, 1978), to reduce socially undesirable behaviors (nose and mouth picking, and head shaking) among institutionalized female adolescents with mild and moderate retardation (Zegiob et al. 1978), to reduce nail biting by a female with moderate retardation (Jackson & Patterson, 1979, 1980), and to maintain independent housekeeping skills in males with mild retardation (Bauman & Iawata, 1977).

Implementing Self-Monitoring: The following steps detail the procedure for effectively implementing self-monitoring:

Step 1. Select a behavior that you and your client want to work on first. Self-monitoring works best on behaviors that do not require new learning by the individual. The major functional purpose of self-monitoring is to allow the natural self-regulatory processes of the individual to operate. So performance of new learning, for example a work skill, will likely not be enhanced because the individual is still learning to perform the behavior competently. However, old behaviors, or habitual behaviors that the individual performs in an automatic way, can be eliminated while positive behaviors can be enhanced. Behaviors such as ruminating thoughts, skin picking, and object throwing will be reduced or eliminated, whereas positive behaviors such as staying on task, or improving work output will be enhanced by helping the individual focus his or her attention on these behaviors. In addition, monitoring of outcomes and consequences (rate of pay, weight loss) has also been shown to produce the desired behavior change.

Step 2. Introduce the idea of self-monitoring. Discuss the nature and purpose of self-monitoring with the client. In some cases it may be useful to give an example of the effectiveness of self-monitoring (perhaps with a previous client). Explain the process and the intended effect at a level the client can understand. Use examples relevant to the individual's situation. Modeling (see the Modeling section of this chapter) may be useful in some cases.

Step 3. Select the self-monitoring process. In general a frequency count is recommended for behaviors that are clearly separable (e.g., negative statements to others, aggressive behaviors, or piecemeal output) and a time interval approach used for behaviors that are continuous (e.g., duration of time in the work area without wandering). Frequency counts are much easier for individuals to understand, and so the ability of the individual to understand monitoring units of time versus discrete behaviors should be considered.

Step 4. Develop a self-monitoring procedure. The procedure for monitoring can be selected from a number of approaches. Self-monitoring charts are commonly used. These charts simply require the individual to make a mark when he or she performs the behavior. Other procedures include transferring a token from one pocket to another, slipping a bead on a string, and putting a peg on a ring. Any clear method for counting either frequency and/or duration is acceptable, with the individual client's ability to grasp the monitoring concept the critical variable.

Step 5. Role-play the procedure with the client. Although the procedure is quite simple, take the time to practice the process with the individual. This is particularly important when a verbal explanation of the self-monitoring procedure is considered insufficient to ensure the client's understanding of what is to be done.

Step 6. Monitor the self-monitoring process. Under no circumstances should it be assumed that the individual understands the process completely. Early and frequent monitoring is a must to ensure that the monitoring process is carried out.

Step 7. Develop some type of reinforcement for successful increase or decrease of the target behavior. As with many other behavior change strategies, maintenance is enhanced with some type of recognition and reinforcement. Reinforcers should be consistent with the individual's abilities and preferences. Frequently self-reinforcement (see Special Considerations below) is very appropriate.

Special Considerations: A number of researchers report the enhanced effectiveness of self-monitoring when combined with some type of self-instruction and reinforcement. Because a major factor in the effectiveness of the self-monitoring approach is thought to be having the individual feel in control of his or her own behavior, self-administered reinforcement (contingent on a set level of self-monitored behavior) seems quite consistent with the self-monitoring approach.

Modeling

Definition: *Modeling is a process in which individuals learn by observation. In this process the behaviors of similar others serve as the stimulus for learning. Individuals learn by watching other individuals perform a behavior, seeing the consequences of the behavior, and then imitating it. Modeling is also called observational learning, vicarious learning, and imitation and generally is thought to be most effective when individuals first watch a model who is similar to themselves perform a task, then* *attempt the task themselves. Modeling can have two effects on the individual: (1) learning a new behavior or set of behaviors, and (2) inhibiting or disinhibiting an already learned behavior.*

According to Bandura (1977) the first stage of learning through modeling is the *acquisition stage.* In order to learn, the individual must accurately attend to and perceive the important features of the model's behavior, which are then coded, symbolically rehearsed, organized, and stored in memory. The second stage of learning through modeling is the *performance stage,* where the individual performs the modeled behavior and is rewarded for it (Bandura, 1977). Although imitation and modeling are common teaching and learning procedures, which are widely used with individuals with mental retardation (Perry & Furukawa, 1986), much of what is done in this area fails to take into account a number of significant factors that greatly influence the effectiveness of modeling.

General Research: Research has examined the effectiveness of modeling with a variety of client concerns. A great deal of research has examined the effectiveness of modeling in treating fear-related behaviors. Klingman, Melamed, Cuthbert, and Hermecz (1984) successfully used modeling with children to deal with their fear of dental procedures. Melamed and Siegel (1975) used modeling to counter fear of an operation in children; Harris and Johnson (1980) used modeling to reduce fear in testing situations; whereas Ladouceur (1983) found that modeling could be used to reduce fear of commonly encountered animals (e.g., cats and dogs).

Other research has focused on teaching social and study skills (Cartledge & Milburn, 1980; McGinnes & Goldstein, 1984) to children. Others have taught problem solving to problem drinkers (Chaney, O'Leary, & Marlatt, 1978) and heroin addicts (Reeder & Kunce, 1976). In general, modeling has been found to be a basic means of modifying a variety of behaviors of individuals of all ages, in many different settings. Similarly, modeling has been used to teach a variety of behaviors to individuals with mental retardation from those as simple as the correct use of the telephone to complex behaviors such as the use of language. The following section will review this body of research.

Special Population Research: Given the fact that individuals with mental retardation and borderline intelligence tend to have difficulty with both written and verbal instruction, it is not surprising that counselors working with these groups have used modeling to help their clients to learn or change important and problematic behaviors. A few examples will help illustrate this research. Stephan, Stephano, and Talkington (1973) used modeling to teach adult females with mental retardation and borderline intelligence (mean age 19) to use the telephone. These investigators found that both videotaped and live models who presented sequenced steps for proper phone use were equally effective. Beisler and Tsai (1983) used modeling to teach language skills such as requesting information, seeking information, greeting, and commenting on the environment to autistic and severely retarded adults with considerable success. Perry and Cerreto (1977) used videotaped models to teach social skills to individuals who are moderately retarded. In this study individuals first saw a videotaped model who demonstrated the component parts of the social skills behavior (e.g., meeting and conversing with people), and then verbally summarized the behavior. This was followed by rehearsal, feedback, and reinforcement.

Johnny Matson and his colleagues have conducted an extensive and programmatic series of studies on the use of modeling, combined with instructions, role playing, reinforcement, and performance feedback, to teach social skills effectively to persons with mental retardation (e.g., Andrasik & Matson, 1983; Christoff & Kelly, 1983; Matson, 1984b). Many of these studies are reviewed in the section in this chapter on social skills training (see Behavioral Rehearsal), but some are worth mentioning here. Matson and Senatore (1981) reported that social skills training, incorporating modeling, was more effective than traditional group psychotherapy for improving interpersonal functioning of adults with mental retardation. Matson and his colleagues have also reported on the use of modeling, paired with other behavioral procedures, in the effective treatment of depression (Frame, Matson, Sonis, Fialkov, & Kazdin, 1982; Matson, 1982), psychosomatic complaints (Matson, 1984a), psychotic speech (Stephens, Matson, Westmoreland, & Kulpa, 1981), and explosive aggressive outbursts (Matson & Stephens, 1978) of children and adults with mental retardation.

Finally, participant modeling has been used successfully to help persons with mental retardation more effectively manage their fears. For example, Jackson and Hooper (1981) treated a 32-year-old female with mild mental retardation (IQ = 57), who had a dog phobia of 20 years' duration, with participant modeling and education. Four coping models were used; the models were individuals with moderate to mild mental retardation. Rigorous measures of change indicated that treatment was effective after eight 20-minute training sessions. Wilson and Jackson (1980) treated a 5-year-old boy with mental retardation's fear of toilets by showing him a student who modeled and then paralleled the client's sequential progress in approaching the toilet. The following is a compilation of procedures used in these studies and the clinical experience of the authors.

Implementing Modeling: The following steps detail the procedures for effectively implementing modeling.

Step 1. Select the behavior that your client needs to learn or have inhibited or disinhibited. Some modeling involves teaching new behaviors or emotional responses to an individual, such as social skills, work behaviors, or confidence. Other modeling inhibits behavior in which the individual currently engages, such as an offensive behavior, or disinhibits a behavior the individual should employ more often, such as assertiveness skills.

When selecting a behavior to teach or modify by modeling, it is also important to consider the capacity of the individual to process and retain information. For example, highly anxious individuals may have trouble learning from a model, as their attention may be distracted by their anxiety. In these cases it still may be possible for the individual to learn from a modeling approach, but other approaches (e.g., relaxation, positive self-talk) may be needed to enhance the modeling.

Modeling that teaches new behaviors. This type of modeling may benefit from multiple presentations of graduated skills. If there is some logical task division, it may be useful to model a component part of the new behavior and then to have the individual practice the new skill with coaching and reinforcement. For example, teaching a work or social skill may require a task analysis so that the component parts of the skill can be individually modeled. A work task may require modeling of several parts (e.g., set-up, completing the task, and clean-up).

Modeling that inhibits a problematic behavior. Here the model should be shown performing the problematic behavior, with the logical consequences of the behavior also demonstrated. For example, showing a model exhibiting verbally aggressive behavior, and having the individual's peers ignore him or her or leave the immediate area. Here, allowing an individual to see both the behavior itself, and the consequences of the behavior, will tend to have an inhibitory effect.

Modeling that disinhibits a desirable behavior. In some cases an individual has a desirable behavior in his or her repertoire, but does not employ it in the appropriate circumstances. For example, showing a model using assertive skills, and having a positive outcome, will tend to disinhibit fear or anxiety that may be associated with the use of assertive skills on the part of the observer.

Step 2. Select a model who is most likely to be imitated. Generally, models who are similar to the observer in terms of gender and age are the most effective. Similarly, models who are in some way seen by the observer as competent and prestigious are more likely to be imitated. Caution should be taken to ensure that the social distance between the observer and the model is not so large that the client/ observer would not see the implications of the modeling for his or her own behavior.

Also, the model should perform the behavior so that it seems attainable by the individual—not so flawlessly executed as to be out of reach of the individual.

Step 3. Develop a presentation procedure for the modeling. The presentation of the modeling can be as simple as having the client watch another similar individual perform the desired behavior in the actual work setting, or as complex as a videotape with a narrator. Videotaped models have generally been found to be as effective as live models, so that convenience may be the deciding factor between live and taped models. Taped models have the benefit of multiple presentation, minimization of distractions, and ongoing discussion with the individual during the repeat viewing of the modeling. A common technique in modeling done with videotaped models is to use a narrator who points out what the individual is doing, in particular highlighting key components of the performance.

Step 4. Provide an incentive for learning and performing the behavior. It is often useful to provide as much incentive as possible to encourage the individual to learn and/or perform the behavior. Showing the model receiving reinforcement and reinforcing the observer when he or she performs the previously modeled behavior are the most common ways of enhancing learning and performance.

Step 5. Repeat the modeling procedure. In many cases repeated modeling will facilitate the learning, and later performance of the modeled behavior. In some cases one observation of the modeled behavior will be sufficient, but in most cases several observations will be the most effective.

Special Considerations: In some cases it may be useful to have groups of individuals view a model. Group discussion afterward may also enhance learning and later performance. Modeling of positive self-talk (see the Cognitive-Behavior Modification section of this chapter) can also be helpful. For example, the model can be shown thinking, or stating out loud, a positive verbal coping behavior. Another approach is suggested by Grinnell and Liberman (1977), who used videotapes of clients themselves performing the behavior. These videotapes were edited so that only the successful and positive aspects of the individual's performance (in a job interview) were made part of the video. This approach is called self-modeling.

Relaxation Training

Definition: *Relaxation training involves teaching a self-control skill (Goldfried & Trier, 1974) that can be used to inhibit or reduce manifestations of stress and anxiety. The relaxation response involves measurable changes in an individual's behavior (e.g., relaxed posture, motionless,* *quiet), physiology (e.g., lowered heart rate, lowered respiration rate, decreased muscle tone), and self-reported experience (e.g., calm, relaxed, peaceful).*

The relaxation training method most commonly used is a shortened version (Bernstein & Borkovec, 1973) of Jacobson's (1938) progressive muscle relaxation technique. This involves alternately tensing and releasing muscle groups, while focusing attention on the contrasting sensations of tension and relaxation. A variation on this approach, called cue-controlled relaxation (Russell & Spich, 1973), pairs a word such as "calm" or "relax" with the relaxed muscle state. After practice the cue word can then be used independently to induce relaxation. In other approaches, relaxation is produced by pleasant imagery, controlled breathing, self-suggestion, sensory awareness, meditation, or biofeedback (Lichstein, 1988).

General Research: Progressive muscle relaxation (PR) has been widely researched as a technique by itself for the treatment of anxiety-related problems, including generalized anxiety, test anxiety, insomnia, chronic pain, asthma, headaches, and hypertension. Three uses have been researched in this regard: (a) setting events, (b) response-independent cueing, and (c) response-dependent cueing. When PR is used as a setting event, clients are trained to relax prior to an activity or stimulus that is anxiety provoking. In this way, it is assumed that the relaxed state will persist and function as an incompatible response to the onset of anxiety. Response-independent cueing is used to prompt relaxation periodically by the use of stimulus or cue words. Response-dependent cueing involves inhibiting anxiety by using cue words contingent upon the onset of symptoms, such as the onset of heart palpitations, sweaty palms, or racing thoughts.

Positive effects of relaxation training are summarized elsewhere (e.g., Lichstein, 1988; Luiselli, Marholin, Steinman, & Steinman, 1979; Poppen, 1988). The consensus shared is that no one relaxation technique is superior, and that all are effective in reducing anxiety. Relaxation training has also been incorporated into a number of behavioral treatment packages, including systematic desensitization (Wolpe, 1958), covert sensitization (Cautela, 1967), anger management training (Novaco, 1975), and stress inoculation training (Meichenbaum, 1975). The specific role of relaxation training in these approaches, however, remains open for investigation.

Special Population Research: Because the incidence of anxiety disorders in persons with mental retardation is significantly higher than in the general population (Ollendick & Ollendick, 1982), clinical use of valid anxiety management techniques is critically important. Persons with mental retardation are assumed to be limited in their ability to cope with social and environmental stressors, which in turn is assumed to increase their vulnerability to anxiety and related emotional disorders (Menolascino, 1977). Several behavioral interventions have been used to treat anxiety in this population, including relaxation training. Although research is meager, and interpretation of the results is confounded by methodological problems (Luiselli, 1980), preliminary data support the validity of relaxation training as a treatment for anxiety-related disorders experienced by individuals with mental retardation or low intelligence (Harvey, 1979; Luiselli, 1980; Rickard, 1986).

In one of the earliest reported studies, Graziano and Kean (1967) used daily massage and the instruction to "relax" to reduce "generalized excitement" exhibited by four children with autism. Although the results are somewhat unclear for interpretation, it appeared that all of the children achieved the relaxation criterion in 43 to 94 days and showed a correlated reduction in excitement. Similarly, an 8-year-old boy with moderate mental retardation who had a foot fetish was treated by an undefined audiotaped relaxation training technique paired with the cue word "relax" (Shaw & Walker, 1979). Significant reduction in the boy's level of arousal when exposed to women's feet was observed by hospital staff and the boy's parents. Braud, Lupin, and Braud (1975) reported that a 6 $\frac{1}{2}$-year-old hyperactive boy, with a WISC Full Scale IQ of 80, was taught to relax via 11 sessions of electromyographic biofeedback. Anecdotal data indicated a reduction in hyperactivity and "emotionality" as long as the child continued to practice the relaxation procedure outside of training sessions.

Rickard, Thrasher, and Elkins (1984) assessed the ability of persons with mental retardation to respond to verbal instructions commonly used in four relaxation procedures, notably, abbreviated PR, controlled breathing (Bernstein & Borkovec, 1973), pleasant imagery (Lazarus, 1970), and counselor suggestion (Bernstein & Borkovec, 1973). Five participants were obtained from each of four IQ groups: 40–54, 55–69, 70–84, and 85–100. All participants received each of the training procedures over the course of three 30-minute training sessions. Self-report and behavioral observation data indicated that individuals with the lowest IQ were the only group that experienced difficulties following the instructions in any of the procedures.

Harvey, Karan, Bhargava, and Morehouse (1978) developed a treatment package, consisting of PR and diaphragmatic breathing, cue conditioning, cognitive procedures, time out, and positive reinforcement, to treat violent temper outbursts displayed by a 38-year-old female with mental retardation. The client reported feeling relaxed after three training sessions. Training to use the cue word "relax" began after 4 weeks of daily relaxation and audiotaped practice. Elimination of aggression was observed in workshop and residential settings. Wells, Turner, Hersen, and Bellack (1978) tested the effects of cue-controlled PR on seizure behavior displayed by a 22-year-old woman with a WAIS Full Scale IQ of 71. Treatment consisted of counselor-administered and self-administered daily relaxation induction. Once a state of relaxation was achieved, the woman was instructed to imagine preseizure auras and seizure activity vividly, then diminish these sensations by repeating the word "relax." Self-report data indicate that seizures and anxiety were effectively reduced outside of the sessions by using the cue word to induce relaxation as an incompatible response.

Marholin, Steinman, Luiselli, Schwartz, and Townsend (1979) assessed the effects of cue-controlled PR on task-oriented, disruptive, and stereotypic behavior displayed by five children with mental retardation and autism. Because the children were nonverbal, the cue to "relax" was given by the teacher while the students were in a relaxed state. Achievement of relaxation was validated by a relaxation checklist. The results indicated that relaxation was no more effective than a Simon-says game in modifying the targeted problem behaviors. Further research is required to determine the efficacy of relaxation training when individuals with mental retardation who also have autism.

Despite methodological shortcomings, preliminary conclusions can be formed based on this review of the literature. These are presented in the order of most to least confidence. First, individuals with mental retardation can be trained to relax. This is most apparent for individuals who function intellectually in the upper range of mental retardation. Second, substantial modifications of traditional relaxation procedures, especially progressive muscle relaxation, may not be required. Third, clinical use of relaxation training with this population is appropriate for treating problems with anxiety, aggression, seizure control, and hyperactivity. Other targets may be appropriate but have not yet been researched. Fourth, treatment causalities have not been reported and, based on research with persons without mental retardation (cf. Lichstein, 1988), are not likely. Fifth, individuals with autism may not benefit from relaxation training.

Implementing Relaxation Training: Because most of the relaxation research with individuals with low intelligence utilized some form of progressive muscle relaxation (PR), this procedure is presented here. Modifications for this special population are based on recommendations made by researchers along with the authors' clinical experience. Common components utilized in all forms of relaxation training (Lichstein, 1988) are also incorporated here.

Clinical studies of PR typically involve 5 to10 training sessions, although more may be required with individuals who have intellectual limitations. Training sessions usually last about 20 to 30 minutes.

Step 1. Assess the need for relaxation training. Form a clinical hypothesis that anxiety is related to the target problem; then validate this impression by behavioral, client self-report, and/or physiological (EMG) indices of anxiety. Standardized measures for the population under consideration should be used. Examples of behavioral observation and self-report measures of anxiety, specifically standardized for individuals with mild mental retardation and borderline intelligence, include the anxiety and internalization scales from the Emotional Problems Scales (Prout & Strohmer, 1991).

Step 2. Secure medical clearance when the disorder is of a medical or quasi-medical nature. In many cases treatment should be coordinated with the client's physician. Examples include headache, acute anxiety attack, essential hypertension, chronic pain, and stomach ulcers.

Step 3. Provide a rationale for relaxation training. Motivating the client is important. A clear and concise rationale that communicates that relaxation training is an effective procedure is often sufficient. Relate the role of anxiety to the problem behavior. Lower functioning individuals who do not understand the rationale may require tangible or social reinforcement to ensure motivation, at least in the early stages of treatment, until the relaxation itself becomes reinforcing. Emphasize that relaxation training involves teaching a skill. Explain that people learn to be tense and, in a similar fashion, they can learn to relax. The slow nature of acquiring a new skill should be stressed to avoid discouragement early in the training process.

Step 4. Create the proper training setting. Training should occur in a quiet, dimly lit room, equipped with a comfortable reclining chair, sofa chair, or couch. Tightly fitting clothing, such as jewelry, belts, and neckties, should be loosened. Quiet, soothing music may be played in the background. It may be useful later to conduct training in a less-relaxing environment to facilitate generalization to real-life settings.

Step 5. Model a calm and relaxed attitude. Creating a relaxed environment will itself induce relaxation. The counselor should use a soft, slow-paced, relaxing voice while instructing the client. The counselor usually remains seated.

Step 6. Relaxation induction. The client is instructed to tense and relax various muscle groups alternately while focusing attention on the contrasting sensations. It may be helpful to model the procedure first for some clients who may be easily embarrassed. No standard order for the muscle groups exists. The following order is suggested:

1. Right hand and forearm
2. Right biceps

3. Left hand and forearm
4. Left biceps
5. Forehead
6. Face
7. Jaw
8. Neck
9. Shoulders
10. Upper back
11. Chest and abdomen
12. Buttocks
13. Right thigh
14. Right calf
15. Right foot
16. Left thigh
17. Left calf
18. Left foot

Each muscle group is tensed for about 5 to 10 seconds and then relaxed for about 20 to 45 seconds. Some counselors use a crisp voice when instructing the client to tense, others maintain a soothing voice throughout the induction. The tension portions are initiated by an instruction such as "When I say 'now,' please . . ." Complete each tension phase with the cue word "relax." It is usually necessary at an opportune point to instruct the client to tense and relax only those muscles that should be under focus. The counselor may decrease the amount of tension-relaxation instruction within and across sessions. Thus, as the client makes progress, there should be increasing periods of counselor silence.

Step 7. Home practice. Practice is considered essential. Training sessions are typically bridged by daily practice sessions assisted by audiotaped relaxation instructions that were recorded during one of the therapy sessions.

The counselor should discuss with the client how to incorporate practice into the home environment. Encourage selection of a distraction-free setting that allows about 20 minutes of private practice. To help ensure that home practice is being conducted efficiently, use of the Relaxation Practice Form is recommended (Figure 5.1). The form uses a 1 to 100 scale that can be explained and modeled in training sessions.

Relaxation Practice Form

Relaxation Rating

Day	Date	Time	Pre	Post
Sun				
Mon				
Tue				
Wed				
Thur				
Fri				
Sat				

Rating

1	50	100
No tension, deeply relaxed	Normal	Extremely tense

Figure 5.1. Form for Record Keeping of Self-Reported Relaxation Progress.

Step 8. Monitor change. Change should be monitored by daily records of pre- and postlevels of relaxation. Tripartite assessment of self-report, behavior, and physiology provides the most precise measure of the effectiveness of a relaxation training program. Self-report for home practice is sufficient. Evaluation of relaxation in training sessions, however, should include self-report (e.g., Relaxation Practice Form), behavioral observation on a measure such as the Relaxation Checklist (Figure 5.2), and physiological indices (rate of respiration, pulse, EMG).

Step 9. Cue-controlled relaxation. This step is introduced once it is clear that the client has learned to relax. This may take several sessions. While the client is relaxed, instruct him or her to repeat the cue word "relax" or "calm" upon each exhalation. The client can then use the cue word to induce relaxation at another time to avoid or interrupt the onset of anxiety.

Relaxation Checklist

1.	Forehead Deeply furrowed or wrinkled	5	4	3	2	1	Smooth
2.	Eyes Deeply wrinkled, squeezed tightly	5	4	3	2	1	Loosely closed, almost fluttering
3.	Neck Veins or muscles visible, extended	5	4	3	2	1	Smooth
4.	Head Held straight, centered, or forward	5	4	3	2	1	Tilted to one side
5.	Arms Closed to body shoulders raised	5	4	3	2	1	Away from body, shoulders forward
6.	Hands Closed fist, clenching chair, tapping	5	4	3	2	1	Open, palms up, resting on lap or chair

7.	Legs Close together swaying, wiggling	5	4	3	2	1	Apart, knees out, no movement
8.	Feet Together, flat on floor, tapping	5	4	3	2	1	Apart, resting on heels, toes out
9.	Breathing Rapid, uneven	5	4	3	2	1	Slow, even

Figure 5.2. Scale of Relaxation Behavioral Markers.

Adapted from "Assessing the Effects of Relaxation Training" by J. K. Luiselli, D. Marholin II, D. L. Steinman, and W. M. Steinman, 1981, *Behavioral Therapy, 10,* 663-668.

Relaxation Training—Example

The following is a fairly representative rendition of PR induction. Prepare the client by having him or her sit in a comfortable reclining chair in a dimly lit room with eyes closed.

Now settle back as comfortably as you can. Please keep your eyes closed during the session. I am going to draw your attention to different sensations in your body. You will become more aware of the sensations of tension and relaxation and gain more control over these states.

I will first instruct you to tighten a muscle group and tense these muscles as hard as you can until I say the word "relax." Then I want you to completely release the tension and return your muscles to a relaxed state. Focus all of your attention on the various sensations coming from your muscles.

First, draw your attention to your right hand. When I say "now," tighten your right hand. Now. Tighten as hard as you can. That's it. Squeeze it tightly. Hold it as tightly as you can. Notice the sensations of tension in your hand and forearm. Feel the strain, the tension (5 to 10 seconds). And relax your hand, let go completely. Relax your right hand and let it rest comfortably on the chair. Note the difference between the relaxation and the tension. Study the difference as you relax more and more. Feel the sensation of relaxation. The more you let go, the more relaxed and peaceful your hand feels (20 to 45 seconds).

Bring your attention to the large upper muscle on your right arm. Now tense this muscle by bending your arm at the elbow and flexing. Feel the tension. Notice how strained the muscle is. Harder. As hard as you can make the muscle (5 to 10 seconds). *And now relax. Let your arm go completely. Study the difference between the tension and relaxation. Allow your arm to feel more and more relaxed* (20 to 45 seconds).

The exact content of the relaxation instruction may vary. The objective is to induce the client's awareness of the contrasting sensation of tension and relaxation. The remaining muscle groups follow a similar pattern. Examples of starting each group are provided.

Tense the muscles of your left hand by tightly squeezing your left fist.

Tense the muscles of your left arm by flexing your elbow.

You can also learn to relax your facial muscles.

First I want you to tighten the muscles on your forehead.

Wrinkle it as hard as you can.

Now squeeze your eyes closed very tightly and wrinkle your nose.

Now clench your jaw and press your tongue against the roof of your mouth.

There are many muscles in your neck.

If you pull them all in a different direction your head will remain in one place.

Notice the shaking or tremor as your muscles pull against each other.

Some clients may require several sessions practicing isolated muscles of the neck instead of all of the muscles simultaneously. This can be done by bending the neck one direction at a time. For example, first back against the chair, then buried down into their chest, and then side to side.

Now direct your attention to your shoulders.

Shrug your shoulders tightly, towards your ears.

Tense the muscles in your upper back.

Arch your back.

Pull your shoulders together as if you were trying to touch them together.

Feel the tension primarily in your upper back.

At this point, a breathing exercise may be incorporated. The client will be instructed to take five deep breaths. Once the client has learned to relax, this is also a good point to instruct the client to repeat the cue word "relax" upon each exhalation.

And now take a deep breath and hold (5 seconds).

Study the tension of your lungs.

Notice your ribs spread out.

The tautness of your stomach muscles.

And relax.

Exhale slowly.

Quietly repeat the word "relax" as you exhale.

Feeling more and more relaxed as you exhale.

Notice the contrast between relaxation and tension.

Continue to breathe normally (10 seconds).

Let's repeat that.

Tense your chest and stomach by pulling your shoulders forward.

Tighten your stomach muscles at the same time.

Tense the muscles in your buttocks.

Tightly squeeze your seat.

Now tense your right thigh.

Do this by holding your foot up and tensing all of your muscles in your thigh simultaneously.

Make your thigh hard.

Tense your right calf by pointing your toes towards your face.

Tense your right ankle by pointing your toes away from your face.

Repeat the same sequence for the left side of the client's body. This completes PR. At this point the counselor may review with the client the various muscle groups and prompt deeper relaxation. During later sessions the cue word "relax" is paired with the relaxed state.

As you sit in the chair please think of the various muscle groups and send messages to them to relax further. First relax your right hand (5 seconds). *Let your right arm relax. Now your left hand* (5 seconds). *Relax more and more. Relax your left arm* (5 seconds). *As we continue feel the warmth spread throughout your body. Relax your facial and jaw muscles* (5 seconds). *And let your neck and throat muscles loosen* (5 seconds). *Let go further and further. Relax your shoulders and back* (5 seconds). *Let go. Let your abdomen, buttocks, and leg muscles all relax* (5 seconds). *Just let your entire body go* (5 seconds). *Further and further. More and more relaxed.*

Do nothing more than sit quietly and softly repeat the word "relax" as you breathe out. More and more relaxed (2 minutes). *Now, I will count from 10 to 0. With each count you will become more alert and awake. When I reach 0 you will be completely alert. 10 . . . 9 . . . 8 . . . 7 . . . , alert, eyes open, and refreshed.*

Special Considerations: Behavioral shaping may be initially required with some clients. For example, it may be necessary to increase slowly the amount of time the client has his or her eyes closed. Instructions to tense and release muscle groups may initially require graduated guidance with subsequent fading of prompts.

If the client has physical limitations that prohibit use of PR, other procedures such as a breathing technique may be clinically indicated. (See Lichstein, 1988.) Individuals with limited verbal skills might benefit from a simplified procedure, such as one developed by Koeppen (1974) for children that utilizes playful animal imagery. Other procedures rely on posturing and positioning the client (e.g., Behavioral Relaxation Training, Poppen, 1988) that may be useful for individuals with limited receptive language skills.

Some clients experience unsettling thoughts or bodily sensations as they learn to relax. The counselor should reframe these (common) reactions as positive indicators that relaxation training is beginning to impact on the client. Acquiring a relaxed state means that uncensored thoughts and reactions are more likely to come into one's awareness.

Before training clients, counselors should be thoroughly acquainted with the relaxation training technique. It is important to understand the nuances of the procedure, potential pitfalls, and the subjective experience of clients. This might be achieved by practicing the technique with nonclients.

It has frequently been noted by the authors that some individuals, particularly impulsive individuals, may tend to take the instructions to tense their muscles to an extreme. Care should be given to ensure that individuals do not overtense their muscles. Cramping and even injury can result in such cases. If an individual is noted to be taking the tensing instructions too literally, the counselor should monitor and teach the client to tense the muscle to a reasonable and therapeutic extent.

Systematic Desensitization

Definition: *Systematic desensitization (Wolpe, 1958) is a frequently used behavioral technique, based on principles of respondent conditioning, for the treatment of phobias, fears, and anxiety. In its most common form, desensitization involves graduated exposure to a feared object or situation, presented imaginally or in vivo, while the client maintains an incompatible response to the onset of anxiety. The counterconditioning response is typically deep muscle relaxation; other antagonistic responses used include laughter, positive imagery, eating, and assertive behavior.*

General Research: Although the specific source(s) of client improvement are unclear, decades of research indicate that systematic desensitization is an effective clinical procedure for the treatment of fear and phobias in adults without retardation (Wolpe, 1973) and children without retardation (Ollendick, 1979). Both in vivo and imaginal (real-life as opposed to by imagination) exposure appear to be effective; some evidence exists for the greater efficacy of live exposure over imaginal and prolonged exposure over brief exposure (Emmelkamp, 1986). Moreover, systematic desensitization appears to be most effective for specific phobias than with more generalized fears such as agoraphobia and social phobia (Emmelkamp, 1982). Systematic desensitization, as developed by Wolpe (1958), is often combined with other procedures, including operant reinforcement, participant modeling, and cognitive restructuring.

Special Population Research: It is assumed that persons with mental retardation experience fears and phobias at a rate higher than that of the general population (e.g., Phillips & Williams, 1975); however, there is a paucity of studies on the prevalence and incidence of fears and phobias in this population (Jackson, 1983). At the very least, the research suggests that persons with mental retardation experience a similar range and intensity of fears found in comparison groups from the general population. Clinical impressions suggest that avoidance and fear reactions commonly interfere with development of adaptive behavior by persons with mental retardation (e.g., Bijou, 1966; Zigler, 1966). Thus, preliminary data suggest that effective clinical treatments for fear and phobia reduction are indicated for this population. The following section reviews a representative sample of this research.

Only one investigation (Peck, 1977) compared a pure form of imaginal or in vivo systematic desensitization with a control or comparison treatment condition. The majority of researchers in this area assumed that it is not possible to use relaxation or imagery procedures with persons with mental retardation, "because they require the subject to follow relatively complex instructions and to be able to generate covert imagery" (Jackson & Hooper, 1981, p. 9). Similarly, Freeman, Roy, and Hemmick (1976) stated "it is generally impossible to train [persons with mental retardation] in either relaxation or positive imagery processes" (p. 63). However, the data presented earlier on relaxation training suggest otherwise. Whether or not limited intellectual functioning rules out the clinical use of imagery techniques is an empirical question not yet systematically investigated.

Most of the research with persons with mental retardation is based on uncontrolled case reports, making interpretation of the efficacy of systematic desensitization with this population impossible. Only a small number of studies used single-subject experimental (Matson, 1981b; Runyan, Stevens, & Reeves, 1985; Waranch, Iwata, Wohl, & Nidiffer, 1981) or between-group designs (Matson, 1981a; Peck, 1977). In these cases, treatment packages were often used without dismantling procedures necessary to identify the components essential for treatment effects. This state of affairs is not unlike research on systematic desensitization with populations without mental retardation. Despite these and other problems (see Jackson, 1983), preliminary data support the use of systematic desensitization, at least in an in vivo format, as the treatment of choice for fears and phobias experienced by persons with mental retardation.

Of the ten case reports found, nine cases were treated for a *specific phobia*. Only one employed imaginal desensitization (Guralnick, 1973). Guralnick (1973) combined imaginal and in vivo desensitization with positive reinforcement to treat a 21-year-old male's (Stanford-Binet IQ of 33) fear of heights (acrophobia). Anecdotal data suggested that the client learned to relax over four sessions using an abbreviated progressive muscle relaxation technique. A 31-item hierarchy of increasing heights, leading to the goal of standing on a chair 20 inches above the ground, was constructed by the counselor. The client first imagined standing at increasing heights while maintaining a relaxed state. Following four sessions of imaginal desensitization, the client generalized to graduated in vivo approximations of increasing height, rewarded by contingent food, candy, and verbal praise. Forty-two sessions were required to meet the criterion.

Freeman et al. (1976) treated a phobia of physical examinations by gradual approximations (11-item hierarchy) using a favored nurse as the anxiety inhibitor. Treatment was reportedly successful after 11 sessions. Jackson and King (1982) employed laughter as the anxiety inhibitor in the successful treatment of a 4 $\frac{1}{2}$-year-old autistic boy's fear of the sounds of flushing toilets. Laughing was used as a setting event prior to flushing different toilets and food and verbal praise were delivered contingent upon the absence of fear. Rivenq (1974) reported that candy was successfully used to inhibit anxiety related to fear of hair. Graduated exposure to pictures of people with increasing amounts of body hair and then to actual people was used.

The remaining case reports used a modified version of in vivo desensitization that involved graduated exposure and contingent reinforcement for approach behavior. Howlin et al. (1973) treated a 5-year-old nonverbal boy's fear of baths and bathrooms by gradual exposure to taking a bath (no formal hierarchy) and contingent parental praise. Treatment was partially successful after 20 weeks. Luiselli (1978) successfully treated a 7-year-old child with autism's fear of riding the school bus by successive approximations (no formal hierarchy) and verbal praise. Treatment was successful after 10 days.

Mansdorf (1976) constructed a hierarchy of 19 items to treat a 35-year-old female with moderately mild retardation's fear of riding in cars. Sessions 1-4 consisted of forming a therapeutic relationship. After the rationale of the treatment was explained to the client, she was then given tokens at the end of each of the following sessions as she progressed to a higher level on the hierarchy. Anecdotal data suggest that treatment was successful after 8 weekly sessions. Only one case report was found that treated a *social phobia* (Chiodo & Maddux, 1985). A 21-year-old female with mild mental retardation (WAIS IQ = 60) was described as excessively nervous around other people and fearful of being negatively evaluated by others. Treatment was successful after four sessions of in vivo desensitization paired with prompts to use adaptive self-statements (e.g., "I'm doing a good job"). Successive approximations to various social situations were used.

Matson (1981b) treated three children with moderate retardation, ages 8 to 10, for a *social phobia* (fear of "strangers and acquaintances") by modified in vivo desensitization techniques. Treatments were conducted by mothers and involved rehearsal, modeling, coaching, in vivo exposure, and contingent tangible reinforcement to shape desensitization of the children's approach to "safe" adults. Successful fear reduction, including generalization to other settings, took 28 sessions.

Peck (1977) selected 20 mildly retarded subjects who had a phobia of rats or heights. Treatments consisted of 15 half-hour sessions and were basically the same as those used with persons without retardation. Subjects were randomly assigned to one of five conditions. Contact desensitization consisted of counselor modeling and guided approximations of approach behavior, using verbal or physical encouragement. Progressive muscle relaxation (Bernstein & Borkovec, 1973) was used in the vicarious symbolic desensitization and systematic desensitization procedures. The vicarious techniques involved videotaped modeling of approach behavior, whereas the systematic desensitization procedure required subjects to imagine approach behavior while maintaining a relaxed state. It is interesting to note that subjects were able to learn to relax *and* utilize imagery techniques. A placebo-attention control and a no-treatment group formed the remaining conditions. Multiple measures of fear suggested that contact desensitization was more effective, as well as more expedient, than all other treatment and control groups. There was also a trend in favor of the three treatments over the control groups. Peck's (1977) findings have been partially replicated by Matson (1981a).

In conclusion, research on the efficacy of systematic desensitization with persons with mental retardation is inconclusive. A bias towards in vivo desensitization was evident although experimental evidence of the greater efficacy of this over imaginal procedures with this population is lacking. Given the above issues, a procedure that utilizes both in vivo desensitization (Wolpe, 1958) and guided participation or contact desensitization is recommended for the clinical treatment of fears and phobias experienced by persons who also have limited intelligence.

Implementing Systematic Desensitization: The following steps detail an approach to systematic desensitization.

Step 1. Select a problem. The first session should include history taking to determine the clinical significance of the client's fear or phobia. Because fear is a normal reaction, and is prevalent in the population of individuals with mental retardation, it is important to distinguish between normal fears and severe debilitating fears and phobias. A useful piece of information in making this distinction is that developmental *trends* of fears found in adults with mental retardation have been found to be similar to the fears experienced by children, when mental age and chronological age comparisons are made (Jackson, 1983).

Step 2. Explain the rationale. Expectancy effects play an important role in systematic desensitization. It is important to emphasize the impairment of adaptive behavior caused by the fear or phobia, that the procedure they are about to begin has been quite effective in reducing fears and phobia in all types of people, and that the counselor expects that it will help them as well.

Step 3. Form a hierarchy. Construct a formal hierarchy of graduated steps leading to approach of the feared situation or object. (See example.) Clients should participate in this step unless they are incapable of doing so, for example, due to cognitive limitations. In these cases, it may be useful to use role-play techniques as a graphic to forming a hierarchy.

Step 4. Behavioral approach test. A pretest of the degree to which the client will approach the feared stimuli should occur. Provide a rationale that this step will allow for a later comparison with a posttest to measure the amount of progress the client makes. Create a simulated situation using the above hierarchy. Instruct the client to approach the stimuli and record the highest step achieved on the hierarchy.

Step 5. Deep muscle relaxation. In order to countercondition the anxiety, the client maintains a state of relaxation while progressing through the steps in the hierarchy. Therefore clients must first be trained to relax using procedures previously reviewed.

Step 6. Imaginal systematic desensitization. Once the client has learned the relaxation response, imaginal systematic desensitization can begin. We have found that the vast majority of individuals with mild mental retardation or borderline intelligence can successfully form the required imagery. However, as with nonretarded persons, it is necessary to assess a person's ability to utilize imagery techniques.

While he or she maintains a relaxed state, instruct the client to imagine approaching the feared stimuli. Use the hierarchy to guide the sequence of the scenes. The counselor should provide substantial verbal descriptions of each scene. Inquire into the client's ability to form these images by asking questions such as "Are you standing in front of the dog now?" or "Is your hand touching the dog now?"

Instruct the client to raise a finger or give a brief verbal comment to signal the *onset* of fear. Prompt the client to then return in his or her imagination to the previous step of the hierarchy. Imaginal desensitization is completed once the client can visualize approaching the feared stimulus without indicating fear.

Step 7. In vivo systematic desensitization. To ensure generalization, the final phase should involve in vivo desensitization. The counselor should accompany the client to the setting where the feared situation can be simulated. For example, we have accompanied clients to a local dance club, to a store to make a purchase, and to a department store to ride the elevator.

Contact desensitization first involves modeled approach behavior by the counselor followed by guided client participation. The client is encouraged to cue a relaxed state and then imitate the counselor's behavior. The absence of client self-reported anxiety is the criterion for advancing through the steps of the hierarchy. Each session is ended by returning to practice the last successful step.

Special Considerations: If the client is unable to utilize imagery, it is still advisable to use graduated in vivo exposure paired with relaxation.

Systematic Desensitization—Example

The following is an example of a behavioral hierarchy used in the treatment of a dog phobia. The hierarchy is used at pre- and posttest Behavioral Approach Tests and during imaginal and in vivo desensitization procedures.

1. Talking to counselor in office about dogs.
2. Talking to counselor in office about dogs outside of the building,

looking at dogs.

3. Talking to counselor outside of office, looking at dogs.

4. Walking towards dog and standing 10 feet in front of it.

5. Walking towards dog and standing 5 feet in front of it.

6. Walking towards dog and standing next to it.

7. Touching the dog.

8. Patting the dog for 5 seconds.

9. Patting the dog for 30 seconds.

10. Patting the dog for 1 minute.

11. Patting the dog continuously for 5 minutes.

12. Scratching the dog on the stomach for 1 continuous minute.

13. Hand feeding the dog.

14. Walking the dog on a leash for 1 continuous minute.

15. Sitting alone in a room with the dog for 5 minutes.

Behavioral Rehearsal

Definition: *Behavioral rehearsal is a specific procedure used to teach new behaviors, typically interpersonal, social, or work skills, in which the client practices the new behavior under the direction of the counselor. This may involve the counselor assuming the role of significant others in the client's life and helping the client in developing and rehearsing more effective ways of interacting with these individuals. It may also involve the practice of work skills. A common variant on this technique is role-reversal, in which the counselor acts the role of the client and the client takes the role of the significant other. In teaching work tasks, behavioral rehearsal typically requires that a detailed task analysis be conducted, and that a multistep approach be used to rehearse the new behavior.*

Behavioral rehearsal is also commonly called role playing. However, we have adopted the behavioral rehearsal terminology to differentiate the strategies described here from other types of role playing such as "psychodrama," where the intention is not to learn new behaviors but rather to work through "symbolic conflicts". Behavioral rehearsal is commonly used in combination with verbal instruction and modeling as the means of acquainting clients with a new skill or behavior, and with verbal praise and other reinforcement to provide the individual with feedback. When applied to the teaching of social skills, this combination has frequently been called social skills training (e.g., Matson, Kazdin, & Esveldt-Dawson, 1980).

General Research: Behavioral rehearsal has been found to be effective in a wide variety of circumstances including reducing anxiety, teaching assertiveness skills, and learning social skills. Problems ranging from dating behavior to test performance have been successfully addressed. O'Leary and Wilson (1975) described a behavioral rehearsal procedure in which clients were involved in role playing or rehearsing assertive responses. The therapist modeled the appropriate assertive behavior and then required the client to engage repeatedly in a graduated sequence of similar actions in the protective confines of the therapist's office. The therapist provided corrective feedback in shaping the desired behaviors. This was done until clients could skillfully and fearlessly display behaviors that were previously missing from their behavioral repertoire. The therapist then encouraged the client to carry out assertive actions, in the naturalistic setting, that were explicitly designed to promote generalization and result in naturally occurring positive reinforcement. Lazarus (1971) reported using behavioral rehearsal to help a man who had been unable to confront his wife concerning any issues whatsoever. This was thought to be causally related to the man's partial impotence. The client learned and rehearsed a carefully prepared speech developed by himself and his therapist. The client then anticipated his wife's most probable responses and rehearsed his response to these. Rehearsal techniques were used to help the client prepare for "tears, interruptions, denials, counterallegations, etc." The client then used his newly rehearsed behavior with his wife, and reported that his wife listened and agreed with many of his concerns. For reviews of this research with adults see O'Leary and Wilson (1975), and Walker, Hedberg, Clement, and Wright (1981).

Special Populations Research: One successful application of behavioral rehearsal has been in the area of teaching new skills such as proper grooming, assertiveness, and work behavior. Petroski, Craighead, and Horan (1983) used behavior rehearsal to improve grooming skills in women with mental retardation. A counselor asked each individual to rehearse sequentially each step of proper grooming previously determined by task analysis. The individual thus rehearsed proper hygiene skills. Results suggested that breaking the task down into steps, and then rehearsing each step in sequence, helped improve hygiene. This approach to task analysis of skills to be taught to an individual has been well documented by Gold (1980). Gold's *Try Another Way* training package details the use of task analysis and behavior rehearsal in individuals with mental retardation. Some of the skills analyzed and rehearsed included shaking hands, refusing someone when he or she tries to borrow or take money, telephone dialing, and stringing a tennis racquet. In this approach a careful analysis of the task is done so that it can be broken down into small component parts for rehearsal.

Behavioral rehearsal has also been shown to be effective in teaching interpersonal skills to individuals with mental retardation. This research typically involves three component parts: (a) instruction, frequently using a model; (b) behavior rehearsal; and (c) some type of performance feedback and reinforcement. For example, Matson et al. (1980) used this combination to teach social skills (e.g., appropriate verbalizations, eye contact, appropriate facial expression, appropriate motor behavior) to two children with mental retardation who had conduct problems. In this study a special education teacher taught certain social skills to the children by way of modeling and rehearsal. The teacher presented each client, in individual sessions, with six social situations, and asked them to try to respond to each. In those cases where the client engaged in inappropriate behavior during practice (rehearsal), the teacher modeled the behavior and then had the client rehearse the situation again. This was done with up to three repetitions. The training improved these clients' social skills and brought them up to or beyond the level of same-age and gender-normal control subjects. Similarly, Matson and Senatore (1981) compared the effectiveness of social skills training (instruction, modeling, and rehearsal) to traditional group psychotherapy in teaching more appropriate verbal skills (decreased complaining and increased positive statements about others) to 35 individuals with moderate and mild retardation. The social skills training proved to be significantly more effective than group psychotherapy. Turner, Hersen, and Bellack (1978) used a similar approach to teach prosocial skills (e.g., words spoken, eye contact, and smiles) to an organically impaired and retarded patient. Turner et al. also provided 6-month booster training sessions to bolster the earlier effects. Other investigators have found similar effectiveness in teaching introductions and small talk, asking for help, differing with others, handling criticism (Bates, 1980), and in effective treatment of depression (Frame et al., 1982; Matson, 1982), psychosomatic complaints (Matson, 1984a), psychotic speech (Stephens et al., 1981), and explosive outbursts (Matson & Stephens, 1978).

Implementing Behavioral Rehearsal: The following steps detail the procedure for effectively implementing behavioral rehearsal. We advocate a process similar to that suggested by the social skills training research as the most desirable for all types of behavioral rehearsal. Thus the following steps take into account the additional components of instruction and modeling.

Step 1. Select a target behavior and ensure that the client agrees that the target behavior needs to be addressed. Client motivation is a must to make behavior rehearsal effective.

Step 2. Explain the modeling process in detail. It is critical that the client understand what the counselor is doing and why he or she is suggesting it when the counselor begins the behavior rehearsal process. In the experience of the authors, far too little attention is paid to setting the stage for the behavior rehearsal. This frequently leads to confusion and a failed intervention. Clients, and not just clients with mental retardation, may take what the counselor says in a role they have assumed too literally, and become upset or angry. Key to this technique is that the "stage is set," and clients are clear about their role in the rehearsal, and why it is being done.

Step 3. Analyze the behavior to be rehearsed to determine if it needs to be broken into separate components. Frequently the behavior to be learned is too complex to be rehearsed in one sitting. In these cases breaking the behavior into discrete steps for rehearsal makes it easier for the client to grasp what he or she needs to learn. These steps can be "put back together" later in the final rehearsal stage. The need for small steps will be determined both by the complexity of the task and by the ability level of the client. What might be a simple behavior for an individual with borderline intelligence may require a number of component steps for an individual with mild retardation. For example, Gold (1980) task-analyzed shaking hands. For certain high-functioning individuals rehearsal might entail only one step, whereas for others it might entail the following: (1) extend the right hand, (2) grasp the greeter's hand, (3) squeeze the greeter's hand, (4) move the grasped hand up and down, (5) release grasp, (6) return hand to relaxed position at side.

Step 4. Provide the individual with some type of instruction in the behavior to be rehearsed. This may entail simple verbal instruction or formal modeling, either by the counselor, some significant other, or by videotape. In many cases this may be done in the form of what has come to be called role reversal, in which the counselor adopts the role of the client and demonstrates a certain behavior. This might be done, in particular, when the client is attempting to learn some social skill with a particular individual, or class of individuals (e.g., dates, authority figures). The counselor is able to model effective behavior, and the client is able to note firsthand how this behavior looks from the view of some significant other.

In teaching skills, instruction and modeling of each component step is necessary. The counselor or trainer may simultaneously provide verbal and modeling instruction.

Step 5. Keep each rehearsed component short and conceptually simple. We have noted that it is not at all uncommon for clients to have difficulty learning a rehearsed behavior. In some cases it may be necessary to redefine the learning to occur in a particular rehearsal segment, and to make it shorter and simpler to grasp. We advocate a flexible approach that takes into account the specific individual, and adjusts to the individual's needs.

Step 6. Rehearse as many times as needed. Be certain that the client understands that he or she is permitted to make mistakes and that the counselor will take all the time necessary to help him or her learn the new behavior.

Step 7. Use additional modeling and instruction as needed. In a great number of situations we can expect that the client will fail to pick up every aspect of the intended rehearsal. Plan to repeat the modeling, and instruction, as a normal part of the behavior rehearsal process.

Step 8. Reinforce the individual for successful completion of each task or component step in the task. Reinforcement will include verbal praise and perhaps a more tangible reinforcer at the completion of the behavioral rehearsal process. In many cases self-reinforcement, in the form of self-praise (see the Cognitive-Behavior Modification section), can be made part of the rehearsal process itself.

Step 9. Provide the client with relevant homework assignments. Once the client has learned a new behavior or skill it is important that it be tried out in a natural situation. Gradually increasing the difficulty of the situation will make an incremental phase–in possible.

Step 10. Discuss what the client has learned and help him or her generalize it to other situations. Once the client has successfully completed a key component of a rehearsal or the entire set of steps, discussion of what he or she learned and how it might generalize to other situations should be used as the concluding component. For example, discussion of how the individual has learned to ask for help from the supervisor may generalize to home, or a careful problem-solving approach to a new work situation may generalize to new nonwork situations.

Special Considerations: Although it is common for the counselor to serve as part of the rehearsal process, this may be problematic in the case of role reversal. Here, when the counselor assumes the role of the client in a role play, it may be impossible for the client to identify with the counselor. In other cases the client may assume that the counselor's successful performance is due to skills or abilities that the client doesn't possess. A peer may serve as the best person to take the client's role in a role-reversal situation.

Cognitive-Behavior Modification

Definition: *Cognitive-behavior modification is a set of techniques designed to modify the thinking or self-talk of the individual. It is used either to increase the number of positive thoughts (e.g., self-motivating or reinforcing) in which the individual engages or to decrease problematic (e.g., irrational, automatic, self-defeating) thoughts in which the individual engages.*

The techniques presented in this section have not received wide use with individuals with mental retardation or borderline intelligence because the techniques require an examination and correction of what might be considered higher, or more sophisticated, mental functions. For example, Luria (1961) suggested that children with retardation are incapable of using "internalized" or "private" speech as a guide to task performance. However, at least four factors suggest the importance and appropriateness of their use. First, the presence of maladaptive thoughts in this group is quite common in clinical situations; second, cognitive-behavior modification is useful with children who are at similar developmental levels; third, these techniques are learned best with the intensive practice often required to ensure that an individual with lower intelligence grasps a relatively difficult concept; and fourth, research has shown that individuals with retardation can be and are influenced by their internal dialogue.

The two techniques discussed in this section have been found by the authors to be quite effective with individuals with mild retardation and borderline intelligence. First we will discuss self-statement modification, which in combination with other techniques is also called self-instructional training, and (2) thought stopping, which is useful in a limited number of cases, but is of great benefit in those cases. Other cognitive methods may be appropriate, in particular Albert Ellis' Rational-Emotive Therapy (1967, 1977), but they do not fall within the scope of this chapter.

General Research: Self-statement modification is most commonly associated with the work of Meichenbaum (1977). Meichenbaum suggested that if we view individuals' thoughts as a type of behavior (self-talk), then it should be possible to help individuals learn to change their self-talk and, as a result, change their behaviors. A large number of research studies suggest both that it is possible to help an individual change his or her self-talk and that changed self-talk can lead to changes in behavior. Modifying self-verbalization has been found to be effective with a variety of client problems including interpersonal anxiety, test anxiety, anger control, pain, depression, and sexual dysfunction. (See Meichenbaum, 1986, for an overview of this research.)

Thought stopping is generally associated with the work of Cautela and Wisocki (1977) and is a self-control procedure designed for the elimination of perseverative thought patterns that are unrealistic, unproductive, and/or anxiety-arousing and either inhibit the performance of a desired behavior or serve to initiate a sequence of undesirable behaviors. Thought stopping has been found to be effective in a variety of situations from obsessive-complusive neurosis (Taylor, 1963) to the treatment of social inadequacy (Wisocki, 1976).

Special Populations Research: Research examining the application of cognitive-behavior modification with individuals with mental retardation or borderline intelligence is not extensive. However, it seems clear to the authors that much of the programming with individuals at all levels of mental retardation focuses on teaching cognitive behavior modification (e.g., teaching the individual new self-talk). Simply, repeatedly praising a lower functioning individual for good performance (e.g., "good work") can frequently result in the client praising or reinforcing him- or herself for similar good work performance—even in the absence of a staff member. Although not extensively researched with individuals with mental retardation or borderline intelligence, the usefulness of these procedures with other special population groups has received a fair amount of research attention.

Self-statement modification has been found to be effective with hyperactive and impulsive children who were taught to use self-talk to regulate their behavior and to "talk themselves through" a difficult task or situation (Meichenbaum & Goodman, 1971). Douglas, Parry, Martin, and Garson (1976) exposed hyperactive children to a model who verbalized self-statements that included "I must stop and think," "What shall I try next?" "See I've made a mistake here—I'll just correct it." The children then rehearsed the statements and finally tried them in a task situation. Hyperactive children who had been trained to use positive and coping self-statements were more successful in task completion.

Peters and Davies (1981) replicated the Meichenbaum and Goodman (1971) procedure with adolescents with mental retardation and found support for the use of Meichenbaum's "self-instructional training" (i.e., self-statement modification taught with modeling and then rehearsed with the counselor) with this group. Thus, contrary to the notion that individuals with mental retardation cannot use internalized dialogues to direct their behavior, this group of adolescents with retardation (12.5 to 18.8 years) showed significant improvement in task performance. Chiodo and Maddux (1985) used self-statement modification that included teaching a 16-year-old female with mild retardation to use positive self-statements ("I am not afraid"), and to think of upcoming pleasurable activities (e.g., sports, dances) to reduce her anxiety level regarding a mock up of a trial in which she was due to participate on an upcoming date. Self-report, GSR data, and behavioral observations suggest that the self-statement modification was effective. Golden and Consorte (1982) also used a combination of techniques that included self-statement modification (e.g., "No one is perfect," "No one can fix everything," "If I'm too frustrated I can come back to this later") and relaxation training and behavior rehearsal (i.e., practicing provoking situations) to decrease violent outbursts among four adults with mild retardation. A significant decrease in outbursts and total elimination of violent behavior were noted in all four subjects in the study.

Little relevant research for the application of thought stopping to the individual with mild retardation and borderline intelligence appears in the literature. However, one study (Campbell, 1973) used a thought-stopping variation to treat disturbing thoughts about a sister's death in a 12-year-old boy. The young boy was taught to count backward each time the disturbing thought occurred, until the thought was controlled or eliminated. Similarly, Walker et al. (1981) treated a young girl's obsessional recurrence of an obscene word using thought stopping.

Implementing Self-Statement Modification: The following steps detail the procedure for effectively implementing self-statement modification.

Step 1. Explain the rationale for self-statement modification. Client motivation is a must to make self-statement modification effective, so it is important that the client understand, in his or her own terms, the rationale underlying this approach. Explain to clients that self-statements are the things they say to themselves (e.g., their thoughts) about something that has happened or is about to happen, and that these self-statements sometimes change how they actually behave. Further explain that sometimes the things people say to themselves can negatively influence how they act. For example, what an individual says before trying a new work task may influence how successful he or she will be when doing the task. A person might say, "I'll never get this right," or they might say, "I am good at work like this, so this will be easy." The counselor might discuss how the counselor's own self-talk has influenced his or her behavior in the past. Asking the client to think of times when a similar effect occurred in his or her own life is frequently useful.

Step 2. Relate the self-statement rationale to the client's situation. Point out where the individual may be engaging in defeating self-statements, or failing to engage in facilitating self-statements.

Step 3. Help the client to identify his or her current self-statements. The counselor should next help the client to examine the problem situations in his or her life where self-statements may be problematic. The counselor and client must analyze the client's current situation to determine when and how self-statements (either their presence or absence) are influencing the client's behavior. This may be done in counseling by simply having the client recall a problematic situation. Role playing a particular situation may also be useful in helping the client to recall the specifics of a problematic situation and, in particular, self-statements made during that situation. It may also help to assign homework in which clients pay attention to what they are thinking in certain critical situations.

Step 4. Assist the client to generate new and more useful self-statements. The client should then be assisted in developing more productive self-statements. In some cases self-statements that are directly counter to a self-defeating self-statement may be useful. In other cases simply identifying self-statements that facilitate the desired behavior will be sufficient. For example, a self-statement to counter anxiety in a social situation might be "I like everyone here," or "I know how to handle this situation, first I . . . ," as directly countering "No one will want to talk to me" or "I am going to say something stupid." Similarly, statements like "My job is important," or "I am (or 'my family is') proud of the good work I do" may facilitate the individual's concentration on task or desire to maintain good work quality.

Step 5. Practice the new self-statements in counseling. To practice the new self-statements, role playing, or even modeling, may help initially. Clients are frequently reluctant to practice their new self-statements. In many cases simple encouragement is enough. In other cases the counselor modeling the new self-statements may help, whereas in some cases a review of the rationale, focusing on the notion of learning new behaviors, will be needed.

Step 6. Help the client internalize the new self-statements. Once a new positive or coping self-statement is developed, the client must learn to make it part of his or her thinking or self-talk. Generally this can be done best by having the client practice the new self-talk out loud, until quite accomplished with it. Next the client should be instructed to say the self-talk quietly to him- or herself, and then finally to practice thinking it, or saying it in his or her head.

Step 7. Role-play the situations where the self-talk can be used. When the client is comfortable with the new self-statements, the counselor and client should role-play situations where the self-talk can be practiced. After the role play, the counselor and client can talk about how the client felt, and make modifications where necessary.

Step 8. Provide the client with relevant homework assignments that allow the application of the new self-statements. The counselor will help the client design "homework" assignments in which the client will try out new self-talk, be aware of its effects, and report back to the counselor what happened.

Step 9. Discuss what the client has learned and help generalize it to other situations. Most any situation clients find themselves in is subject to effects of self-verbalization, so the counselor can attempt to help clients see how they can apply this positive approach to thinking in other common life situations.

Special Considerations: With clients who have particular trouble understanding the self-talk rationale, the authors have found it useful simply to engage the client in a planned series of repetitions of a positive or coping self-statement. For example, one client found the beginning of the work day too stressful, and as a result frequently behaviorally acted out—but only at the beginning of the day. This client practiced, both with day and residential staff, simply saying aloud, and later thinking, "I am a good worker and I want to earn my money." No attempt was made to explain the rationale behind this self-talk, but rather it was treated as simply learning a new behavior with planned practice.

Implementing Thought Stopping: The following steps detail the procedure for effectively implementing thought stopping. This technique is used only in situations that clearly meet certain criteria for application. These criteria are simply that the individual possess perseverative thought patterns that are unrealistic, unproductive, and/or anxiety arousing, and either inhibit the performance of a desired behavior or serve to initiate a sequence of undesirable behaviors. It is also important that the counselor is confident that the individual is capable of understanding the thought–stopping rationale and approach.

Step 1. Determine that the individual possesses some problematic reoccurring thoughts. In the experience of the authors this is not unusual. We have seen thoughts about the death of family members, concern about illness or the client's own death, and negative thoughts about a troubling situation the individual must face. Clearly, some empathic counseling will be called for with certain problems, but as with nonretarded clients, this type of support frequently is not enough.

Step 2. Ensure that the client agrees that the target behavior needs to be addressed. Explain the rationale for thought stopping. Explain the idea that the self-statements the individual is experiencing have no value, and in fact are detrimental to the client. Discuss what negative impacts the thoughts are having. Further explain that eliminating the thoughts should lead to reduction in the problematic behaviors. Explain that the technique you will use will help eliminate these thoughts and has worked well with others in the same situation.

Step 3. Determine exactly what the troubling thoughts are. As suggested in Step 1, it may be useful, and clinically sound, to provide support and understanding about how it feels to experience these thoughts. It is important that the client give precise wording to the thought he or she is experiencing.

Step 4. Give the following instructions to the client. The following instructions are to be given to the client verbatim. They are taken from Wisocki (1985): "Now sit back, relax, and close your eyes. In a few seconds I am going to say the word 'go.' As soon as I say the word 'go,' I want you to deliberately think this thought: (insert client problematic thought). As soon as you begin the thought signal me by raising your right index finger. Do you understand the instruction? Okay. Lean back. Relax. Are you ready? Go" (pp. 120-121).

If the client signals trouble understanding, the counselor should stop the process and discuss the individual problem. In most cases simple misunderstandings can be explained away quite easily.

Step 5. Use the thought-stopping procedure. As soon as the client raises a finger, the counselor is to shout loudly "***stop***." This will generally result in a startle response. Caution should be exercised beforehand to ensure that this type of procedure will not be too intense for the individual. (Most clients seem to find the procedure somewhat humorous, after they get past being startled.) Process the client reaction to the procedure.

Step 6. Use the thought–stopping procedure a second time and process.

Step 7. Teach the client to use the procedure him- or herself. As suggested by Wisocki (1985), say "I'm going to ask you to close your eyes again, but this time I'm not going to shout 'stop'. Try to imagine as well as you can, or try to hear yourself shouting 'stop' very loudly. Keep practicing until you can get a clear picture of yourself shouting 'stop.'" Have the client practice this several times.

Have the client open his or her eyes and determine if he or she had any trouble imagining shouting "stop." If so, have the client practice shouting "stop" out loud. It may be necessary for the counselor to practice with the client at first. Other clients may have trouble with the shouting imagery and may require saying the word out loud, while imagining some other form of stop (e.g., a policeman holding up his hand).

Once the client is able to imagine shouting "stop," have him or her practice imagining the troubling thought and shouting "stop." Several repetitions should be performed. Process the whole procedure with the client completely. Ensure that the client understands why he or she is engaging in the procedure.

Step 8. Give the client homework to practice the thought–stopping procedure in private. Generally the client is asked to practice the procedure several times each day on his or her own. The counselor should check with the client frequently to process his or her success in practicing the procedure.

Step 9. Maintain regular contact during the following weeks. It is not uncommon for clients to experience difficulty, particularly at first, with actual application of the procedure. Encouragement and processing the experience are normally all that is needed.

Step 10. Retrain if needed. In some cases we have found that retraining, in the form of returning to the initial steps, will be necessary for a successful outcome.

Special Considerations: Some clients may find it difficult to practice the thought-stopping procedure at home because of privacy issues and should be allowed time in a private location (e.g., the counselor's office) to practice.

Conclusion

It has been the experience of the authors that the techniques described above can in many cases provide a useful set of tools for client behavior change. It seems likely that other similar techniques may be found to be effective in promoting behavior change in persons with mild mental retardation or borderline intelligence. In fact, for counselors who provide services to this group, we feel that the challenge is to find ways to make effective use of the range of counseling tools available.

Rather than finding counseling with persons with mild mental retardation or borderline intelligence limiting, we feel that it is an ongoing, creative challenge to our abilities as counselors.

References

Abrams, D. B., & Wilson, G. T. (1979). Self-monitoring and reactivity in the modification of cigarette smoking. *Journal of Consulting and Clinical Psychology, 47*, 243-251.

Ackerman, N. W., & Menninger, C. F. (1936). Treatment techniques for mental retardation in a school for personality disorders in children. *American Journal of Orthopsychiatry, 6*, 294-312.

Andrasik, F., & Matson, J. L. (1983). Social skills training for the mentally retarded. In L. L'Abate & M. A. Milan (Eds.), *Handbook of social skills training research* (pp. 418-454). New York: John Wiley & Sons.

Bandura, A. (1977). *Social learning theory.* Englewood Cliffs, NJ: Prentice-Hall.

Bates, P. (1980). The effectiveness of interpersonal skills training on the social skill acquisition of moderately and mildly retarded adults. *Journal of Applied Behavior Analysis, 13*, 237-248.

Bauman, K. E., & Iawata, B. A. (1977). Maintenance of independent housekeeping skills using scheduling plus self-recording procedures. *Behavior Therapy, 8*, 454-560.

Beisler, J. M., & Tsai, L. Y. (1983). A pragmatic approach to increase expressive language skills in young autistic children. *Journal of Autism and Developmental Disorders, 13*, 287-303.

Bernstein, D. A., & Borkovec, T. D. (1973). *Progressive muscle relaxation: A manual for the helping professions.* Champaign, IL: Research Press.

Bigelow, G., Sticker, O., Leibson, L., & Griffiths, R. (1976). Maintaining disulfiram ingestion among outpatient alcoholics: A security deposit contingency contracting program. *Behaviour Research and Therapy, 14*, 378-380.

Bijou, S. W. (1966). A functional analysis of retarded development. In N. R. Ellis (Ed.), *International review of research in mental retardation* (pp. 224-271). New York: Academic Press.

Bornstein, P. H., Bach, P. J., & Anton, B. (1982). Behavioral treatment of psychopathological disorders. In J. L. Matson & R. P. Barrett (Eds.), *Psychopathology in the mentally retarded* (pp. 253-292). New York: Grune & Stratton.

Boudin, H. M. (1972). Contingency contracting as a therapeutic tool in the deceleration of amphetamine use. *Behavior Therapy, 3*, 604-608.

Braud, L. W., Lupin, M. N., & Braud, W. G. (1975). The use of electromyographic biofeedback in the control of hyperactivity. *Journal of Learning Disabilities, 8*, 420-425.

Campbell, L. M. (1973). A variation of thought–stopping in a 12-year-old boy: A case report. *Journal of Behavioral Therapy and Experimental Psychiatry, 4*, 69-70.

Cartledge, G., & Milburn, J. F. (1980). *Teaching social skills to children: Innovative approaches*. Elmsford, NY: Pergamon Press.

Cautela, J. R. (1967). Covert sensitization. *Psychological Reports, 20*, 459-468.

Cautela, J. R., & Wisocki, P.A. (1977). The thought stopping procedure: Description, application, and learning theory interpretation. *Psychological Record, 1*, 255-264.

Chaney, E. F., O'Leary, M. R., & Marlatt, G. A. (1978). Skill training with alcoholics. *Journal of Consulting and Clinical Psychology, 46*, 1092-1104.

Chidester, L., & Menninger, K. A. (1936). The application of psychoanalytic methods to the study of mental retardation. *American Journal of Orthopsychiatry, 6*, 616-625.

Chiodo, J., & Maddux, J. E. (1985). A cognitive behavioral approach to anxiety management of retarded individuals: Two case studies. *Journal of Child and Adolescent Psychotherapy, 2*, 16-20.

Christoff, K. A., & Kelly, J. A. (1983). Social skills. In J. L. Matson & S. E. Breuning (Eds.), *Assessing the mentally retarded* (pp. 181-208). New York: Grune & Stratton.

Cole, C. L., & Gardner, W. I. (1984). Self-management training. *Psychiatric Aspects of Mental Retardation Reviews, 3*, 17-20.

Douglas, V., Parry, P., Martin, P., & Garson, C. (1976). Assessment of a cognitive training program for hyperactive children. *Journal of Abnormal Child Psychology, 4*, 389-410.

Ellis, A. (1967). Rational-emotive psychotherapy. In D. Arbuckle (Ed.), *Counseling and psychotherapy* (pp. 321-369). New York: McGraw-Hill.

Ellis, A. (1977). The basic clinical theory of rational-emotive therapy. In A. Ellis & R. Grieger (Eds.), *Handbook of rational-emotive therapy* (Vol. 1, pp. 3-34). New York: Springer.

Emmelkamp, P. M. G. (1974). Self-observation versus flooding in the treatment of agoraphobia. *Behavior Research and Therapy, 12*, 229-237.

Emmelkamp, P. M. G. (1982). Anxiety and fear. In A. S. Bellack, M. Hersen & A. E. Kazdin (Eds.), *International handbook of behavior modification and therapy* (pp. 349-396). New York: Plenum Press.

Emmelkamp, P. M. G. (1986). Behavior therapy with adults. In S. L. Garfield & A. E. Bergin (Eds.), *Handbook of psychotherapy and behavior change* (pp. 385-442). New York: John Wiley & Sons.

Frame, C., Matson, J. L., Sonis, W. A., Fialkov, M. J., & Kazdin, A. E. (1982). Behavioral treatment of depression in a prepubertal child. *Journal of Behavior Therapy and Experimental Psychiatry, 13*, 239-243.

Freeman, B. J., Roy, R. R., & Hemmick, S. (1976). Extinction of a phobia of physical examination in a seven-year-old retarded boy: A case study. *Behavior Research and Therapy, 14*, 63-64.

Gardner, W. L., Cole, T. J., & Cole, C. L. (1983). Self-management of disruptive verbal ruminations by a mentally retarded adult. *Applied Research in Mental Retardation, 4*, 41-58.

Gold, M. (1980). *Try another way training manual*. Urbana, IL: Marc Gold and Associates.

Golden, W. L., & Consorte, J. (1982). Training mildly retarded individuals to control their anger through the use of cognitive–behavioral therapy techniques. *Journal of*

Contemporary Psychology, 13, 182-187.

Goldfried, M. R., & Trier, C. S. (1974). Effectiveness of relaxation as an active coping skill. *Journal of Abnormal Behavior, 83,* 348-355.

Graziano, A. M., & Kean, J. E. (1967). Programmed relaxation and reciprocal inhibition with psychotic children. *Behavior Research and Therapy, 6,* 433-437.

Grinnell, R. M., & Lieberman, A. (1977). Teaching the mentally retarded job interviewing skills. *Journal of Counseling Psychology, 24,* 332-336.

Guralnick, M. J. (1973). Behavior therapy with an acrophobic mentally retarded young adult. *Journal of Behavior Therapy and Experimental Psychiatry, 4,* 263-265.

Hansen, J. C., Stevic, R. R., & Warner, R. W. (1986). *Counseling: Theory and process* (4th ed.). Boston: Allyn & Bacon.

Harris, G., & Johnson, S. B. (1980). Comparison of individualized covert modeling, self-control desensitization, and study skills training for alleviation of test anxiety. *Journal of Consulting and Clinical Psychology, 48,* 186-194.

Harvey, J. R., Karan, O. C., Bhargava, D., & Morehouse, N. (1978). Relaxation training and cognitive behavioral procedures to reduce violent temper outbursts in a moderately retarded woman. *Journal of Behavior Therapy and Experimental Psychiatry, 9,* 347-351.

Harvey, R. H. (1979). The potential of relaxation training for the mentally retarded. *Mental Retardation, 17,* 71-76.

Howlin, P., Marchant, R., Rutter, M., Berger, M., Hersov, L., & Yule, W. (1973). A home-based approach to the treatment of autistic children. *Journal of Autism and Childhood Schizophrenia, 3* (4), 308-336.

Hurley, A. D., & Hurley, F. J. (1986). Counseling and psychotherapy with mentally retarded clients: I. The initial interview. *Psychiatric Aspects of Mental Retardation Reviews, 5,* 22-26.

Jackson, H. J. (1983). Current trends in the treatment of phobias in autistic and mentally retarded persons. *Australian and New Zealand Journal of Developmental Disabilities, 9,* 191-208.

Jackson, H. J., & Hooper, J. P. (1981). Some issues arising from the desensitization of a dog phobia in a mildly retarded female: or Should we take the bite out of the bark? *Australian Journal of Developmental Disabilities, 7,* 9-16.

Jackson, H. J., & King, N. J. (1982). The therapeutic management of an autistic child's phobia using laughter as the anxiety inhibitor. *Behavioural Psychotherapy, 10,* 364-369.

Jackson, H. J., & Patterson, D. S. (1979). Treatment of nail-biting behavior in a moderately retarded female through use of a self-recording procedure. *Special, 14,* 7-13.

Jackson, H. J., & Patterson, D. S. (1980). Evidence for the long-term effectiveness of a self-recording procedure with a moderately retarded female. A one-year follow-up. *Australian Journal of Developmental Disabilities, 6,* 93-94.

Jacobson, E. (1938). *Progressive relaxation* (2nd ed.). Chicago: University of Chicago Press.

Jacobson, N. S. (1977). Problem-solving and contingency contracting in the treatment of marital discord. *Journal of Consulting and Clinical Psychology, 45*, 92-100.

Jeffery, R. W., Gerber, W. M., Rosenthal, B. S., & Lindquist, R. A. (1983). Monetary contracts in weight control: Effectiveness of group and individual contracts of varying size. *Journal of Consulting and Clinical Psychology, 51*, 242-248.

Johnson, S. M., & White, G. (1971). Self-observation as an agent of behavior change. *Behavior Therapy, 2*, 488-497.

Kanfer, F. H., & Gaelick, L. (1986). Self-management methods. In F. Kanfer & A. P. Goldstein (Eds.), *Helping people change: A textbook of methods* (3rd. ed., pp. 283-345). New York: Pergamon Press.

Klingman, A., Melamed, B. G., Cuthbert, M. L., & Hermecz, D. A. (1984). Effects of participant modeling on information acquisition and skill utilization. *Journal of Consulting and Clinical Psychology, 52*, 414-421.

Koeppen, A. S. (1974). Relaxation training for children. *Elementary School Guidance and Counseling, 9*, 14-21.

Ladouceur, R. (1983). Participant modeling with or without cognitive treatment for phobias. *Journal of Consulting and Clinical Psychology, 51*, 942-944.

Lazarus, A. A. (1970). *Relaxation exercises* (Tape). Chicago: Instructional Dynamics.

Lazarus, A. A. (1971). Behavioral therapy for sexual problems. *Professional Psychology, 3*, 349-353.

Lichstein, K. L. (1988). *Clinical relaxation strategies.* New York: John Wiley & Sons.

Litrownski, A. J., & Freitas, J. L. (1980). Self-monitoring in moderately retarded adolescents: Reactivity and accuracy as a function of valence. *Behavior Therapy, 11*, 245-255.

Litrownski, A. J., Freitas, J. L. , & Franzini, L. R. (1978). Self-regulation in retarded persons: Assessment and training of self-monitoring skills. *American Journal of Mental Deficiency, 82*, 499-506.

Luiselli, J. K. (1978). Treatment of an autistic child's fear of riding a school bus through exposure and reinforcement. *Journal of Behavior Therapy and Experimental Psychiatry, 9*, 169-172.

Luiselli, J. K. (1980). Relaxation training with the developmentally disabled: A reappraisal. *Behavior Research of Severe Developmental Disabilities, 1*, 191-213.

Luiselli, J. K., Marholin II, D., Steinman, D. L., & Steinman, W. M. (1979). Assessing the effects of relaxation training. *Behavior Therapy, 10*, 663-668.

Luiselli, J. K., Steinman, D. L., Marholin II, D., & Steinman, W. M. (1981). Evaluation of progressive muscle relaxation with conduct-problem, learning-disabled children. *Child Behavior Therapy, 3*, 41-55.

Luria, A. (1961). The role of speech in the regulation of normal and abnormal behavior. New York: Liveright.

Mahoney, M. J., & Mahoney K. (1976) Self–control techniques with the mentally retarded. *Exceptional Children, 42*, 338-339.

Mansdorf, I. J. (1976). Eliminating fear in a mentally retarded adult by behavioral hierarchies and operant techniques. *Journal of Behavior Therapy and Experimental Psychiatry, 7*, 189-190.

Marholin, D., Steinman, W. M., Luiselli, J. K., Schwartz, C. S., & Townsend, N. M. (1979). The effects of progressive muscle relaxation on the behavior of autistic adolescents: A preliminary analysis. *Child Behavior Therapy, 1*, 75-84.

Matson, J. L. (1981a). A controlled outcome study of phobias in mentally retarded adults. *Behavioral Research and Therapy, 19*, 101-107.

Matson, J. L. (1981b). Assessment and treatment of clinical fears in mentally retarded children. *Journal of Applied Behavior Analysis, 14*, 287-294.

Matson, J. L. (1982). Independence training vs. modeling procedures for teaching phone conversation skills to the mentally retarded. *Behavior Research and Therapy, 20*, 500-511.

Matson, J. L. (1984a). Behavioral treatment of psychosomatic complaints of mentally retarded adults. *American Journal of Mental Deficiency, 88*, 638-646.

Matson, J. L. (1984b). Social skills training. *Psychiatric Aspects of Mental Retardation Reviews, 3*(1), 1-4.

Matson, J. L., Kazdin, A. E., & Esveldt-Dawson, K. (1980). Training interpersonal skills among mentally retarded and socially dysfunctional children. *Behavior Research and Therapy, 18*, 419-427.

Matson, J. L., & Senatore, V. (1981). A comparison of traditional psychotherapy and social skills training for improving interpersonal functioning of mentally retarded adults. *Behavior Therapy, 12*, 369-382.

Matson, J. L., & Stephens, R. M. (1978). Increasing appropriate behavior of explosive chronic psychiatric patients with social skills training packages. *Behavior Modification, 2*, 61-75.

McGinnes, E., & Goldstein, A. P. (1984). *Skill-streaming the elementary school child: A guide for teaching prosocial skills*. Champaign, IL: Research Press.

Meichenbaum, D. (1975). A self-instructional approach to stress management: A proposal for stress inoculation training. In I. Sarason & C. D. Spielberger (Eds.), *Stress and anxiety* (Vol. 2, pp. 89-124). New York: Wiley.

Meichenbaum, D. (1977). *Cognitive-behavior modification*. New York: Plenum Press.

Meichenbaum, D. (1986). Cognitive-behavior modification. In F. Kanfer & A. P. Goldstein (Eds.), *Helping people change: A textbook of methods* (3rd. ed., pp. 346-380). New York, Pergamon Press.

Meichenbaum, D., & Goodman, J. (1971). Training impulsive children to talk to themselves: A means of developing self-control. *Journal of Abnormal Psychology, 77*, 115-126.

Melamed, B. G., & Siegel, L. J. (1975). Reduction of anxiety in children facing hospitalization and surgery by use of filmed modeling. *Journal of Consulting and Clinical Psychology, 43*, 511-521.

Menolascino, F. J. (1977). *Challenges in mental retardation: Progressive ideology and services*. New York: Human Science Press.

Nay, R. N. (1984). *Multi-method clinical assessment*. New York: Gardner Press.

Neham, S. (1951). Psychotherapy in relation to mental deficiency. *American Journal of Mental Deficiency, 55*, 557-572.

Nelson, R. O., Lipinski, D. P., & Black, J. L. (1976). The reactivity of adult retardates' self-monitoring: A comparison among behaviors of different valences, and a comparison with token reinforcement. *The Psychological Record, 26*, 189-201.

Novaco, R. W. (1975). *Anger control: The development and evaluation of an experimental treatment.* Lexington, MA.: Lexington Books.

O'Leary, K. D., & Wilson, G. T. (1975). *Behavior therapy: Application and outcome.* Engelwood Cliffs, NJ: Prentice-Hall.

Ollendick, T. H. (1979). Fear reduction techniques with children. In M. Hersen, R. M. Eisler, & P. M. Miller (Eds.), *Progress in behavior modification* (Vol. 8, pp.??--??).

Ollendick, T. H., & Ollendick, D. G. (1982). Anxiety disorders. In J. L. Matson & R. P. Barrett (Eds.), *Psychopathology in the mentally retarded* (pp. 317-353). New York: Grune & Stratton.

Peck, C. L. (1977). Desensitization for the treatment of fear in the high level adult retardate. *Behavior Research and Therapy, 15*, 137-148.

Perry, M. A., & Cerreto, M. C. (1977). Structured learning training of social skills for the retarded. *Mental Retardation, 15*, 31-34.

Perry, M. A., & Furukawa. M. J. (1986). Modeling methods. In F. H. Kanfer & A. P. Goldstein (Eds.), *Helping people change: A textbook of methods* (3rd ed., pp. 66-110). New York: Pergamon Press.

Peters, R. D., & Davis, K. (1981). Effects of self-instructional training on cognitive impulsivity of mentally retarded adolescents. *American Journal of Mental Retardation, 4*, 377-382.

Petroski, R. A., Craighead, L. W., & Horan, J. J. (1983). Separate and combined effects of behavior rehearsal and self-other modeling variations on the grooming skill acquisition of mentally retarded women. *Journal of Counseling Psychology, 30*, 279-282.

Phillips, I., & Williams, N. (1975). Psychopathology and mental retardation: A study of 100 mentally retarded children. *American Journal of Psychiatry, 132*, 12-65.

Poppen, R. (1988). *Behavioral relaxation training and assessment.* New York: Pergamon Press.

Prout, H. T., & Strohmer, D. C. (1991). *Emotional Problems Scales.* Odessa, FL: Psychological Assessment Resources.

Reeder, C. W., & Kunce, J. T. (1976). Modeling techniques, drug-abstinence behavior, and heroin addicts: A pilot study. *Journal of Counseling Psychology, 23*, 560-562.

Reiss, S., Levitan, G. W., & McNally, R. J. (1982). Emotionally disturbed mentally retarded people. *American Psychologist, 37*, 361-367.

Rickard, H. C. (1986). Relaxation training for mentally retarded persons. *Psychiatric Aspects of Mental Retardation Reviews, 5*, 11-15.

Rickard, H. C., Thrasher, K. A., & Elkins, P. D. (1984). Responses of persons who are mentally retarded to four components of relaxation instruction. *Mental Retardation, 22*, 248-252.

Rivenq, B. (1974). Behavioral therapy of phobias: A case study with gynecomastia and mental retardation. *Mental Retardation, 12*, 44-45.

Romanczyk, R. G. (1974). Self-monitoring in the treatment of obesity: Parameters of reactivity. *Behavior Therapy, 5*, 531-540.

Rotatori, A. E., Parrish, P., & Freagon, S. (1979). Weight loss in retarded children: A pilot study. *Journal of Psychiatric Nursing, 10*, 33-34.

Rotatori, A., Switzky, H. N., & Fox, R. (1981a). Behavioral treatment approaches to obesity: Successes with the nonretarded and retarded. *Obesity and Metabolism, 1*, 140-158.

Rotatori, A., Switzky, H. N., & Fox, R. (1981b). Behavioral weight reduction procedures for obese mentally retarded individuals: A review. *Mental Retardation, 19*, 157-161.

Runyan, M. C., Stevens, D. H., & Reeves, R. (1985). Reduction of avoidance behavior of institutionalized mentally retarded adults through contact desensitization. *American Journal of Mental Deficiency, 90*, 222-225.

Russell, R. K., & Spich, J. F. (1973). Cue-controlled relaxation in the treatment of test anxiety. *Journal of Behavior Therapy and Experimental Psychiatry, 4*, 47-49.

Shaw, W. J., & Walker, C. E. (1979). Use of relaxation in fetish behavior: An exploratory case study. *Journal of Pediatric Psychology, 4*, 403-407.

Spring, F. L., Sipich, J. F., Trimble, R. W., & Goeckner, D. J. (1978). Effects of contingency and non-contingency contracts in the context of a self-control oriented smoking modification program. *Behavior Therapy, 9*, 967-968.

Stephan, C., Stephano, W., & Talkington, L. W. (1973). Use of modeling in survival social training with the educable mentally retarded. *Training School Bulletin, 70*, 63-68.

Stephens, R. M., Matson, J. L., Westmoreland, T., & Kulpa, J. (1981). Modifications of psychotic speech with mentally retarded patients. *Journal of Mental Deficiency Research, 25*, 187-197.

Stewart, S. R., Winborn, B. B., Johnson, R. G., Burks, H. M., & Engelkes, J. R. (1978). *Systematic counseling*. Engelwood Cliffs, NJ: Prentice-Hall.

Strohmer, D. C. (1987). *Handbook for behavioral contracting*. Albany, NY: New York State Association of Rehabilitation Facilities.

Taylor, J. G. (1963). A behavioral interpretation of obsessive–compulsive neurosis. *Behavior Research and Therapy, 1*, 71-83.

Turner, S. M., Hersen, M., & Bellack, A. S. (1978). Social skills training to teach pro-social behaviors in an organically impaired and retarded patient. *Journal of Behavior Therapy and Experimental Psychiatry, 9*(3), 253-258.

Walker, C. E., Hedburg, A., Clement, P. A., & Wright, L. (1981). *Clinical procedures for behavior therapy*. Engelwood Cliffs, NJ: Prentice-Hall.

Waranch, H. R., Iwata, B. A., Wohl, M. K., & Nidiffer, F. D. (1981). Treatment of a retarded adult's mannequin phobia through in vivo desensitization and shaping approach responses. *Journal of Behavior Therapy and Experimental Psychiatry, 12*, 359-362.

Wells, K. C., Turner, S. M., Bellack, A. S., & Hersen, M. (1978). Effects of cue controlled relaxation on psychomotor seizures: An experimental analysis. *Behavior Re-*

search and Therapy, 16, 51-53.

Wilkins, W. (1971). Desensitization: Social and cognitive factors underlying the effectiveness of Wolpe's procedure. *Psychological Bulletin, 76,* 311-317.

Wilson, B., & Jackson, H. J. (1980). An in vivo approach to the desensitization of a retarded child's toilet phobia. *Australian Journal of Developmental Disabilities, 6,* 137-140.

Wisocki, P. A. (1976). A behavioral treatment program for social inadequacy: Multiple methods for a complex problem. In J. Krumboltz & C. Thorensen (Eds.), *Counseling methods* (pp. 112-149). New York: Holt, Rinehart, & Winston.

Wisocki, P. A. (1985). Thought stopping. In A. S. Bellack & M. Hersen (Eds.), *Dictionary of behavior therapy techniques.* New York: Pergamon Press.

Wolpe, J. (1958). *Psychotherapy by reciprocal inhibition.* Stanford, CA: Stanford University Press.

Wolpe, J. (1973). *The practice of behavior therapy.* New York: Pergamon Press.

Zegiob, L., Klukas, N., & Junginger, J. (1978). Reactivity of self-monitoring procedures with retarded adolescents. *American Journal of Mental Deficiency, 83,* 156-163.

Zigler, E. (1966). Research on personality structure in the retardate. In N. R. Ellis (Ed.), *International review of research in mental retardation* (pp. 212-252). New York: Academic Press.

Zohn, J. C., & Bornstein, P. H. (1980). Self-monitoring of work performance with mentally retarded adults: Effects upon work productivity, work quality, and on-task behavior. *Mental Retardation, 18,* 19-25.

6 GROUP COUNSELING AND PSYCHOTHERAPY

Douglas T. Brown

This chapter will focus on group counseling techniques that can be employed with persons with mental retardation. Most of the techniques discussed can be used with persons with mental retardation who have a mental age of 5 or older. This means that the majority of the applications discussed below will apply to persons with mental retardation with chronological ages of 10 and above. However, much of the literature described is centered on adolescents and adults, with relatively fewer studies devoted to children. This material will be presented in four parts: Part I will describe the general background literature surrounding counseling with persons with mental retardation including developmental, cognitive, and basic affective issues. Part II will present a more detailed discussion of specific counseling approaches that have been employed with persons with mental retardation and the relative utility of each. Part III of the chapter will deal with a variety of counseling programs designed for specific referral issues (e.g., anger management, sexual social skills). Also in this section, a brief review of the efficacy research on group counseling will be presented. Finally, Part IV will present three case studies with differing developmental patterns in order to illustrate the typical group interventions with persons with mental retardation. An annotated bibliography of materials and references of use in group counseling/therapy also will be provided.

Background Literature

Even a cursory review of the literature on counseling with persons with mental retardation suggests that this area has been poorly developed by both researchers and practitioners (Kashubeck, 1989; Spangler, 1982; Spragg, 1983; Vance, McGee, & Finkle, 1977). This is partially due to the fact that the efficacy of psychotherapeutic interventions with normal populations has only recently begun to be established (Brown & Prout, 1989). Of equal importance to this situation, however, is the perceived difficulty of providing services to persons with mental retardation because of their numerous handicapping conditions, especially those involving receptive and expressive language skills. Thus many mental health professionals view persons with mental retardation as essentially unsuitable for counseling, particularly if traditional insight therapies are employed as a means for behavioral change.

In addition, it has been observed by some theorists (Spragg, 1983) that persons with mental retardation are seen by many mental health professionals in a biased manner. First, they are viewed as less emotionally developed and sophisticated. It is assumed that the array of feelings that can be experienced by persons with mental retardation is more restricted than that of normal adults. Second, they are often viewed as a non-cost-effective group for the provision of psychotherapeutic services. Thus they are seen as not benefiting from counseling.

It is interesting to note that a review of the literature clearly shows the prevalence of mental illness among individuals with mental retardation is higher than in the general population (Prout & Strohmer, 1991; Sovner, 1989). Thus it appears that persons with mental retardation are as capable as the general population of developing severe disturbance. The literature is replete with case studies describing bipolar disorders, hyperarousal, anxiety disorders, depression, and a variety of other behaviors associated with poor self-esteem. Therefore, it would be reasonable to assume that persons with mental retardation experience many of the same emotions associated with persons who do not have mental retardation and have many of the same needs including acceptance, love, self-sufficiency, productivity, and belongingness (Whitmore, 1988). The fact that they (due to their limited cognitive abilities) also show difficulty in perceiving social situations accurately, are poor problem solvers, have difficulty in conceptualizing the intentions of others, and have heightened difficulty with their families further complicates their emotional development and the attainment of many of the needs specified above. This results in a number of common referrals for psychotherapeutic interventions. In the author's experience the most common include:

1. aggression and self-destructive behavior;
2. inability to interact effectively with peers, family members, and/or care providers;
3. inability to identify internal emotions and therefore control anger and aggression;
4. expressions of anxiety, depression, and low self-esteem;
5. difficulty in developing social/sexual relationships;
6. difficulty in dealing with normal life stage development issues such as aging, vocational choices, and living arrangements.

Learning Characteristics of Persons with Mental Retardation

The counseling literature for persons with mental retardation traditionally has emphasized the use of scaled-down approaches, usually extrapolated from behavior therapy, reality therapy, or rational-emotive therapy (Spragg, 1984). This is the result of a highly oversimplified notion of the information-processing and retrieval systems associated with mental retardation. For example, attention is of critical concern for most persons with mental retardation. That is, many have significant attention deficits (Detterman, 1979). Attention deficits result in the tendency to be distractible and for stimuli to have variable meaning and impact on the individual. Thus it is probable that persons with mental retardation use only part of the relevant cues available in the environment in problem solving or interpreting social situations. The fact that persons with mental retardation also have poorer short-term memory further complicates the situation. This means that information that is presented may or may not be attended to or may or may not be retained in long-term memory. It also means that the amount of rehearsal needed to enhance long-term memory is substantially greater for persons with mental retardation than for persons who do not have mental retardation.

The ability of persons with mental retardation to classify or to group stimuli (the basis of concept development) is also hampered by attention deficits and associated poor short-term memory. This results in learning that appears to be concrete, limited to the critical aspects of the learning situation only, and devoid of abstract concepts. Added to this is the fact that there is less ability to generalize learning to other similar situations as spontaneously when compared with individuals who do not have mental retardation. That is, information learned in one setting does not readily transfer to a different but similar setting. The concepts of past, present, and future are often confused by persons with mental retardation. Although the concept of present is often understood, the concepts of past, and especially future events are not as clearly understood. Thus, it is difficult to employ traditional therapies that focus on abstract concepts and project these concepts to future life events.

Language in persons with mental retardation is typically deficient. The most common disorders are in expressive language. These include poor articulation, poor speech fluency, restricted vocabulary, and inadequate conversational skills. Fortunately most persons with mental retardation possess significantly better receptive than expressive language skills. This usually means they are interpreting their environment more accurately than would be predicted by their expressive language. In addition, many persons with mental retardation use both oral and sign communication. In the author's experience, some persons with mental retardation communicate more fluently in sign than in oral expressive language. This has obvious implications for the therapeutic process.

Because the rate of learning for persons with mental retardation is slower than for their normal peers, the rate at which they acquire new behaviors of all types will be reduced. Thus it can reasonably be expected that they will show the effects of therapeutic interventions more slowly than persons who do not have mental retardation. When taken in combination, the array of factors discussed above would suggest that persons with mental retardation require therapeutic approaches that are significantly modified and/or newly developed compared to traditional psycho-therapy. Some general considerations for designing an appropriate counseling intervention would seem to be the following:

1. A thorough cognitive assessment should be performed prior to any therapeutic intervention.

2. Any counseling strategy should be implemented only after carefully analyzing the relevant aspects of the particular task that you wish the client to acquire. Thus an analysis of the particular skills involved (e.g., attending, auditory and visual processing, memory skills) should be performed.

3. As Spragg (1983) points out, "the ability to de-emphasize the irrelevant dimensions of a problem and increase the perceptual salience of the relevant cues is important to successful therapeutic intervention" (p. 12). Basically, persons with mental retardation have difficulty both in discriminating important cues and then in generalizing them to later situations.

4. Communication must be improved with persons with mental retardation in order for therapeutic intervention to be effective. Language that is clearly understood and interpreted is a must if any meaningful communication is to occur. Many individuals, including staff, who feel they are communicating with clients with mental retardation are, in fact, only being reinforced by the client through head

nodding. No meaningful communication is taking place. Aside from choosing the appropriate language medium (oral communication, sign communication, or both), material must be presented in a manner that can be understood conceptually or where new concepts are taught if needed. The rule here is to use simple, concise, and repeatable language.

5. In order to overcome the basic memory and recall deficits of persons with mental retardation, repetition of the material is important (Spragg, 1983). Practice not only must be repetitive but must be distributed over an appropriate period of time. Careful linking of the activities from one session to the next is also important for continuity in memory. The linking of new thoughts to previous language is one of the obvious ways to enhance memory processes.

Developmental Issues

As with adults who do not have mental retardation, persons do have mental retardation experience a series of developmental stages that represent both challenging and stressful events in their lives (Prout & Strohmer, 1991). Each of these developmental issues forms the potential basis for the need for therapeutic intervention. Because of the factors discussed above, persons with mental retardation more often have difficulty in achieving developmental milestones or moving through normal stages of self-actualization as described by Maslow (Maslow, 1954). However, many persons with mental retardation tend to experience the same developmental stages experienced by all children and adults but in a more delayed and erratic fashion.

Complicating development for many persons with mental retardation are numerous medical conditions and syndromes that either retard maturation or significantly impede cognitive interventions. Many medical conditions (e.g., seizure disorders, diabetes, cardiac insufficiency, cerebral palsy) require substantially more restrictive care than would normally be the case. Some conditions (Friedreich's Ataxia) result in progressive degeneration and thus result in negative development. The net result of these conditions is that persons with mental retardation often live much more restrictive lives than their non–medically involved counterparts.

In the author's experience, the following developmental stages most often underlie many of the social-emotional problems affecting persons with mental retardation:

1. failure either to enter the adolescent stage of development or to resolve and to grow beyond that stage of development;

2. separation from family and the associated issues of individuation that normally result;

3. relationships with peers rather than with primary caregivers;

4. sexual relationships;

5. long-term relationships including marriage;

6. progressive independence of the type associated with less-restrictive living environments;

7. career and job satisfaction including the resources to choose and plan for living on one's own;

8. economic independence;

9. "mid-life crisis" or dealing with the fact that a particular stage of self-actualization may not be attainable;

10. death of close relatives and/or parents;

11. aging.

Of particular difficulty for persons with mental retardation are their relationships with family members. Families of persons with mental retardation often find it impossible to view their son, daughter, or sibling as a normalized human being. This means that expectations for individuation are minimal or negative. The family member with mental retardation is seen as not capable of achieving the higher stages of development and is often denied access to conditions that would promote or facilitate development and resolution of these life stages. The prevailing view of the family member with mental retardation is that of a child who must be treated and cared for as a child throughout his or her life. Complicating this situation are the usual family dysfunctions experienced by families with nondisabled individuals. Thus, physical and/or emotional abuse of the child/children or spouse, alcoholism, and/or rigid family values are at least as prevalent if not more prevalent in families with a member with mental retardation (Hite, Kleber, & Simpkins, 1985). It can easily be assumed that each individual with mental retardation with whom a therapist may work will harbor a number of unresolved family issues that influence his or her daily behavior.

Career choice and job satisfaction rank high among the more difficult life stages experienced by persons with mental retardation. Persons with mental retardation are often highly restricted in the job choices and career opportunities available to them (Levinson, 1986; Lombana, 1983; Solly, 1987; Stieglitz & Cohen, 1980). This results in lowered economic independence and continued dependence on either family or community resources. Many persons with mental retardation remain unemployed throughout their lives despite the fact that they possess abilities that would be useful to society. An even larger group of persons with mental retardation remain in low-level jobs usually associated with sheltered or semi-independent employment settings. For many in such settings, their career life involves highly repetitive and boring activity that remains substantially unchanged throughout many years. Even for those persons with mental retardation involved in competitive employment, the level of job diversification and job satisfaction is often poor (Lombana, 1983). Therefore, it is not surprising that supervisors often report persons with mental retardation who experience work adjustment difficulty and who exhibit a variety of behavior disorders or emotionally disturbed behaviors. As with all other individuals, persons with mental retardation have a need to feel that they are engaged in productive, meaningful, and worthwhile activity.

Relationships with peers and with members of the opposite sex are the basis for many of the behavior problems associated with persons with mental retardation. As was discussed above, persons with mental retardation often have a reduced capacity for perceiving social situations accurately. This, in combination with their reduced language skill, results in lower levels of peer interaction and more opportunities to misconstrue a social situation. In dealing with heterosexual relationships, persons with mental retardation are more likely to misinterpret the normal social cues associated with such relationships and, therefore, to exhibit inappropriate behaviors. In addition, they often lack fundamental knowledge or acquire inaccurate knowledge regarding heterosexual relationships (Perroncel, 1988). The specific social skills associated with appropriate peer interactions are often the focus of much of the programming in schools and group homes for persons with mental retardation. It is not surprising that persons with mental retardation have difficulty in this area given the fact that higher level concepts are involved in understanding the behavior of others and predicting it.

Because of medical advances, persons with mental retardation are living longer than at any time in the past. This has resulted in many of them entering more advanced stages of development and the attendant problems associated with these stages of development. Dealing with the death of a parent or close relative can be an extremely traumatic life event for an individual with mental retardation. Many persons with mental retardation lack understanding of the basic concepts of life and death because they have not developed a clear concept of future. It is not uncommon to see clients who harbor unresolved conflict for years regarding their parents' death. This often affects their behavior in numerous ways, including anxiety reactions and social withdrawal and depression.

The process of aging and the developmental readiness of a person with mental retardation to deal with biological aging form the basis for another important life stress. In my own practice, I have begun to see, for the first time, a number of persons with mental retardation who experience the equivalent of a "mid-life crisis." These clients, having learned the concept of future, begin to realize that they will not reach certain stages of self-actualization, particularly those associated with marriage and job/career aspirations. The death of a parent often exacerbates this situation, resulting in depression and morbid preoccupation with death. As with adults who are not mentally retarded, the importance of effective therapeutic intervention is critical to the mental health of such individuals.

In summary, persons with mental retardation experience most or all of the same stages of development commonly associated with persons who do not have mental retardation. Effective counseling and therapy depend upon the accurate appraisal of the developmental stages in which a client is currently involved together with knowledge of the key issues that define these stages for that individual. This understanding is as critical to effective counseling as knowledge of the relative cognitive strengths and weaknesses of a given client.

Basic Considerations in Counseling with Persons with Mental Retardation

Not all individuals can be effective counselors with persons with mental retardation. This is particularly true when we are dealing with group applications. It is obvious from the above discussion that any individual providing this mental health service should have adequate training in mental retardation, cognitive assessment, counseling, and special education. Beyond this basic training, those involved with group work must have developed the interactional sensitivity and "systems knowledge" necessary to appreciate the group process. Furthermore, they must be skilled at facilitating that process and, where necessary, directing it. It seems obvious (but is often not the case) that effective therapists with persons with mental retardation should have a strong positive regard for the potential of the individual with mental retardation and a belief in the ability of the individual to benefit from counseling. The usual personality characteristics of counselors (i.e., warmth, respect, positive self-regard) are also assumed. Hurley and Hurley (1987) provide a framework of principles for achieving a good therapeutic relationship when counseling the person with mental retardation. These include (a) accepting the client for who he or she is, (b) understanding reality as the client sees it, (c) accepting the client's life circumstances, (d) being consistent, (e) separating the therapeutic intervention from other aspects of the client's life, (f) keeping the relationship totally devoted to the client, (g) being able to draw the client out, (h) expressing genuine interest in the client, and (i) being a real person with the client.

For therapeutic success to occur, it is important that the therapist interact with the client at his or her developmental level while at the same time retaining the therapist's normal interpersonal style. As with other types of therapy, the ability of the therapist to empathize (put yourself in the place of the client) is crucial to positive therapeutic outcome.

Whitmore (1988) has suggested a number of additional guidelines for the structure of groups. These include the following:

1. Groups should be relatively small, usually no larger than six persons, with ample opportunity afforded for input from all members.

2. Sessions should be relatively brief and more frequent. For example, rather than having 1-hour sessions twice a week, it might be more appropriate to have 30-minute sessions three or four times a week. This maximizes the concept of distributed practice.

3. Groups are best organized on the basis of the developmental levels of their members. This variable is more important than the indicated diagnostic problem or any other reason for the existence of the group. The group can then be organized on the basis of the specific needs of clients (e.g., social skills development, heterosexual social skills, anxiety reduction).

4. Basically, individuals who cannot developmentally fit into a group should be considered for individual counseling. Not all individuals are ready for group interaction nor can some individuals sufficiently disclose in groups.

5. Activities that promote relaxation (e.g., simple games, structured play activity, drawings) should be used to facilitate openness and discussion.

6. If clients exhibit low verbal expressiveness, techniques should be employed with structured activities to facilitate verbal expression as a preliminary to other group therapeutic activity.

7. A set of rules should be developed for sessions that are clear and simple involving appropriate and inappropriate conduct in the group setting. These rules should be portrayed visually and concretely through pictures or drawings. The rules should be displayed during the sessions for all group members to see and to reference as needed.

8. The group leader(s) should learn to utilize a wide variety of activities including modeling, role rehearsal, relaxation techniques, biofeedback techniques, audiotaping, videotaping, and structured games in order to accomplish the counseling objectives.

9. As with any group, the clients should have complete freedom to enter and exit the group as well as the freedom to choose from among a variety of alternative interventions. The clients should be an integral part of the process of the group rather than passive recipients of the therapeutic process.

Counseling Approaches

Traditionally, behavior modification has been the therapy of choice with persons with mental retardation. Deutsch and Placona (1983b) conducted a study in which they compared the efficacy of behavior therapy with that of more traditional individual and group psychotherapy with persons with mental retardation. Specifically, they reviewed the degree of comfort associated with various types of psychotherapy and the perceived benefits of each for both therapist and client. Their findings suggest that when given a choice, both clients and therapists will choose equally among the various techniques including behavior modification, individual therapy, group therapy, and family therapy. Generally, however, they found a preference by therapists for psychotherapy (individual, group, and family) over behavior modification in the types of cases that they examined. This suggests, contrary to popular belief, that mental health practitioners are more open to nonoperant types of therapy than is commonly suggested in the literature. Specifically, it appears that substantial interest in group counseling with clients with mental retardation has developed among mental health professionals during the past 15 years (Fletcher, 1984; Hurley & Hurley, 1986; Robinson, 1973). This is in contrast to earlier reviews (Vance et al., 1977) that suggested minimal interest in group psychotherapy with persons with mental retardation and a paucity of literature in that area.

Spragg (1983) has presented an excellent review of some of the therapeutic techniques commonly considered for use with persons with mental retardation. Traditional psychoanalytic approaches are employed, but with limited success, because they require higher level verbal interpretations and the interpretation of symbolic behaviors and fantasies such as dreams. It does appear, however, that some persons with mental retardation have significant psychological disturbance based on anxiety and presumably subconscious processes that produce that anxiety. Because of its length, complexity, and lack of cost effectiveness, psychoanalytic therapy has not often been implemented with persons with mental retardation.

Both operant and respondent therapies have been extensively investigated with individuals with mental retardation. Considerable success has been shown with techniques such as desensitization, progressive relaxation, and various classical conditioning procedures when used with persons with mental retardation (Prout & Brown, 1989). Desensitization has been especially effective in working with the normal fears and phobias associated with deinstitutionalization, group home, and community placement (Gardner, 1989; Matson, 1981). Because the individual with mental retardation has a limited capacity for the imagery associated with desensitization, many studies have utilized contact desensitization procedures (in vivo) (Spragg, 1983).

Among the group approaches, both nondirective and directive techniques have been employed (Rothberg, Adams, & Boyd, 1989). Generally nondirective approaches have been shown to have limited applicability with persons with mental retardation (Spragg, 1983). This approach assumes that clients have the underlying conceptual skills to introspect and to interact in a group effectively. In examining the content of nondirective groups, Garfield (1982) determined that clients with mental retardation were not dealing with meaningful personal material and that much of the activity in such groups involved peripheral conversation not related to the group.

Directive group therapy appears to be the basis of most of the literature on group therapy with persons with mental retardation. A variety of traditional and eclectic approaches have been attempted including reality therapy, rational-emotive therapy, and a wide assortment of social skills training groups. In contrast to other types of group therapy, therapists in directive groups are seen as highly active and structured in their approach to therapy. Although a significant amount of literature exists regarding directive group applications, the efficacy of these applications is in question because of poor research design (Spragg, 1983). With directive therapies, the current emphasis in the literature appears to be in social skills training, anger management training, and social sexual interaction.

Review of Techniques

A variety of specific directive group techniques have been employed in the literature. In this section, examples of the basic strategies employed will be reviewed.

Role playing is often used as a therapeutic approach in group work with persons with mental retardation (Jageman & Myers, 1986; Schramski, 1984). Role playing is seen by many therapists to improve the verbal communication of the counselee and to increase his or her understanding of his or her own feelings and social interactions. It is thought to improve the client's empathy for the feelings of others and to maximize the client's ability to consider multiple solutions to a problem. Role playing also is seen as a rehearsal in which general social skills are practiced. Schramski (1984) has provided an excellent outline of the various techniques that can be employed in role playing. These include:

1. *Mirroring.* Mirroring allows a client to see his or her personal behavior through the perspective of another person. Thus in mirroring, a group member is asked to mimic the behavior of another group member in a facilitating way.

2. *Soliloquy.* This is a technique in which a client within the group speaks without addressing any particular listener. This technique is constructed in a way to encourage disclosure and confrontation of personal issues.

3. *Concrete Symbolism.* In this technique, the therapist uses concrete objects, pictures, and/or gestures in order to represent more symbolic obstacles to appropriate social interaction among group members. Thus a refusal to interact on the part of two group members might be represented by a physical barrier of some sort.

4. *Doubling.* Doubling is a type of parallel role reversal in which a client or therapist actually takes the part of another client in order to help facilitate the resolution of issues for that client.

5. *Scene Setting.* The therapist takes an active role in setting up a framework (scene) that duplicates a particular social situation in which the group members might commonly interact. Situations like workshop/day activities programs, a dinner setting, or a leisure time setting might be re-enacted in a very realistic manner.

6. *Group Sociometric Exploration.* In this traditional technique, group members are asked to identify other group members in relation to the amount of social intimacy that they have to one another. This process helps to identify socially skilled and socially isolated individuals.

Most role playing takes place in the context of a broader group purpose. This might include general social skills training, sexual awareness training, family issues counseling, or counseling involving anxiety or depression. In any of these situations, the therapist must be certain to assess each client's level of cognitive functioning and to educate a client regarding the general purposes of the group and the expectations for behavior in the group. Particularly with persons with mental retardation, it is important to make clear such simple aspects of group work as how often the group will meet, the length of the sessions, the specific days on which the group will meet, and what will happen should the group be unable to meet.

An excellent example of an in vivo intervention is provided by Hoshmand (1983) in which directive group therapy with role playing was implemented in a sheltered workshop setting. Four "rap groups" were constructed of six to seven members each. Two of these groups represented clients with mild mental retardation, whereas the other two groups focused on clients with moderate mental retardation. Prior to the initiation of group therapy, clients were advised as to the purpose of the group, the concept of confidentiality was explained, the rules for attendance were discussed, each participant was given a name tag, a contract was signed by each regarding their role, and expectations for verbal participation were discussed. The specific content of the sessions included:

Session 1:   Self-disclosure and associated role playing.

Session 2:   Discussion of activities of interest including what each participant liked to do with his or her time.

Session 3:   Description of each participants' social world including significant others and respective interactions with them.

Session 4:   Description and role play of private feelings and thoughts along with self-disclosure regarding these private feelings and thoughts.

Session 5:   Description of oneself as well as discussion of how each client views himself/herself relative to other clients.

These five topic areas were repeated in four cycles for a total of 20 group sessions. All group leaders were instructed to model appropriate responses, solicit but not shape social interaction, and to use active listening and reframing as basic group techniques. Baseline data and subsequent repeated measurements data were collected on a number of group behaviors. Generally the level of participation among group members significantly increased over the 20 sessions. Differences, however, were found across the various groups but were not related to level of retardation. The level of self-awareness and social awareness observed by group facilitators increased significantly over the 20 sessions.

A variety of other interventions have been reported in which group counseling was used with various types of individuals with mental retardation. Lee (1977b) reports the use of group therapy with foster adolescents with mental retardation. Participants in her groups were adolescents with mental retardation who had experienced multiple foster care placements. Group therapy centered around the stress, anxiety, and loneliness associated with such placements. Lee reports the use of a variety of activities including role playing, the use of trips for socialization training, spontaneous parties as a socialization activity, and more traditional group therapy for promoting intimacy and disclosiveness. Lee concluded that "the group promoted ego functioning in many areas including object relationships, tolerance of frustration, judgment, internal controls, and self-confidence" (p. 172). Most of Lee's subjects' were in the mildly retarded range, however.

Some therapists (Gumaer & Simon, 1979), have reported the use of group counseling techniques with students in the moderate to severe range of mental retardation. In their research Gumaer and Simon performed group intervention with students with moderate to severe retardation in the IQ range between 25 and 55 who were morbidly obese. The subjects' chronological ages ranged from 11 to 21 years. Objectives of the group included (a) socialization (getting to know one another), (b) recognizing and discussing obesity in the self, (c) discussing the feelings of being obese, (d) recognizing the personal responsibility for being obese, (e) reviewing food groupings, (f) expressing feelings regarding obesity and the losing or gaining of weight, (g) learning the concept of personal sacrifice as it relates to weight reduction, and (h) closure in which students invited classmates, teachers, and parents to observe the loss of weight and to provide reinforcement for it. Operant reinforcement techniques were also used extensively as part of this group intervention. The results of the study indicate that most group participants experienced a significant weight loss. Reports from teachers and other school personnel suggested that a transfer of learning from the group process to the classroom environment also took place. That is, an improvement in social skills and group interactions in the classroom was observed as a function of the group counseling process.

At least one study has reported group counseling with offenders with mental retardation (Steiner, 1984). In this study 175 male inmates attended group therapy sessions throughout a 4-year period. All clients were identified as having borderline intelligence or mild retardation (IQ range of 55–80). Sessions were structured in an open-ended way because group membership constantly changed. The average number of sessions attended by group members was 4.8. Issues discussed included trust, sexuality, personal abuse, and sentencing. Also addressed were issues of depression and suicidal feelings as well as general frustration with the correctional system. Role playing was used extensively and modeled by the group leader. The results of this intervention suggested that group members, over time, became less egocentric, better able to understand the feelings of others, and better able to express their own feelings. Steiner (1984) suggests that participation in group counseling is a factor related to eventual probation and successful reintegration into the community.

Hazards of Group Therapy

As can be seen from the discussion above, a number of techniques and strategies have been employed in group therapy with persons with mental retardation. Most researchers have utilized behavioral approaches coupled with basic group process therapy techniques. Directive and systemic techniques have been preferred to nondirective, reflective techniques. In the author's experience, a variety of potential hazards face the mental health professional in the formation and implementation of group therapy for clients with mental retardation. These seem worth discussing because they may influence the success rate when using group interventions. They are:

1. A given group member may not respond at all to the group leader or to other group members. Care should be taken in selection of group members in order to maximize the probability of interacting with one another. The simple ability of clients within a group to understand one another (in a linguistic sense) is critical to the therapeutic success.

2. Many clients cannot stay on task—any task. Some clients prefer to remain

on tasks not at all associated with the group therapy situation (either unidentified external or internal stimuli). Some clients exhibit attention deficit disorders, psychotic-like behavior, or echolalic responses during the group therapy responses. Each of these must be dealt with in order for group therapy to be successful.

3. Despite a highly structured situation, some clients will not generalize their skills to other comparable situations. Other clients will show poor retention of their experience in the therapy session or will exhibit odd or inappropriate behavior as a result of it. In some groups with which I have had experience, clients learned inappropriate behaviors by modeling them from the group.

4. Many clients are fixated at an egocentric stage of development. That is, they cannot easily take the perspective of another client or empathize with that client. The primary function of therapy then becomes moving them through this stage of development as a prerequisite to all other therapeutic interventions.

5. Highly aroused, anxious, depressed, and attention deficit disordered clients all have difficulty in group therapy experiences. In particular, clients who experience hyperarousal may find a group therapy situation aversive. It is critical to be able to differentiate among clients who are hyperaroused versus highly anxious versus attention deficit disordered (Sovner, 1989).

6. Many clients are on various psychoactive medications. These medications can either help or hinder group therapy. For example, it is known that neuroleptic medications (e.g., Haldol®, Mellaril®, Thorazine®) may have long-term detrimental impact on the health and behavior of clients to whom they are administered. These medications often result in increased agitation, hyperarousal, and aggression. All of these behaviors can be exhibited in a group therapy session as a result of inappropriate medication. Seizure medications (e.g., Dilantin®, Tegretol®, Phenobarbital, Librium®) may facilitate or hinder group interaction depending upon their individual impact upon clients. Medications used to reduce hyperarousal (e.g., Inderal®, Visken®) may significantly aid a client in social interaction. Obviously a complete review of the drug history and the probable impact of current medications is in order prior to entering into a group counseling program.

7. The quality of group leaders and the structure of sessions will contribute to their success or failure. Poorly trained group leaders who lack basic counseling skills and talk too much may not experience success. Either overly structured or poorly understructured groups will often result in dissatisfaction among group members. Group leaders who have not dealt with their own issues (e.g., family issues or sexual issues) may have difficulty in leading a group counseling session in an unbiased manner.

In summary, there are many factors that determine the success or failure of group counseling with persons with mental retardation. All of these must be taken into account individually and dealt with prior to the structuring of a group session.

Group leaders must be extremely flexible and willing to change as the group develops. Clients who are inappropriate for group counseling should be considered instead for individual counseling or various behavior management programs. As with adults who are not retarded, the readiness for group counseling is a highly individual matter.

Specific Intervention Programs

This section will deal with a number of specific areas in which group therapy interventions have been attempted. These include emotional awareness training, general social skills training, anger management training, sexual social skills training, interventions for anxiety/depression, and family interventions. A brief discussion of the efficacy research on group counseling and psychotherapy with persons with mental retardation will be presented at the end of this section.

Emotional Awareness Training

Emotional awareness training involves the teaching of identification of emotions to clients. That is, clients are taught to conceptualize and discriminate a wider array of emotions. Typically, persons with mental retardation have limited vocabulary in describing their emotions (e.g., "I feel good about something" versus "I feel bad about something"). Thus emotions such as anger, happiness, sadness, jealousy, remorse, grief, and hostility are identified and taught. This is done in a very concrete manner in that clients are shown the body language and facial expressions that are associated with each emotion that is to be learned. Several researchers have presented models for the teaching of emotions to persons with mental retardation (Benson, 1986, 1989; Ludwig & Hingsburger, 1989). Ludwig and Hingsburger (1989) employ the use of feeling faces in order to describe the emotions such as glad, sad, mad, and scared. Clients learn to associate these faces with specific feelings both verbally and internally. In Ludwig and Hingsburger's program, they identify 13 basic feelings for training including depressed, frustrated, thrilled, guilty, excited, intimidated, embarrassed, anxious, annoyed, shy, edgy, apprehensive, disappointed, and irritated. A number of specific situations are used in order to help clients to analyze their feelings. Thus, as an example, "How do you feel when a friend steals some money that belongs to you?" "How do you feel when you are sick and forced to miss an important outing?"

As an adjunct to this process, a game called the Fan Game is employed in which the clients are taught in a group setting to recognize the cues that predict how others feel. In this game, players (group members) are asked to look at a facial feeling expressed by a group member and then pick that feeling from an array of feeling picture cards. Thus, the actual facial expressions of individuals are progressively matched with the representation on feeling cards and discrimination training is achieved over time. In addition, clients are taught to express, in more elaborate body language, their various feelings.

Therapists often employ relaxation training as an adjunct to emotional awareness, as a basic technique in sensitizing clients to their bodies and the effect of emotions on their physiology. Fundamental to this technique is the use of progressive muscle relaxation in which clients are taught to identify specific muscle groups and to relax them. Amazingly, clients with mental retardation can often learn this process more quickly than adults who do not have mental retardation. A positive spin-off of this activity is increased body awareness and better sensitivity to tension and its relationship to emotional outbursts. Another useful relaxation technique has been developed by Monroe (1988) in which a tape and stereophonic tape player were employed. The technique uses a combination of traditional muscle relaxation techniques through guided imagery and produces a relaxing effect, called hemisync, on the brain. The technique was specifically developed for persons with mental retardation in institutional settings. It has been shown to be effective with adults with mild, moderate, and severe retardation.

General Social Skills Training

According to Matson (1984), social skills deficits are a typical result of developmental delays associated with mental retardation. Social skills refer to the ability of an individual to exhibit behaviors appropriate to a variety of settings such as work, home, and social outings. "Deficits in these skills result in lower adaptive functioning and, therefore, prevent a person with mental retardation from achieving normalization" (p. 2). Behaviors such as eye contact, appropriate body language, appropriate initiation of conversation, fundamental greeting skills, and interpretation of emotions are all critical social skills.

As Matson (1984) indicates, both operant and social learning techniques have been employed to aid the person with mental retardation in acquiring social skills. Matson describes his social skills learning curriculum in which modeling and role playing are employed. Staff and other clients demonstrate an appropriate social behavior (such as greeting a new person) and then the target client rehearses that behavior repeatedly. Performance feedback is provided in which the quality of the client's responding is reviewed with suggestions for improvement and appropriate reinforcement for effort. The client is given both tangible and social reinforcement. As with all group counseling situations, every effort is made to generalize the social skill to an in vivo setting. That is, staff members and other clients actively provide cues to help the individual client initiate a particular social skill and reinforce the client for performing it acceptably in a real-life situation.

Lee (1977a) employed group counseling that was primarily verbal in order to have impact on the social adjustment skills of residents with moderate mental retardation in the institutional setting. The group counseling used a social adjustment training program developed by Lee for that purpose. This curriculum emphasized social interaction, personal appearance and mannerisms, perception of feelings, making friends, and social responsibility. A number of baseline measurements were taken, including the Peabody Picture Vocabulary Test—Revised, the Adaptive Behavior Scale, nomination by peers, and nomination by ward staff. A contrast group was employed. Results indicated that, on each of the variables above, the experimental group showed a significantly greater mean score at the end of the 10-session group social skills experience than did the control group. Lee concluded that institutionalized adults with moderate retardation can benefit significantly from structured social skills training.

Foxx and McMorrow (1983) have developed an excellent social skills curriculum entitled *Stacking the Deck*. Their intervention is essentially a game in which group members learn and practice social skills related to three areas: general social activity, social vocational interactions, and social sexual interactions. In each of these areas subskills are addressed including compliments, social interaction, politeness, criticism, social confrontation, and disclosure. The authors suggest that in order for the group intervention to be successful it must be fun for all concerned. The rules for the game must be clear and special rewards must be available for appropriate behaviors. Discrimination training is the key to the acquisition of social skills and group facilitators must be able to reinforce correct responses differentially while ignoring incorrect responses (often a very difficult task). As with other reinforcement systems, reinforcers must be powerful and individually tailored to clients.

Foxx and Bittle (1989) have also developed a curriculum that teaches problem-solving skills for residents in community living settings. This is an excellent adjunct to their social skills training program in which residents are taught to deal with problems in a number of categories including emergencies and injuries, safety, authority figures, peer issues, community resources, and stating one's rights. The curriculum is subdivided in order to target specific populations including the developmentally disabled, individuals with chronic mental illness, brain-injured individuals, and adolescents with emotional disturbance. Many of these disorders are typically found in a residential community care setting. A major advantage of these curricula is that they provide a highly structured system for staff who have only moderate training in group process work.

Although it has been demonstrated that persons with mental retardation have a significant capacity for aggressive behavior, some persons with mental retardation show relatively poor assertiveness skills. These individuals are often withdrawn and lack the appropriate social skills necessary to make their needs known. Even aggressive individuals often choose aggression as a means of meeting their needs in absence of the appropriate assertiveness skills. These social skills include specific types of eye contact, body language, voice inflection, and language fluency (Bergman, 1985; Gentile & Jenkins, 1980). It is known that certain language phrases are indicative of assertiveness whereas others indicate passivity. The training of appropriate assertiveness skills can be a key factor in anger management control and in general social skill acquisition. The lack of assertiveness skills is associated with anxiety, social inadequacy, and depression. Persons who fail to exhibit appropriate assertiveness skills receive less reinforcement and are not positively attended to by their peers. Indeed, much of the attention-seeking behavior exhibited by persons with mental retardation is the result of poor social skills used to gain affection.

Generally the training of assertiveness skills is accomplished in the same manner that other general social skills are acquired. Thus, modeling, behavioral rehearsal, peer feedback, and repetition are all components of assertiveness training. Bergman (1985) has described an assertiveness training program in which six group sessions are undertaken. These sessions include the topics of expressing appropriate affect, expressing feelings with positive statements, expressing needs and desires, expressing anger, saying "No," stating opinions and contradictions, and asserting the self to authority figures. Modeling techniques are employed to demonstrate each of these skills as are a number of in vivo practice and generalization sessions. It is important that persons with mental retardation learn appropriate assertiveness skills as an alternative to aggression or withdrawal. Once they have learned that assertiveness leads to social reinforcement, these skills will be maintained.

Anger Management

Anger management is a logical extension of emotional awareness training. It teaches clients the basic self-control techniques that will allow them to deal with anger-arousing stimuli in social situations. Clearly, anger arousal and the resulting physical violence, including temper tantrums and verbal abuse, are the most common referral problem for the mental health practitioner in working with persons with mental retardation. With most persons with mental retardation, anger management involves both a physiological and cognitive or psychological component.

As was discussed above, many persons with mental retardation suffer from hyperarousal syndrome and thus are easily overstimulated by their environment. What is a painful situation for the client (in terms of overstimulation) appears to staff members to be an unexplained aggressive episode. Intermittent Explosive Disorder (*DSM-III-R*) is also more often associated with persons with mental retardation than with other individuals. This disorder is assumed to have an organic base and produces unexplained, unpredictable, intermittent, and highly aggressive episodes. From a cognitive-behavioral standpoint, many clients learn inappropriate aggressive anger responses through modeling, particularly in institutional settings. Further, as discussed above, the lack of appropriate social perception skills regarding emotions is a predictor to inappropriately aggressive behavior.

Anger management interventions must take into account both the biochemical and cognitive aspects of aggression. Several programs have been developed for cognitive anger management training (Benson, 1986; Foxx & McMorrow, 1983; Gardner & Cole, 1987). Common to all of these programs is the use of relaxation training as a preliminary step together with analysis of the current psychoactive drug regimen for a given client. Gardner and Cole (1987) suggest that environmental factors, internal factors, and reinforcement history need to be examined prior to undertaking anger management training. Thus the obvious environmental antecedents that trigger aggression are examined (e.g., adult demands, negative client interactions) as well as internal affective states such as anxiety or depression. In addition, the conditioning history of a client is very important (Gardner, 1989). That is, clients who have been intermittently reinforced for angry outbursts will be more difficult to countercondition.

Some clients, when exhibiting angry behavior, are in reality attempting to escape from aversive stimulation. Gardner (1989) points out that anxiety is almost always a feature of poor anger management on the part of a client. Therefore, dealing with anxiety through systematic desensitization or comparable cognitive approaches can be critical to reducing angry outbursts. Thus, treatment for anger is a multifaceted process in which group counseling is a single component. When aggression is seen as a function of the environment, then appropriate measures are taken to modify environmental cues for aggression. Conversely, if aggression is seen as a skills deficit, then individual and group skills training is warranted. Benson (1986) has summarized these skills, which include identification of problem situations, teaching appropriate coping statements, relaxation as a precursor to reduction of anxiety and anger, discrimination of environmental stimuli that produce anger, role playing with appropriate coping statements, problem solving for options, and finally, evaluation of the option chosen to handle the anger-producing situation.

Sexual Social Skills

Interest in individual and group sexual counseling with persons with mental retardation has increased during the past 10 years (Griffiths, Hingsburger, & Christian, 1985). Perroncel (1989) has estimated that 80% of adults who have mental retardation have been abused in some way. Persons with mental retardation are often confused about basic issues of intimacy and privacy. Further, they lack fundamental information regarding sexuality in all of its dimensions. As with other areas of social interaction, persons with mental retardation are likely to misperceive the actions of others and to behave inappropriately as a result of that perception.

Perroncel (1988) has developed an instrument called The Social/Sexual Evaluation Profile (S/SEP). This instrument attempts to assess the knowledge and conceptual base about sexuality the client currently possesses. Areas evaluated include gender identity, perception of social cues, accurate perception of affect, appropriate age recognition, incest taboo, staff taboo, impulse control, relative sexual initiative, pleasure associated with sex, conflict associated with sex, general sexual knowledge, general heterosexual knowledge, general homosexual knowl-edge, general knowledge about reproduction, general knowledge about contracep-tion, general knowledge about sexual abuse, and the attitude the individual holds regarding seduction and coercion in sexuality. Using anatomically correct dolls, additional information is collected regarding the person's current and previous interactions. This information forms the basis for further education and counseling regarding sexuality.

Hingsburger (1987) has identified a number of additional issues that are related to sexual counseling with persons with mental retardation. Persons with retardation often have a confused self-concept in that they do not adequately differentiate themselves from others around them. They feel isolated from their peers and lack basic sexual knowledge. Sexuality is seen as a "fugitive behavior" that is not condoned. Many persons with mental retardation have had negative sexual experiences including rape and sodomy. Thus the person with mental retardation does not have a clear understanding of the essence of sexuality or of the societal conventions associated with it.

Hingsburger (1989) has developed a relationship training model for persons with mental retardation in which clients learn to differentiate among different types of relationships, including friendships, love relationships, sexual love relationships, and staff-professional relationships. It is in these areas that the person with mental retardation shows confused and inappropriate sexual behavior. For example, it is common for clients with mental retardation to approach opposite-sex staff members soliciting sexual contact in rather direct and inappropriate ways. Hingsburger's technique also focuses on the rights and responsibilities associated with various types of relationships. That is, individuals have the right to expect reciprocation in various types of relationships but also have the responsibility to provide love, care, and support in their various relationships. The key to relationship training is in teaching persons with mental retardation to distinguish accurately the different types of relationships and to exhibit the appropriate behaviors associated with each. Often persons with mental retardation have difficulty in distinguishing between sexual love relationships and friendship relationships. Much of the clarifying regarding the nature of relationships can occur in a group setting where housemates openly discuss their feelings regarding the behavior of others and the meanings of those behaviors to their relationships. Here language clarification is important. Hingsburger (1989) suggests that clients tend to misuse and misunderstand language associated with relationships. "For example, a client telling a counselor 'I love you' is often told, 'You don't love me, you like me'" (p. 42). Repeated clarifications of this type are important to the ultimate understanding of the terminology associated with relationships.

Of equal importance is the individual staff member's or counselor's attitude regarding sexual relationships. In the author's experience, many counselors are rendered ineffective by their own personal attitudes regarding sexuality. They fundamentally see persons with retardation as being asexual or not having the right to sexual expression. These attitudes are sometimes reinforced by the parents of adolescents and adults with mental retardation who have suppressed their child's sexuality. As with adults who are not mentally retarded, this tends to make the person reticent about being self-disclosing regarding sexual desires and experiences. Thus counselors or staff members should be chosen carefully if sexuality is to be a theme of the counseling process. Even experienced group counselors often need training and education in sexuality before they can be effective in the counseling process.

Counseling regarding sexuality is normally a two-step process for persons with mental retardation. First, an extensive educational curriculum is required (Hingsberger, 1989; Perroncel, 1989). This helps the client to clarify the nature of various kinds of sexuality and to relate these to their own behavior and experiences. Second, role playing is used in a group counseling setting to aid clients in acquiring the appropriate social skills for sexual expression. These include:

1. How to take a sexual initiative;
2. How to distinguish the social cues that indicate either positive or negative responding to a sexual initiative;

3. How to distinguish friendship from sexual interest;

4. How to establish control over sexual impulses and aggressive sexual behavior;

5. Basic grooming and hygiene related to sexual attractiveness;

6. Distinguishing heterosexual from homosexual activity;

7. Distinguishing between coercion and seduction;

8. Understanding the rights and responsibilities associated with sexual activity, including pregnancy and childbearing.

The usual role-playing techniques are used here in order to allow clients to practice working through sexual interactions and to receive feedback from the therapist and peers. Role reversal is often used to help clients gain empathy for one another. The counselor must take an active role in modeling for clients in this situation because much of the behavior is new and has not been socially observed before.

As more enlightened attitudes have prevailed, increasing numbers of married and unmarried couple relationships have developed within the community of individuals with mental retardation. Spragg and Miller (1982) report a group counseling procedure for such couples. In this procedure both married and unmarried couples are seen in groups at various stages in their relationship. The intelligence level of their clients ranged from IQs of 50–85 and the couples in the groups had exclusive relationships. Upon entry in the group, couples were assessed using the Couple Problem Identification Inventory and the Draw a Couple technique, both developed by Spragg and Miller (1982).[1] The authors used a number of traditional group-processing approaches (e.g., role playing, reflective listening) and a series of games. For example, an extrapolation of the "Newlywed Game" was used in which partners are separated, with one person being asked to leave the room while the remaining person was asked a standardized set of questions regarding his or her partner. This process was designed to provide information regarding preferences, habits, and routines that are a part of each relationship. A discussion follows each of these questioning sessions. Spragg and Miller (1982) have found that use of game activities not only helps to maintain interest among couples but also aids in focusing on specific areas of conflict. As with traditional marital therapy, communication skills are emphasized, especially listening skills. Other areas emphasized include mutual problem solving, anger management, and dealing with community pressures.

[1]These inventories are available from the authors.

Anxiety and Mood Disorders

Anxiety reactions and various mood disorders (as defined by *DSM-III-R*) are common behavior patterns seen in persons with mental retardation (Benson, Rice, & Miranti, 1986; Gardner, 1989; Levine, 1985; Sovner, 1989). Clients with mental retardation can develop a variety of organic and environmentally caused anxiety disorders. These can result in a generalized anxiety state and ultimately in depression. Sovner (1989) has suggested that many persons with mental retardation are experiencing heightened states of arousal as a fundamental result of neurological impairment. These are different from learned states of anxiety and from bipolar disorders. According to Sovner, a considerable number of persons with mental retardation suffer from "rapid cycling" bipolar disorders in which they experience mood changes from the depressive to the manic state over fairly short periods of time compared to persons who do not have mental retardation. Basically, in treating anxiety and mood disorders, organic causes including inappropriate drug therapy must be considered before behavioral interventions are undertaken. For example, neuroleptics are known to produce "anxiety-like" states that have no behavioral basis.

From a behavioral standpoint, anxiety may have a variety of causes. Gardner (1989) suggests that much of the anxious behavior exhibited by persons with mental retardation is really an attempt to escape from aversive stimulation. That is, the very environment in which persons with mental retardation receive treatment and programming may be fundamentally aversive to them. This results in other aspects of the environment (including staff members and other clients) taking on aversive characteristics through classical conditioning. Therefore, in this paradigm, it is necessary to look at all the potential cues for anxiety that may have been produced as a result of this classical conditioning process. These include both internal and external behavioral events that may act as cues to anxiety reactions. Careful attention must be focused on seemingly neutral environmental stimuli that may have become cues for anxiety as a result of classical conditioning. For example, in the author's experience, it is common for specific clients or staff to become conditioned as stimuli for triggering anxiety reactions in other clients.

The therapeutic treatment employed with anxiety disorders will vary depending upon the reinforcement history and the types of cues producing the anxiety disorder. Treatment strategies can include systematic desensitization, both imaginary and in vivo; modeling of nonanxious behaviors, both covert and overt; implosive therapy and flooding; and group therapy to desensitize individuals who have developed social anxiety. Gardner (1989) suggests the use of a graduated exposure technique for highly ingrained phobias with as many as 100 trials per day if necessary in order to desensitize the individual to the phobic stimulus.

From a systemic point of view, Gibson (1989) feels that agencies serving persons with mental retardation tend to impose entirely too much control over their clients. This results in the agency becoming a conditioned-aversive environment for their clients. Clients then take on an attitude of learned helplessness, and eventually become depressed. Gibson suggests that therapy focus on creating an internal locus of control for clients and that centers for persons with mental retardation drastically modify their programming in ways that recognize the right of persons with mental retardation to have freedom of choice in participating and in developing their programs. Griffiths (1989) agrees with this approach and suggests that extensive staff training should be performed in order to sensitize staff better to their behaviors that produce anxiety.

In most cases, prevention is far more cost effective than intervention techniques in dealing with anxious or depressed behaviors. Group counseling should focus on issues such as body awareness, identification of tension, self-talk analysis, and the teaching of new self-talk. Clients should also be taught to reinforce themselves when they are relaxed and in nonanxious states. As with all other interventions, training for generalization of the relaxation response to new environments is important if anxiety is ultimately to be reduced. Sometimes generalization of a new skill is facilitated if the client is asked to teach the skill to another peer and then to monitor that peer's progress. Because most anxiety responses are conditioned, a tendency for spontaneous recovery exists and, therefore, a relapse prevention program is appropriate as a follow-up procedure. This can take the form of both individual and small group counseling.

It has been estimated that 14% of clients with mental retardation present with depression as their primary mental health diagnosis (O'Neil, 1982). Depression has many antecedents, both organic and environmental. These clients are depressed and more often require drug intervention (Sovner, 1989). O'Neil has identified several environmental influences that lead to depression in individuals with mental retardation. First, clients often feel that they are unable to control their lives. They are highly dependent upon others and have traditionally been dependent on their parents or caretakers. Second, many clients have considerable apprehension about being molested or harmed by others. This is not surprising given the prevalence of physical and sexual abuse in the history of many clients. Finally, clients can have unrealistic expectations regarding their future plans for vocational or independent living placement. The discrepancy between a client's perceived skills and realistic expectations can form the basis for depression.

O'Neil describes a group therapy intervention in which co-therapists are used, one male and one female, and where group size is from six to eight individuals. Clients participate in 30 weekly sessions. Most of the clients receive individual counseling at the same time that they are in the group. The format of the group includes open-ended discussions and the use of behavioral techniques including modeling, role playing, behavioral rehearsal, and selective reinforcement. Clients are allowed to determine the content of the group, and an ongoing assessment is performed of individual client mood through the use of checklists and self-report forms. The self-report forms are similar to the facial expressions curriculum developed by Benson (1989). O'Neil concludes that group therapy is an appropriate approach with depression for persons with mental retardation because it offers a social skills training component.

Group Therapy Interventions for Families

Family therapy for families with children who have mental retardation is covered elsewhere in this volume. This section will review briefly a few of the group counseling approaches. Group therapy is usually undertaken in instances where the families of children with mental retardation exhibit dysfunctional behavior patterns (Munro, 1985; Robinson, 1973; Tavormina, 1975). Many aspects of the family environment have an impact on the behavior of a person with mental retardation. Individuals with retardation more often remain with their biological family well into later adulthood. Even after persons with mental retardation have been placed in group homes or semi-independent living settings, family issues and pressures can have a significant impact on adaptive behavior. Munro (1985) details some of the typical behaviors exhibited by dysfunctional families. These include chronic dissatisfaction with community-based programs for their child, overt and covert program sabotage, extreme overprotectiveness, hypochondriacal obsessions, open and overt hostility within and outside of the family, symbiotic relationships, and avoidance of the child or sibling with mental retardation. The stress of having a disabled child and being required to maintain that child well into adulthood severely disrupts normal family patterns. It is disruptive to the developmental process of other family members and often results in highly pathological behavior on the part of all concerned.

It is also the case that parents of persons with mental retardation often underestimate the potential of their child and communicate these lowered expectations throughout his or her life. When the child enters community residential or day program placement, the parents resist program efforts to make their child more independent as an adult. Further, other family issues often contaminate the relationship among parents, their child, and the agency in which their child is placed. The most common of these is physical abuse, sexual abuse, and marital discord.

Mental health professionals also find themselves in situations where the parents of persons with mental retardation lack the behavior management skills necessary to provide effective parenting (Tymchuk, Andron, & Rahbar, 1988). Baker and Brightman (1984) describe a program in which parents were trained in behavior modification techniques in order to improve their behavior management skills with their children. The parents were trained in groups lasting for 10 two-hour weekly sessions. Outcome measures indicated that parents improved their knowledge of behavior modification and were able to implement some new behavior control measures effectively. Wide variation, however, was experienced among parents in the acquisition of these skills.

Other group procedures (Robinson, 1973) have focused on parenting skills and on parent feelings regarding the stress involved in having a child with a disability. Robinson suggests that the major goal for parent groups should be to help parents deal with fears and misconceptions regarding retardation. It is especially important to focus on realistic expectations for the child and his or her development as well as the need to deal with issues of identity and individuation prior to placement of the child in a community residential setting. Munro (1985) believes that families of disabled persons require both supportive and confrontive counseling approaches. For severely dysfunctional families, supportive therapy is critical in order to ensure their continuance in group therapy. Many families are so totally overwhelmed by the consequences of having a disabled child that they require a protracted period of compassionate support and empathy regarding their plight. Confrontive strategies are appropriate in instances where families are exhibiting unacceptable behavior (e.g., verbal or physical abuse) or in instances where families are totally sabotaging their child's treatment.

Deutsch and Placona (1983a) present an interesting study of the relationship between family involvement and mental health in persons with mental retardation. Their study concludes that the family context is critical for maintaining the individual's self-concept. Separation from the family in the form of community residential or institutional placement puts significant psychological strain on the individual and the other family members and must be dealt with therapeutically as part of a transition strategy employed by the receiving agency. Thus, as Deutsch and Placona suggest, "it is important for staff in residential facilities that when residents speak of 'home,' whether in realistic or unrealistic terms, it is an issue that must be dealt with effectively or it may develop into a more dangerous problem" (p. 13). Thus staff should respond to any client verbalization of home issues as a signal for therapeutic intervention. Thereafter, family work becomes an integral aspect of residential programming.

For an excellent review of other issues that influence family therapy, the reader is directed to a recent theme issue of the *American Journal of Mental Retardation* on families, edited by Krauss, Simeonsson, and Ramey (1989).

Efficacy

Some of the efficacy research regarding group counseling with adolescents and adults with mental retardation has been reviewed throughout this chapter (Baker & Brightman, 1984; Deutsch & Placona, 1983a,b; Gumaer & Simon, 1979; Hoshmand, 1983; Lee, 1977a,b; Levine, 1985; Spragg, 1983, 1984; Tavormina, 1975; Tymchuk et al., 1988). A few studies have looked at group counseling with persons with mental retardation (DeBlassie & Cowan, 1976; Janus & Podolec, 1982). The evidence, however, for the effectiveness of group psychotherapy with persons with mental retardation is minimal. The experimental methods used for doing research in this area are often anecdotal or lack the quality of instrumentation necessary to measure change over time. The population of individuals with mental retardation is also quite heterogeneous, thus increasing the number of different therapeutic interventions that must be employed. A few trends do appear to emerge from the literature, however:

1. Structured group therapy is more successful in producing behavior change than nonstructured group therapy techniques.

2. Appropriate differential diagnosis tends to predict to more successful therapy.

3. Eclectic models of therapeutic intervention appear to be more effective than orthodox interventions.

4. Techniques that emphasize language and concept development appear to be more successful.

5. Traditional insight therapies are less likely to be successful than other therapeutic techniques.

6. Behavior modification and behavior therapy tend to be more successful than other techniques that have been employed, provided that they are used in conjunction with other techniques such as systemic therapy.

7. Family therapy appears to have positive outcomes, especially if performed early, for the persons with mental retardation.

Considerably more research on group interventions using better baseline measurements and more operationalized intervention techniques will be necessary in order to establish fully the credibility of group counseling with persons with mental retardation.

Case Studies

In this section, three case studies will be presented illustrating clients who are at varying stages of development and have differing diagnoses. An attempt has been made to select clients who have a dual diagnosis, thus having both a mental retardation and a mental health *DSM-III-R* classification. In each instance both individual and group interventions have been employed.

Case I. Male, Chronological Age 41

Hank is a 41-year-old male who has lived in a semi-independent residential setting for the developmentally disabled for the past 17 years. Results of the Stanford-Binet IV indicate that he has a total test composite SAS = 58. Hank exhibits relative strengths in abstract verbal reasoning, quantitative reasoning, and short-term memory. However, he exhibits a significant weakness in verbal reasoning. The Self-Report Inventory (SRI) and Behavior Rating Scale (BRS) of the Emotional Problems Scales were administered. These indicated behaviorally rated elevations on the following scales: thought-behavior disorder, sexual malad-justment, noncompliance, anxiety, and withdrawal. On the SRI, Hank had an elevation on the depression scale (82nd percentile).

Behaviorally, Hank has periodically evidenced behavioral outbursts, usually associated with a specific staff member. On occasion these outbursts have become physically aggressive. Hank has a history of diabetes mellitus. This condition is controlled through diet and oral medication. Throughout the past 10 years, however, Hank has exhibited episodes of refusing to control his diet, resulting in highly variable glucose levels. Hank also exhibits symptoms of cerebral palsy, resulting in retarded psychomotor activity. Staff have consistently reported that Hank experiences difficulty in interacting with women. Periodically, he exhibits inappropriate sexual solicitations and appears frustrated with his lack of success in developing heterosexual relationships. Over time, Hank has become withdrawn and his diabetes mellitus is less controlled than in the past. Hank exhibits a considerable amount of anger and hostility regarding his diabetic condition and refuses to believe that he has the condition.

A review of Hank's daily living pattern suggests that he does not have many close relationships. His social skills are not well developed, but his other adaptive behavior in both personal care and vocational settings is excellent. Hank is highly resistant to staff programming especially if it is structured. He appears to have a very distorted sense of self, both in terms of his expectations for independence and his heterosexual expectations. On numerous occasions, he has approached staff members with unsolicited and unsophisticated sexual advances. He is seen by the staff as having significant authority issues.

On the basis of the psychological evaluation and staff behavioral observations, it was determined that Hank had both a diagnosis of mental retardation and a mental health diagnosis of either depression or dysthymia. Through use of the Boehm Test of Basic Concepts it was determined that Hank had not developed the basic concepts of future and other concepts associated with appropriate social skills. Generally, Hank's verbal conceptualization skills were well below all of his other adaptive skills. This resulted in staff members assuming a higher level of social comprehension than was actually the case. An intervention program was developed with the following components:

1. Hank was placed in a social skills training group in which the Foxx and McMorrow curriculum was employed. The focus of this group for Hank was the identification of emotions and learning labels for different emotions. Learning to express more appropriate body language was also a focus of the program, because Hank's body language was often threatening to those around him. A second aspect of the social skills training was anger management, in which Hank learned progressive relaxation and assertiveness skills.

2. Hank was placed in a second group in which heterosexual social skills were learned. In addition, this group focused on fundamental sexual knowledge as a prerequisite for learning heterosexual social skills.

3. Hank was placed in individual counseling in which the focus was on helping him to understand and accept his strengths and limitations as they relate to his level of independence. For example, Hank was currently placed in a sheltered workshop but desired to be involved in competitive employment. His performance at the sheltered workshop, although adequate, was hindered by his cerebral palsy and reduced his overall work efficiency. This made Hank a poor candidate for independent employment. However, it was decided to undertake a thorough assessment of his current employment situation and to begin training for new and more interesting tasks.

4. Hank was placed on mild antidepressive drug therapy (Amitriptyline) as an adjunct to the psychotherapeutic interventions discussed above.

This case is an example of a multifaceted intervention in which all aspects, psychological, social, and medical, must be taken into account in order to achieve the desired outcome. As a result of these interventions, Hank's social skills improved significantly and his depression abated resulting in his eventual withdrawal from psychoactive medication.

Case II. Female, Chronological Age 33

Karen is a 33-year-old female who is diagnosed with moderate to severe mental retardation and has had a history of anxiety disorder. Karen was seen by staff members as withdrawn, dependent, and unable to benefit from her current programming. She is currently placed in a sheltered workshop setting where she is performing adequately. Karen has a long history of anxiety reactions to various stressful events. These include:

1. withdrawal when angry;
2. inability to confront other residents when angry;
3. compulsive behavior patterns surrounding daily routines and handling of emotional stress;
4. excessive desire to please adult authority figures;
5. inability to perceive social situations accurately;
6. inability to respond flexibly to changes in routine;
7. repression of sexuality and chronic paranoid fear of rape.

Staff express concern that Karen is becoming more anxious in her day-to-day activities and that she may be overwhelmed by her level of anxiety.

Karen was given a complete psychological evaluation. This evaluation indicated that she was functioning in the moderate level of retardation with relative strengths in short-term memory and quantitative reasoning and relative weaknesses in abstract, visual, and verbal reasoning. The results of the Behavior Rating Scale of the Emotional Problems Scales (completed by four staff members for reliability) suggest high levels of anxiety and agitation. Karen is currently not on psychoactive medication. The evaluations resulted in diagnoses of Moderate Mental Retardation and Generalized Anxiety Disorder (*DSM-III-R*). Depression resulting from the long-term Generalized Anxiety Disorder was also considered in the programming effort.

It became apparent that Karen suffered from trait anxiety, which had gradually increased her stress level over the years of her residential placement. This was now complicated by periods of depression and hypochondriacal behavior.

Over the years, Karen had learned a number of acquiescent behaviors. During interactions with other clients and staff members she sought to please them in order to avoid social rejection. Thus she gave the appearance that she understood much of the social and verbal interaction that occurred on a daily basis in the group home. This was not the case because Karen had extremely poor social concept development.

An incident of attempted rape when Karen was 22, coupled with dysfunctional parent attitudes regarding sex, resulted in paranoid ideation regarding the intentions of all male acquaintances. Her interactions with males were characterized by avoidance. A number of obsessive compulsive behaviors regarding food and eating patterns had also developed.

Based on the above information the following program was developed:

1. Karen was placed in a social skills group consisting of male and female members. The purpose of this group was to develop basic concepts regarding the body language of others and its social meaning. This group also had an educational function regarding fundamentals of human sexuality. For Karen, accurate perception of the intention of others and the ability to elicit or self-initiate social contact were key issues in this group.

2. Karen was given intensive training in basic concepts employing both visual and auditory stimuli in order to enhance learning.

3. Karen was taught to use progressive relaxation through the Monroe Institute Tape Series. Progressive relaxation sessions were held three times per day in order to enhance learning. Progressive relaxation was seen as a necessary condition to the initiation of anger management and assertiveness programs.

4. After progressive relaxation had been learned to criteria, Karen was placed in an anger management/assertiveness training group. The curriculum employed in this group was a modification of the Benson Anger Management Series and the Foxx and McMorrow Social Solving Sexual Skills Training Program.

5. Karen was placed in weekly individual counseling sessions in order to facilitate spontaneous discussion of her feelings of anxiety, depression, and frustration that she had experienced during the past week. Coping strategies were part of this counseling.

6. Every effort was used to find new and novel reinforcers for Karen in order to reestablish her reinforcement system and reduce the probability of depression. Tasks within her work setting were gradually changed, as well as many of her activities within the group home setting.

This case is still in process and will require long-term therapeutic intervention because of the tenacious nature of Karen's obsessive behaviors. However, significant reductions in anxiety and expressions of depression have been observed as a result of the therapeutic interventions. Note that this therapeutic intervention was undertaken without the need for psychoactive drug therapy.

Case III. Male, Chronological Age 24

Joe is a 24-year-old male who has previously been diagnosed with severe mental retardation based on his adaptive behavior functioning and the results of the Stanford-Binet IV. He is described by staff as socially adept when motivated but explosive and aggressive when frustrated. Joe is partially ambulatory but uses a wheelchair rather than a walker in most instances. His major strengths include his relatively good socialization, his receptive language, and his ability to learn new tasks. Joe's major weaknesses include slow motoric responding (with a pronounced tremor), variable motivation level, and a series of gross motor difficulties resulting from ataxic cerebral palsy and scoliosis.

In recent evaluations, staff have indicated that Joe's aggressive and noncompliant behaviors have increased. For example, he periodically urinates or defecates in his clothes as a means of expressing anger. This usually follows staff prompting to begin some aspect of his programming. Joe has also exhibited periods of extreme withdrawal and depressive-like episodes in which his social interaction and response to reinforcers decline significantly. Joe responds to a relatively small array of reinforcers, many of which are primary.

The Behavior Rating Scale of the Emotional Problems Scale was administered. The results of this test indicated elevated scores on verbal aggression, physical aggression, noncompliance, withdrawal, depression, and low self-esteem. As a result of this information and previous psychological data, Joe was given a dual diagnosis of Moderate to Severe Mental Retardation and Adjustment Disorder with Depressed Mood (*DSM-III-R,* 309.00).

A review of Joe's family history indicated that he had been rejected by his father because of his physical and mental disability. His father is a Marine officer who provides a highly "macho" image to his sons. Joe found himself in the position of being unable to satisfy his father's expectations or expectations held by other family members. Much of his self-talk surrounded rejection of him by his family. This was a significant factor in his overall behavioral adjustment.

Joe is an excellent example of a client requiring both traditional operant intervention techniques and individual/group counseling. The program intervention designed for Joe was based on the data presented above plus detailed behavioral logs kept by the staff in Joe's residential program. Based on this information, the following program interventions were undertaken:

1. Joe was placed on a multilevel response cost system. The purpose of this system was to aid him in controlling his aggressive and resistant behaviors including his enuretic and encopretic activities. This response cost system had five levels with varying reinforcers being used at each level. A key feature of the system is that all aspects of it were presented on poster board in visual format only. This

was necessary because Joe did not have completely developed concepts of addition and subtraction. Thus access to reinforcers was based on possessing a certain number of pictures of that reinforcer rather than tokens. As an adjunct to this program, when Joe exhibited enuretic or encopretic behavior, staff were instructed to wait him out until he agreed to help in cleaning up his mess. At times this required as much as 4 hours. Ultimately, Joe's enuretic and encopretic behavior disappeared totally.

2. Joe was placed in individual counseling (two sessions per week). The purpose of this counseling was to help Joe identify his feelings regarding his family and to express those feelings openly. As part of this individual counseling, feelings of anger, resentment, and hostility were identified and learned by Joe.

3. Joe was placed in a social skills training group for the purpose of learning anger management, empathy for others, and general skill in using appropriate (nonaggressive) body language dealing with other clients.

4. A program of family counseling was instituted with Joe's parents and his other siblings. Through this program his family was sensitized to the connection between Joe's aggressive/depressive episodes and the relationship that he had with his family, especially his father. As a result of this intervention, the number of visitations by Joe's father increased and these visitations became progressively more positive. Other siblings in the family became more sensitized to the dysfunctional nature of the family behavior pattern. Eventually, Joe's older brother began to develop a close relationship with Joe as a result of the family intervention.

Annotated Bibliography

Foxx, R. M., & Bittle, R. G. (1989). *Thinking it through: Teaching a problem-solving strategy for community living.* Champaign, IL: Research Press.

This is a highly useful curriculum for teaching problem-solving skills to persons with mental retardation. It is designed for use in small groups of four and teaches the person to solve problems commonly associated with group home–living arrangements. The program is designed to aid clients in learning problem–solving techniques by presenting them with commonly experienced problems and then guiding them to choose from a variety of solutions provided by the program materials.

Foxx, R. M., & McMorrow, M. J. (1983). *Stacking the deck: A social skills game for retarded adults.* Champaign, IL: Research Press.

This is a curriculum designed to train adolescents and adults with mental retardation in a variety of social skills. These include general social skills, vocational social skills, and sexual social skills. The curriculum is well organized and easily understood by staff members. It lends itself to measurement of outcomes and provides specific techniques for facilitation in groups.

Gaston, E. T. (1968). *Music in therapy.* New York: MacMillan.

Although not totally devoted to persons with mental retardation, this book is a classic reference on music and movement therapy. It contains comprehensive sections on music therapy for disabled children and adults and an additional section on music therapy for adults with behavior disorders.

Horner, R. H., Dunlap, G., & Koegel, R. L. (1988). *Generalization and maintenance: Lifestyle changes in applied settings.* Baltimore, MD: Paul H. Brookes.

This is an indispensable volume on the techniques that can be utilized for persons with mental retardation and other disabled populations to promote generalization of skills. A broad array of group and individual techniques are discussed and a significant amount of research on generalization is presented. This volume is highly useful for mental health practitioners wishing to improve their knowledge regarding learning and generalization in a variety of applied settings.

Jageman, L. W., & Myers, J. E. (1986). *Counseling mentally retarded adults: A procedures and training manual.* Stout, WI: University of Wisconsin-Stout Press.

This book is a training and reference manual for techniques in counseling applied to persons with mental retardation. It is a highly detailed manual of counseling techniques organized in a step-by-step fashion. Various theoretical orientations are described in terms of the procedures for implementing them. Both individual and group counseling techniques are included. This is an excellent manual for training staff in basic techniques for counseling persons with mental retardation.

References

American Psychiatric Association. (1987). *Diagnostic and statistical manual of mental disorders, revised* (3rd ed., rev.). Washington, DC: Author.

Baker, B. L., & Brightman, R. P. (1984). Training parents of retarded children: Program-specific outcomes. *Journal of Behavior Therapy & Experimental Psychiatry, 15*(3), 255-260.

Benson, B. A. (1986). Anger management training. *Psychiatric Aspects of Mental Retardation Reviews, 5*(10), 51-55.

Benson, B. A. (1989, December). *Anger management training for adults with mild mental retardation.* Paper presented at the Annual Convention of the National Association for the Dually Diagnosed, Washington, DC.

Benson, B. A., Rice, C. J., & Miranti, S. V. (1986). Effects of anger management on training with mentally retarded adults in group treatment. *Journal of Counseling and Clinical Psychology, 54,* 728-729.

Bergman, S. (1985). Assertiveness training for mentally retarded *adults. Psychiatric Aspects of Mental Retardation Reviews, 4,* 43-48.

Brown, D. T., & Prout, H. T. (Eds.). (1989). *Counseling and psychotherapy with children and adolescents: Theory and practice for school and clinical settings* (2nd ed.). Brandon, VT: Clinical Psychology Publishing.

DeBlassie, R., & Cowan, A. (1976). Counseling with the mentally handicapped child. *Elementary School Guidance and Counseling, 10,* 246-252.

Detterman, D. K. (1979). Memory in the mentally retarded. In N. R. Ellis (Ed.), *Handbook of mental deficiency, psychological theory and research* (pp. 727-760). Hillsdale, NJ: Lawrence Erlbaum Associates.

Deutsch, H., & Placona, M. (1983a). *The concept of home and family to mentally retarded individuals placed in residential facilities: Implications for counseling.* Scranton, PA: Keystone City Residence. (ERIC Document Reproduction Service No. ED 233 550)

Deutsch, H., & Placona, M. (1983b). *Psychotherapeutic approaches to dealing with mentally retarded adolescents and adults in community settings.* Scranton, PA: Keystone City Residence. (ERIC Document Reproduction Service No. ED 233 551)

Fletcher, R. (1984). Group therapy with mentally retarded persons with emotional disorders. *Psychiatric Aspects of Mental Retardation Reviews, 3,* 21-24.

Foxx, R. M., & Bittle, R. G. (1989). *Thinking it through: Teaching a problem-solving strategy for community living.* Champaign, IL: Research Press.

Foxx, R. M., & McMorrow, M. J. (1983). *Stacking the deck: A social skills game for retarded adults.* Champaign, IL: Research Press.

Gardner, W. I. (1989, December). *Anxiety disorders: A learning theories perspective.* Paper presented at the Annual Convention of the National Association of the Dually Diagnosed, Washington, DC.

Gardner, W. I., & Cole, C. L. (1987). Managing aggressive behavior: A behavioral diagnostic approach. *Psychiatric Aspects of Mental Retardation Reviews, 6,* 21-25.

Garfield, S. A. (1982). Eclectism and integration in psychotherapy. *Behavior Therapy, 13,*

610-623.

Gaston, E. T. (1968). *Music in therapy.* New York: MacMillan.

Gentile, C., & Jenkins, J. O. (1980). Assertiveness training with mentally retarded persons. *Mental Retardation, 18,* 315-317.

Gibson, S. (1989, December). *Anxiety in children with mental retardation: A developmental perspective.* Paper presented at the Annual Convention of the National Association for the Dually Diagnosed, Washington, DC.

Griffiths, D. (1989, August). *Behavioral therapy for anxiety disorders in persons with mental retardation.* Paper presented at the Annual Convention of the National Association for the Dually Diagnosed, Washington, DC.

Griffiths, D., Hingsburger, D., & Christian, R. (1985). Treating developmentally handicapped sexual offenders: The York behavior management services treatment program. *Psychiatric Aspects of Mental Retardation Reviews, 4,* 49-52.

Gumaer, J., & Simon, R. (1979). Behavioral group counseling and schoolwide reinforcement program with obese trainable mentally retarded students. *Education and Training of the Mentally Retarded,* 106-111.

Hingsburger, D. (1987). Sex counseling with the developmentally handicapped: The assessment and management of seven critical problems. *Psychiatric Aspects of Mental Retardation Reviews, 6,* 41-46.

Hingsburger, D. (1989). Relationship training, sexual behavior, and persons with developmental handicaps. *Psychiatric Aspects of Mental Retardation Reviews, 8,* 33-40.

Hite, M. C., Kleber, D. J., & Simpkins, K. E. (1985, April). *Family constellations of mentally retarded individuals: The changing role of the school psychologist.* Paper presented at the 63rd Annual Convention of the Council for Exceptional Children, Anaheim, CA.

Horner, R. H., Dunlap, G., & Koegel, R. L. (1988). *Generalization and maintenance: Lifestyle changes in applied settings.* Baltimore, MD: Paul H. Brookes.

Hoshmand, L. (1983, August). *"Rap Groups" as a field research method in a sheltered workshop.* Paper presented at the American Psychological Association Convention, Anaheim, CA.

Hurley, A. D., & Hurley, F. J. (1986). Counseling and psychotherapy with mentally retarded clients I: The initial interview. *Psychiatric Aspects of Mental Retardation Reviews, 5,* 22-26.

Hurley, A. D., & Hurley, F. J. (1987). Psychotherapy and counseling II: Establishing a therapeutic relationship. *Psychiatric Aspects of Mental Retardation Reviews, 4,* 15-20.

Jageman, L. W., & Myers, J. E. (1986). *Counseling mentally retarded adults: A procedures training manual.* Stout, WI: University of Wisconsin-Stout Press.

Janus, N. G., & Podolec, M. (1982). Counseling mentally retarded students in the public school. *School Psychology Review, 11*(4), 453-458.

Kashubeck, S. (1989, August). *Paradoxical interventions in counseling: A meta-analysis.* Paper presented at the American Psychological Association Convention, New

Orleans, LA.

Krauss, M. W., Simeonsson, R., & Ramey, S. L. (Eds.). (1989). Research on families [Special issue]. *American Journal on Mental Retardation, 94*.

Lee, D. Y. (1977a). Evaluation of a group counseling program designed to enhance social adjustment of mentally retarded adults. *Journal of Counseling Psychology, 24*, 318-323.

Lee, J. A. (1977b). Group work with mentally retarded foster adolescents. *Social Casework, 58*, 164-173.

Levine, H. G. (1985). Situation anxiety and everyday experiences of mildly mentally retarded adults. *American Journal of Mental Deficiency, 90*, 27-33.

Levinson, E. M. (1986). A vocational evaluation program for handicapped students: Focus on the counselor's role. *Journal of Counseling and Development, 65*, 105-106.

Lombana, J. H. (1983). *Success for mentally retarded students. Sources to upgrade career counseling and employment of special students*. Florida State University, Center for Studies in Vocational Education, Tallahassee.

Ludwig, S., & Hingsburger, D. (1989). Preparation for counseling and psychotherapy: Teaching about feelings. *Psychiatric Aspects of Mental Retardation Reviews, 8*, 1-8.

Maslow, A. (1954). *Motivation and personality*. New York: Harper.

Matson, J. L. (1981). A controlled outcome study of mentally retarded adults. *Behavior Research and Therapy, 19*, 101-107.

Matson, J. L. (1984). Social skills training. *Psychiatric Aspects of Mental Retardation Reviews, 3*, 1-4.

Monroe, R.A. (1988). *Hemi-sync relaxation tape*. Faber, VA: Monroe Institute.

Munro, J. D. (1985). Counseling severely dysfunctional families of mentally and physically disabled persons. *Clinical Social Work Journal, 13*, 18-31.

O'Neil, M. A. (1982, August). *Depression and the mentally retarded*. Paper presented at the American Psychological Association Convention, Washington, DC.

Perroncel, C. C. (1988). *The Social/Sexual Evaluation Profile* (S/SEP). Torrington, CT: Amfortas Press.

Perroncel, C. C. (1989, December). *Social/Sexual Evaluation Profile: Recent developments*. Paper presented at the Annual Convention of the National Association for the Dually Diagnosed, Washington, DC.

Prout, H. T., & Strohmer, D. C. (1991). *The Emotional Problems Scales*. Lutz, FL: Psychological Assessment Resources.

Robinson, L. H. (1973, November). *Group work with parents of retarded adolescents*. Paper presented at the 25th Annual Meeting of the American Association of Psychiatric Services for Children, Chicago, IL.

Rothberg, P., Adams, B., & Boyd, E. (1989, December). *The evolution of a collaborative approach to multimodal counseling to adults with developmental disabilities*. Paper presented at the Annual Convention of the National Association for the Dually Diagnosed, Washington, DC.

Schramski, T. G. (1984). Role playing as a therapeutic approach with the mentally retarded.

Psychiatric Aspects of Mental Retardation Reviews, 3, 25-31.

Solly, D. C. (1987). A career counseling model for the mentally handicapped. *Techniques: A Journal for Remedial Education and Counseling, 3,* 294-300.

Sovner, R. (1989, December). *Pharmacotherapy for anxiety disorders in persons with mental retardation.* Paper presented at the Annual Convention of the National Association for the Dually Diagnosed, Washington, DC.

Spangler, A. S., Jr. (1982, August). *Outpatient services for mentally ill retarded clients in a community mental health center.* Paper presented at the American Psychological Association Convention, Washington, DC.

Spragg, P. A. (1983, October). *Counseling approaches with retarded persons: Current status and an attempt at integration.* Paper presented at the Region IV Conference of the American Association on Mental Deficiency, Snowmass, CO.

Spragg, P. A. (1984, May). *Counseling the mentally retarded: A psychoeducational perspective.* Portions of this paper were presented at the 108th annual meeting of the American Association on Mental Deficiency, Minneapolis, MN.

Spragg, P. A., & Miller, C. (1982, June). *Counseling mentally retarded couples.* Paper presented at the annual meeting of the American Association on Mental Deficiency, Boston, MA.

Steiner, J. (1984). Group counseling with retarded offenders. *Social Work, 65,* 181-185.

Stieglitz, M. N., & Cohen, J. S. (1980). *Career education for physically disabled students: A bibliography.* (A project PREP publication). Research and Utilization Institute, National Center on Employment of the Handicapped at Human Resources Center, Albertson, NY.

Tavormina, J. B. (1975). Relative effectiveness of behavioral and reflective group counseling with parents of mentally retarded children. *Journal of Counseling and Clinical Psychology, 43,* 22-31.

Tymchuk, A. J., Andron, L., & Rahbar, B. (1988). Effective decision-making/problem-solving training with mothers who have mental retardation. *American Journal on Mental Retardation, 92,* 510-516.

Vance, H., McGee, H., & Finkle, L. (1977). Group counseling with mentally retarded persons. *Personnel and Guidance Journal, 56,* 148-152.

Whitmore, K. (1988). *Counseling and psychotherapy with the mentally retarded.* Unpublished manuscript.

7 FAMILY INTERVENTIONS

Harriet C. Cobb and William Gunn

This chapter will provide an overview of issues related to family therapy for families with a member with mental retardation. Specifically, the types of families of individuals with mental retardation will be described, because the functional style of the family has important implications for the manner in which the family copes with its member with mental retardation. Methods for assessing interactions within the family system will be presented, with emphasis on applications for treatment planning. Treatment considerations will also be discussed. This chapter offers a strong assessment focus as the base for family interventions.

The family of an individual with mental retardation should be examined from a systems model perspective, just as families without disabled members can be viewed. Although the obvious difference between these two types of families is the fact that in the family with a member with a disability there is clearly an "identified patient," there are systems principles underlying the dynamics in both kinds of families. As stated by Gargiulo (1985), families of individuals with disabilities are drawn from the ranks of "normal" families. Many of the difficulties in families with children with disabilities are no different from problems found in any family (Meyerson, 1983).

The Family Systems Model

The Systems Perspective

The family systems model is based on the concept of the "ecosystem," the interactional system of living things with their environment. This view focuses on the biological aspects of the organism with a minimal amount of energy required for survival and maintenance of the system. An underlying premise of this approach is that a change in any part of the system affects the system as a whole and its other subparts. Any alteration in the family system requires adaptation. In order for the family to function, basic resources such as information and money are critical. External or internal stressors to the system require higher levels of energy to maintain effective functioning.

The birth into the family of a child with a disability or a later diagnosis of a handicapping condition creates unusual demands on the family system. An understanding of the family system is crucial for effective intervention; to focus only on treatment of the child with disabilities would be highly inappropriate, according to the literature (Berger & Foster, 1986).

It is helpful to conceptualize the entire family structure; hierarchy and boundaries are important assumptions to this philosophy. The concept of hierarchy relates to the notion that effective family systems have clear rules about authority and decision making. Generally speaking, adults have authority over children in decision making. Hierarchy is important to assess in families, because dysfunction can be present when coalitions cross hierarchical levels. For example, a child and one parent can coalesce against the other parent, or one parent can unite with grandparents to create a power imbalance (Haley, 1976).

Boundaries refer to the rules defining the ways members can interact with each other in a given subsystem. Important family subsystems include the spousal system, the parental system, the sibling subsystem, and the individual subsystem (Minuchin & Fishman, 1981). Dysfunction can occur, for example, when parents are so involved in the child-rearing role that they no longer treat each other as husband and wife. Referring to each other as "Mom" and "Dad" rather than by name is indicative of a problem in subsystem functioning.

It is in the entire family's best interest that all its subsystems operate effectively. This means that subsystem boundaries must be clear enough to allow problem solving without interference from other family members, while simultaneously being open enough to permit communication between subsystem members. Spouses must be able to resolve marital differences without input from children or grandparents, and to relate to each other independent of their parental roles. Families have different methods for delineating hierarchies and boundaries (Minuchin, 1974). In the "enmeshed" family, boundaries between different subsystems are vague or nonexistent. It is difficult in this type of system for family members to develop as individuals or even to communicate among themselves because subsystems do not permit freedom of choice or problem solving in an independent fashion. Furthermore, there is little agreement about the legitimacy of each subsystem's authority. So, for example, a son who is worried about not doing well in school may not know whom he can safely confide in about his concerns. The lack of clear boundaries makes it hard for him to know who can help him because family roles are so overlapping.

On the other hand, cooperation between subsystems is nearly impossible in "disengaged" families because subsystem boundaries are too rigid. There is little connectedness in these families; help is difficult to obtain because of a lack of closeness.

Systems and Families with Members with Disabilities

All families progress through cycles, with the family with a member who has a disability progressing through four developmental crises, according to Simeonsson and Simeonsson (1981):

1. an initial awareness of the child's exceptionality;
2. the realistic acceptance of the child's academic capabilities and deficiencies;
3. the postschool adaptation to the individual's living and working arrangements; and
4. the adjustment to the independence of the adult status of the person with a disability in relation to the aging parents.

The first stage in the typical coping process when learning of the limitations of a child with a disability is shock and grief as a response to the loss of the expected healthy child. Some denial may be experienced, with parents "shopping around" for a more favorable explanation of the child's slowness. The initial reaction may then be replaced by anger over feeling unjustly deprived. The grief and anger may deepen into a period of depression before the parents can finally come to terms with the reality of the situation. Parents may feel guilt about giving birth to a child with disabilities and it is not uncommon for them to experience a degree of underlying "chronic sorrow" regarding their child's condition.

With children with mild retardation, the initial diagnosis may not take place until the child is of school age. For many individuals with mild retardation, the etiology of the retardation is of the "cultural-familial" type, which means the parents may well be intellectually limited themselves. This compounds the problem of treatment planning for the mental health professional and clearly means that a variety of community resources will be important in assisting the family in coping with daily living. For the family of the individual with mild retardation of specific organic etiology, the contrast with their expected "normal" child will be perceived as a greater loss.

Awareness of these developmental stages provides a basis for understanding family functioning and gives direction to intervention planning. The therapist should facilitate the parents in setting priorities and acquiring a realistic assessment of their offspring's strengths and weaknesses.

There have been several studies conducted that examine the family with a member with a disability. Longo and Bond (1984) reviewed the literature and concluded that there is no definitive statement that can be made regarding the effect of a child with disabilities or the emotional well-being of his or her parents. Because there are no true normative data on families of individuals with disabilities, it is difficult to describe degrees of dysfunction or psychological health in these families.

Friedrich (1979), however, found that marital satisfaction was the most accurate prediction of successful maternal coping with a child with disabilities. Although it has often been stated in the literature that the birth of a child with a disability has a negative effect on the marital relationship, Longo and Bond's (1984) analysis of the available studies shows a surprising number of couples whose marriage remains stable.

The results of studies that focus on the impact on the siblings of a child with a disability are mixed (Longo & Bond, 1984). In some cases, siblings experience significant stress (Grossman, 1972; Seligman, 1979). However, in other families, the impact on siblings is minimal. The effect of a child with disabilities on his or her siblings is primarily related to the parental responses toward the exceptional child (Gargiulo, 1985). The siblings tend to model expressed feelings and attitudes from the parents, making this a critical variable in sibling adjustment.

According to Chinn, Winn, and Walters (1978), risk for sibling maladjustment occurs when the sibling without disabilities encounters decreased parental attention. This emotional neglect may occur because of the parents' feelings of being overwhelmed with the caretaking needs of the person with a disability. Feeling guilt, the parents may shower attention exclusively on the child with a disability. Consequently, siblings may experience feelings of resentment or jealousy as the exceptional child becomes a rival for parental attention. This may result in the "normal" sibling suddenly becoming a behavior problem, in an effort to refocus parental affection and attention. Siblings may also experience guilt themselves, often because of negative feelings they have toward the brother or sister with a disability.

It is not unusual for siblings without disabilities to feel embarrassed about their brother or sister with a disability if the child's behavior is atypical, particularly in public. This feeling of shame may extend to complete rejection of the sibling who has a disability. Adult siblings may worry about the possible increased likelihood of their own future children being exceptional or of the future responsibility of caring for the sibling with a disability in adulthood (Gargiulo, 1985). However, it is clear from the literature that not all siblings are negatively affected by the family member with a disability. The task of the mental health professional is to assess the manner in which the family members relate among themselves, a procedure discussed in more depth later in this chapter.

The dysfunctional family differs from the functional family in one important way. Although many families are ultimately as able to cope with the stress of an individual with a disability as they are able to handle other stressors, the dysfunctional family is not able to adapt to the stress brought out by this individual's presence in the family. They may be permanently arrested in the beginning stage of the coping process, or simply dysfunctional, with the member with a disability exacerbating an already disturbed interaction pattern (Munro, 1983).

According to Sieffert (1978), two factors may account for severe family dysfunction. The first factor, the personality style of individual family members, may sabotage the normal coping process. For example, a parent or sibling who tends to view most situations or people negatively will direct this discontent toward the individual with a disability. Second, certain circumstances may exacerbate the personality factors. As mentioned previously, the stability of the parents' marriage affects how the entire family responds to the member with a disability. The child may be scapegoated if the marital relationship has not been renegotiated after the child's birth or after the initial diagnosis of the child's limitations.

If the child's mental disability includes significant behavior or medical problems, the accessibility of outside professional resources can be an important influence in adjustment. Without external assistance or relief periods, the parents can "burn out" from the stress of managing the individual alone. However, the impersonal style of many helping agencies discourages families. Without a positive relationship with outside agencies such as schools or social services, the family can feel a sense of alienation and aloneness.

Seriously dysfunctional families appear to be troubled by extreme guilt, hostility, and feelings of inadequacy. They may also simply lack the cognitive and emotional abilities to cope with the individual with a disability. They may deny their negative feelings or scapegoat the disabled family member. In response to the family tension, the member with mental retardation may exhibit behavioral problems. Family homeostasis maintains the problematic behavior and the family resists change because it threatens the family's equilibrium. These families present themselves to professionals as chronic complainers who create crises over minor problems. They demand an excessive amount of attention and are more likely to turn to attorneys or advocacy groups without first attempting to resolve difficulties with professionals in direct service (Munro, 1983). They may attempt to sabotage treatment by passive aggressive behavior such as repeatedly breaking scheduled appointments or refusing to follow through with agreed-upon behavior management procedures. It is not unusual for these families to reinforce dependency in a family member with mild retardation in spite of a definite capacity for a greater degree of independence. Conversely, the individual with a disability may be a victim of unrealistically high expectation and, therefore, a target for the family's frustration and anger.

In some families, the person with a disability will be actively avoided, either by both parents, or by one. In either case, the disabled family member experiences feelings of rejection and may withdraw into depression or respond through disruptive behavior.

Assessment Considerations

Any therapeutic intervention should always be preceded by an accurate identification and assessment of the problem. This is certainly true with family interventions. A close look at the dynamics within the individual with a disability, the family system in which he or she lives, and the external support system (schools, social service, etc.) is crucial for effective family therapy.

Family stress theory provides a helpful framework for thinking about family assessment. The earliest conceptual foundation for research to examine the variability in families was the Hill (1949, 1958) ABCX family crisis model:

A (the stressor event)—interacting with B (the family's crisis-meeting resources)—interacting with C (the definition the family makes of the event)—produce X (the crisis). (1958, p. 141)

Since Hill's earliest conceptualizations, others have expanded the model to reflect a more dynamic process that occurs in families. McCubbin and Patterson (1983) have provided one of the more interesting expansions of the ABCX model, the Double ABCX model. It answered one of the frequent criticisms of Hill's mode namely, that it did not include other stresses occurring during the adaptation period. The Double ABCX model added postcrisis variables in an effort to describe (a) the additional life stressors and strains that shape the course of family adaptation (pile-up), as well as (b) the personal, intrafamilial, and community resources critical to families in effective adaptation.

Aa: The Event and the Pile-Up of Stressors

This expansion is particularly helpful in thinking about assessment of families with member(s) with mental retardation. The birth or trauma that precedes the diagnosis of retardation should not be seen as the only crisis event with everything else seen as adaptation. There are likely a number of other stressors that have occurred since the traumatic event. These may have been severe, requiring immediate response, or just a build up of everyday problems. They can be normative, transitional-type events such as the birth of another child or nonnormative-type events such as chronic illness or disability (Figley & McCubbin, 1983). It is also important to consider events prior to the diagnosis of retardation. One cannot assume a "no stress" baseline family pattern. Accurate assessment must take the historical context into consideration (Walker, 1985).

In counseling or therapy with a family that has a member with a mental disability, assessment must take into account that it did not occur in isolation. A complete history of major events that have impacted the family is important, as well as assessment of progress through normative life-cycle events of individuals within the family.

Finally, assessment of the stressors must include the family's efforts to cope with the hardships or crises. Coping behaviors can themselves become stressors. For example, a mother who gives up her job and career to take care of a child with a disability may introduce financial hardships to the family. The change in roles created in both parents may cause confusion and ambiguity, both within themselves as individuals and in their relationship as a couple.

Methods for assessment of stressors. A careful clinical interview with all members of the family could enable the clinician to discover the events in the family that preceded and followed the diagnosis of retardation. In addition, talking with community agencies, such as schools, that have been involved with the family should provide additional information that may not be volunteered by the family. It is important in this domain as with the other two that more than one member of the family be interviewed so as to ascertain a complete story and, more significantly, to recognize each family member's perception as important.

Two objective paper/pencil assessment instruments that could be used for this purpose are FILE (Family Inventory of Life Events) and the PSI (Parenting Stress Inventory).

FILE (McCubbin, Patterson, & Wilson, 1979) was developed as an index of family stress. Influenced by other, more individual stress instruments such as the Holmes-Rahe scale, FILE has undergone several revisions. The current form is a 50-item self-report instrument that records the stressor events and strains experienced by any member of the family in the past 12 months. FILE includes both objective events such as "Husband and wife retired from work," as well as more subjective events such as "Increased conflict with in-laws." Validity checks for this instrument have been made in two ways. A pile-up of life changes was found to be negatively correlated with desirable dimensions of the family environment, as measured by the Family Environment Scale (Moos & Moos, 1981). Predictive validity was assessed on a population of children with cystic fibrosis, cerebral palsy, or myelomenningocle. It was found that a pile-up of life changes was positively correlated with poor child physical functioning and high family conflict.

The PSI was developed by Abidin (1983). Its primary focus is on looking at characteristics of the parent–child relationship that are seen as stressful by the parent. It will be discussed in greater detail in this section. The PSI contains an optional "life stress" factor, which provides some index of events occurring to the family. It is valuable in identifying the major stressful events and, when combined with how the parent perceives the relationship, offers a more complete picture.

Bb: Resources

The concept of resources has been described as the family's ability to prevent an event or a transition in the family from creating a crisis or disruption (Burr, 1973). The general idea was that if a family's resources were greater than the hardships presented, it would be able to prevent severe problems and adapt positively. It is crucial in assessment of a family and the family–agency relationship with a member with mental retardation to find out what resources and coping strategies exist.

The Bb factor in McCubbin and Patterson (1983) distinguished between existing and expanded family resources. Existing resources are those already part of the family's repertoire and serve to minimize the impact of the initial stressor and reduce the probability that the family will enter into crisis. Existing individual resources might be the cognitive ability of a parent to understand the development of the child. Existing family resources might be togetherness, expressiveness, role flexibility, or shared values.

Expanded family resources are those new resources strengthened or developed in response to the caretaking of a member with a disability in the face of the pile-up of additional stressors. For example, a parent could use his or her knowledge and energy to create a network of support for other parents.

An important resource included in this factor is social support. Social support has been defined as information that a family (a) is cared for and loved, (b) is esteemed and valued, and (c) belongs to a network of mutual obligation and understanding (Cobb, 1976). Families who have and are able to develop sources of social support (church, work, extended family, friends, etc.) will be more resistant to major crises. Parke (1986) distinguished between informal support, which involves friendships and extended family relationships, and the formal support of self-help groups, schools, and agencies. Some research has indicated that intimacy of friendship in informal support is a key variable. Ell's (1984) work provided evidence that the more perceived support a family has the better they will develop their own coping strategies. Vincent (1983) purported that informal support was much more valuable than formal systems.

A systemic view necessitates a multilevel assessment protocol. Keeney (1983) referred to this as ecological assessment and stated that it is important to distinguish among three basic levels.

1. the behavior and characteristics of individuals;
2. social relationships indicated by dyadic interactions; and
3. social group structures that organize the relation among dyadic interactions.

The importance of assessment of individual resources can not be underestimated. Making the distinction regarding the way in which a particular stressor affects individual members of a family allows us to identify those resources that are helpful in stress adaptation. Bandura (1982) identified perceived self-efficacy—judgments of how well one can execute courses of action required to deal with prospective situations—as a critical variable in human behavior. His review of the literature supported the notion that a person's perception of self-efficacy exerts influence in the amount of effort an individual will expend as well as how long an individual will persist under adverse circumstances. Efficacious persons believe they know how to respond in a given situation. This more psychological variable, in addition to, for example, cognitive or financial variables, is an important one to assess in all family members, including the member with mental retardation.

Minuchin (1974) provides a helpful framework for looking at the other two areas of family ecological assessment. In looking at intrafamily variables, he stresses assessment of interactions between various subsystems of the family. These subsystems include the marital (husband–wife) relationship, the parenting (mother–father) relationship, the parent–child relationships, and sibling relationships. It would also apply to evaluation of the family–agency relationships as well as the relationships concerning the family between various agencies. During initial interviews it is important to look for strengths in the functioning of these subsystems as well as the entire family. Examples of questions to be explored are as follows:

1. Are the parents able to provide structure for the children? Do they allow age-appropriate independence?

2. Do the parents provide alternate stimulation and nurturance for the children?

3. Are the parents able to work together as a parenting team and also with agencies? Do they also take the time necessary for their marriage?

4. Are there rigid coalitions between family members that set up barriers to communication and task accomplishment?

Clinical interview assessment should also include exploration of past use of external resources. The genogram (McGoldrick & Gerson, 1983) is a helpful tool in discovering extended family members who have helped in the past and who may be willing to be involved in the present problem. Again, the consistent goal of family therapy is to discover ways the family can assist itself to change, adapt, and grow. Information on how various family members have used outside resources in the past is important data to collect.

Methods for assessment of resources. There are a number of research/clinical instruments that can be used to gather information on resources from family members. It should be noted that they all ask individuals to report on family-level data. Thus, the more family members who participate, the greater the therapist can be sure he or she is getting an accurate picture of the entire family.

McCubbin, Comeau, and Harkins (1981) developed the Family Inventory of Resources for Management (FIRM) scale. It is composed of four scales that have been developed using factor-analytic procedures. These scales tap the dimensions of self-esteem and communication, health, extended family social support, and financial well-being. McCubbin et al. describe the instrument as one that can be used diagnostically to pinpoint the family's strengths for dealing with their situation and to identify resources that need to be increased or strengthened.

The Family Environment Scale (FES) is described by its authors (Moos & Moos, 1981) as a social climate scale. It measures three underlying domains of factors that characterize the family. These factors are its quality of interpersonal relationships, the emphasis on personal growth goals, and the degree of structure and openness to change. The FES has been widely used in both research and clinical settings. It is relatively short (90 items), is standardized, and provides an efficient way of gathering data about family settings. Moos states that it can be used as a screening tool, to compare and contrast families, to formulate case descriptions, and to guide and monitor therapy.

Family cohesion and adaptability are the two primary resource dimensions integrated into the Circumplex Model as formulated by Olson, Russell, and Sprenkle (1979). These researchers have developed an instrument, FACES (Family Adaptability and Cohesion Evaluation Scales), which is now in its third revision, FACES III (Olson, Portner, & Lavee, 1985). Family cohesion assesses the degree to which family members are separated from or connected to their family. Family adaptability has to do with the extent to which the family system is flexible and able to change.

The Circumplex Model postulates four levels of family cohesion ranging from extremely low (disengaged) to extremely high (enmeshed). There are four levels of adaptability ranging from extremely low (rigid) to extremely high (chaotic). "Health" in this model is balanced in the middle levels. FACES III enables a clinician to place a family quickly in a quadrant reflecting their perceived degree of strength on these resource dimensions. Although the instrument is short and easily understood by most family members, its real clinical value is in the way individual questions are answered and not in the total score derived. Individuals respond to questions about the family and these perceptions can be followed up in further interviewing.

There is one caution in using this instrument. Some families of children with disabilities may appear more enmeshed than the average family. In some cases this should be viewed as adaptive strength to band together rather than as a problematic situation.

The last resource assessment instrument is the QRS (Questionnaire on Resources and Stress) developed by Holroyd (1987). It is composed of 285 true/false items; however, there is a shorter version available for clinical and screening purposes. Questions are answered by any member of the family other than the member with retardation. Scores are obtained on 15 subscales that fall into three major areas. The first area is Personal Problems, with scores in poor health, excess time demands, attitude toward the index case, lack of social support, pessimism, overprotection/dependency, and overcommitment/martyrdom. The second area is Family Problems, with scores obtained on lack of family integration, limits on family opportunity, and financial problems. The last area reflects Problems of the

Index Case. Scores in physical incapacitation, activity level, occupational limitations, social obtrusiveness, and difficult personality characteristics are obtained.

The QRS was designed to be used with families with chronically ill or disabled members. Reliability and validity studies have been done using families of children with retardation. The QRS has consistently shown differences between populations with and without disabilities and could be used clinically to help determine what personal and family resources are available at a given time in a given family. The authors note that little research has been published to validate the QRS on adult populations, although it was originally conceived of as being appropriate for these families.

Perception of stress. The perception of stress factor has received very little attention from family stress researchers (Boss, 1986). This perceptual factor affects the degree to which family members make an effort to coordinate their interaction as a group response to the stressor.

Problems with this aspect of the overall model have been identified in the past. The most frequent concern has been about the idea that there is only one definition of any difficult situation. Each family member will see a stressful event in a unique way (Menaghan, 1982). These unique perceptions will either enhance or limit the family's capabilities to deal with the demands created. What is important is an understanding of individual perspectives regarding stressful situations, how these perspectives relate to behavior, and the influence of members' perspectives in combination with each other.

There has been some research looking at different perspectives of family members toward having a member with a disability. Mothers are affected by a child's incapacitation, lack of affective responsivity, and helplessness (Beckman, 1983; Farber, 1975; Rutter, 1975). In contrast, fathers are more affected if the child is male and by concerns about the eventual performance of the child outside the home (Chigier, 1972; Tallman, 1965). Previous research suggests that *both* parents are affected by other factors such as whether the child is their first born (Farber, 1960), severity of retardation (Levinson, 1975), or increased visibility of the child's deviance (Saenga, 1960).

Siblings perceive and adapt to mental retardation in the family in ways similar to those of their parents (Begab, 1969). Farber and Jenne's (1963) research, however, indicates that a child who is the same sex as the child with a disability is at increased risk in terms of social functioning.

It is important to ask each family member carefully about his or her adjustment and perception of the adjustment of other family members to having a family member with a disability. It can help to determine to what extent the presenting problem relates to conflict surrounding this adjustment or rigidity in not adjusting at all. It can also give valuable insight into the family's potential to adjust to present or future difficulties.

Methods for assessment of perception. The best way to assess this factor is a carefully conducted clinical interview in which historical events described by the family are followed up by questions about their perceptions and feelings concerning the event. During this interview the process by which the family responds to questions is important. Who talks first and the most? Does the verbal and nonverbal behavior match for each family member?

Two more objective methods of trying to tease out this factor in assessment of a family have been mentioned previously in the section on Assessment of Stressors. FILE, which is an indication of the number of stressful life events, can be expanded to include a second question on the perception of difficulty in coping with or adjusting to the stressor. This was described first by McCubbin and Patterson (1983) who asked respondents to indicate by each event checked (a) whether the change was anticipated or not, (b) the amount of adjustment (from 0–8) required by the family to cope with the change (a subjective weight), and (c) whether this adjustment continues or is completed. The resulting scores would be some measure of not just what events had occurred but also a subjective assessment of their difficulty.

The PSI (Abidin, 1983), also mentioned in the section on measurement of stressors, is a well-designed measure to gather a parent's perceptions of the stress of raising a child with a disability. Scores in both child and parent domains are obtained. In the child domain a clinician could determine if the parent perceives the child as unable to adjust to the changes in environment, having a depressed affect much of the time, being very demanding, or being highly distractible. This level of difficulty in the child can then be compared to the parent areas, which focus on each parent's perception of his or her own depression, attachment to the child, restrictions imposed by parental role, sense of competence, social isolation, and relationship with their spouse.

Treatment Considerations

Family interventions may involve an array of service delivery to the parents and the individual with mental retardation. Tymchuk (1983) has delineated several models of interventions with parents of persons with mental retardation. The dynamic model is more a counseling or therapeutic model that assumes parental behavior is directly related to how the parents internally or psychologically react to or deal with their child's disability. This model places more importance on the attitudes and feelings of the parents than on actual management strategies for dealing with the child. Laborde and Seligman (1983) call a similar approach that deals largely with parental adjustment "facilitative counseling." The marital relationship of the parents may also receive some attention in this model. Difficulty or inability in dealing with the child and the disability are viewed as psychological reactions or conflicts of the parents. In order to facilitate the parents' adjustment, these reactions and conflicts must be explored, examined, and resolved. The resolution of these conflicts will allow the parents to be more effective in their parenting role.

The behavioral model, in contrast, is more concerned with helping parents improve their parenting skills and deal directly with behaviors presented by their children with mental retardation. Most of the work in this area involves teaching parents how to conduct operantly based behavior modification programs in the home (e.g., how to target and appropriately reinforce specified or desired behaviors). This model is more of a training model than a counseling or therapeutic model.

The family therapy model assumes that the family structure or system is affected by the presence of a family member with mental retardation. The family is dealt with as an interacting system, and therapy may involve all the family members meeting in a group. This model goes beyond the others by including siblings of the child with mental retardation. A more functional family system will facilitate the adjustment of the child with mental retardation as well as other family members.

Early intervention approaches or educational approaches focus on the parents' role in collaborating with educational or developmental programming for their child. Similar to the behavioral model, these focus on training parents to work with their children to maximize their child's cognitive, adaptive, and educational development.

Clearly, dysfunctional families are exceptionally challenging to the mental health professional and necessitate the assumption of the family therapy model. However, there are potentially effective interventions if expectations for positive change are realistic given the family resources. According to Munro (1983), sessions are best when focused on specific "here and now" strategies to assist them in coping, because these families often tend to dwell on the past problems and perceived unfairness of their situation. Professionals must be able to understand and appreciate all of the potential emotions the family has, including the sorrow, anger, and guilt. An appropriate long-term goal is to develop a therapeutic alliance with the family so the professional can function as a partner working with the family to cope with the individual with mental retardation.

Certainly it is important for the therapist to be aware of his or her own feelings about persons with disabilities. It is not unusual for the professional to experience strong emotional responses to the situation, because of the sympathy elicited by the person with the disability or the resistance that may occur on the part of the family. Countertransference can occur when the therapist has unrealistic expectations of the situation or realistic reactions that are countertherapeutic. Becoming overwhelmed by the inertia some families seem to exhibit can lead to "burn out" in the professional. The therapist who works with many dysfunctional families needs to take good care of his or her own mental health and stress management needs. No one can completely avoid some countertransference, but extremely dysfunctional families can be quite manipulative toward the therapist. Maintaining a clear perspective in which the family's needs, not the professional's, direct the relationship is essential.

The initial session with a family is crucial because it sets the stage for future cooperation or resistance. Assessment begins from the first contact with the family, which may be over the telephone. A sense of the emotional state of the parents can be made at this point. It is important for professionals to communicate compassion for the family's situation as well as confidence in their own ability to provide competent assistance.

The therapy should, of course, involve sessions with the entire family present, including the individual with mental retardation. This establishes the philosophy that problems belong to the whole family, who can be integral to the solutions. There will likely be sessions, however, in which only the parents will be present to allow focusing on marital or parenting issues. Sessions done with siblings can also be important as part of assessment as well as treatment.

Individual sessions with the person with a disability also can serve to build a crucial therapeutic alliance and give the family the message that the therapist cares about knowing the individual's characteristics, strengths, and weaknesses well. This is important for building credibility with the family.

Although assessment is ongoing, often in the initial evaluation potential intervention alternatives can be discussed. Professionals can describe the possible approaches to take and instill some hope that positive change can occur if everyone works together. The contracting and treatment implementation can begin. Appropriate treatment may be anywhere from one or two strategic sessions to a long-term maintenance/support approach, depending on the needs of the family and their willingness to participate in therapy. The depth of intervention may range from brief, specific information giving and referral to appropriate services; to counseling and guidance regarding parenting or management issues; to in-depth work at facilitating changes in family interaction patterns. The termination phase may occur after their first session or be a fading process over an extended period of time.

Both supportive and confrontational approaches may be appropriate in working with a specific family. Explicit grieving may go on in the therapist's office for the first time; the professional must be sensitive to the significance of this part of the process. Even the most dysfunctional family encounters legitimate sorrow and frustrations. The therapist can "give permission" for the expression of sadness, guilt, and anger. Teaching family members to be clear about feelings and direct with their messages to each other within a supportive context is an important skill the therapist can encourage.

It is quite common for the family to need understanding and permission to experiment with activities they would not have tried before therapy, such as planning time away from the children or redirecting attention that is overly focused on the individual with a disability. It is essential for professionals to have knowledge of available resources, including educational, residential, or respite care, or to have access to agencies who can provide this information and assistance.

Confrontational strategies may be necessary with dysfunctional families who are clearly sabotaging efforts to help. A "show-down" interview (Munro, 1983) may be necessary to change the direction of escalating conflict. Program strategies can be modified and clarified, with a second opinion referral made by the primary therapist, if necessary. This avoids an atmosphere of defensiveness and encourages family openness to other viewpoints.

Working with families with members with mental retardation requires creativity and flexibility on the part of the professional. The goal must be to build on the attachment that exists at the family's core. Helping the family to develop coping skills as well as to accept assistance and support when needed are lasting ways to help the family to function effectively.

Summary

In summary, assessment of a family with a member with mental retardation is crucial in establishing goals for treatment. This assessment must first include a complete picture of events that have impacted the family. The event of accepting a member with mental retardation deserves focus but only as one major step. The second step is a careful look at resources available to the family. This includes resources specific to dealing with the member with retardation and those specific to dealing with the other difficulties faced by any family. The goal of family therapy is often to help the family become its own best resource. An understanding of existing or potential internal and external resources is crucial in accomplishing this goal. Finally, assessment of different family members' perception of the events that have been influential shows what makes each family unique and what necessitates individualized family treatment in each case.

The following case illustrates many of the issues surrounding the task of providing family therapy for a child with mild mental retardation.

Case Study

John was first referred by the school for therapy at age 11 because of chronic behavioral problems he exhibited in class. John had been identified as seriously emotionally disturbed with mild retardation when he was 6 years old. He was placed in a self-contained class for SED children, and re-evaluations later confirmed the dual diagnosis of both mild retardation and emotional disturbance *(DSM–III-R)* diagnosis: Mild Mental Retardation, Conduct Disorder, Schizotypal Personality Disorder, provisional). Although his academic progress was commensurate with his intellectual functioning, he continued to be a difficult child to manage. The parents are perceived by the school as largely uncooperative and appeared to reinforce aggression in John at home.

This therapist saw the parents first; Donna was an obese, 35-year-old white woman who was clearly in the borderline range of intellectual functioning herself. Her common-law husband, Robert, was a 45-year-old African-American man of above-average intelligence who made an erratic living in the construction business. A complete family history taken at the time of the session revealed that learning and emotional problems were prevalent on both sides of the family. Although Robert did not admit a problem with alcoholism, his wife described him as "drunk" a good part of the time. Donna and Robert were seen individually and as a couple before being seen with their son, John. During the course of therapy, Robert participated in approximately one third of the sessions, which were frequently canceled and rescheduled. Although Donna was quite willing to participate in therapy, Robert was exceedingly mistrustful and rapport was slow to build with him. Their financial situation was precarious. If the school had not covered the cost it was doubtful that they would have paid for the service themselves.

However, both parents appeared to care very much for their son, and although they resisted some basic suggestions the teacher had made regarding providing nutritious snacks for John and seeing that he went to bed at an appropriate time, they wanted John to be "happy." It was clear from the initial family interview that Donna and John were very enmeshed. She was still dressing and bathing him at home, and he sat in her lap at various points during the session. Robert initially was uncommunicative; when he did talk, a speech impediment made him difficult to understand. He and John did not respond to each other with physical affection, although John often asked his father for affirmation when making a statement, "Isn't that right, Daddy?" Robert was the stronger disciplinarian in the family; Donna would occasionally speak sharply to John but, by her own admission, usually indulged him. Both parents were skeptical that allowing John to stay up past midnight to watch X-rated horror videos, because John "wanted" to do so, may have negative repercussions.

Primary goals of therapy were to engage Robert more closely in the parenting of John and to provide assistance and support to Donna in disciplinary matters. The therapist spent considerable time building an alliance with the parents, who later confessed to threatening John at first with punishment for talking to the therapist about family matters. When they were convinced the therapist's goal was not to take John away from them, they became more cooperative and were even able to joke about their early suspiciousness.

The therapist worked closely with the teacher to reinforce good communication between home and school. When John appeared to be well rested and completed homework assignments, the teacher sent a positive note home to the parents. A behavior modification approach where John received points for appropriate behavior was implemented by the teacher.

During the first several months this family was in therapy, a social worker visited the home on a monthly basis to monitor the family's ability to meet John's basic needs. When it became apparent that efforts were being made, the visits ceased. Robert's drinking diminished to occasional weekend binges, which, although still a source of marital conflict, improved the family's day-to-day capacity to function.

It is interesting to note that the Social Services Department placed a deinstitutionalized elderly woman with moderate retardation with a severe seizure disorder in this home to be cared for. This added another variable in therapy as well. "Mary" was approximately at the 8-year-old developmental level. She tantrummed when her cigarettes were taken away from her, and she and John were, at times, rivaling for Robert and Donna's attention. However, Mary's presence in the home provided a diversion for Donna, as well as a good reason for both parents to reinforce some of John's emerging self-help/independence skills. Mary's increased medical needs eventually forced her to re-enter a residential setting after several months.

This change, of course, impacted the system again, refocusing attention on John, who obliged by participating in a minor shoplifting incident with some friends. Robert and Donna's response to this problem was quite appropriate: They coalesced to mete out immediate consequences for John's misbehavior, clearly acting in their "executive" function. The therapist continues to see this family on a monthly basis. John is currently doing well in his school setting, and his parents appear to be managing his behavior appropriately, although occasional crises emerge. This therapist worked primarily on assisting the parents in appropriate management of their child's behavior. Some sessions involved seeing the couple without John, to reinforce their executive function; a few sessions were held with John and his father alone in an effort to involve the father more closely. This family is one who will benefit from continued periodic contact with a mental health professional to help them maintain the gains they have made in becoming a more functional family.

References

Abidin, R. (1983). *Parenting Stress Inventory* (inventory and manual). Charlottesville, VA: Pediatric Psychology Press.

Bandura, A. (1982). Self-efficacy mechanisms in human agency. *American Psychologist, 37*, 122-147.

Beckman, P. (1983). Influences of selected child characteristics on stress in families of handicapped infants. *American Journal of Mental Deficiency, 88*, 150-156.

Begab, M. J. (1969). Casework for the mentally retarded—Casework with parents. In W. Wolfensberger & R. A. Kurtz (Eds.), *Management of the family of the mentally retarded* (pp. 201-217). New York: Follet.

Berger, M., & Foster, M. (1986). Application of family therapy theory to research and interventions with families with mentally retarded children. In J. J. Gallagher & P. M. Vietze (Eds.), *Families of handicapped persons* (pp. 251-260). Baltimore, MD: Paul H. Brookes.

Boss, D. (1986). Family stress: Perception and context. In M. B. Sussman & S. Steinmetz (Eds.), *Handbook in marriage and the family* (pp. 113-127). New York: Plenum.

Burr, W. (1973). *Theory construction and the sociology of the family.* New York: Wiley.

Chinn, P., Winn, J., & Walters, R. (1978). *Two-way talking with parents of special children.* St. Louis, MO: C. V. Mosby.

Chiqier, E. (1972). *Downs syndrome.* Lexington, MA: D. C. Heath.

Cobb, S. (1976). Social support as a moderator of life stress. *Psychosomatic Medicine, 38*, 300-314.

Ell, K. (1984). Note on research—Social networks, social support and health status: A review. *Social Service Review, 3*, 133-149.

Farber, B. (1960). Perceptions of crisis and related variables in the impact of a retarded child on the mother. *Journal of Health and Social Behavior, 1*, 108-118.

Farber, B. (1975). Family adaptations to severely mentally retarded children. In M. Begab & S. Richardson (Eds.), *The mentally retarded and society: A social science perspective* (pp. 247-266). Baltimore: University Park Press.

Farber, B., & Jenne, W. (1963). Family organization and parent-child communication: Parents and siblings of a retarded child. *Monographs of the Society for Research in Child Development, 28* (7, Serial No. 91).

Figley, C., & McCubbin, H. (Eds.) (1983). *Stress and the family. Vol. II: Coping with catastrophe.* New York: Brunner/Mazel.

Friedrich, W. N. (1979). Prediction of coping behavior of mother & handicapped children. *Journal of Consulting and Clinical Psychology, 47*, 1140-1141.

Gargiulo, (1985). *Working with parents of exceptional children: A guide for professionals.* Boston, MA: Houghton-Mifflin.

Grossman, F. (1972). *Brothers and sisters of retarded children: An exploratory study.* Syracuse, NY: Syracuse University Press.

Haley, J. (1976). *Problem-solving therapy.* San Francisco, CA: Jossey-Bass.

Hill, R. (1949). *Families under stress.* New York: Harper.

Hill, R. (1958). Generic features of families under stress. *Social Casework, 49*, 139-150.

Holroyd, J. (1987). *Questionnaire on resources and stress for families with chronically ill or handicapped members.* Brandon, VT: Clinical Psychology Publishing.

Keeney, B. (1983). Ecological assessment. In J. C. Hansen & B. Keeney (Eds.), *Diagnosis and assessment in family therapy* (pp. 157-169). Rockville, MD: Aspen.

Laborde, P. R., & Seligman, M. (1983). Individual counseling with parents of handicapped children: Rationale and strategies. In M. Seligman (Ed.), *The family with a handicapped child: Understanding and treatment* (pp. 261-284). Orlando, FL: Grune & Stratton.

Levinson, R. (1975). *Family crisis and adaptation: Coping with a mentally retarded child.* Doctoral dissertation, University of Wisconsin, Madison.

Longo, D. C., & Bond, L. (1984). Families of the handicapped child: Research and practice. *Family Relations, 33*, 57-65.

McCubbin, H., Comeau, J., & Harkins, J. (1979). *FIRM— Family Inventory of Resources and Management.* St. Paul: University of Minnesota Press.

McCubbin, H., & Patterson, J. (1983). Family stress adaptation to crises: A double ABCX model of family behavior. In H. McCubbin, H. Sussman, & J. Patterson (Eds.), *Social stresses and the family: Advances and developments in family stress theory and research* (pp. 7-37). New York: The Haworth Press.

McCubbin, H., Patterson, J., & Wilson, L. (1979). *FILE—Family Inventory of Life Events and Changes.* St. Paul: University of Minnesota.

McGoldrick, M., & Gerson, R. (1983). *Genograms in family assessment.* New York: W. W. Norton & Company.

Menaghan, E. (1982). Assessing the impact of family transitions on marital experience. In H. McCubbin, A. E. Lauble, & J. M. Patterson (Eds.), *Family stress, coping, and social support* (pp. 90-108). Springfield, IL: Charles Thomas.

Meyerson, R. (1983). Family and parent group therapy. In M. Seligman (Ed.), *The family with a handicapped child* (pp. 285-308). New York: Grune & Stratton.

Minuchin, S. (1974). *Families and family therapy.* Cambridge, MA: Harvard University Press.

Minuchin, S., & Fishman, H. (1981). *Family therapy techniques.* Cambridge, MA: Harvard University Press.

Moos, R., & Moos, B. (1981). *Family Environment Scale Manual.* Palo Alto, CA: Consulting Psychologists Press.

Munro, J. (1983). Counseling severely dysfunctional families of mentally and physically disabled persons. *Clinical Social Work Journal, 12*, 18-31.

Olson, D. H., Portner, J., & Lavee, Y. (1985). *FACES III: Family Adaptability and Cohesion Evaluation Scales III*. St. Paul, MN: Family Social Science, University of Minnesota.

Olson, D., Russell, C., & Sprenkle, D. (1979). Circumplex model of marital and family systems: Empirical studies and clinical intervention. In J. Vincent (Ed.), *Advances in family intervention, assessment and theory* (pp. 129-179). Greenwich, CT: JAI.

Parke, R. D. (1986). Father, families, and support systems. In J. J. Gallagher & P. M. Vietze (Eds.), *Families of handicapped persons* (pp. 101-113). Baltimore, MD: Paul H. Brookes.

Rutter, M. (1975). *Helping troubled children*. New York: Plenum.

Saenga, G. (1960). *Factors influencing the institutionalization of mentally retarded individuals in New York City*. Albany, NY: Interdepartmental Health Resources Board.

Seligman, M. (1979). *Strategies for helping parents of exceptional children*. New York: Free Press.

Sieffert, A. (1978). Parents' initial reaction to having a mentally retarded child: A concept and model for social workers. *Clinical Social Work Journal, 6*, 34-39.

Simeonsson, R., & Simeonsson, N. (1981). Parenting handicapped children: Psychological aspects? In J. Paul (Ed.), *Understanding and working with parents of children with special needs* (pp. 51-58). New York: Holt, Rinehart & Winston.

Tallman, I. (1965). Spousal role differention and the socialization of severely retarded children. *Journal of Marriage and the Family, 27*, 37-42.

Tymchuk, A. J. (1983). Interventions with parents of the mentally retarded. In J. L. Matson & J. A. Mulick (Eds.), *Handbook of mental retardation* (pp. 369-380). New York: Pergamon Press.

Vincent, E. (1983). *Use of support networks by parents of mentally handicapped children*. Unpublished report, Madison, WI.

Walker, A. (1985). Reconceptualizing family stress. *Journal of Marriage and the Family, 47*(4), 827-837.

8 VOCATIONAL COUNSELING WITH PERSONS WITH MENTAL RETARDATION

Edward M. Levinson, Michael Peterson, and Randy Elston

The acquisition of independent living skills, designed to facilitate successful community adjustment and allow individuals with mental retardation to live dignified, normal lives, is a major goal of most services provided to this population. A prerequisite for the attainment of such a goal is the acquisition and maintenance of employment. Employment not only provides individuals with mental retardation with the economic self-sufficiency necessary to function independently in the community, it also provides these individuals with a sense of worth and purpose in life. Hence, vocational counseling has historically been a major component of comprehensive programs for persons with mental retardation. For the purpose of this chapter, vocational counseling will be defined broadly and will be considered to be a comprehensive process that incorporates the practices of vocational assessment, vocational training, and vocational placement, with the goal of facilitating successful adjustment to work.

Legal, Ethical, and Economic Justifications for Vocational Counseling Services

The provision of vocational counseling services to the handicapped population in this country was spurred by federal legislation and can be traced back to the Smith-Hughes Act of 1917, considered to be the beginning of the vocational education system. Followed one year later by the Soldier's Rehabilitation Act, such legislation provided services to disabled veterans and was specifically directed toward facilitating the achievement of gainful employment. These acts are viewed as the beginning of vocational training and retraining services for previously employed individuals with disabilities in this country. The passage of the Vocational Rehabilitation Act of 1943 (P.L. 78-113) signaled a change in the philosophical orientation of vocational counseling for the handicapped. For the first time, services became available to those individuals who had never been employed, and who now needed assistance in gaining employment for the first time. In essence, the act was the first to recognize the eligibility of persons with mental disabilities or mental illness for vocational counseling services. With the passage of the Vocational Rehabilitation Act Amendments of 1965 (P.L. 89-333), eligibility for vocational counseling services was opened up to all persons with disabilities, with a specific emphasis on persons with severe disabilities.

Although this legislation maintained an emphasis on gainful employment as had been the case in the past, there was a broadening of the definition of gainful employment to include sheltered and homebound employment. The Rehabilitation, Comprehensive Services, and Developmental Disabilities Amendments (P.L. 95-602) established new program thrusts in pilot employment services, independent living services, and special service programs for a variety of populations with disabilities. Currently, these pieces of legislation, along with the Education for All Handicapped Children Act of 1975 (P.L. 94-142), the Rehabilitation Act of 1973 (P.L. 93-112), and the 1976 Vocational Education Act Amendments (P.L. 94-482), combine to assure individuals with mental retardation the same rights to vocational counseling services as are enjoyed by their nonhandicapped peers.

Some may believe that personal and ethical concerns for individuals with mental retardation and other populations with disabilities may have motivated such legislation. However, economic concerns related to the high costs associated with supporting unemployed individuals with disabilities have been a motivational factor as well. Individuals with disabilities have consistently been over represented among the unemployed and underemployed (Bell & Burgdorf, 1983; Bowe, 1980). Stark, Baker, Menousek, and McGee (1982) cite U.S. Department of Labor statistics indicating that 87% of the approximately 6 million individuals with mental retardation in this country have the potential to be employed in the competitive labor market, and that 10% are capable of working in a sheltered workshop environment. However, the percentage of individuals with mental retardation who are actually employed is considerably lower. Hightower (1975) estimated that only 21% of persons with mental retardation were fully employed, 40% were underemployed, and 26% were unemployed following completion of school. Batsche (1982) estimated that only two fifths of adults with mental and physical disabilities are employed during a typical year as compared to three fourths of all nonhandicapped adults, and that out of every 100 persons with disabilities, only 25 are fully employed, 40 are unemployed, 25 are on welfare, and 10 are institutionalized or idle. Poplin (1982) noted that of the 30 million persons with disabilities in this country, only 4.1 million are employed; that 85% of employed persons with disabilities earn less than $7,000 per year; and that 52% of this segment of the population earn less than $2,000 per year. The economic and social costs to society of supporting such large numbers of unemployed adults with disabilities is staggering. Poplin (1982) estimated the cost of such dependency to exceed $114 billion per year and believed that this figure was increasing yearly. Batsche (1982) offered similar statistics and estimated that the cost of maintaining an employed individual with disabilities at an institution in Illinois exceeded the cost of educating a person at Harvard!

Given the financial costs associated with continued unemployment among individuals with mental retardation and other populations with disabilities, it is clear why vocational counseling services are a necessary and integral component of comprehensive programs for these populations. However, the social, physical, and emotional benefits to be derived by individuals with mental retardation from successful adjustment to work are not to be slighted by the economic benefits to be derived by society. Research has suggested that an individual's self-worth is intimately related to work performance and work satisfaction (Dore & Meachum, 1973; Greenhaus, 1971; Kananidi & Deivasenapathy, 1980; Super, 1957) and that one's overall adjustment to work is associated with physical and mental health (Kornhauser, 1965; O'Toole, 1973; Portigal, 1976) and overall life satisfaction (Bedian & Marbert, 1979; Orphen, 1978; Schmitt & Mellon, 1980). To be sure, the social and emotional benefits to be derived by individuals with mental retardation as a result of acquiring and maintaining satisfying employment are likely to be as great, if not greater, than are the economic benefits derived by society. The remainder of this chapter will address vocational counseling services for individuals with mental retardation, specifically focusing upon three major areas: (1) issues in vocational development, (2) vocational assessment, and (3) the components of vocational counseling.

Vocational Development

Vocational development has been defined as the totality of factors, psychological, sociological, educational, physical, economic, and chance, that combine to influence the work one performs in one's lifetime (National Vocational Guidance Association, 1985). A number of different vocational development theories have been postulated, and many of these theories assume different theoretical perspectives. It should be stated at the outset that as theories, even the most useful of these are either incomplete, not well substantiated by research, or still in the process of being developed and studied. The reader should be aware that no single theory has emerged as the one "right" or "best" theory of vocational development. What follows is an overview of four major vocational development theories, each representing a different theoretical perspective. Following this overview, the applicability of these theories to the vocational development of persons with mental retardation will be discussed.

Developmental Theory

Theories of vocational development assume the existence of definable, and hierarchical, stages through which all individuals progress in a relatively predictable and orderly way. As is true with other aspects of development, the ages and rate at which individuals progress through these stages will vary. In particular, individuals with mental retardation are believed to progress through these stages at a slower than average rate. The developmental theories of Super (1957) and Ginzberg, Ginsburg, Axelrad, and Herma (1951) will be combined and presented to provide the reader with an overview of the major stages through which individuals progress in their vocational development. Figure 8.1 summarizes these stages.

The first 14 years of life comprise the growth stage, a period during which self-concept develops and self-awareness increases. During this stage, individuals come to develop and understand their interests, abilities, and values and begin to compare these traits to the requirements and demands that exist in various jobs. There is a developing orientation to the world of work, and an understanding of and appreciation for the meaning and value of work. During adolescence, individuals move into the exploration stage, a period of self-examination, role tryouts, and occupational exploration. It is during this stage that individuals make tentative occupational choices, based upon their knowledge of self and of the world of work. These tentative choices are explored and modified via school and leisure experiences, and part-time work experiences. Gradually, the individual comes to decide on a specific vocational choice, acquires the necessary training for entry-level employment in the area, and acquires a job.

Having found an appropriate occupational field in which to work, the young adult now moves into the establishment stage. During this stage, the individual attempts to secure a permanent place in the chosen occupation, possibly making some changes in position, job, or employer, but rarely changing occupations. Having become settled, the individual then concentrates on improving his or her

Figure 8.1. Stages in Vocational Development.

STAGE	GROWTH	EXPLORATION	ESTABLISHMENT	MAINTENANCE	DECLINE
Substage	· Fantasy · Interest · Capacity	· Tentative · Transition	· Trial · Commitment & Stabilization · Advancement	· Preserve Vocational Status & Goals	· Deceleration of Vocational Abilities
Age Range	0-10 11-12 13-14	15-17 18-21	22-24 25-30 31-44	45-64 65-70	71 & on
Primary Task(s)	· Increase Self-Awareness and Awareness of the World of Work	· Explore Various Vocational Options and Implement a Vocational Choice	· Settle and Advance Within Chosen Occupation	· Preserve Vocational Status and Gains	· Cope With and Begin to Adjust to Retirement

work-related abilities and performance, increasing his or her qualifications, and advancing in his or her chosen profession. The mid- to late forties are associated with movement into the maintenance stage, a period of time during which workers attempt to preserve their vocational status and achievements while at the same time fending off competition from younger, upwardly mobile workers in the advancement stage. As age increases, and as physical and mental powers begin to decline, work rate is reduced and the nature of one's work begins to change to accommodate declining capacities. Eventually workers retire and begin to explore part-time work, volunteer, or leisure experiences to satisfy their needs.

Trait-Factor Theories

In contrast to developmental theories that emphasize the process by which individuals come to make vocational choices through their lifetime, trait-factor theories emphasize the factors associated with making a vocational choice at a particular point in time. Holland's (1985) Theory of Vocational Personalities and Work Environments, an example of trait-factor theory, is one of the most well researched of vocational theories. Holland believes that vocational choice is an expression of one's personality, and that people can be characterized by their resemblance to each of six major personality types. Likewise, Holland believes that work environments can be similarly categorized, and that six major work environments exist that correspond to each of the six personality orientations. These six personality orientations and work environments are as follows:

Realistic. Realistic people enjoy and excel at mechanical activities that involve use of tools and machines. They are physically agile, practical, and prefer to avoid social situations that require use of their weaker verbal abilities. Realistic work environments require use of mechanical abilities and tools and stress concrete, persistent, physical behavior. Examples of realistic work environments are farms, machine shops, trucking companies, and auto repair shops.

Investigative. Investigative people are intelligent, curious, studious, and theoretical. They value and enjoy mathematics and science, tend to deal in the abstract, and prefer to work alone. Investigative work environments require use of abstract and analytical abilities and usually involve work in scientifically oriented disciplines. Typical jobs found in investigative work environments are chemist, biologist, physician, and mathematician.

Artistic. Artistic individuals are creative and original thinkers who enjoy autonomy, independence, and opportunities for self-expression. They often exhibit nonconformist attitudes and values. Artistic work environments stress expressive and imaginative use of various art forms. Common jobs found in these work environments include painter, musician, writer, and dancer.

Social. Social individuals are concerned about the welfare of others and are generally friendly, sociable, sympathetic, understanding, and reassuring. They possess strong verbal skills, enjoy positive interpersonal relationships, and enjoy being with people. Social work environments stress the ability to understand and change human behavior, and emphasize helping people. Typical jobs in social work environments include teacher, counselor, nurse, and social worker.

Enterprising. Enterprising individuals are often self-confident, energetic, enthusiastic, and assertive. They enjoy and excel at tasks that require them to lead, persuade, influence, and direct others. Enterprising work environments require use of verbal skills for the purposes of convincing or influencing people. Most business-oriented occupations are enterprising in nature. Typical enterprising jobs are salesman, banker, politician, and business executive.

Conventional. Conventional types of people have a preference for clearly defined, well-organized, highly structured activities. They are often meticulous, orderly, dependable, and systematic. Conventional work environments require the routine, systematic, and often concrete processing of verbal and mathematical information. Typical conventional jobs include accountant, bank teller, secretary, and computer operator.

Holland believes that there are no "pure" types; that is, every individual is to some extent a combination of the traits inherent in each of the six personality orientations. However, Holland does believe that each individual will have a predominant personality orientation conforming to one of the six types, and will also possess, to a more limited degree, some of the characteristics inherent in each of the other types. Holland believes that people are best suited for jobs that are "congruent" with their personality orientations. That is, realistic types of individuals are best suited for realistic types of jobs, social types of people are best suited for social types of jobs, etc. Holland believes that the degree of congruence that exists between one's personality and one's work environment will influence work performance, job satisfaction, and job stability. Consequently, assisting an individual with vocational choice involves identifying that individual's primary personality orientation, and then identifying and providing opportunities for the individual to explore jobs that are congruent with his or her personality orientation. As can be ascertained from such a procedure, trait-factor approaches rely heavily on testing and providing individuals with occupational information.

Social Learning Theory

The social learning theory of vocational development (Krumboltz, 1979) emphasizes the importance of behavioral concepts and learning theory to vocational choice. Because these principles are discussed in more detail in other sections of this volume, only a brief description will be provided here. Specifically, four factors are believed to influence vocational development and vocational choice: (1) *inherited characteristics*, such as race, sex, physical appearance, or special talents; (2) *environmental conditions and events*, such as the number and type of vocational training opportunities available, family factors, or educational experiences; (3) *learning principles*, including both operant and classical conditioning; and (4) *task approach skills*, skills, values, work habits and cognitive and emotional responses that mediate behavioral outcomes. These factors combine to influence "self-observation generalizations," preferences for one kind of activity or another, and vocational planning strategies (such as interviewing, applying for a job). In summary, social learning theory advances the notion that reinforcement, punishment, modeling, and other behavioral principles influence vocational development and vocational choice.

Decision Theory

Decision theory, drawn from the works of Gelatt (1962), a colleague of Krumboltz, emphasizes use of a rational, step-by-step decision-making process to make vocational choices. It is based upon the concepts of value (the desirability of an object or outcome) and probability (the likelihood that a given event will occur). Gelatt (1962) believes that deciding requires a prediction system for determining possible alternative actions, the possible outcomes of actions, and the probability of the outcomes; a value system for examining the desirability of the outcomes; and decision criteria for evaluating and selecting the decision. Four basic categories of information are necessary to make an informed decision: knowledge of possible alternative actions, possible outcomes of each of these actions, a knowledge of the probability that each action will result in the expected outcome, and relative preferences. Using such information, the client uses the following steps to make a vocational choice (Krumboltz & Baker, 1973):

1. Identify goals and define the problem.
2. Agree to achieve the goals set forth.
3. Generate alternative solutions to the problem.
4. Collect information about alternatives to the situation.

5. Examine the consequences of the options.

6. Reevaluate the goals, alternatives, and consequences.

7. Make the decision or tentatively select an alternative based upon new developments and new opportunities.

8. Generalize the decision-making procedures to other problems.

Theoretical Perspectives and Persons with Mental Retardation

Little research has been specifically done on the application of the previously described vocational theories to the population of individuals with mental retardation. Certainly, because these theories target the nonhandicapped population, application of them in full to individuals with mental retardation would appear to be inappropriate. The vocational development of individuals with mental retardation may not be orderly and systematic as is suggested by developmental theory. Generally, individuals with mental retardation have been restricted in their vocational exploration and limited in terms of their range of experiences. Consequently, individuals with mental retardation may progress through the developmental stages cited at a slowed rate, or not at all. Similarly, Holland's (1985) theory, as do most trait-factor approaches, emphasizes testing and the provision of occupational information to clients. As will be discussed in the next section of this chapter, testing may be one of the least desirable forms of assessment to utilize with individuals with mental retardation. The heavy reliance upon self-direction also present in Holland's theory also reduces its utility with individuals with mental retardation. As is true with decision-making theory, as well, the person with mental retardation's intellectual limitations usually render the independent use of occupational information and decision-making strategies ineffective.

Although inappropriate when applied in full, each of these theories offers a perspective that can be modified and adapted for use with the population of individuals with mental retardation. Age ranges aside, developmental theory would seem to suggest that increasing self- and occupational awareness, facilitating occupational exploration, implementing an occupational choice, and facilitating adjustment within that occupation would be sequentially appropriate developmental tasks for individuals with mental retardation. The stages at which each of these tasks are appropriate for an individual with mental retardation may differ significantly from what is the norm, and may be influenced by degree of retardation and range of occupational and life experience. Decision theory may be most appropriately applied within this developmental framework at logical decision points, such as the time at which decisions need to be made about which occupational areas an

Figure 8.2. Interrelationships Among and Application of Vocational
Theories to Mental Retardation

DEVELOPMENTAL THEORY

1. Increase Self and Occupational Awareness	2. Explore Various Vocational Options	3. Implement a Vocational Choice	4. Settle and Advance Within Occupation

• Decision-Making Theory •   Decision-Making Theory •

1. Decide on Vocational Options to Explore

1. Decide on Vocational Options to Pursue

2. Generate Alternatives

2. Generate Alternatives

TRAIT-FACTOR THEORY
UTILIZE TESTS AND OTHER ASSESSMENT PROCEDURES TO
Compare Traits of Individual with Traits Required
for Success in Various Jobs

3. Collect Information About Options

3. Collect Information About Options

4. Examine Consequences of the Options

4. Examine Consequences of the Options

5. Make a Decision

5. Make a Decision

6. Generalize Decision-Making Procedures to Other Situations •

6. Generalize Decision-Making Procedures to Other Situations •

SOCIAL LEARNING THEORY
Utilize Learning Principles to Facilitate Acquisition of Vocational Adaptive Behavior,
Consistent with Developmental Tasks

individual with mental retardation should explore further, which of these are realistic options, and which of these options should be pursued. Although individuals with mental retardation may not be able to apply such a decision-making approach independently, those assisting these individuals can utilize decision-making theory as a guide to making such decisions, and can involve the client with mental retardation in the process. Trait-factor approaches seem to have their greatest utility within this decision-making framework, specifically in terms of identifying realistic options for individuals. Testing and other forms of assessment can be utilized to identify the specific traits possessed by the individual, and how these traits compare to the traits required for successful adjustment to various occupations and jobs. From such an assessment, realistic options can be identified. Social learning theory would seem to have its greatest utility in training individuals with mental retardation to function within a previously identified and appropriate occupational training program or job. The behavioral and learning principles that form the foundation of social learning theory can be utilized to facilitate acquisition of the skills necessary to complete the vocationally appropriate developmental tasks specified in developmental theory. Figure 8.2 describes the interrelationship among and application of the various vocational theories discussed to the population of individuals with mental retardation. Regardless of theoretical orientation, a key in doing effective vocational counseling with individuals with mental retardation is an effective and useful vocational assessment. Issues and approaches toward conducting this type of assessment with individuals with mental retardation are discussed in the following section.

Vocational Assessment

The completion of a comprehensive vocational assessment is a necessary and prerequisite condition in establishing any vocational education or training program for individuals with mental retardation. In fact, a 1974 review of vocational education for the handicapped indicated that all successful vocational training programs utilized some form of vocational assessment (Parker, 1974). Vocational assessment may be defined as "a comprehensive process that utilizes work, real or simulated, as the focal point of assessment and vocational exploration, the purpose of which is to assist individuals in vocational development. Vocational evaluation incorporates medical, psychological, social, vocational, and economic data in the attainment of the goals of the evaluation process" (Vocational Evaluation and Work Adjustment Association, 1975, p. 86). Given the comprehensiveness of this process, it is clear that vocational assessment must involve a variety of professionals in data-gathering chores, and most probably needs to be conducted over a significant period of time. Consequently, Dahl, Appleby, and Lipe (1978, p. 103) offered the following definition of vocational assessment: ". . . a comprehensive process conducted over a period of time, involving a multi-disciplinary team . . . with the purpose of identifying individual characteristics, education, training, and placement needs, which provides educators the basis for planning an individual program, and which provides the individual with insight into his or her vocational potential."

The purposes and goals of vocational assessment are many and varied. Rudrud, Ziarnik, Bernstein, and Ferrara (1984) identify four major purposes of vocational assessment: diagnosis, placement, prediction, and prescription. Elaborating on these purposes and goals, Peterson (1981) notes that vocational assessment can (a) determine whether individuals have adequate prerequisite skills for various types of vocational education programs, (b) suggest effective teaching techniques and instructional modifications for special individuals, and (c) suggest needed support services for individuals. More specifically, he states that vocational assessment is necessary to develop vocational education plans and objectives, and to facilitate successful transition from training programs to jobs. Vocational assessment data can be used to establish both long- and short-term vocational goals for individuals with mental retardation; to identify discrepancies between an individual's present skill level and the skills necessary in order for that individual to function successfully in a targeted occupational area; to identify appropriate vocational services, program placement, and curriculum content necessary to develop deficient skill areas; and to identify effective methods of implementing instruction and vocational services to facilitate quick, efficient skill acquisition.

A number of factors need to be considered in establishing and implementing comprehensive vocational assessment programs for individuals with mental retardation. Certainly, the physical facilities and resources that exist in the setting in which the program is to be established will influence the nature of the vocational assessment services provided. Because vocational assessment is a multidisciplinary endeavor, the types of professionals employed and the nature of their expertise will influence who will be responsible for which aspect of data gathering. For example, school-based vocational assessment programs typically interface the vocational assessment and special education triennial reevaluation process (the latter is an evaluation mandated by the law, the purpose of which is to determine the student with mental retardation's continued eligibility for special education services) and involve personnel who are already responsible for gathering data necessary for completing these reevaluations. Because there is such overlap among the kinds of data that must be gathered to complete both types of evaluations, the school-based professionals involved, including psychologists, guidance counselors, and regular, special, and vocational education teachers, simply expand their traditional data-gathering strategies to gather vocationally relevant data as well. This results in a time- and cost-efficient process for completing both forms of evaluation (Levinson & Capps, 1985). Because individuals with mental retardation rarely leave their immediate area to obtain jobs, another factor that must be considered in the establishment of vocational assessment programs is the local job market. The types of locally available jobs in which individuals with mental retardation may be successfully placed will have a likely effect on both the types of vocational training programs that are available in the immediate area, and in turn, the type of vocational assessment equipment and strategies that are employed in the assessment program. Last, it must be noted that vocational assessment programs for individuals with mental retardation will differ to some extent from those that are typically appropriate for nonhandicapped individuals. In addition to some differences in the techniques and strategies employed, it is imperative that vocational assessment procedures for individuals with mental retardation incorporate training into the evaluation process (Wehman & McLaughlin, 1980). Because individuals with mental retardation frequently enter vocational assessment with a very limited set of vocational experiences, their entry-level behaviors are frequently deficient in terms of the interests, aptitudes, attitudes, and other learning abilities that are required for them to demonstrate, during the vocational assessment process, their full vocational potential. Consequently, individuals with mental retardation need the opportunity to develop, during the assessment process, the skills upon which their vocational potential will be measured.

Comprehensive vocational assessments of individuals with mental retardation typically include an evaluation of mental ability, academic achievement, sensory processes and motor skills, vocational aptitudes and interests, and adaptive behavior and social skills. Because research has suggested that individuals with mental retardation fail to obtain and hold jobs because of a lack of functional living skills and appropriate work habits (Dahl et al., 1978), the latter area is especially important to assess. Assessment of this area frequently includes evaluation of self-help skills, such as dressing, eating, or toileting; consumer skills, including money handling, banking, and purchasing; domestic skills, including household maintenance; health care; community knowledge, including travel skills and telephone usage; job readiness skills, including interviewing skills and on-the-job information; vocational behavior, including job performance and productivity, work habits and attitudes, and work-related skills; and social behavior on the job, including interactions with co-workers and supervisors. A variety of assessment techniques are employed to gather data in each of these different areas and include interviewing, paper-and-pencil tests, performance tests, work samples (tasks common to a number of jobs within an occupational area that are performed by a client under the supervision of a trained observer), simulated work experiences (real jobs performed by a client in a highly sheltered and supervised situation), and work experiences (actual on-the-job experiences). Comprehensive vocational assessment programs make use of all of these various data-gathering strategies; however, the data-gathering technique emphasized within an assessment program frequently depends upon the philosophical approach taken in conducting vocational assessments.

Vocational Assessment Approaches

Traditional assessment of individuals with mental retardation has focused upon the assessment of specific traits, such as aptitudes, interests, and work habits, which are then used to predict vocational potential. However, as Halpern and Fuhrer (1984) have summarized, the practice of using test scores to predict future performance has not been justified on the basis of current research. Very often there is very little direct relationship between the behaviors sampled by a test and the behaviors required for successful performance of a job. Consequently, use of the former to predict the latter is often inappropriate. Another problem with such traditional assessment is that it focuses on the products of past learning (Halpern & Fuhrer, 1984). Such an approach assumes that an individual's previous experiences have been sufficient for such learning to occur. With individuals with mental retardation, however, such an assumption would appear to be inappropriate, given the often limited range of vocational and life experiences possessed by these individuals. Wehman and McLaughlin (1980) agree and note that no one test can demonstrate the work potential of an individual with mental retardation as effectively as a continuous and direct measurement of performance. They note that many individuals with mental retardation will only show their full potential after initial training under optimal reinforcement conditions.

In contrast to traditional assessment, Halpern and Fuhrer (1984) recommend use of a more contemporary approach to assessment, one that emphasizes the direct assessment of the actual competencies and skills required for successful performance of specific jobs. Such an approach, which they term a process (rather than product) assessment approach, requires the outcomes of assessment to have a direct relationship to program planning, and that the process of instruction necessary to bring about acquisition of specific competencies and skills be included in the overall assessment program. Peterson (1981) agrees and offers a similar dichotomy: a guidance approach, which is viewed as developmental in nature, and which emphasizes potential for learning and change, and decision making; and a testing approach, which is diagnostic in nature, and which emphasizes the degree to which an individual's characteristics match the characteristics necessary for success in specific work environments. Peterson, like Halpern and Fuhrer, advocates use of the former approach in assessing the vocational potential of individuals with mental retardation.

Perhaps the most common form of vocational assessment, one consistent with the traditional product or testing approach, is trait assessment. Trait assessment relies on the use of various tests to identify the specific traits possessed by an individual. This "trait profile" is then compared to the "trait profile" required for success in specific jobs. From such a matching process, realistic jobs or training programs are identified. In contrast, functional skills assessment emphasizes use of work samples, situational assessment strategies, and observational strategies to determine the degree to which an individual possesses the skills necessary to perform a specific job successfully. Whereas trait assessment would assess the "amount" of intelligence, eye-hand coordination, and so on, required to function successfully as a plumber, functional skills assessment would assess the presence or absence of specific skills, such as using tools to fix a stopped-up drain, necessary for success in the job. A learning assessment approach to vocational assessment emphasizes the assessment of learning potential, and attempts to determine whether an individual is capable of learning the specific skills required for success in a specific job, and which learning or behavior change strategies might be most effective in facilitating acquisition of such skills. A community-referenced assessment approach (Rudrud et al., 1984) attempts to identify what local job opportunities exist for which employment of individuals with mental retardation may be appropriate and realistic, which of these the individual prefers, which skills of this job the individual can and cannot perform, and the individual's progress toward acquiring the skills necessary for performance of the job. Two models of assessment that integrate and utilize a variety of these approaches quite successfully are the comprehensive multidisciplinary approach to school-based assessment, and the vocational evaluation process followed in rehabilitation facilities. These approaches are described below.

School-Based Vocational Assessment: A Comprehensive Multidisciplinary Approach

It is recommended that all vocational assessments completed with individuals with mental retardation be comprehensive and ongoing in nature, utilize a variety of assessment and data-gathering methods, and involve a variety of personnel. Ideally, such assessments should begin as early as the 6th grade and be interfaced with the individual with mental retardation's special education triennial reevaluation (given the overlap in the information gathered in these evaluations). What follows is a recommended, two-phase vocational assessment program, which integrates and utilizes a variety of the assessment approaches previously described. Prior to establishing such a program, jobs that exist in the local community, in which individuals with mental retardation could be successfully placed, must be identified. Training programs consistent with such employment opportunities must then be established. Individuals with mental retardation ideally should have an opportunity to explore such training programs in order to gain some familiarity with them prior to assessment. The assessment program herein described has the purpose of identifying realistic vocational placements for individuals with mental retardation, and in assisting in the identification and acquisition of skills necessary for successful functioning in these placements.

Phase 1. A Phase 1 vocational assessment should be completed during the 6th, 7th, or 8th grade (depending upon when the student's triennial reevaluation is scheduled) and should involve a variety of personnel including a psychologist; vocational evaluator; rehabilitation counselor; social worker or guidance counselor; and vocational, special, and regular education teachers. (See Levinson & Capps, 1985, for a description of the advantages of interfacing these processes.) This team should gather information relative to the student's cognitive and academic functioning, vocational interests and aptitudes, fine and gross motor skills, and work habits and social skills. The Phase 1 assessment provides a preliminary screening of students for the purpose of identifying a variety of realistic vocational placement options. Data are gathered utilizing a variety of techniques including interviewing, observation, tests, behavior rating forms and skills checklists, and a review of records. Overreliance on the use of tests during this phase is problematic, in that many students with retardation who are in these early grades have not had an opportunity to develop many of the skills being assessed by these tests. Consequently, use of tests should be supplemented with use of skills checklists, behavior rating forms, and observational and interviewing strategies. This is especially true for students with more severe retardation. Data relative to each assessment domain (cognitive, academic, etc.) should be gathered by more than one professional utilizing more than one data-gathering technique. Such "triangulation" of data sources increases the reliability and validity of the data gathered. For example, both a school psychologist and a vocational evaluator may gather data relative to vocational interests, one utilizing an interest inventory, and one utilizing interviewing and observational techniques. Should the data gathered by these two professionals be consistent, despite the use of different data-gathering techniques, one can be relatively certain that the results are not specific to either the technique used to gather the data or the data gatherers.

Once all data have been gathered, the multidisciplinary team meets to integrate it, and to identify a number of realistic training programs for which planning may be initiated. Such planning should involve, for each identified program, a sequential listing of skills necessary for success within that program. Such planning should be done jointly by the special education teacher, the vocational education teacher(s) of the identified programs, and at least one other professional thoroughly familiar with the assessment data gathered (probably the vocational evaluator). This team should use these skills to specify objectives for students that could then be written into a vocational component of the student's individualized education plan. The teacher initiating instruction (probably the special education teacher) should then pretest the student on the identified skills and begin teaching skills that are lacking. Instruction should be a continual process of teaching a skill, testing to assess acquisition, and teaching until mastery. Once mastery is reached, the next sequential skill would be taught. Yearly progress would be assessed, and objectives modified and rewritten accordingly. This would be done by the planning team as part of the annual revision of the student's IEP. Mastery of the various skills required for success in the identified vocational programs, combined with interests manifested by the student during training, will allow the planning team to begin focusing instruction on more appropriate vocational options as time progresses. Premature narrowing of options should be avoided. The major advantage of beginning the Phase 1 assessment early in a student's school career is that it provides ample time for vocational exploration (via instruction), focusing of vocational preferences, and acquisition of skills necessary for success in the preferred training program. It also allows for a continuous, ongoing assessment of instructional and teaching strategies that are most effective in facilitating skill acquisition.

Phase 2. The Phase 2 assessment is completed in the 9th, 10th, or 11th grades; is again interfaced with the student's special education triennial reevaluation; and utilizes such assessment techniques as work samples, situational assessment, simulated work experiences, and work behavior observation. It is a lengthier, more time consuming and more expensive assessment than is Phase 1. The Phase 2 assessment allows students to apply their acquired skills to real or simulated work, prior to their placement in an actual vocational training program. It allows the student's planning team to make a final determination of the appropriateness of the vocational training program being considered, and what instructional or programmatic modifications may be necessary to increase the student's chances for success in the program. Although the vocational evaluator would primarily be responsible for completion of this assessment, results would be integrated with data gathered by other personnel during a multidisciplinary team staffing. Final recommendations for vocational training placement, along with instructional and programmatic recommendations, would be made at this time.

Vocational Evaluation in Rehabilitation Facilities

Vocational evaluation is defined by the Council for Accreditation of Rehabilitation Facilities (CARF) as a service or program which is provided on a systematic, organized basis for the purpose of determining the individual's vocational objectives, assets, limitations, and behaviors in the context of work environments in which the individual might function, and specific recommendations which may be used in the development of the individual's program plan. Vocational evaluation typically includes an assessment of aptitudes, interests, occupational social skills, work habits, psycho-motor skills, educational/academic skills, and vocational learning style. Vocational evaluation is often the first phase of an individual's rehabilitation program, the results of which are used to develop an individualized written rehabilitation program (IWRP). An IWRP is a plan developed between a rehabilitation counselor and a client that designates services and techniques/ methods that will be used to assist the client in formulating and achieving realistic vocational goals. As such, it is similar in purpose and structure to individual education plans for school-aged children with disabilities.

In many rehabilitation facilities, the vocational evaluation process is a multidisciplinary, team-oriented process that consists of five phases: a review of background information including previous psychoeducational, medical, and vocational testing; vocational evaluation program planning; vocational assessment; vocational exploration; and vocational counseling.

Clients participating in vocational evaluation are often placed in one of several vocational evaluation tracks (academic, nonacademic; individual, group), depending upon disability type, the severity of the disability, academic functioning, and level of career maturity. Different assessment techniques are utilized in these different tracks in an attempt to "tailor" the assessment programs to the individual needs of the client. The assessment techniques utilized include traditional pencil-paper tests, performance tests, work samples, and situational tryouts. Following the completion of the assessment, clients review assessment results under the supervision of a rehabilitation guidance counselor, and participate in a career exploration program appropriate for their level of career maturity. As part of exploration, clients identify occupations that are appropriate for them and acquire knowledge about these occupations. Appendix A provides a brief description of commonly used vocational tests.

Assessment Modifications

As a part of both school-based and facility-based vocational assessments discussed above, it is necessary to make modifications in the assessment procedures used. Botterbusch (1976) offers a number of useful suggestions on how assessment techniques, especially tests, may be modified for persons with mental retardation. Among these suggestions are:

Simplification of instructions. Assessors can review instructions prior to testing and change any words that may be difficult for the individual with mental retardation to understand. Complex sentences can be simplified, and additional instructions, visual aids, or demonstrations can be added.

Use of pretrials. Assessors can orient individuals with mental retardation to tests they will be taking, prior to actual administration of such tests. "Mock tests," whose purpose is to familiarize the assessee with test instructions and procedures, can be used. Although such a mock test should contain items similar in content, format, and difficulty level to ones used in the actual test, the items should not be the same.

Repeating instructions to the administrator. Test administrators can ask the assessee to repeat test instructions to determine how well these instructions were understood. Because retarded individuals have difficulty remembering complex instructions, these instructions can be broken down into segments, and each segment can be repeated back sequentially.

Color coding. Some paper-pencil and performance tests can be color coded for greater understanding. For example, instead of having to explain the difference between right and left, test administrators may simply color each side differently and refer to the "white" side and "black" side.

Marking answers in the test book. Poor motor skills sometimes lengthen the time required for individuals with mental retardation to mark answers, and this often detracts from their performance. Test administrators can mark answers themselves, thereby eliminating this burden.

Low-literate and nonverbal test forms. Because persons with retardation do not read at the levels required for the successful administration of certain tests, nonreading, pictorially based instruments or low reading–requirement instruments can be used.

It should be noted that use of such assessment modifications invalidates the norms associated with many tests, because these tests were not standardized utilizing such modifications. Consequently, use of such norms following implementation of these modifications is often inappropriate.

Evaluating the Effectiveness of Vocational Assessments

It is interesting to note that relatively few studies have been conducted on the efficacy of vocational assessment services. Those that have been conducted focused primarily on a vocational evaluation center model because curriculum-based vocational assessment and multilevel models are in very early stages of development. Nadolsky (1972) obtained feedback concerning the perceived efficacy of vocational evaluation in centers from rehabilitation counselors who indicated that the service was valuable. He later compared a systematic decision-making process of vocational evaluation with the process used by the JEVS (Vocational Research Institute, 1973) work sample system and concluded that the former process was more effective in the long run.

Some evaluation studies have pointed out significant problems in the delivery of effective vocational evaluation services (Nadolsky, 1972). Gold (1972) indicated concerns about the use of vocational assessment measures that do not incorporate direct instruction as part of the assessment process, and practitioners have reported problems of individuals with severe disabilities who were assessed as having no "vocational potential" but who were subsequently successfully employed via supported employment programs (Gemmel, 1987; Gold, 1972; Moon, Goodall, Barcus, & Brooke, 1986).

Other studies have focused more specifically on vocational evaluation in school settings. Menz (1978) evaluated the results of a high-risk youth group program in Wisconsin and found that involvement in a vocational evaluation program resulted in reported improvements in attitude and behavior of students. Neubert (1986) studied the use of vocational evaluation results in three school districts and drew the following conclusions: vocational evaluators played a major role in assisting the majority of students with disabilities to gain access to vocational programs; lack of coordination between special education and vocational education was problematic; support services in vocational education were critical in facilitating access to and success in vocational education; lack of appropriate curriculum adaptation in vocational education hindered access to vocational programs; vocational evaluation reports did not appear to be used for planning IEPs with students nor were vocational objectives included as significant components of IEPs; and recommendations from vocational evaluation were utilized when there were administrative directives or support for this to occur. Cobb and Phelps (1983) similarly reviewed IEPs in Illinois to determine if vocational evaluation data were present on IEPs and concluded that use was limited. Repetto (1986) conducted a similar study in Missouri related to placement and assessment in vocational education programs via a survey of vocational resource educators in the state. She concluded that "students are more likely to enter business and office, machine shops, health services and marketing and cooperative education programs if they have had a formal (versus informal) vocational assessment" (p. 13). Stodden, Meehan, Hodell, Bisconer, and Cabebe (1986) are in the process of conducting a large investigation of the effectiveness of vocational assessment in its impact and use with special education teachers. Their preliminary report indicates similarly that vocational assessment results have had limited impact on the development of IEPs for students with disabilities who were enrolled in work study programs. IEPs, in fact, varied little from school to school.

In summary, it seems clear that vocational assessments done with individuals with mental retardation need to be multidimensional, geared to the ability level of the individual being assessed, and, perhaps most important, once collected, used as part of the counseling and planning process. Having discussed the vocational assessment process, we now turn our attention to issues in conducting effective vocational counseling with individuals with mental retardation.

Vocational Counseling

Vocational counseling is necessary to facilitate the development of appropriate vocational goals and selection of appropriate vocational services for individuals with mental retardation. Vocational counselors working with persons with mental retardation should have a commitment to the community integration of persons with mental retardation. This includes a belief that persons with mental retardation, both mildly and severely disabled, should have opportunities for interactions with nondisabled persons in integrated settings. The goal of such community integration is involvement in work, home, and community activities where the ratio of persons with and without disabilities is the same as the ratio in the community as a whole.

Counselors working with persons with mental retardation must recognize that these persons must take, to the maximum extent possible, responsibility for the choices and decisions that are made. Vocational counseling and services are not something to be done "to" an individual. Rather, vocational counseling and services are designed to assist an individual in meeting his or her own goals. Persons with mental retardation too often have been considered incapable of making choices, and professionals and family members have assumed responsibility for making such choices. Certainly, individuals with mental retardation may have difficulty processing information to make decisions and may need assistance from others in simplifying and clarifying decisions and options. Two very real dangers exist in this process, however. Parents and professionals may encourage a person with mental retardation to accept options in which the individual is not interested, or individuals may be left to flounder and to select options that are clearly unrealistic in light of local resources and opportunities. Vocational counselors must walk a tightrope between these two extremes.

Last, the provision of ongoing support services on the job should be recognized as a viable and appropriate part of vocational services to persons with mental retardation. Relatedly, a commitment to provision of services that facilitate career development, retraining, or job transfers should also be provided. Recognizing this, the remainder of this chapter describes the procedures, considerations, and resources necessary to ensure the provision of comprehensive vocational counseling services to individuals with mental retardation.

Components of Vocational Counseling

Vocational counseling with persons with mental retardation includes the following components: (a) identification of vocational interests and goals, and making plans for employment; (b) counseling during vocational training; and (c) vocational counseling during job placement. Each of these major components of the vocational counseling process is described below.

Counseling to Identify Vocational Goals and to Make Vocational Plans

Counselors conduct vocational interviews and vocational information-gathering activities to assist persons with mental retardation and their families in identifying appropriate vocational goals and services. In some cases, the vocational counseling process may be relatively short, in which an initial interview is held, information is gathered, and plans are developed. However, with persons with mental retardation, vocational counseling will most often occur on an ongoing basis as the individual is involved in services. Such "follow-along" counseling and support services have been essential in programs that effectively serve persons with mental retardation, including vocational education (Phelps & Lutz, 1977), transitional work adjustment in rehabilitation facilities (Marr & Means, 1984), and community-based training and supported employment programs (Moon et al., 1986).

Vocational counseling requires that the counselor gather as much information about the counselee as possible. Such information includes data obtained from the initial interview, including sociocultural, educational, and previous vocational information; medical reports; specialist reports; psychological reports; and vocational assessment results (McGowan & Porter, 1967). Because vocational assessment was discussed in depth in a previous section, it will not be detailed here. Suffice it to say that many of the assessment strategies and techniques discussed in that section are used by the vocational counselor to gather the data necessary for assisting individuals with mental retardation in establishing realistic vocational goals. It should be noted, however, that many of the assessment strategies previously discussed can be used by the vocational counselor to facilitate a greater degree of self-awareness, occupational awareness, and general understanding on the part of the client. This, in and of itself, is often an important goal in the counseling process. It is clearly a prerequisite for realistic and informed decision making. What follows is a description of techniques that can be utilized within a counseling framework to build the knowledge necessary for individuals with mental retardation to assist in the counseling process. Included are a discussion of vocational interviews, vocational interest inventories, exploratory and decision-making programs, and community-based activities.

Vocational counseling interviews. Often, the most useful and direct method of obtaining information about client interests and goals is simply to ask. A semistructured format is often used in such interviews and specifies certain types of questions and points of discussion but allows for exploration and discussion between the interviewer and the student (Pruitt, 1986). One instrument based on such a semistructured format, the Vocational Decision-Making Interview (Czerlinsky & McCray, 1986; Czerlinsky, Strohmer, Coker, & Engelkes, 1981; Strohmer, 1979), has been found to be helpful in assessing career choices and decision-making readiness. Interviews should be structured around the local employment options available and can be conducted with a group of peers, or in the presence of significant others. Vocational counseling interviews may be most effective when they are associated with experiential learning on the part of the client.

In the initial vocational counseling interview, the counselee is the major source of information. Rapport should be established and the counselee should feel free both to express him- or herself and to begin to talk about personal issues (McGowan & Porter, 1967). As much information as possible should be obtained during this interview concerning the past history of the counselee. During the initial interview, the counselee may or may not express a vocational choice. Many persons with mental retardation have not worked before and do not know what kind of work they are capable of performing. If an interest is expressed, the reason behind the vocational choice should be explored carefully. Choices may be due to the influence of a parent, relative, or friend (Dubrin, 1983). Often, vocational choices selected by the counselee as a result of influence from others are inappropriate in that these choices are either too complex or are too simple for the counselee. Such inappropriate choices are often the result of unrealistic expectations that are held by significant others in the counselee's life.

Vocational counselors may have difficulty in communicating with the counselee with mental retardation during the initial interview and throughout the counseling process. Because most counseling methods rely heavily on verbal communication, alternative modes of communication may be required. The counselor may need to simplify language in order to assist the counselee in better understanding what is said. In addition, alternative communication methods such as communication boards, signing, gesturing, pictures, drawings, models, objects, or role playing (Jagerman & Myers, 1986) may be used.

It is important that parents be involved with the mentally retarded counselee in the vocational counseling process (Wehman, 1981). Parents need to understand

280 COUNSELING AND PSYCHOTHERAPY

what will be involved in obtaining employment for the counselee, and the changes this employment is likely to bring about within the family. Parents can play a major role during the initial interview, and throughout the vocational counseling process, because they are more likely to understand the counselee better than anyone else. However, caution is advised relative to parental involvement. According to Wright (1983), parents may bring attitudes into the counseling process that may be counterproductive due to fear and awe of the counseling relationship. They may also feel that they may be blamed for the counselee's problems and that their guilt as parents may be exposed. In addition, parents may try to speak for the counselee instead of letting the counselee speak for him- or herself.

Vocational interest inventories. When used properly, interest inventories can help clients focus on their interest areas and provide a point for discussion and decision making. Vocational interest inventories do not tell clients what they "ought" to do in any way. Interest inventories are simply a method of organizing likes and dislikes of the client. They can be used by the client and counselor to identify occupations consistent with the client's patterns of likes and dislikes.

For individuals with mental retardation who have limited reading ability, the Reading Free Vocational Interest Inventory is one of several picture-based interest tests that are appropriate for use. It has norms that were specifically developed on samples of individuals with mental retardation. For individuals who read on a 4th-grade level, the Self-Directed Search-Form E, which is based on Holland's (1985) theory of vocational personalities described earlier, provides information that can facilitate occupational exploration (Peterson, 1986).

Observation in exploration experiences. As individuals with mental retardation are involved in work, home, and community activities for exploration and skill assessment purposes, valuable information may also be obtained concerning their interests. This may occur via interviews in which individuals are questioned regarding their interest in a particular activity. Observing individuals while they are engaged in these activities is also useful. Much information about interests is often communicated nonverbally. Behaviors that often indicate interests include: intense attention to task and fascination with an activity; high levels of mental or physical energy related to a task; and smiling, laughing, and showing enjoyment of the task. Observation of such nonverbal behaviors is especially important in assessing the interests of individuals who have poor verbal skills or who have difficulty verbalizing their ideas.

Prevocational and vocational exploration classes. Specific classes may be and have been established in some states to facilitate vocational and, in some cases, life-style exploration and decision making on the part of individuals. All of the activities listed above may be included in these classes. Additionally, curricula specifically designed to facilitate career exploration are available for use by counselors. Brolin and associates (1986) have reviewed and compiled many curriculum materials that may be used for this purpose. Additionally, occupational exploration curriculum guides are available from vocational curriculum centers in most states.

Community-based activities. Involvement of individuals in community activities may be done via an organized program of experience-based career education (EBCE), work experience/work study programs, or community-based special education. In EBCE, individuals are placed in a series of community job sites over a series of weeks for exploration and personal skill assessment purposes. A teacher coordinates this process and provides periodic in-class time where the students may discuss their experiences and come to a greater understanding of factors that are related to job choice. Work experience and community-based special education are similar but focus to a greater degree on skill development (Calhoun & Finch, 1976).

After the counselor and client have assessed the client's interests, strengths and weaknesses and desired areas for employment, many, if not most clients will require some type of vocational training. Vocational counseling is critical during this phase of the individual's program.

Counseling in Vocational Training

A number of services are available to assist persons with mental retardation in developing vocational skills. Vocational counselors are aware of and, in many cases, are directly involved in such services. These include: life-centered career education; vocational education; work adjustment; community-based training and supported employment; and job placement, counseling and assistance.

Life-centered career education. Career education programs are designed to facilitate vocational development during the school years and, more specifically, to facilitate acquisition of the skills necessary to make realistic and informed career choices. However, as the career education movement progressed, the focus increasingly was limited to career choice. Considerations of community participation and skill development were minimized. As professionals developed career education programs for individuals with disabilities, however, it was clear that a focus on preparation for independent living, not just employment, was necessary. This includes preparation for the roles of homemaker and family member, the participation as a citizen and volunteer, and the engagement in productive leisure and recreational pursuits (Brolin, 1986). A variety of individuals have developed materials and programs for the career education of students with disabilities. Brolin's life-centered career education approach, however, has been the most widely used. This curriculum is designed to facilitate exploration and preparation of handicapped students in three broad areas that can be infused into the regular academic program of the school and/or taught in special classes. These areas are daily living skills, occupational guidance and preparation, and personal-social skills. The curriculum is organized around 22 competencies and 102 subcompetencies identified as important for adult living.

Functional, community-based special education. Individuals with disabilities have historically had difficulty making the transition from school to adult life. Consequently, special educators have responded by using an approach to curriculum that is both functional in content and community based in service delivery. Such a curriculum in elementary or secondary schools assists students in learning skills related to work, home, and community functioning. Rather than just teaching basic academic and social skills, a functional curriculum specifically teaches students to apply those skills in real work situations. Thus, students are not only taught math skills and social skills in the classroom, but are assisted in using math skills to balance a checkbook and develop positive social relationships with family and community members. This renewed emphasis on functional application of skills is very consistent with the life-centered career education approach developed by Brolin and his associates (Falvey, 1986; Wilcox & Bellamy, 1987) and is especially necessary with individuals with mental retardation, who have limited ability to apply and generalize skills learned in classrooms to the real world.

Community-based functional special education approaches have assisted students with mental retardation, particularly those with more severe disabilities, to achieve a variety of community skills that were not previously thought possible. For instance, students have learned to perform aerobic exercise (Stainback, Stainback, Wehman, & Spangiers, 1983), photography for leisure purposes (Giangreco, 1983), to shop for groceries and to budget using calculators (Nietupski, Welch, & Wacker, 1983), and to purchase items in a restaurant (Storey, Bates, & Hanson, 1984). These studies illustrate the effectiveness of this approach.

Additional research has indicated that a combination of school-based simulations and community-based functional instruction is most effective (McDonnell, Horner, & Williams, 1984). Evidence also indicates that community-based instruction may also facilitate long-term community integration of persons with severe disabilities (Brown et al., 1986).

Vocational education. Vocational education provides education and training for semiskilled, skilled, and technical occupations requiring less than a college degree. The Carl Perkins Vocational Education Act mandates services that assist handicapped students in entering and successfully competing in vocational education programs. These include: (a) access to the full range of vocational programs offered; (b) information to students and parents regarding opportunities in vocational education provided no later than the 9th grade; (c) vocational assessment of interests, abilities, and special needs; (d) curriculum adaptations and support services to assist students in being successful in regular vocational education programs; (e) career development counseling; and (f) services to facilitate the transition from school to employment or further education. Vocational counselors may assist students with mental retardation in all aspects of this process. Numerous projects, publications, and personnel training programs have provided resources that may be of assistance in providing vocational education for students with mental retardation (Gugerty & Tindall, 1980; Miller & Schloss, 1982; Phelps & Lutz, 1977).

Several studies have indicated that support services in vocational education may assist students with mental retardation and other special students in successfully completing vocational education classes. Asselin (1987) conducted a national study that indicated that over half of states are conducting program evaluation of support programs in vocational education with overall positive results.

Work adjustment. Work adjustment training programs are designed for individuals who lack basic work behaviors and social skills needed to maintain employment (Neff, 1968). Many persons with mental retardation often lose their jobs, not because of an inability to perform job tasks, but because of skill deficits in the emotional-personal area of functioning (Ballantyne, 1985).

Work adjustment has been defined as a "treatment/training process utilizing individual and group work, or work related activities, to assist individuals in understanding the meaning, value and demands of work; to modify or develop attitudes, personal characteristics, and work behavior; and to develop functional capacities, as required in order to assist individuals toward their optimum level of vocational development" (Anthony, 1979). Thus, work adjustment uses real work situations to assist individuals in developing appropriate work and interpersonal behaviors that will assist them in obtaining employment.

Individuals learn appropriate work behavior skills via the use of a variety of behavioral, instructional, and counseling techniques implemented by paraprofessional work supervisors, trained work adjustment counselors, and other specialists. Although the focus of such programs is most often on learning work behaviors in the actual work environment, most programs also include classes and group counseling in a variety of areas related to home and community functioning.

Although such programs are most often associated with services conducted within rehabilitation facilities, work adjustment involves an approach that can be used in almost any setting where real work activity can be used as a behavior change medium. Work adjustment techniques can be included in functional, community-based special education; in vocational education classrooms; in community-based training and supported employment; and in related areas. As the supported employment initiative has focused on community-based training, all such programs have included work adjustment training as an integral part of job task skills training (Moon et al., 1986).

Once vocational and work adjustment training activities are completed the client and counselor turn their attention to perhaps the most critical aspect of the entire process. Assessment and training, no matter how effectively done, are of minor importance if the long-term vocational counseling process does not end with effective job placement counseling. The following section deals with issues of providing vocational counseling for job placement.

Vocational Counseling for Job Placement

Vocational counselors, and others, have responsibilities to assist the person with mental retardation in obtaining and maintaining employment. Job placement is the major goal of all vocational services. A first step in facilitating job placement of individuals with mental retardation is the identification of an appropriate employment option.

Employment options for persons with mental retardation. The vocational options for persons with mental retardation are many and are expanding as vocational services for this population improve. Options can be categorized as: (a) competitive employment without support in regular community jobs, (b) supported employment in regular community jobs in which ongoing support services are provided, and (c) sheltered employment.

COMPETITIVE EMPLOYMENT. Persons with mental retardation have held a wide range of competitive jobs for many years. Strickland (1964) found that 436 students with mental retardation 16 years of age or older had been successfully placed in 99 different jobs in Texas during a given school year. These jobs included, among others, beauty shop assistant, soda fountain clerk, nursery assistant, mechanic's helper, and beauty attendant helper. Brickey and Campbell (1981) found that properly selected and trained persons with mental retardation could work successfully at McDonald's Restaurants. Gold (1973) and Moon et al. (1986) have shown that individuals with severe mental retardation can do complex, meaningful work if given appropriate training and opportunities. This includes work that was, in the past, thought to be beyond the capability of persons with mental retardation. As a result, the counselee with mental retardation has more vocational options to choose from today than ever before.

SUPPORTED EMPLOYMENT. Supported employment is a new approach to job placement and follow-up for persons with more severe disabilities. In supported employment, individuals are placed on jobs with special assistance from "job coaches" and are simultaneously provided with ongoing follow-up support. This may include the availability of a professional to assist in solving problems that may develop on the job, assistance in retraining, and so on. The availability of appropriate ongoing support services can assist individuals in maintaining jobs that they might otherwise lose. The supported employment model has evolved as a result of numerous demonstration projects. Over the years, progressive rehabilitation facilities have used variations of this approach via enclaves in industry, work crews, and other arrangements, where work training was provided in the community and some degree of ongoing support services made available. With the passage of the 1986 amendments to the Rehabilitation Act, however, supported employment has been added as a new component to the vocational rehabilitation service delivery system. A variety of "systems change" projects have recently been funded throughout the country to focus on changes that range from providing sheltered employment to persons who have more severe work handicaps to providing supported employment in integrated work settings. A number of variations of supported employment exist that vary in the degree of social integration provided. These include: individual supported jobs, enclave in industry, work crews, unpaid work, and clustered part-time employment.

In the *individual supported jobs* approach, intensive on-the-job training is typically provided one-on-one by a special trainer who gradually fades intervention efforts and assists existing supervisors and co-workers to take over training and supervision (Moon et al., 1986). Ongoing supports are provided to assist the individual in maintaining employment.

In an *enclave in industry*, a small group of special workers most often work as a unit within a regular industry or business. Supervision and training may be provided by the industry but is more typically provided by supervisors hired by a rehabilitation facility, public school, or other service agency. Workers may be hired into the regular industry setting as they meet production, quality, and behavioral standards. Opportunities are provided in this approach for interaction with nondisabled persons via completion of work tasks, breaks, and so on.

Work crews are similar to enclaves. However, work crews are most often mobile and move from place to place performing work. Examples include lawn maintenance and janitorial work crews.

Fredericks (1986) has developed a variation of the supported jobs model, termed *clustered part-time employment*, in which single-skill tasks are identified in a number of businesses and a series of part-time jobs negotiated for a specific individual. For instance, a variety of machine shops may have periodic needs to sort metal screws and other materials. Pooling the needs of several such shops may result in somewhat stable part-time employment. Such single-skill tasks may provide excellent jobs for individuals with severe mental disabilities. Brown, Shiraga, York, and Kessler (1985) have advocated the use of *unpaid, extended training* and, in some cases, *unpaid employment* as an option for individuals whose work and behavioral skills are not sufficient for them to meet the requirements of paid employment. He indicates that the intrinsic value and self-esteem generated by work and the opportunity for social interaction with nonhandicapped persons is, in and of itself, of sufficient benefit to the individual with mental retardation.

To date, research concerning the effectiveness of supported employment for persons with mental retardation is promising. However, the service is new and many questions regarding long-term support services and other issues have not yet been adequately addressed. Hill, Wehman, Kregel, Banks, and Metzler (1987) studied the employment outcomes and economic impact for individuals with moderate and severe mental retardation who had been employed via an individual jobs approach to supported employment and concluded that consumers benefited financially and that significant tax dollars were saved. Noble and Conley (1987) used data from a number of sheltered and supported employment programs nationwide to compare some of the major forms of supported employment with adult day care and sheltered workshops. They concluded that all forms of employment provided more earnings to the individuals and were less costly to operate than day care centers. On the other hand, Lam (1986) conducted one exploratory study in which he compared sheltered employment and support work and concluded that the former was more cost effective and provided more work hours to individuals in the program.

SHELTERED EMPLOYMENT. Sheltered employment refers to businesses or industries run by human services agencies that primarily employ disabled persons to perform service or small contract work. Sheltered rehabilitation facilities that use sheltered work as a transitional tool for work adjustment and vocational skills training may be roughly divided into three categories—sheltered industries, sheltered workshops, and work activity centers. These differ primarily in the production and behavioral skills required and the level of wages paid. Although employment of persons with disabilities in settings in which they are segregated from persons without disabilities has been questioned by professionals and parents (Brown et al., 1985), many feel that sheltered employment must be maintained as an option for individuals with mental retardation.

A variety of approaches exist that can be used to facilitate job placement of individuals with mental retardation. Selection of an appropriate approach depends upon the needs and characteristics of the individual. Approaches include: (a) job-seeking skills training, (b) job-matching and referral services, (c) job adaptation, and (d) community-based training and supported employment.

JOB-SEEKING SKILLS TRAINING. In this approach to job placement, the primary role of the vocational counselor is to provide assistance to the individual in developing skills related to job seeking. It is then the responsibility of the individual to seek out his or her own job. In most cases, however, job-seeking skills training is provided in concert with any number of placement-related services.

Typically, job-seeking skills training will include a number of content areas based upon a task analysis of the job-seeking process. Farr (1989) developed a job-seeking skills curriculum that included information and exercises related to the following: understanding employer expectations; collecting and presenting personal data and information; application forms and how to answer them; developing job leads, using telephone contacts; interviews; and organizing the job search. Job-seeking skills training is often provided in a class during and after which individuals actually seek jobs. A number of other job-seeking curricula have been developed and used with persons with mild mental retardation as an effective part of the vocational counseling process (Kimeldorf & Turnow, 1984; Multi-Resource Centers, 1971; Vocational Development Center, 1979). Azrin and Bezalel (1980) developed the job club model as a behaviorally based adaptation of job-seeking skills training. In this approach, individuals are provided both job-seeking skills training and active support in the job-seeking process. The counselor works with a small group of individuals who commit to a full-time job search. Clients are involved in half-day sessions in which they make contacts over the telephone to develop job leads, improve job-seeking skills, develop resumes, and so on. During the other half of the day, they go on job interviews. Clients receive assistance from the counselor and clerical services for the development of resumes. A buddy system is used, and an attempt is made to develop family support. Particular focus is placed on developing and using personal and professional networks of contacts to develop job leads.

Research has shown this approach to be effective with a wide variety of individuals with special needs including individuals with mild mental retardation.

The job club and related forms of job-seeking assistance appear to be effective methods of job placement for persons with mild mental retardation and related disabilities. Azrin, Flores, and Kaplan (1977), for instance, conducted a study using a matched-control experimental design. At the end of 2 months, 90% of the job seekers had obtained employment versus 55% of persons who did not participate in the program. More traditional job-seeking skills training had also been effective, though at rates not as high as the job club (Keith, Engelkes, & Winborn, 1977; McClure, 1972). According to Vandergoot (1987), a primary factor in the success of these approaches is the strong support, guidance, and reinforcement provided by the counselor.

However, many persons with moderate to severe retardation will need significant assistance in job development and job seeking from professional counselors and, consequently, may benefit from only selected aspects of job-seeking skills training.

JOB MATCHING AND REFERRAL SERVICE. This type of placement resource provides a service where job openings are collected and matched to the interests and capabilities of job applicants. In some cases, individual counseling will accompany such services, though the degree and quality of such counseling may vary tremendously. Vocational counselors working with persons with mental retardation may access such services to identify local placement options for their clients.

JOB MODIFICATION. The job modification approach to job placement is a type of selective placement approach that focuses on adaptation of the job tasks to the needs and limitations of the individual. Provision of "reasonable accommodation" for qualified persons with disabilities is legally required of contractors with the federal government and recipients of federal public funds (Sections 503 and 504, P.L. 93-112). Adaptations include environmental accessibility, job task modification, and use of adaptive aids. Job modification is especially important to persons with mental retardation who have physical disabilities. Adaptations are often inexpensive and simple to implement and are often recommended by creative counselors, employers, job coaches, or others. Rehabilitation engineering centers around the country are currently being funded that develop adaptive aids for various functional needs. Additionally, the National Rehabilitation Information Clearinghouse provides an on-line service to identify job accommodations via ABLE-DATA.

COMMUNITY-BASED TRAINING AND SUPPORTED EMPLOYMENT. These two approaches were discussed earlier under vocational services and combine both vocational training and job placement assistance. Community-based training involves on-the-job training and varies in the degree of professional counseling service provided. In traditional work-study programs in public schools or on-the-job training programs in vocational rehabilitation centers, an agreement is developed with employers for a training site in which most of the job training is completed. Training is provided by the employer. The role of the counselor is to conduct periodic site visits to monitor counselor progress, and to assist in solving job-related problems. In more intensive approaches to community-based placement, however, job coaches will actually spend substantial amounts of time on the job providing direct training and assistance, assisting supervisors in learning how to work with the individual, coordinating support with the family, and facilitating a gradual fading of assistance (Moon et al., 1986).

Individualizing the Job Placement Process

Given these various approaches, it is clear that vocational counselors working with persons with mental retardation must provide and coordinate job placement assistance based upon the individual needs of the client. Research has shown that the development of specific, individualized plans for job placement results in higher placement rates and shorter time spent in the placement process in vocational rehabilitation agencies. Such plans should identify job goals and objectives, potential barriers to placement, job development roles and responsibilities, and other specific approaches and services needed.

In working with persons with mental retardation, special attention will need to be paid by counselors to the following issues:

- orientation of the individual to the placement process;
- orientation of family members for the purpose of enlisting support and dealing with fears and concerns;
- identification of roles and responsibilities regarding job development among the counselee, family members, and the counselor;
- development of plans for on-the-job training including needs for job adaptation and community-based training;
- needs for ongoing support and follow-up.

Careful consideration of these issues will facilitate effective and successful job placement of persons with mental retardation.

In summary, vocational counseling with individuals with mental retardation is most appropriate when conceived of as consisting of several multidimensional stages: counseling during assessment, planning, training, and placement. One special case of this extensive model of vocational counseling that has received considerable attention in recent years is vocational counseling during the transition from school to work. This issue is discussed below.

Vocational Counseling and Transition from School to Work

Vocational counseling must occur within a broader, developmental context of transition from school to work. A variety of individuals, including special education teachers, psychologists, vocational evaluators, parents, and others, may actually be involved in a vocational counseling process with persons with mental retardation at different points in time. Increasingly, individuals who work with more severely retarded individuals are suggesting that a community-based, functional special education curriculum aimed at independent functioning in work, home, and community situations should begin early in a student's school career.

Transition from school to work has been a recent federal initiative. Leadership has been provided through the Office of Special Education and Rehabilitation Services (OSERS) in concert with other agencies—particularly the Administration on Developmental Disabilities, the National Institute of Mental Health, the Department of Labor, and others. Public Law 98-199, the 1983 amendments to P.L. 94-142, included the addition of Section 626, Secondary Education and Transitional Services for Handicapped Youth. Under this act, some 90 demonstration projects have been funded nationwide and a Transition Institute has been established at the University of Illinois to evaluate these projects and provide technical assistance to transition efforts throughout the country.

Will (1984), as Assistant Secretary of OSERS, developed a model of transition from school to work that has been used as the cornerstone of policy development and implementation in the transition initiative. This model included three major service paths: (a) no special services, in which students participate and utilize existing services available to the general public, such as the employment service, vocational-technical schools, etc.; (b) time-limited special services, such as vocational rehabilitation, which provide specially designed training and assistance for handicapped students for a limited period of time; and (c) ongoing support services, such as various approaches to supported employment, in which follow-up and interventions are provided to assist an individual in maintaining a job. Will's model has a total focus on employment. Home, community, and leisure skills and interests are important only to the degree that they are directly linked to employment outcomes.

Halpern (1985) developed an adaptation of the Will model which he described as "transition from school to community adjustment." This approach maintains the three service paths described by Will but includes three outcome components: (a) employment; (b) home/residential; and (c) interpersonal networks. For Halpern, the home/residential component includes functioning at home, accessing community services, and engaging in recreational and leisure opportunities. Social and interpersonal networks include aspects of human relationships such as daily communications, self-esteem, family support, emotional maturity, and intimate relationships.

Case Study

Mary, an 18-year-old special education student identified by a school psychologist as having mental retardation, was referred to an area vocational rehabilitation counselor by her classroom teacher. The school system Mary attended did not have a school-based vocational assessment program. During the initial interview Mary indicated that she had never worked and really did not know what she wanted to do, or what she could do. The counselor explained to Mary that she could find out what type of work she would like, and could do, if she would be willing to go through a vocational evaluation. The vocational evaluation process was fully explained and Mary indicated that, if it was okay with her parents, she would go through the evaluation. Her parents agreed, the referral was made, and the evaluation was initiated.

During the intake interview the evaluator found Mary to be shy, but friendly and cooperative. Mary indicated that she thought she might like to work with people but could not identify any specific work in which she was interested. Throughout the evaluation process the evaluator noted that Mary's dress was appropriate for the evaluation setting, but her hair often appeared unkempt. In addition, Mary's speech was very low and difficult to understand. She was also reluctant to attempt any tasks if there was a chance of failure. Only after encouragement did Mary's attitude and performance change.

The evaluator decided that because Mary had mental retardation, a multi-method assessment approach would be required in order to determine Mary's true vocational capabilities. Trait assessment was utilized initially. Psychometric test results placed Mary at a mid-3rd-grade level in both reading and arithmetic. Her only interest areas, according to an interest test, were mechanics and athletics.

Mary's dexterity test results were low. She was administered the Personal Capacities Questionnaire orally, but responses were questionable. Mary was either unaware of her own capabilities or reluctant to respond.

If the evaluator had stopped Mary's evaluation at this point, few vocational recommendations could have been made because little information was gleaned from psychometric testing which utilized work sampling equipment.

Consequently a functional skills assessment was initiated. Mary was administered the janitorial, food service, and bench assembly work samples. The janitorial work sample included window washing, dust mopping, damp mopping, and buffer operation. Although her work was somewhat slow, the quality of the work was adequate. However, Mary indicated that she was not interested in janitorial-type work.

Mary was reluctant to begin the cooking work sample, but with encouragement she completed the unit. The tasks included mixing batter and baking a cake in a microwave oven. Again, Mary's work was somewhat slow but the quality of the work was adequate. She expressed some interest in this vocational area.

Mary began the bench assembly work sample but did not complete it. She indicated that she did not like working with nuts and bolts, and that she really did not want to attempt any other work samples.

It was determined that Mary's ability to follow audiovisual instructions was fair, but her retention of directions was weak. Her reaction to work pressure or job change was poor. However, once she initiated a task she was reasonably persistent.

After completion of the work samples, results were again discussed with Mary. She indicated that she wanted to be a cook and that she was not interested in other vocational areas. Although significant information had been gained from the cooking work sample unit, additional information was required to determine if cooking was a feasible vocational choice. Therefore, situational assessment at a local rehabilitation center was suggested. Mary agreed and was assessed by the food service staff for 1 week. Based on Mary's performance, the food service staff felt Mary had the capability to become a cook with proper training and time. The staff also noted that Mary's personal hygiene and other independent living skills were somewhat weak, possibly due to dependency on her parents.

Based on the results of Mary's evaluation, it was recommended that she consider training under sheltered conditions with an initial goal of independent living skill development. In addition, work adjustment training and vocational training in the area of food service was recommended. It was suggested that Mary be placed on the job in the community, utilizing the individualized supported employment approach upon completion of training.

After receiving the vocational evaluation report, the counselor set up an appointment with Mary and her parents. The counselor very carefully explained and interpreted the results of Mary's vocational evaluation. It was suggested that Mary could benefit from training in independent living skills, personal, social, and work adjustment skills, and vocational training at a local rehabilitation center. Both Mary and her parents agreed that the training she could receive at the rehabilitation center would be of benefit and would help lead to gainful employment.

Once accepted into the rehabilitation center, Mary took part in personal, social, and work adjustment courses for half a day and received vocational training in the area of food service during the remainder of the day. She learned the basic skills of cooking. Within 6 months, Mary had made enough progress to seek employment in the community. Placement was made at a local restaurant and individualized supported employment was initiated. Mary required assistance for 2 weeks, after which the job coach began fading from the work site. Mary's confidence grew, her personal and social skills improved, she began to develop positive relationships with others, and she gradually developed into a successful cook.

References

Anthony, W. A. (1979). *The principles of psychiatric rehabilitation.* Amherst, MA: Human Resource Development Press.

Asselin, S. B. (1987, October). *Roles of vocational resource/support personnel: A national perspective.* Paper presented at a conference on Career Development for Exceptional Individuals, Nashville, TN.

Azrin, N., & Bezalel, V. (1980). *Job club counselor manual.* Baltimore: University Park Press.

Azrin, N., Flores, T., & Kaplan, S. (1977, December). Job finding club: A group assisted program for obtaining employment. *Rehabilitation Counseling Bulletin, 21*(2), 130-139.

Ballantyne, D. (1985). *Cooperative programs for transition from school to work.* Washington, DC: U.S. Government Printing Office.

Batsche, C. (1982). Vocational education of handicapped youth: State of the art. In T. H. Hohenshil & W. T. Anderson (Eds.), *School psychological services in secondary vocational education* (pp. 235-276). Blacksburg, VA: Virginia State Department of Education and NASP.

Bedian, A. G., & Marbert, L. D. (1979). Individual differences in self-perception and the job-life satisfaction relationship. *Journal of Social Psychology, 109,* 111-118.

Bell, C., & Burgdorf, L. (1983). *Accommodating the spectrum of individual abilities.* Washington, DC: U.S. Commission on Civil Rights Clearinghouse Publications.

Botterbusch, K. (1976). *A comparison of seven vocational evaluation systems.* Menomonie, WI: University of Wisconsin-Stout, Stout Vocational Rehabilitation Institute, Materials Development Center.

Bowe, F. (1980). *Rehabilitating America toward independence for disabled and elderly people.* New York: Harper & Row.

Brickey, M., & Campbell, K. (1981). Fast food employment for moderately and mildly retarded adults: The McDonalds Project. *Mental Retardation, 19*(3), 113-116.

Brolin, D. (1986). *Life centered career education: A competency based approach.* Reston, VA: The Council for Exceptional Children.

Brown, L., Rogan, P., Shiraga, B., Zanella Albright, K., Kessler, K., Bryson, F., VanDeventer, P., & Loomis, R. (1986). A vocational follow-up evaluation of the 1984-1986 Madison Metropolitan School District graduates with severe intellectual disabilities. In L. Brown, R. Loomis, K. Zanella Albright, P. Rogan, J. York, B. Shiraga, & E. Long (Eds.), *Educational programs for students with severe handicaps* (Vol. XVI, pp. 97-132). Madison, WI: Madison Metropolitan School District.

Brown, L., Shiraga, B., York, J., & Kessler, K. (1985). *Integrated work opportunity for adults with severe handicaps: The extended training option.* Madison, WI: University of Wisconsin and Madison Metropolitan School District.

Calhoun, C., & Finch, A. (1976). *Vocational and career education: Concepts and operation.* Belmont, CA: Wadsworth.

Cobb, R. B., & Phelps, L. A. (1983). Analyzing individualized education programs for vocational components: An exploratory study. *Exceptional Children, 50,* 62-64.

Czerlinsky, T., & McCray, P. (1986). *Vocational decision-making interview: Administration manual.* Menomonie, WI: University of Wisconsin-Stout, Research and Training Center.

Czerlinsky, T., Strohmer, D. C., Coker, C., & Engelkes, J. E. (1981). *Assessing vocational decision-making in the rehabilitation process: Instrument development.* Menomonie, WI: University of Wisconsin-Stout, Rehabilitation Research and Training Institute.

Dahl, P. R., Appleby, J. A., & Lipe, D. (1978). *Mainstreaming guidebook for vocational educators.* Salt Lake City: Olympus.

Dore, R., & Meacham, M. (1973). Self-concept and interests related to job satisfaction of managers. *Personnel Psychology, 26,* 49-59.

Dubrin, A. J. (1983). *Bouncing back: How to handle setbacks in work and personal life.* Englewood Cliffs, NJ: Prentice-Hall/Spectrum.

Falvey, M. (1986). *Community-based curriculum.* Baltimore, MD: Brookes.

Farr, J. M. (1989). *The work book.* Bloomington, IL: McKnight.

Fredericks, B. (1986). Part-time work for high school students. *Teaching Research 15*(1), 1-7.

Gelatt, H. B. (1962). Decision-making: A conceptual frame of reference for counseling. *Journal of Counseling Psychology, 9,* 240-245.

Gemmel, J. K. (1987). *Field reports on transition project.* Unpublished report. Portland: University of Southern Maine.

Giangreco, M. (1983). Teaching basic photography skill to a severely handicapped young adult using simulated materials. *Journal of the Association for the Severely Handicapped, 8*(1), 43-50.

Ginzberg, E., Ginsburg, S. W., Axelrad, S., & Herma, J. L. (1951). *Occupational choice: An approach to a general theory.* New York: Columbia University Press.

Gold, M. (1972). Research on the vocational rehabilitation of the retarded: The present, the future. In N. R. Ellis (Ed.), *International review of research in mental retardation* (pp. 89-124). New York: Academic Press.

Gold, M. (1973). *Try another way: A training manual.* Champaign, IL: Research Press.

Greenhaus, J. H. (1971). Self-esteem as an influence on occupational choice and occupational satisfaction. *Journal of Vocational Behavior, 1,* 75-83,

Gugerty, J., & Tindall, L. (1980). *Puzzled about educating special need students? A handbook on modifying vocational curricula for handicapped students.* Madison, WI: Wisconsin Vocational Studies Center.

Halpern, A. (1985). Transition: A look at the foundations. *Exceptional Children, 51,* 479-486.

Halpern, A. S., & Fuhrer, M. J. (1984). *Functional assessment in rehabilitation.* Baltimore, MD: Brookes.

Hightower, M. D. (1975). Status quo in certain death. *Journal of Rehabilitation, 42,* 32-35.

Hill, M., Wehman, P., Kregel, P., Banks, D., & Metzler, M. (1987). Employment outcomes for people with moderate and severe disabilities: An eight year longitudinal analysis of supported competitive employment. *Journal of the Association of Persons with Severe Handicaps, 12*, 182-189.

Holland, J. L. (1985). *Making vocational choices: A theory of vocational personalities and work environments.* Englewood Cliffs, NJ: Prentice-Hall.

Jagerman, L. W., & Myers, J. E. (1986). *Counseling mentally retarded adults: A procedures and training manual.* Menomonie, WI: University of Wisconsin-Stout, School of Education and Human Services, Materials Development Center.

Kananidi, M. S., & Deivasenapathy, P. (1980). Self-concept and job satisfaction among the self-employed. *Psychological Studies, 25*, 39-41.

Keith, R. D., Engelkes, J. R., & Winborn, B. B. (1977). Employment seeking preparation and activity: An experimental job-placement training model for rehabilitation clients. *Rehabilitation Counseling Bulletin, 21*, 159-165.

Kimeldorf, M., & Turnow, J. (1984). Job search education: Meeting the challenge of unemployment. *Journal for Vocational Special Needs Education, 7*, 7-10.

Kornhauser, A. W. (1965). *Mental health of the industrial worker.* New York: Wiley.

Krumboltz, J. D. (1979). A social learning theory of career decision making. In A. M. Mitchell, G. B. Jones, & J. D. Krumboltz (Eds.), *Social learning and career decision making* (pp. 19-49). Cranston, RI: Carroll Press.

Krumboltz, J. D., & Baker, R. D. (1973). Behavioral counseling for vocational decisions. In H. Borrow (Ed.), *Career guidance for a new age* (pp. 235-284). Boston: Houghton Mifflin.

Lam, C. S. (1986). Comparison of sheltered and supported work programs: A pilot study. *Rehabilitation Counseling Bulletin, 30*, 66-82.

Levinson, E. M., & Capps, C. F. (1985). Vocational assessment and special education triennial reevaluations at the secondary school level. *Psychology in the Schools, 22*, 283-291.

Marr, J. N., & Means, B. L. (1984). *Behavior management manual: Procedures for psychological problems in rehabilitation.* Fayetteville, AR: University of Arkansas, Arkansas Rehabilitation Services, Arkansas Rehabilitation Research and Training Center.

McClure, D. (1972). Placement through improvement of clients' job-seeking skills. *Journal of Applied Rehabilitation Counseling, 3*, 188-196.

McDonnell, J. J., Horner, R. H., & Williams, J. A. (1984). Comparison of three strategies for teaching generalized grocery purchasing to high school students with severe handicaps. *Journal of the Association for Persons with Severe Handicaps, 9*, 123-133.

McGowan, J. F., & Porter, T. L. (1967). *An introduction to the rehabilitation process.* Washington, DC: U.S. Department of Health, Education, and Welfare, Vocational Rehabilitation Administration.

Menz, F. E. (1978). *Vocational evaluation with adolescents: Description and evaluation of a program with reluctant learners.* Menomonie, WI: University of Wisconsin-Stout, Research and Training Center.

Miller, S., & Schloss, P. (1982). *Career-vocational education for handicapped youth.* Rockville, MD: Aspen.

Moon, S., Goodall, P., Barcus, M., & Brooke, V. (1986). *The supported work model of competitive employment for citizens with severe handicaps: A guide for job trainers.* Richmond, VA: Virginia Commonwealth University, Rehabilitation Research & Training Center.

Multi-Resource Centers. (1971). *Job seeking skills workbook.* Minneapolis, MN: Author.

Nadolsky, J. M. (1972). *Development of a model for vocational evaluation of the disadvantaged.* Auburn, AL: University Printing.

National Vocational Guidance Association. (1985). Vocational and career counseling competencies. *Vocational Guidance Quarterly, 34,* 131-134.

Neff, W. (1968). *Work and human behavior.* New York: Atherton Press.

Neubert, D. A. (1986). Use of vocational evaluation recommendations in selected public school settings. *Career Development for Exceptional Individuals. 9,* 98-105.

Nietupski, J., Welch, J., & Wacker, D. (1983). Acquisition, maintenance, and transfer of grocery item purchasing skills by moderately and severely handicapped students. *Education and Training of the Mentally Retarded, 18,* 279-286.

Noble, J., & Conley, R. (1987). Accumulation evidence on the benefits and costs of supported and transitional employment for persons with severe disabilities. *Journal of the Association of Persons with Severe Handicaps, 12,* 163-174.

Orphen, C. (1978). Work and nonwork satisfaction: A causal-correlational analysis. *Journal of Applied Psychology, 63,* 530-532.

O'Toole, J. (Ed.). (1973). *Work in America: Report of a special task force to the Secretary of Health, Education, and Welfare.* Cambridge, MA: MIT Press.

Parker, S. (1974). *Programs for the handicapped.* Washington, DC: U.S. Government Printing Office.

Peterson, M. (1981). Developing a model of vocational assessment for use in public school in Texas. *Vocational Evaluation and Work Adjustment Bulletin, 14,* 100-107.

Peterson, M. (1986). *Vocational assessment of special students: A procedural manual.* Storkville, MS: VOC-AIM.

Phelps, L. A., & Lutz, R. (1977). *Career exploration and preparation for the special needs learner.* Boston: Allyn and Bacon.

Poplin, P. (1982). The development and execution of the vocational IEP: Who does what, when, to whom. In T. H. Hohenshil & W. T. Anderson (Eds.), *School psychological services in secondary vocational education: Roles in programs for handicapped students.* Blacksburg, VA: Virginia Tech. (ERIC Document Reproduction Service No. 215245).

Portigal, A. H. (1976). *Towards the measurement of work satisfaction.* Paris: Organization for Economic Cooperation and Development.

Pruitt, W. (1986). *Vocational evaluation.* Menomonie, WI: Walt Pruitt Associates.

Repetto, J. (1986). *The effects of assessment and handicapping conditions on program placement in Missouri's area vocational technical schools.* Paper read at the convention of the American Vocational Association, Dallas, TX.

Rudrud, E. H., Ziarnik, J. P., Bernstein, G. S., & Ferrara, J. M. (1984). *Proactive vocational habilitation.* Baltimore, MD: Brookes.

Schmitt, N., & Mellon, P. M. (1980). Life and job satisfaction: Is the job central? *Journal of Vocational Behavior, 16,* 51-58.

Stainback, S., Stainback, W., Wehman, P., & Spangiers, L. (1983). Acquisition and generalization of physical fitness exercises in three profoundly retarded adults. *Journal of the Association for the Severely Handicapped, 8*(2), 47-55.

Stark, J. A., Baker, D. H., Menousek, P. E., & McGee, J. J. (1982). Behavioral programming for severely mentally retarded/behaviorally impaired youth. In K. P. Lynch, W. E. Kiernan, & J. A. Stark (Eds.), *Prevocational and vocational education for special needs youth: A blueprint for the 1980's* (pp. 122-193). Baltimore, MD: Brookes.

Stodden, R. A., Meehan, K. A., Hodell, S., Bisconer, S. W., & Cabebe, S. (1986). *Vocational assessment research project.* Honolulu: University of Hawaii.

Storey, K., Bates, P., & Hanson, H. B. (1984). Acquisition and generalization of coffee purchase skills by adults with severe disabilities. *Journal of the Association for Persons with Severe Handicaps, 9,* 178-185.

Strickland, C. (1964). Job training placement for retarded youth. *Exceptional Child, 31,* 83-86.

Strohmer, D. C. (1979). *The Decision Making Interview (DMI).* Menomonie, WI: University of Wisconsin-Stout, Rehabilitation Research and Training Institute.

Super, D. (1957). *The psychology of careers.* New York: Harper & Row.

Vandergoot, D. (1987). Review of placement research literature: Implications for research and practice. *Rehabilitation Counseling Bulletin, 30,* 243-267.

Vocational Development Center. (1979). *Job seeking skills: A curriculum and guide.* Menomonie, WI: University of Wisconsin-Stout, Stout Vocational Rehabilitation Institute.

Vocational Evaluation and Work Adjustment Association. (1975). Vocational evaluation project final report [Special edition]. *Vocational Evaluation and Work Adjustment Bulletin, 8.*

Vocational Research Institute. (1973). *Jewish Employment Vocational Service Work Sample System.* Philadelphia, PA: Author.

Wehman, P. (1981). *Competitive employment: New horizons for severely disabled individuals.* Baltimore, MD: Brookes.

Wehman, P., & McLaughlin, P. J. (1980). *Vocational curriculum for developmentally disabled persons.* Baltimore: University Park Press.

Wilcox, B., & Bellamy, G. T. (1987). *The activities catalog: An alternative curriculum for youth and adults with severe disabilities.* Baltimore, MD: Brookes.

Will, M. (1984). *Bridges from school to working life.* Washington, DC: Office of Special Education and Rehabilitation Services.

Wright, B. A. (1983). *Physical disability - A psychological approach.* New York: Harper & Row.

APPENDIX: Vocational Tests

Vocational Interest Inventories

Title	Description	Publisher
Wide Range Interest Opinion Test	This is a picture-based inventory appropriate for age 5 yrs–adult that measures interests in a wide range of occupational areas. It can be administered individually or to groups in about 40 minutes. However, it possesses weak psychometric characteristics and does not report specific norms for individuals with mental retardation.	Slosson Educational Publications

| Reading Free Vocational Interest Inventory | This is a picture-based inventory appropriate for use for ages 13 yrs–adult that measures interest in unskilled, semiskilled, and skilled occupations. It can be administered individually or to groups in approximately 20 minutes. It possesses adequate reliability but questionable validity. It has specific norms for individuals with mental retardation. | The Psychological Corporation |
| Self-Directed Search Form E | This inventory, written at a 4th–grade reading level, is appropriate for use with ages 15 yrs–adult and assesses interest in a wide range of occupational areas. Its self-administered format may need to be modified for use with individuals with mental retardation. Administration time is approximately 45 minutes, and psychometric characteristics are adequate. | Psychological Assessment Resources, Inc. |

Geist Picture
Interest Inventory

This is a picture-based inventory appropriate for use with ages 14–adult. It can be administered individually or to groups and assesses interest in 12 occupational areas. Psychometric characteristics are reported to be adquate.

Western Psychological
Services

Vocational Aptitudes

Non-Reading Aptitude
Battery

This nonreading, multiple aptitude battery was developed for educationally deficient individuals ages 15–adult. It can be administered to individuals or to groups in about 2 hours. Scores are related to General Aptitude Test Battery scores for which norms are available on more than 460 occupations. Psychometric adequacy is questionable.

U.S. Employment Test
Battery Service

(continued)

Crawford Small Parts
Dexterity Test

This individually administered instrument designed for adolescents and adults measures eye-hand coordination and fine finger dexterity. Reliability is reported to be adequate, but little validity data is reported. Little standardization information is provided.

The Psychological Corporation

Pennsylvania
Bi-Manual Worksample

This individually administered test measures finger dexterity for individuals 17 yrs or older. Administration time is approximately 15 minutes. Psychometric characteristics are reported to be adequate.

American Guidance Service

Purdue Pegboard

This test of manual dexterity can be administered to individuals or groups of individuals 15 yrs or older in approximately 10 minutes. Little information on the standardization sample is provided, and psychometric characteristics are questionable.

Science Research Associates

Prevocational and Social Skills

San Francisco
Vocational Competency
Scale

Purports to assess the vocational competency of persons with mental retardation age 18 yrs and older. Consists of 30 items, which are rated by an individual who has observed the client. Administration time is approximately 15 minutes. Norms were derived from 562 male and female workshop clients with mental retardation. Reliability is reported to be adequate but no validity studies are presented in the manual.

The Psychological Corporation

(continued)

Social Prevocational
Information Battery

Designed to measure competencies required
for successful community adjustment of
junior and senior high school educable
students with mental retardation. Administration time is approximately 3 ½ hours
and norms are provided for public school
educable students with mental retardation.
Psychometric characteristics appear to
be adequate.

CTB/McGraw-Hill

Work Sample System

JEVS Work Samples

Provides 28 work samples specifically
designed for special populations and is
administered over a 5–7 day period.
Can be administered to groups, and
individuals. Normed on 1,100 individuals.

Vocational Research
Institute

VIEWS (Vocational Information and Evaluation Work Samples)	Provides 16 work samples specifically designed and normed for individuals with mental retardation. Incorporates training assessed to a specified level of competency prior to performance assessment. Includes industrial time standards for comparison of client performance.	Vocational Research Institute
Singer Vocational Evaluation	Provides over 20 work samples for handicapped, nonhandicapped, and disadvantaged individuals. Assesses interests, abilities, aptitudes, and tolerances for specific job areas that are related to the DOT.	Singer Education Division

(continued)

MICRO-TOWER

Provides 13 work samples designed for clients of educable mental retardation through the normal range of intelligence. Can be administered to groups and takes 3–5 days to complete. Provides scores on five aptitude areas: verbal, numerical, motor, spatial, and clerical perception.

MICRO-TOWER
Institutional Services

INDEX